KU-050-707

CHICHESTER INSTITUTE OF
HIGHER EDUCATION LIBRARY

WS 2145309 8

WITHDRAWN

TITLE

CHURCH

CLASS No.

283.42

JAN99

LIBRARY

WITHDRAWN

A Church for the Twenty-First Century

CANTERBURY BOOKS

General Editor: Robert Hannaford, Professor of Christian Theology in the Bishop Otter Centre for Theology and Ministry at the Chichester Institute of Higher Education

This series of books explores topics that have a direct bearing upon the development of the Christian tradition of thought. The books will address theological issues directly related to the faith and practice of the Christian community and explore the interpretative significance of Christian theology for modern life and thought. The contributions are drawn from a number of different theological disciplines and schools of thought and should be of interest both to the specialist reader and the educated general public.

Already published

Further titles in preparation

A Church for the
Twenty-First Century
Agenda for the Church of England

Edited by

Robert Hannaford

Gracewing.

First published in 1998

Gracewing
2 Southern Avenue, Leominster
Herefordshire HR6 0QF

All rights reserved. No part of this publication may be reproduced, stored in a retrieval system, or transmitted in any form, or by any means, electronic, mechanical, photocopying, or otherwise, without the written permission of the publisher.

Compilation and editorial material © Robert Hannaford
Copyright for individual chapters resides with the authors.

The right of the editor and the contributors to be identified as the authors of this work has been asserted in accordance with the Copyright, Designs and Patents Act, 1988.

UK ISBN 0 85244 300 5

Typeset by Action Publishing Technology Ltd,
Gloucester, GL1 1SP

Printed by Redwood Books,
Trowbridge, Wiltshire, BA14 8RN

Contents

Part Three: Faith and Praxis

Notes on Contributors

Paul Avis is a parish priest and Sub-Dean of Exeter Cathedral, Vice-Chairman of the Church of England's Faith and Order Advisory Group, Honorary Research Fellow in the Department of Theology of the University of Exeter and Director of the Centre for the Study of the Christian Church. His recent publications include *Authority, Leadership and Conflict in the Church* (Mowbrays) and *Faith in the Fires of Criticism: Christianity in Modern Thought* (Darton, Longman and Todd). He has also edited *The Resurrection of Jesus Christ* (Darton, Longman and Todd) and *Divine Revelation* (Darton, Longman and Todd).

Keith Bladon trained as a Chartered Accountant in a large provincial practice after graduating from the University of Liverpool. Following experience overseas, working in a large international practice, he returned to this country where he worked in industry and eventually returned to practise, becoming managing partner in a medium-sized firm of Chartered Accountants. He retired in 1992 after a period in private consultancy. Currently a Reader-in-training in the parish of St Nicholas, Hereford, and Chairman of the Diocesan Synod House of Laity, he is also a former Chairman of the Hereford Diocesan Board of Finance and served in this capacity as a member of the Church Commissioners' Consultative Committee of Diocesan Board of Finance Chairmen and Secretaries. He is a member of the Central Board of Finance and its Executive Committee and has been a member of the General Synod since 1995. He also works as a free-lance writer, journalist and broadcaster.

Timothy Bradshaw taught Christian Doctrine at Trinity College, Bristol. He is now Tutor in Doctrine and Dean of Regent's Park College, Oxford. The author of several books and articles, including *The Olive Branch: An Evangelical Anglican Doctrine of the Church* (Paternoster), he is also a member of the International Anglican–

vii

Orthodox Dialogue and the English Anglican–Roman Catholic Committee.

Wesley Carr is Dean of Westminster Abbey. He was previously Dean of Bristol and before that Canon Residentiary of Chelmsford Cathedral where he was Deputy Director of the Cathedral Centre for Research and Training and the Bishop's Director of Training. He has had an extensive involvement with ministry issues in the Church of England, including membership of the Advisory Board of Ministry and several of its committees. He is a member of the General Synod. He is the author of a number of books on the church's ministry and pastoral practice and on several other topics.

Leslie J. Francis is D.J. James Professor of Pastoral Theology at Trinity College Carmarthen and University of Wales Lampeter, and Dean of Chapel at Trinity College. He combines research interests in pastoral theology, religious education and social psychology. His recent books include *Research in Religious Education* (Gracewing), *Drift from the Churches* (University of Wales Press), *Church Watch* (SPCK), *Personality Type and Scripture* (Mowbrays) and *All God's People* (Gracewing).

Robin Gill is Michael Ramsey Professor of Modern Theology in the University of Kent at Canterbury. He is the author of a number of books including *Moral Leadership in a Postmodern Age* (T & T Clark), *A Textbook of Christian Ethics* (T & T Clark) and *Christian Ethics in Secular Worlds* (T & T Clark).

Robert Hannaford until recently Senior Lecturer in Theology at Canterbury Christ Church College and honorary assistant priest in the parish of Harbledown, Canterbury, is now Professor of Theology in the Chichester Institute of Higher Education. He has taught at Exeter and Oxford Universities and was formerly tutor in Christian Doctrine at St Stephen's House, Oxford. A specialist in Systematic and Philosophical Theology he has published several articles and edited collections on Ecclesiology and Anglican Theology. He has been a member of the General Synod since 1997.

Gordon P. Jeanes is Sub-Warden of St Michael's Theological College, Llandaff, and Lecturer in Church History, University of Wales, Cardiff. Previously, after parish work in South Wimbledon and Surbiton in the diocese of Southwark, he was Chaplain of St Chad's College and Cuming Fellow in Liturgy in the University of Durham. He has written widely on matters of liturgy, in both historical studies and current theological and pastoral issues, and is a member of the Church in Wales Standing Liturgical Advisory Commission.

Lynne Leeder read theology and law at Girton College, Cambridge.

During that period she studied canon law with E. Garth Moore and completed a thesis on the seal of the confessional. A member of Lincoln's Inn, she practised at the Chancery Bar before joining the Government Legal Service. She has also acted as legal adviser to the government of Sierra Leone and is currently working on a project to simplify legislation. She was a contributor to *The Deacon's Ministry* (Gracewing) and *Through a Glass Darkly* (Gracewing), and is also a contributor to legal journals. She is the author of *A Handbook of Ecclesiastical Law* (Sweet and Maxwell).

Margaret Selby graduated in theology at the University of Durham. After working as tutor at Lightfoot House in Durham she was accepted by CACTM in 1959 for accredited lay ministry. Since then, she has worked in a team ministry in Cowley, as a community worker in inner Birmingham, as a University Chaplain, and as a Director of Training in Sheffield before going to the College of the Resurrection as Director of Pastoral Studies.

Christopher Smith read theology at Cambridge and was ordained priest in 1969. He served in the Diocese of Liverpool for many years, as curate at Our Lady and St Nicholas' parish, as Team Vicar of St Andrew's, Tower Hill in the parish of Kirby and, most recently, as Rector of Walton. He is currently a Canon Residentiary at Sheffield Cathedral.

Mary Tanner is currently the General Secretary of the General Synod's Council for Christian Unity. She has served on a number of bilateral theological conversations including the Anglican–Roman Catholic International Commission and the Porvoo and Meissen Conversations. For the last eight years she has served as Moderator of the World Council of Churches' Faith and Order Commission. Before taking up full time ecumenical work in 1982 she taught Old Testament and Hebrew.

Preface

The purpose of this collection of essays is to present the reader with an account of important aspects of the life of the Church of England as it prepares to enter the next millennium. The contributors assess the current state of the church and raise important questions about its future direction. They represent the range of traditions within Anglicanism and all, except two from the Church in Wales, are members of the Church of England. While none have fought shy of raising sharply critical questions, all write of a church that they love and honour. In the best traditions of Anglicanism they make full use of critical scholarship but, as this volume is offered to the church at large and not just to the scholarly community, they have avoided the use of highly technical language.

The volume comes at a time of considerable change in the life of the Church of England. The General Synod has just given final approval to the National Institutions Measure which establishes for the first time a national executive body charged with overseeing the life of the church. Many see this as an un-Anglican innovation, importing into our tradition a curial model of government. Others wonder how far a single executive body will be able to harness the life of an increasingly plural church. The Elizabethan settlement of the sixteenth century secured a future for the Church of England as the national church of the English people. The boundaries of membership were drawn fairly wide so as to include all but the most extreme of Catholic and Protestant churchmen and women. Those who remained outside were persecuted and excluded from full participation in the State. It would be inaccurate to deny that many were Anglicans by conviction, but the fact remains that, unlike the churches of the continental Reformation where consent was secured on the basis of clear confessional theological statements, political establishment played a key role in building the identity of the English church. Once secularism

emerged as a powerful force in the nineteenth centufy, political establishment gradually weakened as a factor in the identity of the Church
of England. It is no coincidence that the nineteenth century witnessed
the emergence of theological pluralism within the church; separate
'parties' developed, each with its vision of what it means to be the
Church of God. The gradual withdrawal of the State from the life of
the Church has removed the constraints that held the extremes of
churchmanship in check. This, together with the cultural pluralism of
modern England, constitutes perhaps the greatest challenge for the
contemporary Church of England. Quite simply, and perhaps for the
first time in its post-Reformation history, the Church of England faces
questions about the kind of church it conceives itself to be. Is it to be
a church simply for the converted or will it continue to provide a
refuge for all who are seeking a spiritual dimension to their lives?

In one way or another pluralism features as a key factor in all of
the essays that follow. Wesley Carr considers the complex structure
of the Church of England and raises particularly critical questions
about the church's life at the national level. He is sceptical about the
Turnbull Commission's assessment of the relationship between the
various structural levels of the church, arguing that it has misconceived the idea of the national working of the Church of England.[1]
Keith Bladon surveys the Church of England's material and financial
resources. He is sharply critical of the church's leadership in these
matters and is doubtful whether all the lessons of the Church
Commissioners' disastrous involvement in property speculation have
been learnt. He also makes reference to the implications of the
church's increasing dependence upon parochial giving. On the principle that there can be no taxation without representation, he predicts
an uncertain future as the parishes demand an increasing say over how
their money is spent. A similar future is predicted by Lynne Leeder
in her examination of the legal position of the church. She examines
the legal and canonical implications of the Church's changing relationship with the State and society in general. In particular she takes
note of the long-term implications of the changing structure of
community life in modern Britain, a factor that is noted by more than
one contributor. The parochial system is premised on a geographi-
cally-based notion of community. This has already been compromised
by factors such as churchmanship, with Anglicans 'shopping around'
to find a church that matches their own tradition. In society as a whole
communities are increasingly defined by interests, work and leisure
rather than by physical location. This has serious strategic implications for the structure and organisation of the Church of England.
Ministry and mission are still conceived primarily in terms of

geographically-defined parishes, but this is already being challenged by factors such as church planting and what Wesley Carr terms 'para-parishes'. Representation, a crucial factor in modern Anglicanism, is also premised on the traditional structure of parishes and deaneries but this is likely to become increasingly problematic.

In his contribution Paul Avis considers the question of spiritual leadership in a society which appears to have turned its back on traditional forms of authority. Without neglecting the importance of conciliar authority in Anglicanism, Avis's essay hinges on the question of episcopal authority. Cultural fragmentation and the voracious appetite of the communications media for news impose enormous demands upon the bishops. They are expected to speak for their communities; the question is, how can they speak with one voice for a church which is increasingly divided on questions of faith and morals? Avis acknowledges the importance of effective communication but insists that too little attention is given to the question of what is to be communicated.

Following a sustained discussion of social change over the past fifty years, Margaret Selby and Christopher Smith consider the implications of different ecclesiological models for our understanding of the mission of the Church in England. Like Tim Bradshaw they also consider the implications of social change for the shape of the church's mission at the parochial level. Bradshaw offers a vision of ministry that is deeply traditional and radical at the same time, suggesting various ways in which the Church of England should respond to and embrace pluralism. He notes the implications of increasing theological polarisation in the church and speculates that the church will be forced to embrace more flexible models of ordained and non-ordained ministry. Tentative models of experimentation such as the use of informal worship sessions for young people may point the way forward for the future modelling of the church at the local level. Bradshaw's is the only essay in this volume in which church-manship plays an explicit part and this calls for some explanation. Ministry is obviously a matter of deep concern for the whole Church but since a clear majority of ordinands now stand in the evangelical tradition it was felt appropriate to include this as a key factor in this particular contribution.

In his contribution Leslie Francis offers a comprehensive analysis of the Church of England's involvement in education and schooling. He considers the results of various studies of the effectiveness of Church of England schools, noting that they have at best a neutral effect on the religious beliefs of their students. He points to the need for further work on the development of a theology of education and for greater clarity on the part of the church about the purpose of its involvement in schools. In a final section he examines the church's considerable investment in higher education. It comes as a surprise to many Anglicans to learn that tens of thousands of students receive their higher education in Anglican institutions. Virtually all of the Church of England's Colleges of Higher Education offer a wide-ranging curriculum and several now award their own degrees. The likelihood is that there will be an Anglican university in England in the not too distant future. Until relatively recently it was customary for the church to ignore its own colleges and to relate instead to the secular universities. This was understandable when validation for courses of ministerial training was only possible from the secular institutions but in the case of many of the colleges this no longer applies. Furthermore theology is under considerable pressure in a number of existing universities and it makes greater sense for the church to cultivate its own resources.

Uniformity of worship was an early victim of the emergence of the Evangelical Revival in the eighteenth century and, to a greater extent, the Oxford Movement in the following century. For better or worse the Book of Common Prayer no longer occupies the liturgically unifying place that it once did in the Church of England. Churchmanship is not the only factor contributing to liturgical change and development. Social and cultural pluralism is also a major consideration in the search for an appropriate form of common prayer for the next millennium. The experience of the mass media is instructive in this respect. Fewer and fewer programmes are aimed at a genuinely mass audience. Programme makers increasingly target particular cultural groups which are defined in terms of age, interests, ethnic origin, and gender or sexual orientation. Liturgists are now confronted with an enormous challenge: how to compile forms of worship that are faithful to Christian tradition and at the same time culturally accessible to the widest range of people. As this volume appears, the Church of England is in the process of finding a replacement for the *Alternative Service Book*. Gordon Jeanes has wisely avoided offering specific comment on this project but his careful analysis of the current situation and his identification of a common liturgical core will come as a helpful contribution to this debate.

When the time comes to write the history of the modern Church of England's involvement in ecumenical affairs the picture will be a mixed one. Two major attempts at unity in England came to nothing: the Anglican–Methodist Unity Scheme in 1969 and again in 1972, and the Covenant for Unity in 1982; but in 1997 the Porvoo Common Statement established a new relationship with the Nordic and Baltic

Lutheran Churches. The General Synod recently agreed to pursue official conversations with the Methodist Church but the tone of the debate on this matter was measured rather than enthusiastic. Many placed great store by the considerable achievements of the two Anglican–Roman Catholic International Commissions but the Roman Church has been slow in responding to the ensuing Agreed Statements. Mary Tanner surveys the current position and sets out an agenda for the future. The churches in England need to develop a common understanding of the kind of unity they are seeking. The lack of such a 'portrait of unity' engenders suspicion amongst those who fear the loss of their traditional ecclesial identity. The Church of England in particular needs to see that different ecumenical advances are consistent and coherent with one another. She points out, for example, that the question of the inter-Anglican implications of the Porvoo arrangements, which only involve the British and Irish Anglican Churches, appear to have been overlooked. This underlines the need for the Anglican Communion itself to develop more effective structures of unity.

When asked to identify what is distinctive about their own approach to theology Anglicans often point to theological method and particularly the role of reason as the key component. Since the place of reason in theology is at its clearest in the theology of culture, I have chosen to take this as the focus of my own discussion of the theological life of the Church of England. Following a survey of recent trends in Anglican theology, I consider the implications of cultural pluralism and the growing awareness of the historically contingent nature of reason for a contemporary theology of culture. It is clear that the ethical climate within western societies is undergoing profound change: cultural pluralism, developments in medical technology, the increasing rejection of traditional forms of authority, are all having an effect on church and society. This is particularly true in sexual ethics where attitudes have changed dramatically during the past fifty years. Behaviour which would once have guaranteed social exclusion is now commonplace. Robin Gill takes up this theme, noting that it is likely to be the most troublesome issue facing the Church of England over the next few decades. His work on recent attitude surveys underscores the difficulties facing Christian leaders as they strive for a consensus on ethical matters. While younger church members evince more liberal attitudes, the older and numerically more significant members are markedly more conservative in their approach. Anglican leaders appear to be in an impossible position. If they take a firm line they are in danger of alienating the young, but if they take a more liberal line they are likely to be accused of secularisation by the majority. Of all the issues facing the church the question of homosexuality looks set to be the most intractable. Gill is sharply critical of the 1991 House of Bishops' report *Issues in Human Sexuality*, arguing that the bishops seem to be more concerned with the avoidance of public scandal than with questions of ethical principle. He concludes his discussion by identifying certain abiding Christian virtues which are balanced differently in changing historical circumstances.

Finally, some explanation of the procedures involved in compiling this volume are called for. The project is a personal initiative on the part of the contributors. They write as Anglicans but not at the behest of any interest group or body within the Church of England. In that sense the book is offered as a constructive contribution to the debate about the future of the Church of England and not as a manifesto. Indeed, while the authors have written to a common brief, no effort has been made to secure a common theological or critical voice. Hopefully, careful editing has removed any repetition or incoherence but the words of each essay stand in their own right. Every effort has been made by the writers to make the volume as accurate and topical as possible. However, people write at different speeds and the process of time might well have overtaken some of the practical illustrations used by the authors. In mitigation it should be pointed out that this is the price to be paid for writing about the actual life of the church. That having been said, all of the contributors have taken the long-term view and they should be judged in terms of the depth of their analysis and judgement and not by the narrower criteria of short-term topicality.

Ash Wednesday, 1998

Note

1. *Working as One Body: the report of the Archbishops' Commission on the organisation of the Church of England* (Church House Publishing, London, 1995).

Introduction: The Theological and Historical Context

Robert Hannaford

This collection of essays about the condition of the Church of England on the edge of the next millennium focuses upon a number of practical and theological issues. All the issues discussed, from organisation and finance to theology and ethics, are crucial to the identity and working of the Church of England. Inevitably each author has concentrated upon his or her field of enquiry but it is important not to overlook the larger, ecclesiological, picture. The Church can be studied in the same way as any other complex social organisation, and there is much to be gained from this. However, such approaches, by definition, exclude any sense of the Church's apostolic calling. While pressures of time and space mean that it was not possible to include any explicit discussion of ecclesiology in this volume, the authors take it as read that they are talking about the Church of God and not simply another human organisation. While they address in one way or another matters of practical concern they do so against the backdrop of the Church's mission under God. Although this introduction falls short of providing a comprehensive ecclesiological framework, it does raise the question of an appropriate theological perspective for reflection on the Church and its effectiveness. Ecclesiology represents the Church as the tangible, historical, outcome of the divine–human mystery of Christ. It is important that this should be understood as the ultimate point of perspective for any study of the actual historical life of the Church.

The enormous challenges facing the Church of England need to be set within an historical and theological context. History reminds us that the Church is always confronted with crisis, and theology identifies this as the inevitable and unavoidable consequence of its eschatological positioning at the point where this age meets the reality of the age to come. As those who are already experiencing the power of the new age of the Kingdom, Christians are made more and not less aware of their shortcomings. Theologically this suggests that all reflection on the actual historical experience of the Church must match sober reflection with the celebration of God's grace and power.

'The Church as it now stands, no human power can save.' This sentiment refers not as one might suppose to the apparently crisis-ridden church of our own day but to the church of the early nineteenth century. To reformers such as Thomas Arnold, the author of the statement, the Church of England appeared moribund and incapable of reform. In point of fact his pessimism was misplaced, for the nineteenth century proved to be a period of considerable reform and change in both Church and State. New programmes of church building were set in hand, additional dioceses were created, the question of the unequal distribution of clerical stipends was addressed and serious attempts were made to assess the spiritual condition of the nation.

It is tempting to regard one's own age as peculiarly fraught with problems and challenges, and members of the Church of England are no exception to this rule. The national press both feeds and responds to this pessimism. During the week in which this introduction was first drafted various stories appeared to confirm this impression. The installation of a new Bishop of Newcastle provided the occasion for a further story about the Church of England's apparent confusion over sexual ethics and homosexuality in particular. The bishop-elect had uttered remarks on the subject to which some took exception. Even before his arrival in the diocese three parishes stated that they would not be able to accept his authority as bishop. One of these parishes had planned to have a lay worker ordained to serve in an unlicensed post and was only inhibited from doing so by the legal action of the acting diocesan bishop. The week also saw stories suggesting that the Church of England was attempting to conceal the extent of decline in its own membership. The Statistics Unit of the Church of England had omitted figures for regular Sunday worship from a summary of statistics published in February 1998. The press chose to ignore the fact that the unit is investigating new ways of measuring the changing pattern of church attendance.[1]

Anglicans pride themselves on their attention to history in matters of theology but seem unwilling to adopt an historical perspective when considering the current state of the Church of England. Anyone leafing through the pages of R.P. Flindall's excellent documentary history of the Church of England from 1815 to 1948 will be struck by the parallels with our own times.[2] The church of the last century, like ours, was anxious about the growing gap between its own life and that of the rest of the nation. The Census of Religious Worship published in 1851 suggested that about five and a half million people in England and Wales, mainly drawn from the urban working class, were not churchgoers.[3] The nineteenth century was also a period of intense theological debate. The controversy following the publication of *Essays and Reviews* in 1860 was perhaps the most notable. The book was 'an attempt to illustrate the advantage derivable to the cause of religious and moral truth, from a free handling, in a becoming spirit, of subjects peculiarly liable to suffer by the repetition of conventional language and from traditional methods of treatment' and attracted a formal remonstrance from the Archbishop of Canterbury and 26 bishops. A little earlier, in 1853, F.D. Maurice's refusal to equate eternal death with eternal punishment in his essay on *Eternal Life and Eternal Death* led to his dismissal as Professor in Divinity at King's College, London.[4] In the 1920s the ground of controversy shifted from particular doctrines to the wider question of the nature of the Christian revelation itself and its expression in scripture and creed. Many Anglo-Catholics saw Modernism as a threat to the historic faith, and successfully petitioned the Archbishop of Canterbury to establish a doctrinal commission. Although they had hoped for an authoritative statement of the common mind of the church, the report, which was not finally published until 1938, contented itself with setting out the various theological viewpoints then current within the Church of England.[5] The report confirmed the impression, already gaining ground in the previous century, of a church profoundly divided on matters of theology. Theological differences, particularly over the ecclesiological implications of historic Anglican formularies, also surfaced in a number of disputes about relations with other non-Anglican churches. The Tractarians objected to the establishment in 1841 of a joint bishopric in Jerusalem for Anglicans and members of the non-episcopal Prussian National Church.[6] Although this was warmly welcomed by many Evangelicals, Anglo-Catholics insisted that it represented a threat to the integrity of the Church of England's episcopal polity. Similar objections were raised about the proposals put forward at the conference held at Kikuyu in British East Africa in 1913. At this missionary conference of Protestant churches a scheme was proposed for the union of various missionary societies which made no explicit mention of episcopacy. Bishop Frank Weston of Zanzibar, a leading Anglo-Catholic, objected to the scheme and particularly to the fact that the two Anglican bishops involved had given communion to members of non-episcopal churches at the concluding service of the conference.[7] The nineteenth century also witnessed the gradual erosion of the church's authority in matters of public morality with many in the church seeing the Divorce Act of 1857 as marking the State's effective abandonment of the scriptural basis of ethics.[8]

The historically sensitive will see the echoes of these controversies in our own age. Now as then many in the church are exercised by the continuing pace of secularisation. Our own Decade of Evangelism bears comparison with the National Mission of Repentance and Hope launched by Archbishop Davidson in 1916. Our own efforts to identify a suitable framework for channelling the national life of the church recall the revival of the Convocations of Canterbury and York in 1852 and 1861 respectively, and the Enabling Act of 1919 which established the National Assembly. Even the tenor of recent theological controversies, such as that following the publication of the 1976 Doctrine Commission report, *Christian Believing*,[9] or more recently over the disciplining of a clerical member of the Sea of Faith network, recalls the passion and sometimes even the language of earlier theological debates. Tractarian refusal to countenance any compromise on the historic episcopate find almost its exact parallel in modern-day Anglo-Catholic objections to the Anglican–Methodist Unity Scheme, the Covenant for Unity and, more recently, the Porvoo Common Statement. The debate which began in the middle of the last century about divorce and its consequences looks set to be overtaken by the discussion of wider questions of human sexuality, but the fissure opened up in the nineteenth century between traditional Christian morality and secular ethics is more pronounced than ever.

A sense of history can help to set our contemporary concerns and anxieties in an appropriate time frame. We should not expect to find speedy solutions to problems that have beset our church for at least two hundred years, and certainly not without paying careful attention to the lessons of past experience. A sense of historical perspective can also help to obviate the almost hysterical obsession with problem-solving that bedevils our church. 'It was ever thus' is not a counsel of despair but a necessary reminder of that contingency which God has determined for his Church in this age. The Church awaits the fulfilment of the Lord's promises, but gospel hope should not be confused with the very human yearning for tidy and effective ecclesial systems. The pursuit of better church order and government needs to be set within an eschatological as well as an historical context. Since the Church is established within history it cannot avoid engaging with the kinds of questions that concern any human society, but its frame of reference includes eternity as well as time. The Church naturally embraces all that is best and constructive in human learning and ingenuity but this is not to be confused with its ultimate goal and purpose. Although the Church is set within time and history it exists for the sake of that which is ultimate and final, God's Kingdom of reconciliation and peace. The Church serves a Kingdom which it neither owns nor controls. On the contrary, it is God's Kingdom that establishes the ultimate context for all action and decision-making in the Church.

We habitually think in terms of means and ends, in the Church no less than in society. It is always tempting to see questions of church order and governance as simply a means to the true end of the Church. Paradoxically, this has the effect of making such questions seem both vital and inconsequential at the same time; vital because of the urgency of our task and the need for effectiveness in mission and evangelism; inconsequential insofar as they are viewed as contingent means to an absolute end. In contrast to this, eschatology knows nothing of means and ends; God's Kingdom is simply *the* end. Whatever serves the Kingdom is already a sign of that end; there can be no means to this end which are not also an anticipation of the end itself. The Church is appropriately termed an instrument of the Kingdom, but as the body of Christ it is already an effective sign and sacrament of the Kingdom's fulfilment. This insight is powerfully expressed in the ARCIC II agreed statement on *Church as Communion*:

> Communion with God through Christ is constantly established and renewed through the power of the Holy Spirit. By the power of the Spirit, the incomparable riches of God's grace are made present for all time through the Church. Those who are reconciled to God form 'one body in Christ and are individually members one of another' (Rom. 12.5). By the action of the same Spirit, believers are baptised into one Body (1 Cor. 12.13) and in the breaking of bread they also participate in that one body (1 Cor. 10.16–17; 11.23–29). Thus the Church 'which is Christ's body, the fullness of him who fills all in all', reveals and embodies 'the mystery of Christ' (cf. Eph. 1.23; 3.4, 8–11). It is therefore itself rightly described as a visible sign which both points to and embodies our communion with God and with one another; as an instrument through which God effects this communion; and as a foretaste of the fullness of communion to be consummated when Christ is all in all. It is a 'mystery' or 'sacrament'.[10]

The Church proclaims *and* anticipates the Kingdom that is to come in its own life. All that serves and embodies our communion with God and one another points to that final moment when God will be all in all. Many would point to the sacraments, and especially the eucharist, as the principal expression of this communion but the sacraments are inclusive and not exclusive; they signify the eschatological orientation of the whole life of the Church. This explains why attention to the unity of the Church and the effectiveness of its mission are matters of eschatological significance and urgency, but it also sets our concern about these matters in their proper perspective. Anxiety about organisational or structural questions, even – maybe, especially – when the goal is the proclamation of God's Kingdom, is totally inappropriate in relation to the Kingdom of ends.

The words of Jesus in the Sermon on the Mount apply to the Church as much as to Christian individuals: 'Therefore, I tell you, do not be anxious about your life, what you shall eat or what you shall drink, nor about your body, what you shall put on. Is not life more than food, and the body more than clothing?' (Matt. 6.25). The whole point of this passage is missed if it is interpreted simply as an ethical injunction concerning the intrinsic value of poverty. The concluding verse of this particular section of the Sermon makes it clear that the passage refers to the new eschatological context in which Christians find themselves: 'But seek first his kingdom and his righteousness, and all these things shall be yours as well' (Matt. 6.33). Anxiety about even the basic essentials of life is inappropriate for those whose attention is fixed on the dawning of the new age of the Kingdom. The implications for ecclesiology are fairly clear: anxiety about the effectiveness of the Church and its mission betrays a lack of trust in the promises of God and in the power and reality of the Kingdom at work in the life of the Christian community. The middle section of our passage from the Sermon on the Mount could be transcribed as follows: 'Which of you by being anxious can add to what God is already achieving through the mission and ministry of the Church?' (cf. Matt. 6.27). We are right to take very seriously matters of Church order and governance, but not to the point where this passes over into anxiety. Anxiety betrays a lack of confidence and trust in the grace of God at work in the life of the Church. In the end it is grace which constitutes the human community of the Church as the sign and sacrament of God's eschatological Kingdom, and his grace is sufficient. As sign and sacrament of the end of all things the Church is already an effective instrument of divine grace; nothing that we do can either nullify or improve upon the work of grace. In Christ we see that the sufficiency of grace includes rather than excludes our humanity and

freedom; in that sense Christian discipleship and effort plays a constitutive role in the divine–human mystery of the Church. Dependence
upon divine grace can never be an excuse for passivity and quietism
but it does exclude the despair and weariness that sometimes infects
our relationships with the body of Christ. Our acknowledgement of
the mystery of the Church means believing that it is already in an
important sense a sign of the end and not merely a means to that end.

Eschatology injects a necessary sense of urgency into our mission
but it also militates against feverish activism by enlarging our perspective. Fulfilment and perfection are God's eschatological gift and can
never come as a result of human action and deliberation. Since the
Church proclaims a Kingdom that is not of this world it should
observe an appropriate humility and reserve in its own counsels. The
challenge for the Church is not that of achieving organisational perfection but of bearing witness to the coming Kingdom within the
constraints of history. The mission of the Church is not rendered
impossible until it is perfected. On the contrary, its very incompleteness serves the mission of God in Christ. The apostle Paul realised
this well, recognising that his weakness was a sign of the power and
efficacy of God's grace (2 Cor. 12.9; 4.7–12). Even what we perceive
to be our weaknesses and deficiencies serve the purposes of God. The
Church's potency as a sign of the Kingdom depends entirely upon the
power of God's love. It is when we are weak and recognise our
incompleteness as a community that we demonstrate our need of God.
To say otherwise comes dangerously close to suggesting that the
Church ceases to be the Church when it manifests incompleteness. In
signifying 'what is lacking' the very incompleteness of the Church
serves the mystery of God's will, pointing beyond the Church to the
fulfilment that it too hopes and yearns for.[11]

Notes

1. *The Church of England Today: A Summary of Current Statistics* GS Misc
   513 (Church of England Statistics Unit, London, 1998).
2. R.P. Flindall, (ed.), *The Church of England 1815–1948: A Documentary
   History* (SPCK, London, 1972).
3. ibid., pp. 124–35.
4. ibid., pp. 149–51.
5. ibid., pp. 370–5, 416–20.
6. ibid., pp. 100–4.
7. ibid., pp. 299–307.
8. ibid., pp. 152–4.
9. *Christian Believing: The Nature of the Christian Faith and its Expression*

     in Holy Scripture and Creeds (SPCK, London, 1976).
10. *Church as Communion*. An Agreed Statement by the Second Anglican–Roman Catholic International Commission (Church House Publishing/Catholic Truth Society, London, 1991), 17.
11. For a more detailed discussion of this theme see my 'Ecclesiology and Communion' in R. Hannaford (ed.), *The Future of Anglicanism: Essays on Faith and Order* (Gracewing, Leominster, 1996), pp. 55–89.

Part One:
Organisation and Structure

1

The Church of England in the Next Millennium: Structure and Organisation[1]

Wesley Carr

Introduction

Any attempt at informed speculation about the shape of the Church of England in the twenty-first century has ultimately to issue in proposals for its organisation. But organisation always follows task: it does not determine it. And if the task is unclear, then sound organisational proposals are impossible. It is necessary, therefore, initially to hypothesise an underlying ecclesiology for the Church of England. This is notoriously difficult. But the fact of such difficulty itself expounds the distinctively English Anglican understanding of the Church. Its distinguishing mark is the way that it is a community of people called out both by God to worship and service and by society for a specific function. The Church of England exists less because of any decision of some who consider themselves to be members than on the will, or even need, of the society that forms its context to use it as a means for religious expression. In its believing the Church of England chiefly acts on behalf of others. Around this core idea swirl social change and ecclesiastical debate.

During the twentieth century three major stages in the life of the Church of England can be discerned.[2] Prior to 1914 it was a national church, its activities at every level permeating and being permeated by English society. People attended; the clergy were influential; and the church was strong in areas such as education, health and welfare. The next phase was marked by a preoccupation with becoming a lively denomination. Lay participation increased, especially as a result of the

3

Church Assembly and later synodical government. The Church began to speak to national life rather than for it. New dioceses were formed and a more self-consciously Christian liturgy emerged. Since the 1980s the third change is occurring. The multi-ethnic and multi-faith society with its prevailing cultural pluralism is giving way to a world of non-institutional and private religion. Within the Church of England the influence of this culture creates new tensions between notions of order and an emphasis on self-expression which organisationally borders on anarchy.

If this analysis is largely accurate, then the identity of the Church of England has already become problematic and suggesting suitable new structures becomes almost impossible. For even allowing for the inevitable delay in institutional response to change, it is unlikely that a new organisation can be devised for this third-stage church. The difficulty would be compounded by the financial pressures being experienced by the church as much as by many other bodies. But this is not the whole picture. Through all these stages the task of the Church of England has remained the same. It continues to exist, more than probably any other church (certainly those in England), on the basis of the interchange between it and its context.[3] The style and even locus of this interaction may alter. But it remains distinctive. If that fact provides the fundamental ecclesiology, the consequential organisational structure may be devised on the basis that the church is an open system. If, however, the Church of England in the twenty-first century will become (or even has become already) closed, the structure will be different, probably unrecognisable. On this point, therefore, a decision is required before any discussion of structures.

The mark of an open system is that attention is paid to the relationship between the way in which behaviour within an organisation is directly related to the way that the institution as a whole interacts with its environment. The environment is included in any analysis of the system as a whole.[4] When considering the organisation of a church some such approach is essential. For from an organisational perspective a church is composed from the beliefs held about it and what it represents, not only by its members but by others in its context. But that environment, like the beliefs of the members, is a mix of rational and irrational beliefs and expectations, most of them unexpressed and even inexpressible. All churches work in this dynamic setting.[5] But the Church of England is unusual in that it has incorporated this task into its ecclesiology. This task also gives practical meaning to the generalised idea of an established church.

Any approach to the church's organisation, therefore, has to take this interaction into account. The current environment may be characterised thus. There is a decline in public religious practice. But this does not necessarily imply a similar reduction in religious belief. The impact of secularisation on religion has not produced its apparently inexorable conclusion. Indeed, this failure may prove to be one of the most significant factors for the Church of England in the next century. For it leaves the church without a convenient excuse to explain people's withdrawal from it. It also forces a reconsideration of religion as a phenomenon and the relationship of the Christian churches, especially the Church of England, to it.[6] It may be, therefore, that in the face of continuing religion and the waning of belief in science, the predominant 'religion' of the twentieth century, society will need some institution to handle on its behalf the irrational and confusing dimensions of human life.[7] For the time being in England it may also be surmised that this is likely to be primarily the Church of England, whatever ecumenical developments take place. This seems a reasonable assumption on which to base a discussion of the organisational structure that the church requires. And if it proves false, then the organisational questions will be unimportant. I will, therefore, assume in what follows:

(1) that religion will continue as a phenomenon;
(2) that the Church of England will continue to offer to deal purposefully with such religion. It is difficult to know whether this is as likely as the first proposition. The continuing conventional affirmation of the parochial system, for instance, is not necessarily a commitment to this specific task;[8]
(3) that, therefore, the primary task[9] of the Church of England is to provide opportunities for religious behaviour. This is the critical point at which the distinctively Christian interpretation of life to which the church witnesses is brought to bear on all aspects of living. This is a major statement about the nature of the church and its task. It also is a task around which those with differing theological emphases may unite.

This practical establishment has a major impact on organisational thinking about the Church of England. For most of its components operate as charitable bodies. The church is, therefore, deeply involved in civil and charitable law, not just its own arrangements. These two add to the inevitable bureaucracy and skew even the brightest organisational proposals.

In discussion of the organisation of the Church of England three components are usually given attention: the parish, the diocese and the national church. Floating, and often disputed, is the deanery. These are useful distinctions, but they need to be used with care. In the

Church there is a natural tendency to homogenise rather than to differ-entiate and to endorse one specific icon at the expense of others.[10] The image of the body of Christ, for example, ceases to hold different parts together and celebrates inseparability. The churches have elevated this into a liturgical expression of fellowship. When consid-ering organisation, however, it is important not to confuse the different tasks of these parts of the overall institution and elevate one into a presumed primary task. It is also essential to have a clear grasp of the structural relations between them.

In recent discussions, and notably in the Report of the Archbishops' Commission on the Organisation of the Church of England (1995),[11] the principle of subsidiarity has been invoked. This is a theological concept, formally expounded in 1931 by Pius XI:

> The following most important principle in moral philosophy remains fixed and immovable. Just as in respect of those things which can be carried out by individuals through their own exertion and industry, it is unlawful to seize them and hand them over to the community, so also in respect of those which can be effected and undertaken by smaller and lower level communities (*inferioribus communitatibus*), it is unjust to divert them to a greater and higher association (*altiorem societatem*). It is similarly a serious wrong and overturns due order. For any social activity by its strength ought to afford support (*subsidium*) to the members of the social body and certainly never destroy them or take them over.[12]

This idea is organisationally important. It does not, as is popularly supposed, describe levels in a structural hierarchy. It is concerned with how support is provided in and strength built into a system and with the underlying grace and justice of such behaviour. Subsidiarity, therefore, is to do with tasks and where they are appropriately located and not with levels of activity. If levels are given undue prominence, the tendency will always be to look for structural parallels between them rather than to create an effectively interactive organisation. In the Church, as elsewhere, systems are not straightforwardly parallel with each other: they are structurally complementary.

Synodical government

The twentieth century has seen some of the greatest changes in the church's structure since the Reformation. Any future organisation will build on this foundation. Some factors are historical, such as the trans-formation of society during and since the Victorian era. Not separable, but conveniently considered separately, are the attitudes and beliefs of that society. The Church of England is always enmeshed in social change in a distinctive fashion. It is also in a profound way caught up in the general place assigned to religious belief in the West. Because of its nature this church can neither stand against nor endorse the prevailing mores and beliefs. Consequently it may seem to vacillate. Such uncertainty may not be a virtue, but organisationally it may be taken as evidence of life.

During the nineteenth century communications were transformed, notably by the new media and the railways. One effect was that the various parts of the church began to function in a different fashion. Bishops, for example, became accessible to their clergy and, even more significantly in due course, to the parochial laity. The idea of managing the church was given prominence through the series of commissions that reported. The Convocations, originally an integral part of the national political establishment, were revived as church bodies, Canterbury in 1852 and York in 1861. But because they were increasingly regarded as concerned with church affairs, their limitations as clerical bodies were exposed. Parliament retained ultimate control, but was no longer the sole debating chamber for church matters. Consequently in 1885 a House of Laity was associated with the Canterbury Convocation, although York only followed in 1892. From this period dates one of the most significant phenomena of the twentieth century – 'ecclesiastical laymen':

A man like Lord Halifax influenced the history of the Church of England far more by his presidency of the English Church Union than from his seat in the House of Lords ... They were men of public spirit and energy, willing to give time to unpalatable subjects for the sake of their church, and without them the Church of England could not have reorganised itself to encounter the twentieth century.[13]

Since then this structure has been elaborated and a steady movement towards independent government of the Church of England has ensued. In 1919 the Enabling Act created the Church Assembly, something which had been strongly urged by Archbishop Benson in 1890.[14] This was superseded by synodical government. The Synodical Government Measure (1969) put in place a graduated representative system – Parochial Church Council, Deanery, Diocesan and General Synods – in which each part was intended to relate to each other. In so doing the Church of England not only took a further step in the process begun at the end of the nineteenth century. It also acknowledged, for the most part inadvertently, one other change: the increasing influence of the Anglican Communion, in the churches of which some form of synodical government was already the norm.

Some distinctively English factors, however, remain, among which three are notable. First, most of this system has been superimposed on existing structures. The General Synod, for example, did not replace Parliament, where church affairs are still debated and to which legislative decisions have to be referred. Second, the Church Commissioners retain funds which are for church work (loosely defined) but which under the law they have discretion for administering. This means that the financial structure of the church, although various organisational stratagems have been devised to bring it together as well as may be, remains split between historic resources (largely the Church Commissioners), contemporary giving (the people in the parishes) and the spending bodies (the departments of the General Synod and the dioceses). The third mark of the English synodical system is its pervasiveness. The model of the General Synod is a compromise based on a mix of the British parliamentary system, the history of the convocations and bishops who have not been expected to do very much. The same pattern applies elsewhere: the diocesan synodical system parallels it closely, where the old diocesan conference has been replaced; the deanery synodical system represents a compromise between old structures, such as the clergy chapter and the ruridecanal conference, and the new needs of a voting system. The parish is probably least affected, although the role of the parochial church council has become more powerful. At the national and diocesan level, at least until recently, the shape of boards and councils roughly corresponded. Indeed it was sometimes argued that to have diocesan boards which shadowed the national ones gave the total system greater coherence and congruity.

A partial review of synodical government was attempted in 1988.[15] Its brief was restricted to a consideration of the infrastructure of the General Synod. It has proved to be a largely ineffectual effort that compounded the problems. It was vitiated for three reasons. First, its brief was too limited. The infrastructure of an organisation cannot be isolated from consideration of its task.[16] Too many complexities were overlooked or ignored as falling outside the brief, and the outcome was an unsatisfactory tinkering with an already complicated bureaucracy. Second, at the time there were few indications of the serious financial anxieties that were about to afflict the church. And although the review group identified a number of problems inherent in the committee structure, the Synod itself resisted the major recommendation that finance and policy should be brought together. Proposals to abandon Church House, Westminster and to move the synod departments to the Church Commissioners' building were also rejected. Lord Bridge chaired a full review of synodical government which was published towards the end of 1997, although the Turnbull Commission (of which he was a member) was given advance information.[17] The report recommended among other things the abolition of the convocations and the statutory requirement for deanery synods to be part of the formal structure of synodical government as well as a reduction in size of the General Synod. It received a stormy reception at its take-note debate in the November 1997 General Synod. It is uncertain how far its proposals are likely to be adopted.

The Parish

One function of any organisation is to channel power into constructive activity, action that is based on authority, without diminishing the energy available. So for instance, the enthusiasm and commitment of worshippers is powerful. The parochial system is designed, more unwittingly than deliberately, to allow that erratic vigour of believers and others to be channelled into creative activity. So worship, social action, learning and teaching all emerge as the activities of a congregation in the wider context of the parish. The parish priest is appointed to the cure of souls in the parish as a whole and not to the congregation alone as a sign both to the church and to the world of the stance of this particular church. He or she reminds all that the life of the Church is not an end in itself. The parochial system is not merely a way of organising: it is a theological statement about the nature of the Church as the Church of England perceives this. It is, in a sense, the lived doctrine of what this church believes itself to be called to be.

It is sometimes thought that an emphasis on the parish system implies only one type of working by the church – pastoral action among residents. But the parochial system is not that. 'Parochial' describes an attitude and set of assumptions rather than a geographical entity.[18] In organisational terms it means that the structures begin from a task and not from presuppositions about an institution. In the case of the Church of England that task is taken to be about serving people in the parishes and para-parishes,[19] whether they are formally connected with the church or not. There is a correspondingly minimal notion of membership in Anglican ecclesiology. This is partly a residuum of a time when it could be assumed that all people were Anglican unless they declared to the contrary. But it is also part of the thinking of a church that forms itself by negotiation at the boundary between people's beliefs and feelings, however rarely expressed, and the gospel resource of the Christian community. Organisationally the parish is the ecclesiological unit where power is channelled into authority structures. Those are basically two: that of the congregation expressed through the parochial church council and the church's activities, and that of the parish priest, who is not appointed to that congregation but to the parish. There is, therefore, a proper tension between what each represents. And from such complementarity (a better notion than the contemporary vogue theme of collaboration) creative action results.

The second aspect of that power has recently become more prominent. It is in the parishes, chiefly in practice today in the congregations, that finance is generated. There has as yet been no time fully to evaluate the effect of the swift switch from a church which uses inherited money to subsidise its parochial services to one which wholly relies on current giving. It is sometimes said that the Church of England should not rely on its historic resources, since that allows people to escape the demands of Christian commitment. That is, however, not an accurate assessment of the case. For if the church is parochially structured, then its existence both in the here and now and in its inherited role identifies it. The giving of previous generations to build a capital base is a task-related activity, for it has made it possible for two things to happen. First, the church can continue to assign priests to parishes where there is little or no prospect of the church sustaining itself. And second, the deployment of the priestly resource has not depended on the wishes of the congregations; the church's strategic use of its priest has been free of that control. Whether this state of affairs has now gone or not remains to be seen. But the Social Security Committee of the House of Commons may have been right when it reported that the fiasco over the loss of money by the Church Commissioners might have brought about the demise of the parochial system.[20] It will take a great deal of care and education to ensure that the power of money is channelled to the service of the church's task and that it does not constitute an excuse for abandoning the demands of such a ministry.

The Diocese

By contrast the diocese is a notion in the mind rather than a working entity. A diocese can do nothing other than be a unit of government. Such developments as the post of Diocesan Secretary misleadingly imply that dioceses have a discrete existence. But it is difficult to discern what a diocese can do. Its life is focused in the key role of the diocesan bishop. At this point the Church of England's claim to be an episcopal church becomes real. It is not surprising, therefore, that on the agenda of every Lambeth Conference[21] the issue of bishop and diocese appears. One confusion, however, arises from the word 'local'. For example, in 1988 the report of the Conference states: 'Within the wider context of the mission and ministry of the whole church, the diocese is often seen as basic to the life and unity of the local church. This unity is personified and symbolised in the office of the bishop. Under God the bishop leads the local church in its mission to the world.'[22] But in working terms 'local' in England is parochial. Here the bishop's involvement is not specific: it is participatory.

When a parish priest is inducted he or she receives from the bishop the cure of souls which is 'both yours and mine'. This phrase indicates a shared responsibility. But this obviously does not mean shared working. The bishop is not going personally to work in two hundred or so parishes in his diocese. Even were the church to restructure itself into a series of smaller dioceses, the issue remains. For the phrase, like the principle of subsidiarity, refers to working connections. It is relational, describing how the ministry functions with proper authority. The parish priest is responsible for what the church does in the parish. His or her ministry is, therefore, collaborative with that of the lay people. They complement each other. But the parish priest is also a boundary figure: it is his or her specific responsibility not only to speak for but to the church. An incumbent does that through being in touch with the Church Catholic, that larger entity of which the local church is part and which, assisted by his representative ministry, it also embodies. Organisationally this is achieved by connecting the parish priest to the wider Church through his or her connection with the bishop. He in similar fashion represents the wider Church (the Church Catholic) to the parishes of his diocese. Theologically that is the basis of catholic practice: organisationally it is recognised that the primary, though today not sole, form of such connection has to be personal – it resides in the relationship between parish priest and bishop. In that sense the cure of souls is the responsibility of both: the bishop can do nothing without the parish priest and vice versa.

The basic working unit of the Church of England is the parish; but its primary organisational structure is the diocese.[23] If this church is 'episcopally led and synodically governed' it is important to recognise that 'episcopal' does not merely refer to bishops. It describes the relationship between the bishop with his oversight (*episcope*) and the parish priest as a contributor to that. For the Church of England,

therefore, in the future as much as in the past, the critical nexus is
that between bishop and incumbent. Both are boundary figures, i.e.,
they are responsible for bringing a wider perspective to bear on what
is respectively for each of them local. Theologically this wider
perspective is the catholic tradition, as manifest in the four marks of
the Church – unity, holiness, catholicity and apostolicity. Practically
it is seen by their customarily being appointed from outside the immediate context. Recent discussions about the church's ministry have not
paid as great attention to this as is necessary for the Church of
England. Interestingly confusions have arisen at the level both of
bishop and parish priest.

The role of the bishop has been confused by the proliferation of
suffragan bishops. What was intended as a temporary expedient has
become so foundational to the life of the Church of England that the
role is now seen for some as an apprenticeship to becoming a diocesan bishop. In January 1996 twenty-one diocesan bishops had
previously been suffragans. Not only has such an appointments system
changed the apparent significance of the suffragan role; it has also
altered assumptions about what it is to be a bishop today. In addition
it has generated a group of people who have little recent experience
of being ultimately responsible for anything in the church and whose
mind set is accordingly limited. A further problem is the new concept
of parallel episcopacy offered by the provincial episcopal visitors.
Two of these (subsequently a third was added) were appointed after
the decision to ordain women. It is unclear whether the future of episcopacy in the Church of England is now to lead in unity or to
authenticate difference. It is also too early to say whether the provincial episcopal visitor represents a new form of episcopacy with
different authority or a genuinely new insight in ecclesiology. But
both these developments carry unexamined implications for the
government and organisation of the Church of England.

The position of the parish priest has been under similar pressure.
Positive developments, especially that of the ministry of the laity,
have occurred in many churches during the second half of the twentieth century. But the culture of the church is now in danger of
absorbing this ministry within the church rather than seeing it primarily as a witness in the world. The new ministries of non-stipendiary
minister, and even more local non-stipendiary minister, have not been
assessed for their impact on the basic concept of the parish priest. The
financial demands on parishes have been in some cases interpreted as
suggesting that the clergy are the major cost and, by implication,
might be dispensed with. Changed employment practices in society
have stirred questions about the nature of the incumbent's employ-

ment. Theological questions have been asked about ordination, especially in the ecumenical context. All of these issues have their intrinsic significance. The overall effect, however, has been to reduce confidence in the role of the parish priest both in the church at large and in the men and women themselves. The crucial organisational question facing the church is how structurally to create a climate of confidence and responsibility in the parish priest and bishop and renew the total concept of *episcope*, that of the bishop and incumbent together giving each other help and strength.

The Church of England tends to compensate for perceived weaknesses by proliferating systems. It has done this in two ways. First, it has passed a great amount of legislation and encouraged wide debate through the synodical system. Secondly, throughout the twentieth century bishops have become more accessible both because there are more of them and because they are more active in their dioceses. One consequence has been that the diocese, in the sense of the bishop, his staff and the diocesan office and its bureaucracy, has impinged on the parishes more than hitherto. There has been an increase in the number of diocesan officers and services. And as activity expanded, the number of committees and boards to make officers accountable burgeoned. That development has come to a sudden stop. Money has always been a problem. But it has not been so serious a constraint as it has recently. The new and prospective limitations, both in terms of finance and available people, that have followed the highly publicised problems of the Church Commissioners in 1994, have created a disjunction. Dioceses are rapidly slimming their bureaucracies. The relationship between national bodies and the dioceses is being rethought. Those between diocese and parishes have been or are being reconsidered and revised. Many dioceses have undergone major restructuring in order to deploy reduced resources to the best effect. But amid this activity two aspects of the system need to be distinguished. On the one hand the nexus of bishop and parish priest remains crucial. Great attention is paid to it in terms of personal relations. Contact between bishops and clergy has rarely been greater. At the same time relationships between the diocese and the parishes have become more stressful because more demanding, often with impositions that feel intrusive. As a result neither bishop nor parish priest is able to mobilise their personal relationship as a way to manage the boundary between parish and diocese. Both begin to feel manipulated and caught by a sense of loyalty rather than making this part of the system work.

The National Church

Similar questions face the church nationally. The background to any consideration of the future structure of the Church of England in that regard is now the report commissioned by the archbishops in 1994. *Working as One Body* was published in September 1995 and immediately provoked discussion. The outcome, however, will remain uncertain into the next century. For there is widespread recognition that something has to be done. The present structures of the Church of England in the dioceses and in the General Synod are widely held to need reform. So if, as now seems likely, change follows the Commission's proposals, there will be a long period of discovering their effect. If Turnbull is rejected, something else will inevitably be required.

The Commission was 'invited to recommend ways of strengthening the effectiveness of the Church's central policy-making and resource direction machinery.' It was novel in that the archbishops endorsed it in their Foreword. 'This report sets out a clear way forward which we believe would enable the Church to be better equipped for the challenges of the next millennium. The broad thrust of its overall conclusion ... is one which we support.' Following the first debate, responses were unusually invited to be sent to the archbishops. The General Synod was informed that detailed proposals would emanate from a group already in existence – the Lambeth Group. This had been established with the quite different task of responding to the criticism of the Church Commissioners' management of their finances. It was made clear, therefore, that this was not just another report: behind it lay determination for change from the Archbishop of Canterbury himself and a group of twentieth-century ecclesiastical laymen.[24]

The report provided an overview of the way in which the Church of England was structured in 1995 at what it called 'the national level'. Its descriptions of the various parts were excellent and will be a key reference for future studies. Among the main operators it noted the archbishops and their offices, the House of Bishops, the General Synod, the Church Commissioners, the Central Board of Finance and the Pensions Board. The authors concluded that three key problems must be addressed: 'There is a lack of confidence in the central performance of the Church especially, in recent years, the Church Commissioners. National responsibilities are split between too many bodies; it is too difficult to get the necessary decisions taken. There is little drive and direction from the national bodies.'[25]

Several recommendations were made covering aspects of the

Church's administration. But the central and original proposal was that the archbishops should chair a 'new National Council; this would take an overview of the needs and resources of the whole Church, ensure that necessary decisions are taken and that things get done, not just talked about'. There would be consequential changes in the authority and activity of all other bodies. *Working as One Body* invoked the principle of subsidiarity, the concept of 'the national church' and made the ecclesiological claim that Anglican churches, including the Church of England, are 'episcopally led and synodically governed'.

Turnbull has taken subsidiarity to give legitimacy to a hierarchy rather than to interpret the interactive nature of a structure. So, for example, the Commission rightly perceived that the mutuality of the parish priest and parochial church council (indeed the whole local congregation, too) is the foundation of the church's work. In this setting things get done. The report then moved to the next 'level' – the diocese. Yet here the concept of bishop-in-synod was introduced in a way that made it closed to scrutiny. A mutuality is discerned between bishop and diocesan synod which is superficially similar to that between incumbent and church council but at another level. But the function of a diocese is of a different order of task: it is primarily a linking and servicing body to enable the work of the church to be carried out in the parishes and the para-parishes. Once, however, this step has been taken in thinking about the diocese, it is a small one to think in similar terms about the work of the church at a national level. There, so the argument runs, the House of Bishops in the General Synod represents a further example of the basic mutuality that marks all the church's systems. But the idea that the church 'works' is even more incongruous at a national level than at the diocesan. Individuals and institutions contribute to the life of the nation. Obvious instances include the public role of the Archbishop of Canterbury, a national shrine like Westminster Abbey, or the contribution of bishops in the House of Lords. But they are joined by other influences. For instance, the Church of England has been famous for its charismatic priests with contacts and able preachers, who have similar impact. Throughout England the cathedrals add their distinctive contribution to the national religious scene.[26] But none of these, individually or collectively, represents a national level of working that can be organised. Such work is dispersed and achieved through influence not structures. The authority for it is moral and earned, not structural.

The Turnbull Commission assumed parallel activities at each 'level' of a hierarchy which does not exist. Those working in the parishes do not believe that the diocese does similar things but at a 'higher' level. And dioceses – that is primarily the diocesan bishops – will not recognise a higher active authority to be formalised in an Archbishops' Council. There are many problems with this latter concept, but the first area of discussion should be, in the words of *Quadragesimo anno*, about the 'important principle of moral philosophy'. The question is not, therefore, will such a Council work, but is it theologically and dynamically right? There seems to be a wish that the Archbishop of Canterbury might be more active and provide a hands-on type of leadership. The report assigns both archbishops a specific executive authority. But this is difficult to identify apart from their roles as diocesan bishops.[27] But that leadership when the work of the Council is described, is not that of a national church but of a superior body within a hierarchy. It is intended that the Council should match policy and finance and manage resources for ministry. But nothing suggested will make the church more clearly articulate the Christian faith to the English nation. The reason is that the Commission has extrapolated ways of working through a series of supposed levels of church life rather than explored the dynamic interrelation of the parts that make up the Church of England. For the role of an archbishop is not that of a parish priest writ large at some national level; nor is that of the diocesan bishop amplified. There are different expectations of these roles, not just different intensities.

The Role of the Bishop

The role of the bishop is the crucial link in the Anglican system. It connects the national expression of the Church Catholic, specifically the notion of the Church of England, with the working units of the parishes and para-parishes. 'Catholic' thus refers less to any succession than to the interaction between today's working churches and the wider system of which they are part.[28] In spite of developments in church government the significance of the bishop has remained largely unaltered, although the demands have changed. In any organisational thinking, therefore, it is vital to clarify the diocesan bishop's roles.

Historical legitimacy is claimed for the theme of bishop-in-synod, which is currently in vogue. The model is then applied to all aspects of the bishop's role, or, better, series of roles. 'The distribution of authority ... has led Anglicans to develop decision making structures which embody, or seek to embody, this principle of open access to the criteria. Hence the idea (in Anglican history not a new idea) of bishop-in-synodical consultation. Clergy and laity too are part of a normal process of decision-making'.[29]

This claim for the concept of bishop-in-synod, whether for Anglican synods in general or for the history of the Church of England, is questionable. It seems to have originated in 1836 as a pragmatic solution to a political problem of church government when W.G. Broughton was appointed the first (and as it turned out last) Bishop of Australia. Bereft of a Parliament to which to refer, he was advised to use as an expedient a created synod. Yet the idea has gathered force since the advent of synodical government in England. Richard Hooker is a seminal writer on this Church's ecclesiology. But he has to be read in his historical context. He was concerned with royal supremacy and parliamentary representation. Even in his own time, 'Richard Hooker's judicious defence of the Royal Supremacy attained almost the status of an official Anglican *apologia*. But the reality differed from the ideal.'[30] The issue of supremacy is no longer central; its impact, however, on the theory of episcopacy is. The role of the General Synod is not simply that which once belonged to Parliament and the Crown adjusted for today's more democratic times. The role of the bishop is also in many key facets different from that which Hooker adumbrated. In particular

> ... from the days of Whitgift and Hooker apologetic and polemical concerns have stood at the centre of attention. By comparison little energy has been devoted to examination of the actual workings of episcopacy ... which might support a critical understanding of the role of bishops in the church. One result of this situation has been that claims are made for episcopacy which are not in all, or even in most cases, justified by the practice of Anglican Churches.[31]

Not only is the weight put on the concept of bishop-in-synod historically questionable. It is also less useful practically than might first appear. Leadership may require someone to be ahead of the rest rather than always awaiting a moment of consensus. That might never come: or it might come, but too late. In fact there are many aspects to the complex role of the bishop that have no synodical dimension. For example, the decision to ordain or not is nothing to do with the function of bishop-in-synod: it is the act of one who holds office as bishop in the Church of God. At a dynamic level, rather than a legal one, some facets of the bishop's role lie beyond the synodical system. He carries moral and spiritual authority and some legal powers in his corporate person. But just as Hooker's idealism did not find practical expression in the Church of England, so too the contemporary theory of bishop-in-synod is weak. This is partly because the synodical system as a whole is not as consultative as its progenitors might have expected. This is largely a consequence of the distinctive dynamic nature of religious life. A church is an organisationally curious institution. It is made up of people who volunteer; no one can insist that they belong.[32] They associate because of a personal and unexaminable commitment, based on a transcendent belief which is more than the organisation and its members. And these mostly unarticulated beliefs are often sufficient to keep them together until fission becomes unavoidable. What is more, they do not know each other's beliefs in any depth. The organisational system is hierarchical, chiefly because in dealing with God a church needs some people to be believed to be able particularly to be in touch with God, although that does not make them morally or spiritually superior. And ultimately this curious institution exists, it believes, to serve in various fashions those who are neither members nor may have any intention of joining. Once this fundamental irrationality (the word is not used pejoratively but technically) is recognised, progress can be made on organisational structures. One such step is to realise that those who are recognised as leaders (in this case the bishops) are assigned moral authority and influence, which exceeds and may even supplant any structured authority.[33]

'Episcopally led and synodically governed' is a reasonable shorthand for an ideal state of affairs; but what hides under the word episcopal needs testing. There are three aspects to this word which need to be distinguished. First, there is the role of diocesan bishop. In this he works with his fellow clergy and heads the administration of the units which make up a diocese. More importantly he sets a tone and creates an ethos for the period that he is diocesan. That is why the role of bishop is both structural and at the same time infused with the person. In the Church of England this person is given power and authority, which is largely (but not wholly) confirmed by law. He functions in a Janus-like fashion, looking inwards to the churches and structures of the diocese and at the same time informing them and keeping them in touch with the wider policies of his church. He cannot, therefore, do what he likes, although the range of constraints and their force vary.

There is, secondly, the role of the bishop chiefly looking outwards from the work in the diocese. This takes on two major facets: one is the way in which he relates to other bishops. There is a commonality of actions which can mutually inform one another. There is also good reason why bishops should have some common approaches. A major instance of this is ordination. It is the prerogative of the individual bishop within the canons to ordain whomsoever he wills, provided they are qualified. But during the twentieth century a national system of selection and training has emerged. To achieve this the bishops severally surrendered some of their powers to facilitate a co-ordinated approach to ordination. This has led to the selection work of the Advisory Board of Ministry and its predecessors.

The second aspect to this outward looking of the bishop is that it is the base for his national platform. The obvious instances of this are those bishops who sit in the House of Lords. But there are many other national platforms, occasions when a bishop is expected to speak, comment or write. Their authority for doing this derives chiefly from their knowledge of the cure of souls and their learning. The key to understanding the role of the bishop is that he is a pastor and teacher, not ideally but actually. These are the twin foundations of their leadership. Two instances may be noted. Dr John Habgood, when Archbishop of York, acquired a national reputation as a thinker, which was reinforced by his role as archbishop. But most episcopal comment is better derived from their knowledge of the ground in their diocese. In October 1995, for example, the Bishop of Sheffield effectively commented on national policy on housing estates in the light of specific information from one of his parish priests.

The third aspect to the role of bishops is as members of the House of Bishops, one part of the synodical system. Within this the bishops have a special place which derives from their office as described earlier. But structurally there is no problem about this. Practically, however, a confusion prevails between orders and authority. This House includes a number of suffragan and assistant bishops, one of whom until recently carried only the authority of a parish priest.

When the roles of the bishops are analysed in this way, it becomes clear that in the contemporary structure the second role is the most problematic. This is exercised at the point where the authority of the individual diocesan interacts with that of his colleagues and where the notion of national leadership is for better or worse exercised. But this gathering of bishops is not the same as the House of Bishops. The two meetings have different tasks and responsibility. Attempts have been made to acknowledge this difference by holding bishops' meetings. But membership of these has been confused by the presence of all suffragans and assistant bishops. Their orders may be similar but the organisational issue is always that of authority. In that they differ.[34]

Finance

There is no disputing that during the twentieth century the financing of the Church of England has become increasingly problematic. From

1945 onwards the idea of raising parochial giving has been regarded
as a priority. In part this was due to financial exigencies, especially
in a time of high inflation. In part, however, it was also an increasing recognition, largely under the influence of ecumenical and
international Anglican closeness, that a live church cannot (or at least
should not) exist on the legacy of the dead. This theological motif ran
through that mix of mission, evangelism and fund-raising that constitutes the stewardship movement. Coupled with the greater
acknowledgement of the distinctive role of the laity, giving became a
priority. And the success has been remarkable, not least in the switch
during the period 1994 to 1996 of almost the whole cost of clergy
stipends onto diocesan (that is parish) budgets. Nevertheless, Turnbull
was correct when it commented:

> The support which the Church Commissioners have in the past been
> able to provide may have served to obscure the fact that the funda-
> mental responsibility for the maintenance of the ministry rests with
> the bishop and his diocese ... The reduction in the Church
> Commissioners' income has laid bare a need, which was always
> there, for the Church to find new endowments to finance its expen-
> diture; and for it to take an overview of its total financial position.[35]

A number of factors have affected the finances of the Church of
England. One is the loss of confidence in the Church Commissioners
after the débâcle of 1992. The exposure of the lack of basic management surprised many. And in a body like the church, in which in the
absence of information trust assumes that things are all right, this
came as a greater shock. It had a secondary effect of reducing confidence in all central bodies, including those in diocesan offices. At the
same time as learning about their new financial responsibilities,
parishes have discovered their control over the church. It will soon
also be clear that they have greater influence over the church's
ministry. Some, such as the Evangelical group, Reform, and some
parishes resisting the ordination of women, have foreseen applying
doctrinal criteria as to whether they will give to the church at large or
not. Such a new situation makes management of the church's finances
appear potentially difficult. But just as the church exists because of
the *consensus fidelium*, so the management of finances and resources
is likely to follow confidence in the basic systems rather than be an
issue on its own.

A Prospect for the Future

The devil, it is said, is in the detail. Without a full investigation it is impossible to draw up a model structure for the Church of England as a whole. And to attempt this external consultancy is essential. Internal church reports have proved neither profound nor successful. What is more, the way that they are handled exposes a serious flaw in the synodical system. The process usually follows this pattern: an issue is identified; a commission or working party produces a report, which is often good, and another group is invited to draw up legislative proposals. But in so doing, and working within the constraints of law, it often fails to perceive the dynamic effect of what it is proposing and its impact on the concept (or, we might even say, 'feeling') of the church as a whole. This quasi-parliamentary process is inappropriate for a church. However, with such caveats, certain pointers as to what will be organisationally necessary in the next millennium can be indicated. No structure can perfectly draw together its systems. The reasons have already been explored. The parts of the system are not as discrete in practice as they are in theory. It is the nature of a voluntary organisation that individuals occupy a series of roles that are difficult to disentangle. Third, and following from this, the human dynamics of a parish, diocese or other church body are peculiarly complex because they deal with beliefs and are therefore not easily harnessed to the task.

The key to the structure of the Church of England will continue to lie in the work of the priests and people in the parishes and the extent to which it is enabled by the linking, pastoring and teaching work of the diocesan bishops. Although confidence may have dwindled in its episcopal leadership, the church has no alternative option. The flow of power into authority needs to be demonstrated by the flow of financial resource and therefore also power. It may be that diocesan boundaries will need adjustment and administrations be shared. There are arguments for and against smaller dioceses and regional administrations. But such suggestions do not go to the core issues. Therefore for the time being the basis would appear to remain the forty-three English dioceses and bishops. Through their work with the parochial clergy mission will be sustained and new ideas generated. It is, therefore, important not to confuse these activities with whatever the House of Bishops and the General Synod might do. Such clarification would also make the task of the synods, especially the General Synod, clearer. For it is through the synodical system that the consensus of the church is accountably enunciated. It is always possible that a bishop might with confidence discern and articulate the mind of the church in his diocese. But today people are nervous about such representation if they cannot publicly scrutinise it. It is therefore likely that the trend towards more debate that has persisted through this century will be sustained and refined. But in terms of work the overall organisation needs to ensure that the ten thousand or so parishes are effective for worship, ministry and mission.

The parishes

These basic units are the organisational key. Two primary systems may be usefully distinguished, the apostolic and the diaconal.[36] The former includes all the operating strategies that create opportunities for encounter. These range from such obvious systems as the vicar's visiting or preaching through to those familiar access points like the choir or Sunday school. Whatever a church's specific social setting the task remains the same – that of providing opportunities. The means by which this is achieved will vary considerably. Most other activities in a church constitute the diaconal system. This includes committees, administration and every other part of the system that facilitates the apostolic work of the church. A parochial church council is involved in both systems. With the incumbent it is responsible for the mission of the church in that locality. But much of its time is necessarily given to diaconal matters – providing the servicing of the church. Mission is often contrasted with maintenance – a distinction that in terms of providing opportunities may sometimes be clarifying but is usually false. Their interrelatedness needs to be affirmed at a time when talk is increasingly of a shift from pastoring, with its corollaries of worship, ritual and teaching, to that of mission.[37]

The practical problems facing the parish structure are familiar and are unlikely to change very much in the near future. Certainly the geographical and numerical size of parishes will increase and amalgamations will continue. It is also likely that styles of ministry will differ according to local condition. The number of stipendiary clergy is set to decrease for the forseeable future.[38] But it does not follow that such a reduction will inevitably continue. Neither does their style of activity have to remain the same. The demands on these public ministers have changed in the past two decades. But in common with other institutions the Church of England has invested in continuing ministerial education. This has notably been one area in which the dioceses have not cut their budgets.[39] The issue, therefore, with the primary working unit of the Church of England is less one of organisation and more a matter of confidence and appropriate resource.

The diocese

Dioceses have already responded rapidly to changed circumstances, especially those forced on them by financial problems and the changed availability of clergy. Bristol offers a typical example of what is being done and what will probably apply into the next millennium.

The diocese faced three problems. First, decision-making was difficult. The diocesan organisation was typical of that period. The Diocesan Synod met three times a year, with the Bishop's Council meeting about six or seven times. The Diocesan Board of Finance also met three times a year and the Finance Committee about nine times. There was the usual range of committees and boards, some of which were statutory. Members of the Diocesan Synod and others were elected to these, each of which met four or five times a year. The diocesan officers were accountable to their boards. The bishop had his staff meeting, which met monthly. The structure was suffused with enthusiastic inertia. It had developed, or even been unconsciously designed, so that people could speak about the need in the church to trust one another without any obligation to do so. Every decision could be re-examined at any point. The Diocesan Synod would try to manage executive decisions; the Finance Committee could always question, defer and even revise a decision of the Synod if money was involved; the Bishop's Council could receive reports, but any decision had to be referred to the Diocesan Synod. The bishop might wish to initiate a programme, but could not do so since officers, who were believed to act in his name, could invoke their accountability to their Board if they did not wish to do something. This confusion resulted in a deep sense of missing communication. The people in the parishes, clergy and laity alike, felt excluded from decision-making and claimed ignorance about those that were made. Organisations in difficulty frequently invoke communication and trust. So much attention was given to the mechanics of how to get messages to and from the parishes. But since the parishes were unsure what they wanted to say and the diocesan bodies were confused about what they wished to communicate, other than exhortations, this usually came to nothing. The third factor was money. The parishes were aware that they were providing the quota and wished to have a greater say in the way that money was spent.

Following consultation a new system was introduced. Its basis was

that the Church of England is synodical and that therefore any structural alterations must begin with that presupposition. The first clarity
was to bring finance and policy together. This was easily accom-
plished symbolically by making the membership of the Diocesan
Synod and the Board of Finance identical. The members' experience
was that at every meeting of the Synod, for example, they were
reminded through having to alternate roles that they themselves were
responsible for financing any proposals. The practical effect,
however, was more obvious in the Bishop's Council. This body had
three discrete functions, each of which had to be held in mind when
other functions were being mobilised. It is advisory body to the bishop
(Bishop's Council), financial board of the diocese (Board of Directors
of the Diocesan Board of Finance) and standing committee of the
Diocesan Synod. Since its chief function is to consider policy matters
for the diocese, its major point of reference again became the ministry
and mission of the parishes. But because finance and policy were now
held together, the realism of policies and the financial constraints
under which all work were both alike in mind. Structurally this work
is focused in an annual priorities review, which was the key to the
whole enterprise. Each year the Bishop's Council establishes a priorities group. This is chaired by someone with no financial interest,
preferably a lay person who is not a member of the Council. The other
four members are drawn from the Council and include the chairman
(but not secretary) of the Diocesan Board of Finance. The group is
given one parameter, namely what the Council considers a reasonable
amount that the parishes can raise two years' hence. This is usually a
figure for inflation plus a percentage. The Priorities Group receives
from every spending body on the diocesan budget a brief report on
past activity, proposed new activity and financial needs. These reports
come from the Diocesan Bishop on how he sees clergy deployment,
the Diocesan Secretary on the needs of the administration, and from
the Chairmen of the various departments. Each of these appears
before the Group to present their case for scrutiny. The Priorities
Group offers the Council its confidential report, which includes a
review of activities, a statement of requests and a series of policy
options, if the Council is to remain within its proposed financial parameters. The Bishop's Council has this as its sole item of business for
the meeting, which is held overnight in December. The report is
debated; often new ideas emerge or weaknesses in the work appear.
Medium and short term strategies can be devised, out of which comes
what is known as the steer. The Council gives back to the spending
bodies its judgements on their requests for final comment. Then it
produces for the Diocesan Synod its proposals which will determine

the diocesan budget and policy two years' hence. That is debated in March, when any changes can be made by the Synod. The final policy and budget are drawn up for approval in July. In practice because the Diocesan Synod knows that hard discussion has already gone into what is presented to it, the debate is usually about major issues rather than minutiae.

The third change has been to emphasise the work of the parishes and para-parishes. This is where the local church functions and where resources need to be applied. As a result, most boards and councils have been abolished. Those which are statutory now have their work carefully defined. In place of the others there is a Parish Resource Team, headed by the Director of Training, and including for the time being a Children's Officer, a Mission Officer, the Stewardship Adviser and the Director of Ordinands, although this membership may change according to need. This group, as its name implies, exists to support and encourage those engaged in the primary task of the church, the clergy and laity in the parishes. Its staff are accountable as officers of the bishop. He, therefore, knows what is being done in his name and they in turn know where their responsibility lies. A monitoring board of elected and appointed members meets three times a year to receive reports and offer advice to the team.

This is not a model diocesan structure. But it demonstrates what can be achieved if tasks are discerned and appropriate confidence established in an ecclesiastical system.

The synodical system

A large question hangs over synodical government. One of its major weaknesses is that it allows (even encourages) those who are for any reason discontented with their parish, deanery or diocese to voice their personal opinions in a different forum. They can sustain the delusion that their views have potential significance and others, often the media, may assign them spurious value. This is most noticeable in the deanery synods. Studies have suggested that for all its apparent potential, the deanery has too confused a set of tasks to be effective either as a working body in the church's apostolic task or a diaconal support.[40] The Bridge Report reaches a similar conclusion. In the General Synod this weakness appears in question time and private member's motions. This (as with much of the synodical system) is based on a parliamentary model of representation and behaviour, not one that stands the scrutiny of the Christian ideal. Question time in the General Synod has sometimes degenerated into abuse. The Bishop of Birmingham has noted that 'no Church can be healthy whose elected representatives show so little respect towards the office of their chief pastor. The institutionalisation of mistrust is evident in every piece of synodical legislation which further restricts the power of bishops to exercise their pastoral office freely.'[41]

The debating and legislative system of the synod, especially the General Synod, requires an input that is relevant (i.e., related directly to the distinctive experience of the Church of England) and managed. But the primary locus of power for work is the parish, the focus of structure the diocese and bishop, and the national dimension is more ethos than activity. In the light of these distinctions the function and structure of the General Synod becomes clearer. First, it is part, but not the sum, of the synodical system which is designed to encourage and enable debate. It is essential therefore that the activity of the parishes as focused by the dioceses should be the major source of material. But this needs to be balanced by the input from the bishops who hold a wider representative role on behalf of the Church. In practice this would mean that motions before the Synod would come from only two sources – the diocesan synods and the bishops. Once this task is clearer, the Synod could function effectively on one annual meeting of a week's duration. The constraints of time would contribute to more focused debate and better decision-making.

There is however, a second area of questioning to which Turnbull drew attention – the proliferation of bodies in the centre. The issue, however, is less the number of boards, councils and committees than the unclarity of the tasks that they perform. The key issues are the redistribution of resources to the working units of the church and the maintenance of the supra-parochial institutions such as the bishops and cathedrals. Whatever the detailed structure that emerges for the church it must not discount a key aspect. This is the use of minds and abilities to stimulate ideas and enable the Church of England to remain creative. This, like the church's national role, has historically been a distributed activity. It is a further consequence of dispersed authority. Some ideas are generated by voluntary associations. The history of the missionary movement within the Anglican Communion, for example, is one of voluntary societies, rarely of the church as an organisation. The idiosyncratic parish priest should never be underestimated.[42] The boards and councils of the Synod have themselves been productive. They have often been criticised, but this is less for having original ideas than because people in the world and the church at large were unclear about the authority of their productions. But the thinking on ministry, mission and social affairs has often been of a high order. The problem is where it is owned, much depending in recent years on what the General Synod does with it. It seems recently to have become more alert to the danger of embarking on a course of action by default, that is, formally taking note and referring the document to a committee for proposals for action.

One key area offers an example of how the exercise of a major facet of episcopal responsibility has by mutual agreement of the bishops been centralised. This is the recruitment, selection and training of the ordained ministers. Although questions are occasionally asked, this process has served the church well and it would be a loss if it were demolished. If the parish priest/bishop connection is the fulcrum on which everything turns, issues of how many priests, what quality and type of training, what career patterns, what style of ministry and deployment, are all matters of policy and of action. The current confusion has been exemplified by difficulties in knowing what to do about theological education and specifically the respective responsibilities of the bishops, the Advisory Board of Ministry, and the General Synod. Two reports followed hard on one another.[43] Few, if any, doubt that because they ordain, the bishops are severally and collectively responsible to the church for the ordained ministry. Yet these reports were commissioned by the House of Bishops. They were thus caught from the start within the synodical system. As a result the bishops had little freedom and time to think or to be advised. The position of the Advisory Board of Ministry, which structurally should have been advising the bishops on these matters, was usurped. When the steering group for suggesting ways forward was created, a long debate ensued as to where it should report. The confusion exemplified the problems of locating authority for such decision in the church. Ultimately the core question is whether the numbers of stipendiary clergy will be limited. That would imply the replacement of an open-ended policy on vocations with a planned human resource recruitment programme. Control would also have to be taken of the theological training enterprise. At present this is highly diversified, although the overall task of training about eight hundred candidates is a small educational task.

But all these issues are matters of belief rather than of management. More practically significant is how policy and finance are to be brought together. This has already happened in a number of dioceses. At the so-called centre, however, the problem is compounded because there is no agreement about the task of this centre and into what system it fits, the diaconal or apostolic. This lack of clarity allows it to be used by different groups and individuals for their own purposes, since no one has to discern the corporate body. In practice the centre is diaconal and it will, therefore, have to fit the shape of the structure that it is to serve. This, like many other facets of an episcopal church, even if synodically modified, hinges on the role assigned to the bishops and their competence in assuming it.

The bishops

The role of the diocesan bishops is the fulcrum on which the organisational structure of the Church of England rests. It is arguable that the fact that the Turnbull report was required at all represents a loss of confidence in the present group of bishops. But bishops may be appointed because there is no clarity among the selectors about what the church as a whole requires. With a clearer sense of the task of the church it is possible that a group of bishops could emerge in which more confidence would repose. All the functions of the proposed Archbishops' Council (to use the term now adopted in the legislative proposals following the Turnbull report) in an episcopal church fall within the natural remit of its bishops. The bishops gathered as a meeting and structured for work are the place where national and international issues are raised and first discussed. Advice on church and other topics is also tendered there and the matching policy and resource is begun. It is curiously apposite that the one group in the contemporary church that has experience of this is the collection of diocesan bishops. For they already have to do this in their dioceses. A further key task is the formulation of resolutions requiring legislation or debate by the General Synod.

But a group like this needs proper servicing. By contrast the Synod needs very little. It has been an organisational nightmare that the boards and councils have been those of the General Synod. Their reports and ideas, often useful and good, inevitably push for executive action. But the Synod is incapable of that. Sometimes, too, it is better that ideas should not be acted on. The support structures should be shifted to the bishops, and through them to the dioceses and the public work of the church. They would be served by two types of officer and board. The first would be something like the present Advisory Board of Ministry, which is both advisory and executive in a primary area of episcopal responsibility – the ordained and lay ministries of the church. The others would be bodies concerned with such topics as ecumenical affairs, Anglican issues and social responsibility. These would resource the bishops, and through them the church in the dioceses, ensuring a higher level of technical competence than can at present be sustained. The bishops' performance as national figures would be improved (they would know better what they were talking about) and as diocesan links they would bring new perspectives into the working systems of the church. A further benefit would also be the need for fewer diocesan advisers, thus allowing some diocesan structures to be dissolved. How the office of the arch-bishops would fit into this remains unclear. Most current thinking gives insufficient attention to the increasing demands that the Anglican Communion has placed on that office since the time of Archbishop Tait. But the dioceses of Canterbury and York need their bishops and in the provinces there may be an embryonic form of more regional structures. The regional grouping of bishops, which is already coming informally into being, may take on greater organisational significance. But these are all matters of evolution in relation to a clearly perceived task rather than of structure.

In return much of the material that the General Synod and the system at large would discuss – initiatives, reports and proposals – would derive from informed diocesan synods and bishops with a larger outlook. The church could then claim with justification that debates in the General Synod and proposed legislation were on issues that arise within the mind of the church. It would allow recognition that consensus is a complex of ideas produced by various interactions, religious, secular, national and local. Such a conviction matches the Anglican concept of dispersed authority. That does not mean that there is no authority or that it cannot be articulated.[44]

They would also be advised on the financial resources available to augment their diocesan work and the money assigned to the national work of the cathedrals and bishops. Here the servicing of the bishops, to enable work, and the servicing of the centre come together. It is clear that no longer can the church, in any configuration, do every-thing that may be expected of it or that interested parties might wish it to do. This means that any future system must include a means of proposing priorities for the limited financial and human resource that the church possesses. An annual review of priorities and proposed financial allocation, similar to that proposed above for the diocese, would be a simple affair to set up. The central financial body of the Church of England (see below) would require a permanent audit department. An extension of that would be an annual prioritisation exercise carried out by a small group appointed by the Synod, consist-ing of those who were not part of spending departments. Before this group those responsible for spending of any sort would appear. The final connection between resource and activity would be proposed to the Synod, where decisions would be taken.

Financial resources

The reduced confidence in those responsible for the church's finances, especially the Church Commissioners, is an unfortunate background against which to take decisions about the future. This has not solely been a response to the well-advertised losses. It is also expressed anger against the paternalist attitude that has marked the dealings of the Commissioners. There seems no obvious reason to suggest the disbandment of the Church Commissioners, even if this were technically possible without a long, wearying debate and even dispute with Parliament. The report of the House of Commons Select Committee on Social Security, while highly critical, also avoids this suggestion.[45] However, whatever the history of the church's inherited money, it is clear that from 1995 onwards, and certainly into the twenty-first century, the Commissioners will have a lesser role to play in day-to-day funding. Most, if not eventually all, their assets will be required for pension liabilities as well as for the payment of the bishops and part of the costs of cathedrals, neither of which link into the giving base of the parishes. Given the notion of a national role that has been outlined, reservation of historic funding to enable bishops and cathedrals to continue to contribute is wise. Any other resource for the work of the church in parishes cannot be left to the whim of the Commissioners or even that of the Synod. That will be an executive decision.

It is doubtful, however, whether the Church of England can continue its national ministry (i.e., its parochial structures) without some mechanism for distributing funds nationally. Any idea of self-sufficient parishes, and even self-sufficient dioceses, will congregationalise this church. It may be that this will happen in the twenty-first century. But if so an identifiable Church of England will have gone.[46] If that demise is believed to be undesirable, some mechanism for distributing and allocating finance is required. For that purpose a single central body is needed. It seems likely that this might itself be the Archbishops' Council through a new Finance Committee. A reformed Church Commissioners would remain for limited purposes. It seems probable that so far as church people are concerned, attitude will be crucial and much will depend on the way in which the Commissioners are reformed. But if a defined but limited function in finance became their sole preoccupation and the so-called pastoral side was delegated, their traditional expertise might be usefully recovered.

Conclusion

The organisation of a church is peculiarly complicated. It may be a divine institution, but it is earthed in the world. One consequence is that churches adopt contemporary managerial models to a greater degree than they may recognise or admit. That is neither good nor bad: it is inevitable. But when change becomes essential there is always the risk that, reacting against one model, the church will excessively identify itself with a new one. This, for example, is a major weakness in *Working as One Body*. Having rightly perceived that the parliamentary model that underlies the synodical system leads in the context of the church to paralysis, the Turnbull Commission shifted to a corporate, even curial, model in its proposals. It is unlikely that this will succeed, not least because of a gut antipathy to centralism. Its thrust is already being modified as the debate continues. And ecclesiastically the Church of England is uncomfortable with any hint of a Roman Catholic style of papalism. This matches the political discomfort that keeps Britain distant from the European Community. And the suggested design, especially of the Archbishops' Council, is also similar to the government of the United States, with an unelected executive and an elected assembly. But their record of working together is not impressive, especially at the end of the twentieth century.

The key to any structure for the Church of England must be the sustaining of diversity. This variety is not the range of theological opinions that can be discovered so much as a rich set of access points to the gospel. The basic systems have to take account of individual bishops, eccentric priests, cathedrals, lay communities and such like. Looked at in this light 'episcopally led and synodically governed' is a slogan and not something on which to construct an organisation. Nevertheless, these two elements – bishops and synods – are the core of any structure for this church. For the next phase of its life, therefore, the characteristics of the structure will probably include:

> No Convocations but a slimmer General Synod, meeting once a year for business and debate. Motions would arise from only two sources – the bishops, acting collectively, and diocesan synods, representing the variety of church life. There would be no private members' motions or reports from boards or councils. The latter would cease to exist, being replaced by advisers to the bishops. Their work would be monitored by small boards elected by the synod.
>
> All other energy would be devoted to the controlling notion that work is primarily in the parishes and para-parishes. There both

power, especially as represented by money, and the authority of the gospel are chiefly located. This area of the church's life would remain, as it has been for most of its existence, subject to permanent review and reordering on a diocesan basis.

Bishops would lead first by teaching and pastoring. To do that better they would corporately have the benefit of quality advice.

Diocesan synods would consist of a fully representative membership from the parishes, but no deanery synods. Diocesan officers and boards would work on the same pattern as above, but allowing for the different task of enthusing and enabling parishes.

National finance will be the responsibility of only one central body. The Church Commissioners would, apart from their legal responsibility to account to Parliament, only deal with the General Synod office and the dioceses. Their function would be the provision of such resource as possible, rather in the manner of a trust fund for the church.

The General Synod would annually appoint a group to scrutinise every aspect of the central activities of the church and advise on the options and potential priorities that lie before the bishops and the synod. This would work with advised financial parameters budgeting three years in advance.

This summary and the argument that preceded it, however, is based on a series of beliefs. Possibly the most important of these is that, just as the remorseless impact of secularisation has not issued in the expected outcome, so the trends outlined in the introduction to this chapter will not obliterate religion or encourage the Church of England to withdraw further from the difficult and messy task of offering to handle religious expectations. No organisational suggestions for a church can be made that do not take into account the curious and distinctive nature of faith and commitment. Indeed, the structure of a church must always be designed to maximise opportunity for the expression of that faith and for inviting such commitment. So long as the tradition remains 'diverse and infuriatingly influencing and responding to the history and variety of our society in a manner which is both symbiotic and prophetic'[47] the Church of England will continue to be structurally less than perfect, in some ways annoyingly inefficient, but always organisationally intriguing.

Notes

1. I am grateful to Lesley Farrall and Peter Marshall and Tim Stevens for advice on an early draft of this paper.

2. P. Sedgwick, 'The Future of the Church of England and the Turnbull Report', unpublished. See also R. Gill, *The Myth of the Empty Church* (SPCK, London, 1993), especially ch. 1.
3. G. Davie, *Religion in Britain since 1945. Believing without Belonging* (Blackwell, Oxford, 1994). See also J.H. Moses, *A Broad and Living Way. Church and State: A Continuing Establishment* (Canterbury Press, Norwich, 1995).
4. On open systems see E.J. Miller and A.K. Rice, *Systems of Organization. The Control of Task and Sentient Boundaries* (Tavistock Press, London, 1967).
5. B.D. Reed, *The Dynamics of Religion. Process and Movement in Christian Churches* (Darton, Longman and Todd, London, 1978). A.W. Carr, *The Priestlike Task. A Model for Developing and Training the Church's Ministry* (SPCK, London, 1985).
6. R. Gill, *Competing Convictions* (SCM Press, London, 1989).
7. E.R. Shapiro and A.W. Carr, *Lost in Familiar Places. Creating New Connections between the Individual and Society* (Yale University Press, New Haven and London, 1991). A.W. Carr, *A Handbook of Pastoral Studies* (SPCK, London, 1997).
8. See, for example, the pastoral letter *Ministry* published by the House of Bishops on 12 January 1994.
9. The concept of primary task is descriptive. It delineates what an institution has at any moment to do in order to continue in its distinctive existence. For the Church of England such a primary task will be about providing opportunities for religious activity. What the church then decides to do with those opportunities is up to it; this would constitute an agreed aim. So, for instance, it might be argued that any request for infant baptism represents an engagement with the environment and the primary task of the church is being demonstrated there – providing an opportunity for religious expression. Because of that, the church can engage in its evangelistic task, however it conceives that, by interpreting that approach. But it is on the basis of being willing to allow or encourage the religious activity that the church's continuing engagement with people at all depends. Hence that is the primary task, what it must do; the interpretation is the aim, which it believes that it is called to do. See A.W. Carr, *Brief Encounters. Pastoral Ministry through Baptisms, Weddings and Funerals* (SPCK, London, revised edition 1994).
10. The point was made by C.A. Lewis, Dean of St Albans, in the debate in the General Synod of 29 November 1995.
11. *Working as One Body. The Report of the Archbishops' Commission on the Organisation of the Church of England* (Church House Publishing, London, 1995). It is widely known as The Turnbull Report after its Chairman, Michael Turnbull, Bishop of Durham.
12. Pius XI, 'Quadragesimo anno', in H. Denzinger, *Enchiridion Symbolorum. Definitinum et declarationum de rebus fidei et morum* (Editio xxxiv), (Herder, Freiburg, 1966), p. 732. My translation with the assistance of Canon P.F. Johnson.

13. O. Chadwick, *The Victorian Church* (Adam & Charles Black, London, 1970). Vol. 2, pp. 364ff.
14. It is popularly called this, but the full title is 'The Church of England Assembly (Powers) Act'. The permanent monument to the movement towards a single assembly is Church House, Westminster, which was intended to accommodate the single assembly. The foundation stone was laid in 1891.
15. *The General Synod Infrastructure Review: Report of the Review Officer and the Observations of the Review Group*, GS827 (Church House Publishing, London, 1988).
16. The mistake is not peculiar to the Church of England. In 1992 the World Council of Churches began a review of its activities without first reconsidering its vocation. In 1996 the Central Committee has asked for this work to be done in time for the next Assembly, which will be on 'The Common Understanding and Vision of the World Council of Churches'.
17. *Synodical Government in the Church of England: A Review*, The Report of the Review Group appointed by the Standing Committee of the General Synod (Church House Publishing, London, 1997).
18. It seems that the connection between 'appertaining to a parish' and 'small-mindedness' was first made about the mid-nineteenth century.
19. The term 'para-parish' is a way of referring to all forms of interactive ministry in addition to that customarily thought of as parochial. Industrial and other chaplaincies are the most obvious examples, but see also Angela Tilby's idea of a 'national parish' as exemplified in the media, in A.W. Carr (ed.), *Say One for Me. The Church of England in the Next Decade* (SPCK, London, 1992), pp. 72ff.
20. *The Operation of Pension Funds: The Church Commissioners and Church of England Pensions. The Second Report of the Social Security Committee.* (HMSO, London, 1995), p. xxxvi.
21. The Lambeth Conference is a gathering of all bishops in the Anglican Communion. It has been held about every ten years since 1867.
22. *The Truth Shall Make You Free: Report of the Lambeth Conference* (SPCK, London, 1988), p. 61.
23. For a discussion of these issues see E.J. Miller and W.G. Lawrence (with a postscript by A.W. Carr), 'A Church of England Diocese' in E.J. Miller, *From Dependency to Autonomy: Studies in Organization and Change* (Free Association Books, London, 1993), pp. 102–19.
24. Although John Habgood signed the Foreword, he had retired before the debate began. There was one woman among the membership (a Diocesan Secretary), but the rest were prominent men in the church.
25. From the summary produced with the Report.
26. This is re-affirmed in *Heritage and Renewal. The Report of the Archbishops' Commission on Cathedrals* (Church House Publishing, London, 1994).
27. The ecumenical implications of any change here are worth monitoring. The style of episcopacy that has evolved in the Church of England is a key in the commendation of episcopal government in conversations with

Reformed and Lutheran churches. Some Roman Catholics also admire it.

28. For an ecumenical amplification of this point see *Together in Mission and Ministry. The Porvoo Common Statement*, GS 1083 (Church House Publishing, London, 1993), especially ch. IV.

29. S.W. Sykes, *Unashamed Anglicanism* (Darton, Longman and Todd, London, 1995), p.173.

30. *Episcopal Ministry. The Report of the Archbishops' Group on the Episcopate* (Church House Publishing, London, 1990), p. 213.

31. R.A. Norris, 'Episcopacy', in S.W. Sykes and J.E. Booty (ed.), *The Study of Anglicanism* (SPCK, London, 1988), pp. 296–313. The quotation is from p. 307.

32. That church people are volunteers is organisationally important. This observation contributes to, but should not be confused with, the sociological classification of modern Western churches as voluntary movements. For the latter see J. Kerkhofs, 'Leadership in a Voluntary Movement', in J. Kerkhofs (ed.), *Europe without Priests* (SCM Press, London, 1995), pp. 143–62.

33. See A.W. Carr, 'Irrationality and Religion' in J. Krantz (ed.), *Irrationality in Social and Organizational Life* (A.K. Rice Institute, Washington, 1987), pp. 76–90. Reprinted in Carr, *Handbook*.

34. The extreme instance of this confusion was Colin Buchanan, Vicar of St Mark, Gillingham. He sat in the House of Bishops, eligible for election because being in episcopal orders he was Honorary Assistant Bishop in Rochester. He was a suffragan in Birmingham for four years before becoming an incumbent and has since been appointed suffragan bishop of Woolwich.

35. *Working as One Body*, p. 84.

36. Reed, *Dynamics*, pp. 198ff.

37. See S.W. Sykes, 'An Anglican Theology of Evangelism', in *Unashamed Anglicanism*, ch. 11. On the connections between mission, pastoring, teaching and worship see A.W. Carr, *The Pastor as Theologian. The Integration of Pastoral Ministry, Theology and Discipleship* (SPCK, London, 1989).

38. *Numbers in Ministry*, GS Misc 451 (Church House Publishing, London, 1995).

39. *Advisory Board of Ministry Annual Report 1994* (Church House Publishing, London, 1995), pp. 27ff.

40. Papers from a major project in the Hitchin Deanery which was undertaken during the late 1970s in collaboration with Elliot Jaques and Gillian Stamp of Brunel University and St George's House, Windsor, are at Windsor.

41. M. Santer, *Church Times*, 29 June 1990.

42. M. Hinton, *The Anglican Parochial Clergy. A Celebration* (SCM Press, London, 1994).

43. *Theological Training: A Way Ahead. A Report to the House of Bishops of the Church of England on Theological Colleges and Courses* (Church House Publishing, London, 1992). *Theological Colleges: The Next Steps.*

Report of the Assessment Group on Theological Colleges (Church House Publishing, London, 1993).

44. The classic statement on this is found in *The Lambeth Conference Report 1948* (SPCK, London, 1948). The elements of authority are Scripture, tradition, creeds, the ministry of word and sacraments, the witness of the saints and the *consensus fidelium*.

45. *Report of the Select Committee.*

46. Frank Field MP, Chairman of the Select Committee, was right to ask whether the exposed weakness of the Church Commissioners as a result of the fiasco of 1992, would in practice lead to the demise of the parish system and hence of the Church of England. He and his committee had a clearer notion of what the Church of England is than the General Synod. See n. 20 above.

47. C.A. Lewis, private correspondence elaborating his speech in the General Synod. See n. 10 above.

2

'The Gracious Gift';[1] Church of England Finances and Resources

Keith Bladon

Introduction

Any analysis of the Church of England finances as the twentieth century draws to a close has to be seen in the shadow of the celebrated revelations concerning the Church Commissioners' financial losses, which broke upon an unsuspecting public, even an unsuspecting Archbishop of Canterbury, in July 1992. The repercussions have been explosive and will no doubt rumble on into the twenty-first century. Many commentators have seen the consequences as potentially devastating. Parliament has found time to examine the position and proffer the view that in the period from the mid-1980s to 1992 the leadership of the Church Commissioners has in all likelihood contributed more than anything else towards the destruction of the parish system of the national church.[2] Powerful sentiments, indeed, but very much in line with the opinions expressed in countless newspaper articles, and in radio and television programmes. 'The Church as it now stands no human power can save', is a quotation which hardly exaggerates the stance taken by some of the tabloid newspapers when more was revealed of the inept management by the Church Commissioners. Yet this quotation dates back to the 1830s when Thomas Arnold was demonstrating the church's desperate need for reform as England moved into the industrial age.[3]

Sadly, many in the church, including some holding high office, have only a superficial understanding of how the recent losses arose. There is a school of thought which questions whether this lack of understanding really matters. Surely we should be looking forward, not back. The mistakes of the past have been recognised and acknowledged, and although no-one has accepted personal responsibility for them, that is of no significance. What is important now is that we should draw a line under the whole episode and look to the future with confidence. This we are able to do under the new leadership of the Church Commissioners, which is clearly set on a more open and prudent course. In a few years' time we shall look back on the failure of the property development investment strategy as a mere blip on a long and distinguished record which the Commissioners can rightly claim. Tragically, this is precisely the attitude which allowed the property débâcle to take place, and ignored the numerous warnings from people of the calibre of Archdeacon Derek Hayward, formerly Diocesan Secretary of London, Mr H.S. Cranfield, a former Commissioner elected by the General Synod, whose concerns on the conduct of the Commissioners span a period of over 20 years, and Mr Trevor Stevenson, also a former Commissioner elected by the General Synod, who noted that as recently as April and May 1994, Commissioners who were not on the key committees found that they were excluded from access to those committees' papers. As the Parliamentary Social Security Committee observed, 'This Committee can only wonder why the warnings of people of such standing were consistently ignored and why their views were marginalised.'[4] The analysis of past events put forward in this paper is an attempt to construct that essential foundation on which to base an examination of the options which face the Church of England, standing, as it does, at a cross-roads.

Before the Church Commissioners

To comprehend not just the recent past but also proposals for the future of the Church Commissioners, it is necessary to look at how the Commissioners came into being. We will see the reasons for Thomas Arnold's outburst, but first we must go back briefly to Tudor times when the church's allegiance was turned by Henry VIII from Rome to the English Crown. By making Church and State synonymous, the King was able to plunder the vast accumulation of wealth which the church had built up over the previous thousand years, since long before the days of a unified state in England. One small part of this plunder was the revenue from the First Fruits and Tenths which had been paid by ecclesiastical benefices to the papal curia and which Henry appropriated in 1534.

Gradually over the next 170 years there emerged, in embryonic form at first, some semblance of a national conscience, a sense of right and wrong in society, what today we may call public opinion. By the beginning of the eighteenth century, the huge disparity in the endowment of benefices had become a matter of such concern that it provoked a response from within the church. Moved by two of her bishops, Anne used the income from the First Fruits and Tenths to create a fund to augment the livings of the poorer clergy, a fund which came to be known as Queen Anne's Bounty. In spite of subsequent Parliamentary grants and private benefactions, much of the benefit was absorbed, so it is said, by a costly bureaucracy.

As in the eighteenth century, so again at the time of Thomas Arnold, it was misuse by the church of its wealth that fuelled demands for the reform of the church. The inequitable distribution of its rich endowments was a scandal which brought public odium on those bishops who enjoyed the vast incomes which enabled them to socialise with the wealthiest in the land. Although many in the church saw the need for reform, no serious proposals were put forward. Some took the view that the church was an essential bulwark against revolution and nothing must be done to weaken its position for fear that the whole process would get out of control. Others, and certainly this applied to most in positions of power and influence within the church, recognised that reform would inevitably undermine their own privileges. Procrastination seemed more attractive than the prospect of having to wrestle with the problems that reform would undoubtedly spawn. Another difficulty was that the church lacked within its structures the mechanism by which these matters could be discussed and addressed. The Church of England was little more than a loose federation of dioceses. The bishops reigned supreme, each in his own diocese with his own hierarchy to support his authority. At the centre was a gaping void.

Parliament itself was remodelled by the Reform Act of 1832, following which a Royal Commission led to the setting up of the Ecclesiastical Commissioners with the task of making additional provision for the cures of souls in parishes where such assistance was most required. Sir Robert Peel's intention had been that the Ecclesiastical Commissioners should be few in number, but powerful in influence and so provide a strong and effective central financial administration for the church. At the outset, the Commissioners were the two archbishops, three bishops, the Lord President of the Council and seven Government ministers. In spite of vigorous opposition from within the church on the grounds that it had a built-in lay majority which was subject to political appointment (and removal), the Ecclesiastical Commissioners worked rapidly and ruthlessly and were soon making sweeping proposals for the reform of church finances. The endowments of bishoprics were completely redistributed to create much more equality, and the financing of cathedral chapters was overhauled by reducing the large number of endowed canonries, often held on a non-residential basis by clergy with other positions in the hierarchy. The money thus saved was used to augment the many poor livings and to provide for the endowment of new parishes and two new bishoprics in the rapidly-expanding towns of the Midlands and the North.

So successful were their early proposals, that in spite of passionate clerical opposition to the whole concept of payment of the clergy being brought under some form of central control, the Commission quickly became a permanent body. However, the price to be paid for church acquiescence was a high one. The Commission was expanded to include all the bishops of England and Wales, three deans and two ecclesiastical judges. In 1850, an Estates Committee was formed with wide powers to manage the property acquired by the Commission, and three Church Estates Commissioners – two salaried, one not – were given complete control over all leasehold property.[5] Gradually they gained the confidence of the clergy, and by the end of the nineteenth century more than a third of the parishes in the land were benefiting from their distributions.

The Church Commissioners

In 1919, the Church Assembly was established and given the right to pass Measures which, with the assent of Parliament, have statutory force. A generation later, the Church used these Measure-making powers to create the Church Commissioners, 'To promote the more efficient and economical administration of the resources of the Church of England by uniting the Corporation of the Governors of the Bounty of Queen Anne ..., and the Ecclesiastical Commissioners for England ....'[6]

Apart from the granting to the Church Commissioners of authority to invest in equities, whereas previously the church's assets were represented by property, the 1947 Measure did little more than merge the two bodies, restating the total ban on distributing capital. The Commissioners were required to make only such distributions as were prudent from the income available after deducting their own proper expenses. The sweeping powers transferred to the Church Commissioners were, and remain today, largely unrestricted by other legislation, such as the Charities Acts, or the duties placed upon trustees by the Trustee Acts. The expectation implicit in the Measure was that the new Church Commissioners would continue to operate in much the same manner as their predecessors.

The enlarged body of the Ecclesiastical Commissioners, as established in the 1840s, was replicated and extended in the 1947 Measure. In addition to the seven Government ministers, including the Prime Minister, the Lord Chancellor, the Chancellor of the Exchequer and both Law Officers, other Commissioners included the Speaker, the Lord Chief Justice, the Master of the Rolls, the Lord Mayors of London and York, two aldermen of the City of London, and the Vice-Chancellors of the Universities of Oxford and Cambridge. The Crown nominated four distinguished laymen, as did the Archbishop of Canterbury. Church representation was massive: both Archbishops, all 41 diocesan bishops and five deans or provosts elected from amongst their number, together with ten other clergy (including a number of archdeacons), and ten laity appointed by the Church Assembly. The 92 Commissioners were joined by three Estates Commissioners, the first two appointed by the Government and the third by the Archbishop of Canterbury, who presided over the whole assembly. Executive responsibility was entrusted to the three Estates Commissioners, of whom the First Estates Commissioner is effectively Chief Executive. The Second Estates Commissioner is by custom a Government back-bencher and acts as Parliamentary spokesman for the Commissioners, who are responsible, not to the church, but to Parliament. The Third Estates Commissioner is more concerned with pastoral responsibilities. A Board of Governors was supported by a structure of five committees, including the Assets Committee which, while subject to rules laid down by the Board, had the specific power and duty to act independently in all matters relating to the management of the Commissioners' assets.[7]

This cumbersome structure was archaic even at the moment of its inception, yet it survived almost unscathed for 50 years and, but for the journalistic revelations of the 1990s, would no doubt have continued into the twenty-first century. It is a tribute to the skill and dedication of successive Church Estates Commissioners and their staff that the new body quickly established a reputation which enabled it to retain the trust and confidence of church people, and particularly the clergy. The Commissioners' legal and quasi-judicial functions have always been performed to a high standard. As the paymasters of the clergy, including the bishops, the Commissioners have carried out their administrative duties efficiently and sympathetically. Above all, until the mid-1980s, the management of their large investment portfolio was considered to be shrewd and soundly based, if not spectacular. However, established on Civil Service lines, the organisation has always been expensive to run.

In spite of their success, the Commissioners failed to withstand the growing pressures of inflation. By the 1960s, many stipends, even after increasing augmentation by the Church Commissioners, were becoming inadequate for the growing proportion of clergy without private means. Although the Commissioners had been able to replace a modest contributory pension scheme for the clergy by a non-contributory scheme, retirement still raised the spectre of homelessness and poverty for clergy unable to make any provision for their older years out of their meagre stipends.[8] Increasingly, clergy wives had to take paid employment to make ends meet, but this option was not always available.

Rampant inflation led to the publication in 1972 of a report which indicated that parishioners would have to find in 1975 anything up to twice as much as they did in 1970.[9] Exacerbated by the oil crisis of 1973, the inflation forecasts proved wildly optimistic. No longer were the living laity to be exempt from making meaningful contributions to the cost of clergy stipends. This remained true even though the number of candidates offering themselves for ordination was dropping significantly, with the resultant prospect of a steady contraction in the stipendiary ministry, which in turn made the large-scale amalgamation of benefices, particularly in rural areas, inevitable. All this came on top of a long and continuing period of decline in church attendances, so that fewer lay people were being asked to pay much more for reduced numbers of clergy and less frequent services.

The General Synod, which in 1970 had replaced the Church Assembly, refused to be daunted by mere financial difficulties, and grasped the nettle. A medium-term programme of increasing stipend levels year by year, by more than the rate of inflation, was introduced. The clergy were in future to be required to retire on reaching 70 and were to be allowed to do so from the age of 65. The need for enhanced pension arrangements was accepted, and in 1980 General Synod enthusiastically adopted pension 'aspirations' proposed by the Commissioners themselves, which envisaged moving to a clergy retirement package promising a pension of two-thirds of national minimum stipend, realistic help with housing and a lump sum on retirement.

Ends and means

As far as can be ascertained, the pension aspirations commitment was entered into without any serious attempt to establish the likely costs.

Certainly no estimates were presented to the Synod.[10] Here lay the seeds of impending disaster. Consider for a moment the essential arithmetic of church finance in the early 1980s. The Church Commissioners had responsibility for a very large, but closed, fund – there was no new money coming in. They had committed themselves to substantial improvements in both stipends and clergy pensions at a time when the number of pensioners was already growing inexorably. Unless they proposed to reduce their support for bishops or cathedrals, which they did not, or were willing to cut their own costs, which did not occur to them, they would have to switch an increasingly large proportion of their income from stipend support to pensions. The time could be envisaged when virtually all their income would be required to meet their pension obligations – and yet they never did the sums! This is not the wisdom of hindsight. At the time, many of us involved in church finance at diocesan level felt a duty to go round warning people that the Church Commissioners would not be able to sustain their support for stipends. Watsons', the firm of actuaries consulted by the Church Commissioners some 14 years later, reported that, 'The accumulating unrecognised liabilities can be likened to a time bomb waiting to go off: poor performance within the asset portfolio merely shortened the fuse.'[11] Curiously, the Commissioners themselves appear to have been sublimely unaware of the time bomb.

The immediate consequence of all this for parishioners was that the contribution they were asked to make towards the support of their stipendiary clergy rose sharply, even though the number of clergy continued to decline. It is the diocese which has the responsibility for collecting the money from the parishes, and in the early 1980s it was not uncommon for the assessments made by the dioceses on the parishes to rise by 20 per cent or more per annum above the rate of inflation. There was much grumbling but, to their credit, they found the extra money. Then the picture began to change. Stipends and pensions continued to improve. The cost of pensions continued to rise steeply, but the demands on parishes for increased contributions began to abate to something much closer to inflation rates. Praise for the achievements of the Commissioners was fulsome and almost universal, and anyone minded, however gently, to question the basis of their success was regarded with great suspicion.

We now know how the 'miracle' was achieved. The Commissioners had inherited a large property portfolio which they had maintained at a level which many would regard as too high. However, in the mid-1980s there were clear signs that, after a long period in the doldrums, the property market was beginning to take off and valuations were starting to rise sharply, particularly in the retail sector where higher rents were underpinned by boom conditions in the high streets. In these circumstances, property development offers high potential returns. This was perceived to be a window of opportunity for the Commissioners. But there was a problem. Because they managed a closed fund, the only way to put money into property development was to switch funds already invested elsewhere – and that involved selling assets which would in the short term reduce income. Property development companies overcome this problem by borrowing the funds required, using their other assets as collateral. To succeed, the profits arising from the development have to be sufficient to cover the interest paid on the borrowed money. If they get their timing right, this presents no problem; but conversely, if they get their timing wrong and boom turns to bust before the development is completed, they could go to the wall. Because they had so much of their assets in property, the Commissioners, or more accurately the Assets Committee, began to see themselves as a property company. From that point onwards it was but a small step to seeing themselves as a property development company, and doing what all property development companies do: borrowing the funds required to finance the developments.

Initial forays into property development were successful and appeared fully to justify the strategy. The temptation then is to increase the scale of activity on the basis that the greater the risks you are prepared to take, the larger the potential profits become. The Metro Centre in Gateshead was a huge out-of-town shopping complex requiring an investment running into hundreds of millions – too big for the Church Commissioners to handle on their own; but when their partners fell by the wayside it was too good to miss so the Commissioners took on the whole risk – and got away with it! There was no stopping them now! Further projects followed, with total disregard for the signs that the economy was overheating, that the boom would not last for ever.

The achievements of the Church Commissioners' financial miracle in the 1980s were spectacular. They were able to fulfil the pensions aspirations while at the same time increasing the support they provided for stipends, sometimes by even more than inflation. In addition they picked up the extra costs arising from the application of national insurance contributions to clergy stipends and from the introduction of the Community Charge. Further grants were made towards housing costs, equity sharing loans were made available to dioceses for the purchase of houses, even car loans were introduced to help the clergy replace their cars, and ongoing support was given to the Church Urban Fund.

However, there must surely have been some disquiet, perhaps within the Assets Committee itself, at the means by which these benefits had been achieved. With the rush into speculative property development, it was necessary to establish as many as 37 subsidiary companies to enable the Church Commissioners to maintain their status as an exempt charity. As well as providing a smoke-screen to conceal what was really going on, these wholly-owned companies were used to create bogus fees and dividends which enabled the Commissioners to get round the prohibition on making distributions in excess of their income.[12] As the Parliamentary Select Committee was to comment in 1995: 'The outcome of these acts proved to be as disastrous for the Commissioners' assets as it was ethically suspect.'[13]

The reckoning

When the property bubble finally burst in 1990, the Commissioners were left with several development projects in hand: some in the course of construction, others, such as Ashford Great Park, not even started although substantial sums had already been committed in site acquisition costs, etc. Those that were coming on stream for letting suddenly presented a much lower income potential, even if tenants could be found, and established retail properties suffered a rise in vacant accommodation as tenants could no longer sustain their rental obligations. The Commissioners' borrowings were so horrendous, some £500 million at the peak, that interest payments alone accounted for more than a third of their sustainable income. The constant outflow of funds, absorbing an increasingly high proportion of a diminishing income, are the classic symptoms of a failing property development company that got its timing wrong.

The Commissioners' problems were further compounded by their continuing commitment to excessively high and increasing levels of distributions. To reduce their borrowings, they were forced to sell those properties that were most marketable in a rapidly falling market – for the most part those producing the best returns of income, or income potential. To increase their income, they switched investments into high-yielding gilts, with little prospect of capital growth, but even this could not enable them to square the circle. Being precluded from using their capital, they somehow had to generate still more income to meet their commitments. To their shame, they came up with what they called 'temporary income' – the exact nature of which they refused to disclose. Only later did we find out, with almost total incredulity, that this was a euphemism for 'coupon-trading' or 'dividend stripping'. These technical terms describe a process of purchasing fixed interest securities just before an interest payment is due to be received, and then, immediately after receipt of the interest, selling the securities at a price inevitably reduced by the absence of the imminent receipt of interest. By taking the whole of the interest received into income, and the whole of the resulting loss on sale to capital, the Commissioners were effectively using capital to purchase income. The legality of these operations has never been tested in the courts.

By the autumn of 1991, the First Estates Commissioner was touring the dioceses warning Boards of Finance that from 1992 there would be substantial reductions in the Commissioners' support for stipends. As we contemplated the ruins of our forward budgets, we pondered on how the Commissioners had so misjudged the situation as to be forced into what were clearly panic measures. Probably for the first time, most of us seriously began to question the Commissioners' financial management, and by the Spring of 1992 a paper submitted to a regional conference of diocesan chairmen and secretaries demanding an urgent enquiry into the Commissioners' investment activities met with unanimous support.[14] We did not know how we might convince the bishops of the validity of our concerns in the absence of the very evidence such an enquiry might elicit, but as it turned out, our efforts were overtaken by events.

On 11 July 1992, the time bomb went off. It was detonated by John Plender's major piece of investigative journalism, published with full prominence in the *Financial Times* under the headline 'Unholy Saga of the Church's Missing Millions'. The explosion ripped through the calm of a blissfully ignorant General Synod which by no coincidence was in session in York at the time. The revelations of mismanagement and under-performance over many years were so unexpected that the resultant shock wave was even more devastating in its effect. As far back as 1983, the Commissioners were getting their timing wrong by, for example, jumping into US real estate development at a time when the dollar was riding high. Many of their later decisions were equally ill-advised. Their errors of judgement were compounded by quaint, almost bizarre, practices which had no place in the management of major funds in the late 20th century. John Plender postulated, 'on a rough calculation that under-performance could have cost the clergy anything between £50 million and £100 million a year in today's money over the course of the decade'.[15]

The Archbishop of Canterbury promised swift action to respond to the allegations in Mr Plender's article and quickly set up, on his own initiative, a Committee of Enquiry (the Lambeth Group), under the chairmanship of John Waine, then Bishop of Chelmsford, but also Deputy Chairman of the Board of Governors. Fears of a whitewash were reinforced by the appointment of other Commissioners, including Brian Howard, Deputy Chairman of the Assets Committee, which was at the very heart of the enquiry, to fill three of the remaining eight seats making up the Group. The independence of the enquiry was further undermined by the appointment, as consultants to investigate the Commissioners' investment activities, of Coopers & Lybrand, a leading firm of accountants, who as auditors of the subsidiary companies had been responsible for much of the Commissioners' creative accounting policies. Thus both Mr Howard and the accountants were being invited to play key parts in judging the consequences of their own actions.[16] To be fair, the Coopers & Lybrand team, led by Peter King, interpreted the very narrow brief they had been given in the widest possible terms, and in spite of an inevitable gloss, their report and that of the Group as a whole, published in July 1993, revealed a state of affairs at Millbank which was almost beyond belief. The Assets Committee were portrayed as a bunch of well-meaning amateurs, totally out of their depth and yet unaware of their own shortcomings. As permitted by the Church Commissioners Measure, they acted almost independently of the remainder of the organisation. The Board of Governors, the Archbishop of Canterbury included, were not even kept informed about, let alone involved in, many of the major decisions taken by the Assets Committee. However, it is important to recognise that the problems arose almost exclusively in the management of the property and fixed interest investment portfolios. The Commissioners' management of their equity investments has consistently been of a high order.

There are those who see little wrong with what the Church Commissioners were doing in the 1980s. Surely they were only trying to make the most of what had been entrusted to them – like the good stewards of our Lord's parables. They were just unlucky, that's all. Sir Douglas Lovelock, who had inherited the nightmare scenario in 1983, defended his role as First Church Estates Commissioner in these terms:

> everything was done in what we believed to be the interests of the Church. The Church wanted us to pay higher pensions, they wanted the stipend to go up, they wanted the Community Charge to be met, they wanted £1 million a year for the Church Urban Fund, they wanted free car loans for the clergy, and on and on and on we could go. They were all good causes which the Church had wanted, and

in some cases, like the pensions improvement, the General Synod had itself decided upon. To do these things, we needed more income. We thought we could safely change the basis of our capital in order that more income could be obtained. As things have turned out we went too far in that direction, but every single thing was done to meet a request from the Church and to help the Church. There was no wrongdoing, there was no sleaze. Nobody gained from it or got any commission from it.[17]

It is true that the evidence of the Accountants' Report to the Lambeth Group supports Sir Douglas's assertion, but the Parliamentary Committee remained unimpressed: 'It [the Accountants' Report] did not cover fraud, although the Church Commissioners proved such an easy target to developers to whom they entrusted vast sums of capital that fraud was probably superfluous.'[18] Perhaps good stewardship requires more than good intentions. The end never justifies the means.

A question of integrity

The Lambeth Report made many recommendations for improving the quality of the expertise available to the Commissioners and strengthening their internal procedures. It also addressed more fundamental concerns such as the need for a greater degree of prudence (even) than a pension fund; the Commissioners should avoid borrowing; the practice of generating 'temporary income' through 'coupon trading' should cease. Turning to wider issues, the Lambeth Group commented, 'We believe that the Church would benefit from a simpler organisational structure'.[19]

All the recommendations were accepted by the Church Commissioners. Most were implemented with commendable dispatch. By the time the Lambeth Report was published, the process of reducing borrowing and repositioning the investment portfolio so that there was less dependence on property was already under way. This involved a crash programme of selling property, mainly commercial property, at a time when the property market was at its lowest ebb. Many of the Commissioners' 'losses' which arose on revaluation of the assets after the collapse of the property boom were now converted into real losses as the prices obtained on disposal were little more than the reduced valuations. However, from an accounting point of view, the new management under Sir Michael Colman, who took over as First Estates Commissioner in April 1993, was able to record modest gains as sale proceeds exceeded the book values shown in the balance sheet.

The church's organisational structure was addressed by a Commission set up by the two archbishops under the chairmanship of Michael Turnbull, successively Bishop of Rochester and of Durham. The task was addressed diligently and expeditiously, and the Turnbull Report, *Working as One Body*, was published in September 1995, within a year of the Commission's appointment.

Coupon trading presented the church with a more acute problem. In accepting the recommendations of the Lambeth Report, the Commissioners proposed to phase out coupon trading as quickly as possible, implying that they would not be able to meet even their reduced commitments without some coupon trading in the short term. Sir Michael Colman made no secret of his discomfort with the continuation of coupon trading.[20] The bishops were left with a dilemma. They were faced with three options. They could say to the church at large that there would have to be a further immediate sharp cutback in Commissioners' support for stipends. This would involve an equivalent prompt increase in the levels of giving, over and above what was already being asked, with the risk of not being able to maintain so many stipendiary clergy in post (for example by not filling vacancies as they arose) if giving did not increase sufficiently or quickly enough. Experience in my own far from affluent diocese gave firm grounds for believing that most churchgoers were expecting a further appeal such as this after all the publicity concerning the Commissioners' losses, and would certainly do whatever was necessary to ensure that they did not lose their parish priest. Many chairmen of Diocesan Boards of Finance (DBFs) took the cautious view for which they are well-known and told their bishops that they could not guarantee success and therefore they must advise against this course of action. They needed more time. However, the Church Commissioners were prepared to be as helpful as possible in this situation and therefore offered a second option. Although precluded by statute from distributing capital to sustain support for stipends, there is no legal restriction on the use of capital to make loans to dioceses, particularly if interest is charged at a rate sufficient to involve the Commissioners in no loss of income. The Commissioners were prepared to tailor such loans to the requirements of individual dioceses so that they had the extra time they needed. Obviously the loan option could be used as a fallback situation if the appeal for further increases in giving did not generate a big enough response quickly enough. This would have avoided any risk to stipendiary posts. Again, the DBF chairmen, not wishing to involve themselves in commitments to pay back loans and interest, gave this proposal the thumbs down. The third possibility was to continue coupon trading. This was much the easiest alternative and to their great discredit the House of Bishops took the soft option and told the Church Commissioners that the church could not find the extra money which would allow them to stop coupon trading. In spite of all the declarations of intent to the contrary, this costly and despicable practice continued at a significant level until Parliament passed the Church of England Pensions Measure which enabled the Commissioners to spend their capital lawfully.

Subsequent experience across the length and breadth of the Church of England has demonstrated that churchgoers are prepared to give more generously to meet the needs of the church. They have responded magnificently. But then, why shouldn't they? The living church is still greatly subsidised by the giving of past generations. Even today, the Church of England asks for less financial commitment from its members than possibly any other church in Christendom.

From the outset, the bishops must have known their decision lacked integrity. They now know it was unnecessary. The Church of England's highest authority, the House of Bishops, has demonstrated its willingness to flout the spirit (and possibly the letter) of the law, not for the sake of any high-blown principle, but merely for the sake of perceived expediency. What moral authority remains to the bishops of the Church of England?

The hand of God?

In the 1980s, the nation was overwhelmed with the Thatcherite *laissez-faire* philosophy of free competition and the pursuit of personal advancement. This preoccupation with self-interest is just a short step from worshipping Mammon. Far from speaking out against this culture, certain elements in the church followed the trends in the secular world and by their example condoned them. Only in this way is it possible to explain how good Christians in the Commissioners, and amongst the bishops, were prepared to countenance speculation, a form of gambling, on a large scale with someone else's money; to believe it was right to use the giving of past generations as collateral to borrow money to finance speculation; even to contemplate a programme of converting capital into income in direct contravention of the undoubted spirit, if not the letter, of the law, and to do all these things in the name of Christ's Church. No bishop, and but one commissioner, has had the integrity to offer to resign, and that offer was not accepted. As we know well enough, for evil to triumph it is necessary only for men and women of goodwill to remain silent. We are entitled to speak up and ask what sort of church is going into the next millennium – a church in which almost anything goes, or a church that speaks for God and puts him at the centre of everything it does?

Money, or wealth, is not something we possess as of right. Nor is it the invention of Satan. It is entrusted to us by God that we might use it in his service and to his glory. Often, we hear the clergy say that decisions must not be driven by finance but by the Spirit, implying that the Spirit cannot and does not speak to us through money. Yet our Lord taught in parables more often on the subject of how we handle wealth or riches than on any other single topic. If it is true that we are mere stewards, or trustees, of God's bounty, our response to the duties placed upon us by trusteeship reflects the spirituality of our commitment to God. As our Lord put it so succinctly, we cannot serve two masters.

There are some who see the hand of God behind the travails of the Church Commissioners in the early 1990s. The loss of so much money has given those of us who make up God's Church of England a jolt. It has shaken us out of our lethargy. It has made us sit up and take stock of the situation, to look at where we are, and where we are going. There is a new determination to face up to realities. One consequence is that the pattern of the church's ministry in the twenty-first century may be more relevant to the nation's needs and the church's resources.

Counting blessings

Already the sense of panic engendered by the Commissioners' losses is receding. Now is the time to remind ourselves of the resources which our Lord has placed at the disposal of his Church. In order to quantify them it is necessary to attach monetary values wherever possible. This is not to propose a widespread disposal of assets to release their full potential. However, by valuing our assets we force ourselves not to take them quite so much for granted, to recognise that although most of them came to us 'for free', they nevertheless represent the sacrifices of millions of people over many generations, freely given for the glory of God and for the work of his Church. In acknowledgement of this debt which we owe to our predecessors, we have a duty to ask whether we are making the best possible use of these historic resources. If we are not, we are not only letting down the host of Christian witnesses in this land before us, we are failing to fulfil our Lord's command to be good stewards. How we carry out our financial responsibilities is very much a reflection of our willingness to be guided by the practical outpouring of the Spirit.

There are, however, several problems when monetary values are attached to resources. First is their transient nature. Even at so-called low rates of inflation, the real value of monetary units halves every 15 to 20 years. Secondly, because we are dealing with very large figures, we are overwhelmed by their size which is beyond our range of experience. Finally, there is always a wide range of resources which defy meaningful quantification in monetary terms. There is not much we can do about this final difficulty except acknowledge its existence and try to replace quantitative assessments of value by more subjective qualitative judgements. Perhaps the first two obstacles to understanding can best be addressed by expressing monetary values in terms of equivalent values which we are more able to recognise. Thus at the time of writing we may work on the assumption that the bricks and mortar value of Buckingham Palace is of the order of £100 million – it being possible to rebuild or replace Buckingham Palace by a palace of similar standing for such a sum. The figure may lack precision but it will suffice for our purposes.

At first sight, it is apparent that the bulk of the church's financial resources are in the hands either of the Church Commissioners or the parishes. Certainly in terms of liquidity, the ability to convert assets into cash, this is true, and the Church Commissioners are very much the dominant partner. It is therefore inevitable that the future of funds currently entrusted to them is crucial to any financial analysis of a possible agenda for the church in the twenty-first century. Good stewardship requires us to use our understanding of how and why the mistakes of the recent past arose, in order to ensure that such mistakes can never be repeated.

As the twentieth century draws to a close, the assets of the Church Commissioners will grow beyond the £3 billion figure first achieved a decade earlier.[21] Now we would be looking at, say, thirty Buckingham Palaces (BPs), a decade ago more like forty. By contrast the total assets of the church's 13,000 parishes perhaps amount to no more than a dozen BPs.[22] Cathedrals and other greater churches, together with certain Central Funds, can probably muster the best part of a further two BPs, and the dioceses, which now administer the historic glebe funds, together with various smaller funds for the payment of stipends and provision of housing, etc., are responsible for assets totalling some three BPs.[23] In financial terms, therefore, the loss by the Commissioners of about ten BPs is substantial in relation to the 47 BPs which remain.

However, these financial assets of the church are little more than the visible part of the iceberg of total resources. Beneath the surface, and therefore much less open to scrutiny, is what we might call the fixed plant of the church – the church buildings, parish halls, bishops' and parsonage houses, which the living church has been given for free as part of past legacies. The prospect of placing a value on the 15,000 places of worship available to the Church is daunting – perhaps as much as 300 BPs. The figure, whatever it is, is very large and not particularly meaningful, but it does force us to consider whether we are making the best possible use of such vast resources. Is it right that so many churches should remain locked and unused for most of each week? The parish halls are, of course, much better utilised, and represent a further resource, say another ten BPs. The ten thousand plus clergy houses represent at least another 15 BPs over which present avenues of accountability leave much to be desired. On top of this there are several hundred bishopric or cathedral houses administered by the Church Commissioners and cathedral chapters which might conservatively be valued at a further couple of BPs. Public accountability in respect of these buildings is almost non-existent. Thus, ignoring its vast resources of places of worship, the church has the benefit of other buildings perhaps totalling 27 BPs in value.

Enough has surely been said to demonstrate that the resources placed at the disposal of the church are more than adequate to the task in hand. And yet the greatest resource of all available to the Church of England is its million-strong band of regular worshippers.[24] They are the instruments of God's will in the world, increasingly they provide the income on which the work of the church depends, and they are 99 per cent lay. It is no longer realistic to expect the clerical 1 per cent to accept the lion's share of responsibility for furthering the Kingdom, willing as they may be. Nor is it realistic for the 1 per cent who are clergy to regard themselves as the only people entrusted by God to ensure the church's survival. Unless these two barriers are broken down, and quickly, there can be little immediate prospect of a sustained reversal of the long decline which the church has experienced.

The servant church?

One of the most consistent features of the Christian churches in the twentieth century has been the inexorable decline in support in the affluent West, more than matched by the equally inexorable growth of Christian churches in the impoverished Third World. The Church of

England will finish the twentieth century with only a third of the number of regular churchgoers that it had at the beginning. More than half the loss will have occurred since 1960. The graph of clergy numbers shows more peaks and troughs, it is true, but again the underlying trend is unmistakably downwards. There will be fewer than half the number of stipendiary clergy, under the age of 65, at the end of the twentieth century than there was at the start, and here the sharpest fall will have been in the last decade.[25] It really is becoming impossible for the church to maintain the concept of the stipendiary minister working alone in his parish. This is certainly true in rural areas where the process of uniting small parishes into single benefices has already gone too far in some places, with the result that small communities of Christians feel increasingly isolated and abandoned. In the large urban centres and suburban housing estates, the sight of the vicar sitting in his still overlarge 'green-book' house,[26] beleaguered behind his high-security fence, increasingly cut off from the community he serves, is no longer a rarity. The church urgently needs to rethink its strategy and if a financial jolt is the means by which the Spirit awakens the church to this need, so be it.

The process of adjustment has, of course, been going on for some time. As long ago as 1963, 'The Paul Report' drew attention to the wasteful deployment of clergy away from the areas of greatest need – the large centres of population.[27] The 'Sheffield' formula of allocating clergy between dioceses was devised and introduced a decade later to address the worst of these anomalies. In 1983, 'The Tiller Report' saw the decline in numbers of stipendiary clergy as inevitably leading to a flowering of lay ministry in what John Tiller called 'The Ministry of the Whole People of God'.[28] What is new is the realisation that it just is not going to be possible to 'get by' without the implementation of radical new ideas on patterns of ministry. The financial implications will be substantial.

The Church of England is greatly blessed by the quality of its clergy. There is also a new breed of clergy, called to the ministry in mid-career and therefore bringing with them great gifts acquired in the secular world. Most clergy feel frustrated that their traditional ministry touches only a tiny proportion of the population. Somehow, they have to be released from the straitjacket of 'maintenance' to fulfil their mission in the wider community. Similarly, the church is greatly blessed in the quality of its laity. Numbers are not everything, and probably never before have the Church of England laity been so actively committed to their church. In the church's hour of need the calling to be part of a royal priesthood is touching growing numbers of the laity. Increasingly, lay people are finding themselves in a position to serve the church and, through the church, the wider community. More people are taking early retirement, or are in part-time employment, or sadly between jobs or in the ranks of the long-term unemployed. They have much to offer. More mechanisms are needed to enable the church to use their gifts to best effect.

Amongst the hierarchy and the senior clergy there is widespread evidence of the deep suspicion they have of what they call 'managerialism' in the Church. One example is provided by the Revd M.G. Fuller, who in a letter to the *Church Times*, wrote:

> My experience, having left industry to be ordained, after 20 years as a senior executive in a large international corporation, was that I was subjected by the theological college to a de-skilling process; a number of other students who had been in similar positions felt the same. In my parish there are a number of highly-skilled and senior lay people from all walks of life who are considered to be at the top in their particular disciplines. Are their skills drawn upon by the diocese? Not a bit of it.[29]

There has to be a genuine partnership between clergy and laity, stipendiary, part-stipendiary and non-stipendiary, to create a truly servant church. Lay people want to be taken seriously, they want to play a full part. This involves many clergy in the stipendiary ministry with a difficult adjustment of their role. A senior cleric, extolling the virtues of collaborative ministry, said recently that more and more he found he was able to use lay people in worship. He meant well, of course, but it won't do. The laity are not there to be 'used' by the clergy, to assist the priests as some sort of substitute clergy. If lay people are to play their full part they will need all the help they can get – from the clergy. Priests in the Church of England have a vital role to play in enabling the laity to be the body of Christ. Will the clergy, particularly those whose training of many years ago did not prepare them for the new situation, be willing to share responsibility with the laity?

The pay package

The financial implications of new patterns of ministry are very much the consequence of, and in no way the justification for, change. With the fall in the numbers of full-time stipendiaries comes a decline in the stipends bill, which is the biggest single element in the church's expenditure. So surprising was the loss of over 300 full-time stipendiaries in 1995 that nearly every diocesan Board of Finance recorded an unexpected surplus. Although arising from circumstances which are of concern to all, DBF chairmen welcomed the relief. It was, we hope, an unusual occurrence, a time when ordinations fell far below retirements and the net loss of clergy to posts outside the church was exceptionally high. It is thought that the air of financial insecurity following the revelations of Commissioners' losses was in part responsible. However, there is the ongoing prospect of the number of stipendiaries falling by anything up to two hundred a year, every year, for the foreseeable future. Insofar as these represent permanent losses, in addition to stipends, there are considerable savings in housing costs as well as the longer-term pensions considerations. The immediate savings in expenditure are going to be large enough to help smooth the introduction of a properly-funded clergy pension scheme. Of less significance, but not to be overlooked, the reduced number of ordinands in training has led to underspends on the Central Board of Finance (CBF) training budget and made it easier for the CBF Apportionment on dioceses to be reduced in real terms.

The pensions mess has been addressed with remarkable expedition. As recommended by the Lambeth Report, the Church Commissioners asked a leading firm of Consultant Actuaries, R. Watson & Sons, to examine the Church Commissioners' liabilities and Investment Strategy. The Watsons' report confirmed the findings of the earlier Coopers & Lybrand report to the Lambeth Group that the Commissioners had been over-distributing their income for some time and that even with improved investment performance their current level of commitments was unsustainable. Watsons' recommended that the distinction between income and capital, which they felt was artificial and unnecessarily constraining to the adoption of the most suitable investment policies, should be replaced by a formal recognition of the need for the Commissioners to protect the real value of the assets and hence the real level of income available for distribution. In addition, they recommended that contributions should be collected to finance the cost of pension benefits accruing in future.[30] The DBF chairmen had already come to much the same conclusions and at an informal meeting in Peterborough in March 1995 they endorsed the findings of the Watsons' report and accepted the principle of a properly-funded clergy pension scheme in respect of future service, with contributions to be paid by the dioceses as part of the clergy remuneration package. They did so on the clear understanding that the Church Commissioners would provide transitional assistance, on a tapering basis, by increasing their stipend support grants over a period of up to six years. However, the Commissioners would not have sufficient income to enable them to do this and maintain their other expenditure so the DBF chairmen backed the removal of the restriction on the Commissioners' distribution of capital. Perhaps for the first time the DBF chairmen (and secretaries) had been instrumental in determining policy which was subsequently adopted by General Synod, in principle, some four months later. This has paved the way for the speedy preparation of the necessary Pensions Measure, in spite of initial reservations by the House of Commons Social Security Committee. The new Scheme will apply only to pension liabilities arising from service after the start of the Scheme, in 1998, responsibility for pension benefits arising from service before that date continuing to rest with the Church Commissioners out of their total funds. In order to make as seamless as possible the join between what will be, in effect, two different pension schemes, both will have essentially the same benefits based on years of eligible service and a national stipend benchmark for the previous year. For the first time, the old unfunded Scheme will be subject to statutory provisions, in just the same way as the new Scheme, this being part of the 'deal' negotiated with interested Parliamentarians. Both schemes will now be subject to the statutory Minimum Funding Requirement under the Pensions Act 1995, and both will be restricted by the regulations relating to Limited Price Indexation which will impose an upper limit of 5 per cent on annual benefit increments.[31] Only the source of funding will differ.

Initially the contribution to the new funded Scheme will be fixed at just under 22 per cent of stipends. At first sight this looks like a formidable amount of extra money to ask the parishes to find, bearing in mind that the stipends bill can account for anything up to 80 per cent of diocesan budgets. However, the extra transitional support will enable dioceses to phase in the additional cost over a number of years, tailored within limits, to their own requirements. Over that transitional period, the expected fall in the total number of stipendiary clergy available of about 2 per cent per annum will lead to stipend savings which will halve the impact of the pension contributions. A further significant factor is the revision of the basis on which the Church Commissioners allocate their stipend support grants to the dioceses. This has been worked out in close consultation with the Diocesan Boards of Finance who have very responsibly agreed that the lion's share of future grants will at last go to the dozen or so dioceses where the need is greatest. In this way the major part of the extra costs of the pensions contributions will fall on parishes in the more prosperous parts of the country.

Clergy fears that the parishes may not find the required pension contribution, leaving their retirement benefits to suffer, are unfounded. In practice, the pension contribution will be part of the diocesan budget like any other expense. If a diocese is unable to raise from its parishes the cash needed to balance its budget, then expenditure will be cut. This may well involve a reduction in the number of stipendiary clergy on the diocesan payroll, by not filling vacancies or by extending interregna for example, but for all stipendiary clergy in post the pension contribution will be paid, just as their stipends will be paid.

Of much greater concern is the willingness of parishioners, particularly in times of recession, to fund a clergy pay package which, including its pension element, can be perceived as being more generous than that which the laity themselves enjoy in their secular employment. Many employers are finding the cost of a final salary pension scheme impossible to sustain in a harshly competitive environment, particularly as ever more demanding statutory requirements introduce an unacceptable degree of open-endedness to the ultimate costs. Their response is to require their employees, who in most cases are in no position to resist, to switch to a money purchase scheme in which the ultimate benefits are determined not by final salary but by the size of the individual's personal fund which has accumulated over the years. This type of pension limits the employer's contribution to the fixed percentage of salary agreed as part of each individual's contract of employment. It is perhaps a little strange, therefore, that the church has ignored such considerations and has opted for the potentially open-ended commitment to a final salary scheme such as those enjoyed by the Civil Service and other public employees and which are funded out of current taxation. Whether the church's final salary scheme will be sustainable in the long term remains to be seen. It is worth noting that the Pensions Measure does not rule out the possibility of changing to a money purchase scheme at a later date.

A pension contribution approaching 22 per cent of salary is high by secular standards. However, the clergy are not paid a 'salary' which rewards them for the job they do, but a 'stipend' which is intended only to meet the expenses of maintaining a relatively modest lifestyle. Thus the high percentage contribution can be justified by the relatively small stipend to which it is related. On the face of it, the stipend represents a great sacrifice by the clergy who could earn much higher salaries in secular employment. Closer examination reveals that, unless a Nelsonian blind-eye is turned to part or all of the housing element in the clergy remuneration package, the full cost of paying and housing each stipendiary minister is remarkably close to comparable employment costs in the secular world. This is best explained by turning the statement round and looking at what costs are saved if a stipendiary clergy post is abolished. In addition to the stipend, the savings, expressed in terms of percentages of stipend, include: National Insurance Contribution (8.2 per cent), Pension Contribution (21.9 per cent) and Training costs, both initial and continuing, averaged over the working life of the priest (7 per cent). The permanent loss of a clergy post leads to a house becoming surplus to requirements. Sale of the house produces major savings: Repairs, Maintenance, Insurance, Taxes, Water Rates, etc. (18 per cent), periodic Improvements to the house not reflected in the market value (5 per cent), and of course the sale proceeds themselves, if invested, would produce, at a conservative estimate, an income equal to about 96.5 per cent of the basic stipend.[32] For each clergy post lost, the total saving to the church is more than 2½ times the stipend! Faced with the loss of approximately 2 per cent of the stipendiary clergy each year for the next few years, no wonder the DBF chairmen are remarkably sanguine about the introduction of a contributory clergy pension scheme!

There is, of course, another side to the coin. The loss of so many stipendiary clergy will lead to much greater flexibility in patterns of employment in ministry. Some houses will be retained to provide a 'house for duties' in support of a non-stipendiary minister. Indeed the distinction between stipendiary and non-stipendiary is bound to become more blurred as the number of appointments on a part-time stipendiary basis increases. No longer will all parochial ministry be linked to tied-house accommodation, although in certain areas this will remain essential. Increasingly, clergy will be employed on contracts more comparable to secular employment. We have already seen that shorn of housing and some other peripheral benefits the stipend could be more than doubled without any additional cost to the church. The expansion of lay ministry, some of it paid, or part paid, will add significantly also to lay training costs. More of the parish administration tasks previously carried out by the clergy will be performed by lay people, some paid, or at least partly paid. Some work may be contracted out to people like lay evangelists, youth workers, etc., who are directly employed by parishes, or deaneries, outside the normal diocesan structures. It may well be found that such appointments are more cost-effective and more responsive to specific needs than the traditional parish ministry. In many cases, decisions will be taken at local level based on funding also provided by local congregations. The church will have to be very careful to ensure that congregationalism is kept in check without stifling parochial initiatives.

The body of Christ

As we have seen, the one certainty is that patterns of ministry will change as we move into the third millennium. It is essential that the church has the organisational structure to manage change. It cannot be sensible to ask each diocese to start from scratch, reinventing the wheel which best suits its own circumstances. There has to be effective machinery for gathering and evaluating creative thinking from across the whole church, evolving new strategies, consulting with informed opinion at every level so that all feel involved in the decision-taking process, and then when the way forward seems clear taking the necessary decisions and ensuring proper implementation. We are, together in the church, the body of Christ and we must work together as one body. This theological approach underpinned the Report of the Turnbull Commission, appropriately entitled *Working as One Body*, which examined the church's central organisation. They emphasised the theology of the gracious gift, that God in his goodness has already given to the Church the resources it needs to be God's people, and to live and work to his praise and glory. The Church is not a democracy, nor is it a line management hierarchy. Authority in the Church is located not in the hierarchy exclusively but in the whole body of the faithful, united in the sacraments.[33] To dismiss the Turnbull proposals as creating an all-powerful central 'curia' is to misunderstand the Report. If the Church of England's central organisation was to function as a 'curia' it would be denying the whole basis of synodical government. Any attempts to exclude the people from the decision-taking processes, to enforce decisions which the faithful are not prepared to own, is likely to be counterproductive in terms of the resources which God has graciously given to his Church. Quite rightly, the church has to come to terms with this new situation. No longer does the hierarchy alone have sole control over these resources.

The process by which decisions concerning the new Clergy Pension Scheme were taken is an example of this fresh approach in action. For its success it depended on a full disclosure of all the relevant information to those who would be heavily involved in the implementation of any decision. Based on a good understanding of the position in the parishes as well as at the centre, the green light was given at a meeting at which no member of the hierarchy was present. If circumstances change in the future there is sufficient flexibility built into the scheme to enable key decisions to be reviewed later. This process may appear to undermine the authority of the bishops in what is, after all, an episcopal church. In fact most of those present at the informal meeting would have discussed the issues involved with their bishops beforehand. The support of the bishops for the decision that was taken was just as vital as that of the parishes. The bishops in any case had an effective veto but there was no reason for them to use it. Through their control of the necessary financial resources, the parishes also have an effective veto but because they, or their representatives, have been consulted they can own the decision and we can be confident their veto will not be used. Thus the people of God work together as the body of Christ.

Unfortunately, there are few grounds for optimism that the vision of the Turnbull Commission will see ultimate fulfilment. If the church is to work together as one body there has to be trust between all parties, there has to be an openness and a transparency in all decisions, there has to be a full exchange of information and there has to be total accountability. As the Turnbull Commission itself commented, 'Whereas the natural inclination of those with authority and power may be to protect themselves from criticism, the structures which require consultation make them vulnerable.'[34] Powerful vested interests at the heart of the church have no wish to see their influence or freedom of action restricted. Many clergy, fearful of the already awesome power of the bishops over their careers, have no wish to see the church adopt an effective central organisation which in their eyes may appear to extend the power of the hierarchy. Nominally, at least, the Church of England is still part of the State, with Parliament wielding considerable influence over its decisions and the Government controlling every senior appointment within the church. The State shows no willingness to surrender any of its powers over the Church of England. If the people of God really are to be involved together, working as one body, there has to be a genuine transfer of authority away from these vested interests. The determination to make Turnbull work has yet to manifest itself.

Indeed, recognition of the power of one of these vested interests, the Church Commissioners, appears to have led the Turnbull Commission to conclude that any proposal for the total abolition of the Church Commissioners would be unlikely to succeed. In consequence, their Report is seriously flawed by the recommendation that, 'the Church Commissioners should be retained as an independent trust as guardians and stewards of the centrally-held historic assets of the Church (their 'core' function) but that their other functions should be transferred to the National (now to be known as Archbishops') Council.'[35] Many see it as ironic that the Turnbull Commission, which owed its appointment solely to concern arising from the mismanagement by the Church Commissioners of the 'centrally held historic assets of the Church', should propose that this function alone should be retained by the Church Commissioners. We do not know the arguments that led the Turnbull Commission to this conclusion, although it may be significant that Sir Michael Colman, as First Church Estates Commissioner, was himself a member of the Commission. By taking to its logical conclusion the strategy set out so powerfully in the Report, it could have been expected that the Church Commissioners would share the same fate as the Central Board of Finance (CBF), whose management of its responsibilities has been above reproach. If the Finance Committee of the Archbishops' Council is to have overall responsibility for all the central financial policies of the church, there is no place for the Church Commissioners any more than for the CBF. There are good grounds for believing that Parliament would have understood the reasoning and, with great reluctance no doubt, would have accepted the proposal. The alternative would have been to appear to defend an organisation that had demonstrably failed to fulfil its responsibilities of trusteeship to both Church and State. The Social Security Committee itself expressed concern at the apparent complacency within the church with regard to the failings of the Church Commissioners.[36] No doubt some Parliamentarians would have been moved to insist that any proposal to wind up the Church Commissioners must be considered in the context of a wide-ranging review of relations between the State and its established Church. This is a separate issue which in any event will have to be addressed sooner rather than later, as we shall see.

The 'new' Church Commissioners

The quality of the present leadership of the Commissioners is such that the Church may well be lulled into a false sense of security. Sir Michael Colman and Patrick Locke (Secretary to the Commissioners) have put in place a professional and dedicated team. Management of the property portfolio has been strengthened, a finance 'director' has been appointed, an internal audit committee established and, to some extent at least, the appalling lack of openness and accountability has been addressed. However, these reforms are capable of instant reversal at the whim of another First Estates Commissioner. Sir Michael Colman himself confirmed the crucial nature of his office in evidence to the House of Commons Social Security Committee, 'a great deal of the problem lies in the hands of those people in a position of responsibility, like myself ...'.[37] He was referring to the role of auditors, but the comment is capable of wider application.

The First Estates Commissioner and Mr Locke have been willing to discuss the future with considerable candour.[38] Indeed, Sir Michael spoke with passion on the responsibilities of the church to support areas of greatest need. Horrified at the way the Church Commissioners were viewed in the past as general providers, he personally would wish to see such assistance focused where it is most required. Mr Locke emphasised that in terms of the annual expenditure of the church as a whole, the income of the Commissioners is sufficient only to meet a relatively small part, less than 20 per cent. They clearly saw their organisation as something of a bulwark against some of the problems thrown up by synodical government where the church can find itself dominated by pressure groups, and in which a small number of activists, usually living close to London and therefore able to participate regularly in committees, have a disproportionate influence on decisions. The Commissioners' dual accountability, as they saw it, to the church and to Parliament is a strength, although they acknowledge that they were very much in the middle and would be servants of the dominant master. However, Parliament and the church should be working together. So long as we have an established church, there are advantages in retaining some State appointments of Commissioners. On the other hand, disestablishment should not lead to disendowment. Unlike Ireland and Wales, the Church of England has no surplus of endowments.

Ever since their appointment in 1972 as the Clergy Stipends Authority the Commissioners have had a structure for direct consultation with dioceses. Building on this, and following the publication of the Lambeth Report, the Commissioners invited certain DBF chairmen and secretaries to make up a Consultative Committee with which they could discuss the way forward. They may not have been representative, but the Consultative Committee has certainly opened up further avenues of direct consultation with the dioceses. It took the lead in forging the decision on the future funding of clergy pensions, and subsequently on the redirection of Commissioners' allocations away from the more affluent dioceses. Attention has now turned to questions of mutual support between dioceses, leading hopefully to the more affluent providing assistance for those where the need is greatest. This would be some compensation to the less well-off for the severe cutbacks in the Commissioners' support for stipends on which they depend so heavily. How much will come of this initiative remains to be seen but these developments undoubtedly represent new and exciting manifestations of the outpouring of Christian love in action. They also exemplify the Turnbull approach of direct consultation with those most involved with the implementation of decisions – in this case the DBF chairmen and secretaries, who are likely to be given a formal consultative role in the proposed 'Finance Forum'. It would be good if the General Synod was prepared to be similarly self-effacing. Elected representatives sometimes pay little attention to the views of those who have to implement their decisions.

Much has been made of the Commissioners' mistakes in the management of property investments, but it would be very wrong to suggest that the main thrust of their stewardship has been misguided. A great deal has been achieved, and in particular the principal objective for which their predecessors were established, the elimination of the inequitable distribution of endowments, has been spectacularly fulfilled. The clergy are assured of a reasonable, if not generous, stipend, decent housing and an adequate pension in retirement. Bishops and cathedrals have rightly given up much but still enjoy substantial support on which they can rely. The Commissioners carry out their administrative and pastoral functions with great care and efficiency.

In the wake of encouraging developments since 1993 can we now be sure that the leopard has changed his spots, and relax? Alas, we cannot!

Probably the most worrying feature is the way the Church Commissioners have dealt with the steering group responsible for overseeing the implementation of the Turnbull proposals. While professing support for the proposals, their representations to the group appear to seek to retain as much freedom of action and to reserve to the Commissioners as many functions as possible. These objectives are pursued almost to, and perhaps beyond, the point of obstruction. Such duplicity makes the whole concept of the Commissioners and other central church institutions working together as one body something of a sham. Moreover, whilst the steering group have to give due weight to the views expressed on behalf of the Commissioners, there are serious questions as to the validity of the submissions made in the name of the Church Commissioners. For example, a central feature of the Turnbull proposals is a unified staff structure by which the staffs of General Synod and its boards and councils, Lambeth Palace, the Church Commissioners and the Pensions Board are pooled, and work together, as far as possible under one roof and under a single personnel management department with all that that implies for career development.[39] The steering group have been told that this is not acceptable to the Church Commissioners. To accommodate the Church Commissioners' position, the proposals have been modified to provide for a common employer, under which a single body would provide an employment and personnel service to the other bodies under their joint direction. Far from working as one body, this adds another layer of management to the existing structure and is more akin to working as one more body! However, it seems the situation is even worse than this. Apparently, the representations by the Commissioners to the steering group were made without prior consultation with the Commissioners' own General Purposes and Finance Committee, which is responsible for personnel matters, and without the knowledge of the Commissioners' Board of Governors. Actions such as these were precisely the target of so much of the criticism of the Commissioners' internal procedures in the Lambeth Report, whose recommendations have been implemented, or so we are told. How can the Church be assured that the mistakes of the past will not be repeated when the mechanism which allowed those mistakes to be made is clearly still in place and functioning as it always did? There is nothing in the Turnbull proposals which would, by itself, prevent a repetition of past mistakes.

Another serious concern which strikes at the heart of the twin requirements of trust and accountability is the continuing ethos of secrecy which still pervades what may be called the 'Millbank culture'.[40] It is a legitimate concern of the church whether the Commissioners were wise to reduce their portfolio of commercial properties so swiftly in view of the depressed state of the property market at the time. Perhaps the benefits of being able to reinvest in a rising equities market justified such haste. We do not know and cannot tell, because the Commissioners refuse to divulge the detailed information necessary for such an assessment. Again, we do not know to what extent the improvement in the value of their assets since 1993 has been due to an excessive writedown of assets before 1993. Do the Commissioners have something to hide?

Even more remarkable is the attitude regarding the Church Commissioners' twenty-year forward projections, in which the church as a whole must have a vital interest. The investments currently entrusted to the Church Commissioners will generate a substantial and growing income for the church. The liability for pensions benefits under the current unfunded scheme will continue to absorb a large part of this income, but it will not last for ever. The projections themselves have been circulated to dioceses, it is true, but marked 'Confidential'. Precise details cannot be quoted because in response to a request to lift this restriction, Sir Michael Colman replied, 'It is important that, although we are willing to share our management information with dioceses, the information should not be freely available for publication'.[41] No reason is offered. Perhaps Sir Michael is concerned that the wider church should not become aware of the sharp swing away from stipend support and towards increasing funding for bishops, cathedrals and the Commissioners' own administration. No doubt he would wish to avoid a public debate on the over-cautious estimates of future income which are certain to be exceeded by wide margins in all but the most exceptional years. Other assumptions on which the projections are based are equally suspect.

Interestingly, financial information published by the Commissioners is often given a misleading 'gloss'. Two examples may illustrate this point.

During 1996, a particularly good year for investments in UK equities and agricultural land, the total value of Church Commissioners' assets thankfully rose to the monetary level first achieved seven years earlier before the property bubble burst. These figures were described by Michael Alison, on his retirement in 1997 as Second Estates Commissioner, as 'very significant, if only to put a lid on the earlier so-called loss'.[42] His upbeat remarks led *The Times* newspaper to headline their report: 'Church recovers fortune lost in 80s market crash'.[43] No mention was made of the not-inconsiderable effects of inflation and market growth in the intervening seven years, a period in which the FTSE-100 index of UK equity prices has doubled. Thus the Commissioners continue to mislead the public by their refusal to acknowledge that the damage resulting from past mistakes is so long-term as to be virtually permanent.

Again, a newsletter reporting progress on the new clergy pension arrangements referred to the use of the Commissioners' assets to fund the existing scheme and transitional support for the new scheme, 'The rest will continue to be used to generate the Commissioners' support for the nation-wide ministry, especially in the needier areas'.[44] The 'needier areas' must mean the bishops, the cathedrals and the Church Commissioners, or are they being economical with the truth?

Such criticism of the 'new' Church Commissioners is not welcomed in many quarters. The priority must be to restore the confidence of the faithful in the sagacity of the Commissioners. Criticism, whether well-founded or not, may have an adverse affect on levels of giving and must therefore be discouraged. Such sentiments strike at the very basis of synodical government and without full accountability, by the Commissioners no less than any other body in the church, the future is bleak indeed.

Depressingly, the bishops are unlikely to back any moves to bring the Church Commissioners, their paymasters, into line. With episcopal support, the Commissioners will retain most of their functions. Does the church have to wait for a second financial disaster before the future of the Commissioners can be looked at again? There is no possibility at present of the laity being willing to bail out the church, or the Church Commissioners, a second time. General Synod must be much more vigilant than it has been in the past. The overall investment performance of the Commissioners must be compared with appropriate benchmarks for the management of similar funds. Failure to achieve an acceptable return must raise questions as to the Commissioners' competence to continue as investment managers. Similar considerations will apply in future to the Pension Board's management of the contributions to the new funded scheme. The commercial logic of splitting funds between several competing managers is almost unassailable. Never put all your eggs in one basket! There must be much more transparency, much more accountability and an end to half-truths and misinformation. If the Commissioners are found to be failing in their duty they will become a festering sore disfiguring the body of Christ in the Church of England. In those circumstances, the Archbishops' Council will have to be resolute and grasp the nettle which Turnbull failed to grasp, and lance the carbuncle by winding up the Church Commissioners, even if it involves a showdown with Parliament.

The State and the Church's money

As things stand, there is no agreement as to what would happen to the funds in the Commissioners' care if they were to be wound up. This is fertile ground for misunderstanding and distrust between Church and State and really should be addressed in any event. More than three-quarters of a century has elapsed since the 1919 settlement between Church and State. Both have changed out of all recognition since then. Surely the time is ripe for a review and re-negotiation.

How urgent it is for church and Parliament to address this issue is revealed very clearly in the Social Security Committee's Fifth Report, their second examination of Church of England pensions. Philip Mawer, the Secretary General of the General Synod, defended legislation for the new pension fund by Measure, rather than by a Bill which could be amended by Parliament, in these terms: 'When the 1919 settlement was reached, it was made clear that Parliament could, if it so wished, continue to legislate on Church matters. In fact, Parliament has not done so since the 1919 Act was passed and clearly there would be concern about any development which appeared to reverse the settlement.'[45] This produced a swift rebuff from the Social Security Committee, 'The argument that by not using its powers since 1919, Parliament has in some ways surrendered its ability to legislate on Church matters by way of a Bill shows a faulty appreciation of how the British Constitution works'.[46] Earlier in the same report, the Social Security Committee referred to the Church Commissioners' assets in these terms: 'As these assets have been bestowed by Parliament through primary legislation ...'[47] Parliament's involvement was the consequence of the establishment of the Church of England as part of the State in the Tudor settlement, which many would argue is now more than 400 years out of date, and which still requires that Parliament must approve all Church of England 'legislation'. Arguably, the only funds 'bestowed' on the Church by the State are the assets of Queen Anne's Bounty which Michael Alison, then Second Estates Commissioner, estimated as, 'representing something like one-third, or more, of the Commissioners' total portfolio'.[48] Even these assets represent revenues appropriated by Henry VIII and handed back to the church by Queen Anne in 1704.[49] In fact, there can be no serious doubt that the Church Commissioners' assets belong to the Church.

Parliament's historic role has been to speak for the people of the church. Under the Tudor settlement the House of Commons was the voice of the laity – a role that cannot be justified today when only a minority of MPs are active members of the Church of England. Until very recently, Parliament has appeared to recognise that in the current circumstances it would not be appropriate for it to play an active role in church affairs. In the 1980s and early 1990s when so much was going wrong at the Church Commissioners, neither Parliament nor the Government ministers who were themselves Commissioners showed any interest. A letter from 10 Downing Street dated 3 March 1994 sets out the Government's attitude, 'The Prime Minister and those of his colleagues who are Commissioners by virtue of an office held in Her Majesty's Government have in practice no day-to-day involvement in the business of the Commissioners. As Commissioners they are not personally or individually liable for the Commission as a corporate body.' They have power, but accept no responsibility! What must also be made clear is that it is totally indefensible for a small group of Parliamentarians to claim to speak for the church against the wishes of the church's elected representatives sitting in the General Synod. Sadly, church leaders appear to have little stomach for such plain speaking.

It is difficult even to refer to these matters without opening up the whole question of disestablishment. The reluctance of church leaders to address this question is shared by the laity who feel that in some vague way their faith is authenticated by the seal of State approval and that such Christian influence as remains in State affairs would be diminished by disestablishment. Whether they would feel quite so sanguine if the powers of the Supreme Governor of the Church fell to be exercised, under the Constitution, by an Islamic Fundamentalist Prime Minister is open to doubt, but can be dismissed as being only a remote possibility. However, much more likely in the foreseeable future is the prospect of an avowedly atheist Prime Minister exercising his or her constitutional powers with regard to the church, powers that include the appointment of the archbishops, the bishops, two of the Church Estates Commissioners, and virtually every other senior office in the church.

There is a growing debate on the British Constitution, the future of the monarchy, reform of the House of Lords, and other matters impinging on relations between Church and State, such as the changes, if any, to the Coronation Oath and the acceptability of Prince Charles as the future nominal Supreme Governor of the church. In view of the obvious need for the church to reach a new accord with Parliament in regard to the role of Parliament, if any, in the governance of the church and the management of the church's historic resources, the growing pressure for constitutional reform provides a heaven-sent (God-sent?) opportunity. It is an opportunity which church leaders appear to be too timid to take.

These issues should not be addressed in stark terms of establishment or disestablishment. There is need for a calm, rational and informed debate on the nature of establishment which best serves the requirements of the church and the nation in the twenty-first century. Coexisting within the United Kingdom is a very different model of quasi-establishment, a national church without any of the overtones of State interference to which the Church of England is subject. Can we learn anything from the Church of Scotland and its relations with the State and with Parliament? What is clear is that the present position cannot long survive.

Taxation is a further aspect of Church–State relations that requires attention. Far from the benign attitude of the State towards the Church which the Government likes to portray, the true position is rather different. The churches have suffered grievously as a result of the Government's policy of switching from direct to indirect taxation. This has had the double-whammy effect of reducing the income tax reclaimable on covenants and increasing, both in scope and rate, the VAT payable by the churches. It has been estimated that the Church of England alone now pays in VAT at least six times as much as the Government contributes to the maintenance of the church buildings. Additional National Insurance contributions have been levied on clergy stipends and local tax relief on parsonage houses has been phased out.[50] Some dioceses even find themselves in the manifestly unjust position of having to pay both National Insurance Contributions and VAT on their Registrars' fees because they are deemed to be related to the holding of an office under the Crown. The Treasury admits that there is no machinery for regularly reviewing how fiscal policy affects the churches, as there is for more powerful interest groups.[51] Whilst it is true that English Heritage are now able to offer more assistance for church repairs and community-based improvements, this is entirely due to Lottery money. A good case can be made for generous State support for the maintenance of our national heritage of cathedrals and historic churches, instead of the heavy burden of taxation placed on such work at present under the VAT regulations. As part of any review of Church–State relations, the Church of England, on behalf of all the churches, and many charities, could speak up at the highest level for a more fair-minded attitude to the taxation of voluntary bodies.

Trust and accountability

Any dispassionate analysis of the church's financial position leads to the conclusion that God has provided his people with the resources the church needs to carry out its mission. Complacency has taken a severe jolt. Any comfortable assumption that the church can continue to carry out its ministry solely in the time-honoured, traditional, but increasingly ineffective, manner has been shattered by the sharp decline in the numbers of full-time stipendiary clergy available. Yet the human resources of the church are again more than adequate for the task in hand. It is crystal clear that the church of the future will have to make much better use of the resources which God has provided than it has done in the past. The key to success in the servant church of the twenty-first century is accountability: accountability before God and accountability to one another. The two go hand-in-hand.

Little may have been asked financially of Church of England lay people in the past, but now they have demonstrated a willingness to increase levels of giving in order to retain the best parochial ministry that can be provided. There are good grounds for believing that the financial resources of the church which God has entrusted to the laity will be released, but only on condition that such funds are put to best use, and not squandered by the church. The laity themselves will insist on being the judges; they will require to be involved in the decisions; consultation will have to be for real or the funds will be withheld. Sadly, the laity have learned by experience that they cannot trust others with the financial resources of the church. As John Plender, the journalist whose article detonated the Church Commissioners' time-bomb, wrote in evidence to the House of Commons Social Security Committee:

> Men and women in the pew are expected to take on the residual risk in meeting the pension liabilities and other costs of maintaining the clergy. These are open-ended liabilities; and the fact that they are not liabilities in the strict legal sense does not make them any less onerous for those who accept a moral obligation to meet them. In the commercial world no person or company would be likely to take on such a financial commitment without some say or adequate representation in the management of the assets.[52]

The Church of England, whether it likes it or not, is in the same world as 'the commercial world'. The same rules apply and the church will have to learn to be accountable, at every level, and for everything it does.

Decisions regarding the allocation of the income from endowments managed by the Church Commissioners have been taken in the past by the Commissioners themselves. As they are not accountable to the church this arrangement is no longer acceptable. It is for the Archbishops' Council, answerable to the General Synod, to determine the church's priorities and to consider policies in relation to the resources available, having consulted widely and fully as appropriate. It is true that the Commissioners are bound by certain trust obligations to the needy, but there is no reason why the Archbishops' Council should not give due attention to such requirements. The Commissioners' record in this regard is, in any event, open to challenge. Their reluctance to relinquish decision-taking to the Archbishops' Council is particularly sad when compared with their willingness to consult with dioceses on stipends and pensions – the one role that will be transferred to the Archbishops' Council. Accountability to God has never been optional. Accountability to each other, working together as one body, is more elusive.

There needs to be a fresh approach to the way the church is run. Currently, the bishops are not only responsible for directing every aspect of church life; they are also closely involved in the day-to-day administration. This places enormous burdens on most bishops, who simply do not have the time and space to stand back and reflect through prayer and meditation, to receive the inspiration of the Holy Spirit so essential to the fulfilment of their episcopal responsibilities. Even our Lord had to detach himself from the multitude to pray alone from time to time. Archbishop David Hope echoed similar concerns when making a passionate plea for a rethink of the way the House of Bishops addresses its agenda.[53] Meanwhile, the church now has a very able team of dedicated and professional administrators in every diocesan office as well as in its central organisations. Although they are far from underemployed, their work is hampered by the requirement for episcopal oversight in everything they do. Somehow the church has to develop the ethos of trust, and this has to start at the top. If bishops are not prepared to trust their diocesan secretaries to carry out the policies determined by the hierarchy and endorsed by the synods, how can we expect the stipendiary parochial clergy to trust the laity to handle the myriad of administrative duties which take our priests so much away from their responsibilities of pastoral care? Trust does not involve a *carte blanche* – there must always be full accountability, but without trust the church cannot fulfil its calling.

Trust, with or without accountability, is in remarkably short supply in the Church of England. Not only are the bishops unwilling to entrust their permanent staffs with the responsibilities of management, they are not prepared to trust to anybody directly accountable to a synod, matters relating to their own stipends and expenses, something the rest of the clergy have been obliged to do. Is it any wonder that the clergy have so much distrust of the bishops that they continue to seek the protection of their freehold which to many seems to be contrary to the teachings of our Lord? Can the laity be blamed for suspicion of 'the diocese' and indeed every church authority outside the parish?

A resurgent church?

The Chairman of the Turnbull Steering Group, Alan McLintock, is very well aware of the agenda facing the church as the twentieth century draws to a close. There are many good things that are happening: the rising levels of giving, realism regarding pensions, the improved performance of the Commissioners' investments and the hope of a growing spirit of co-operation as a result of the Turnbull initiative. However, much remains to be done. The goal of Christian unity continues to present difficulties, and more theological work is required; the churches, including the Church of England, have to do more to pool their resources, to think ecumenically; there are huge sectors of the population untouched by the Christian Churches, and this is particularly true with regard to young adults.[54] These are major challenges and all require the input of more resources, human and financial. On a modest scale, the Church Urban Fund is doing sterling work in the inner cities, but again it is hampered by lack of money. The problems of rural poverty and depopulation highlighted in the report *Faith in the Countryside*, have not begun to be addressed. Yet the church has a ready pool of willing servants whose skills are under-utilised; the church has thousands of buildings in every corner of the kingdom which are under-utilised; and the church has a major capital fund, which can be expected to produce a growing income and which has the potential for being under-utilised. When will the people of God use God's gifts to the full? Surely a fresh approach is required. By increasing Commissioners' allocations to support the ministry in the needier dioceses, are we really putting resources where the need is greatest, or are we merely subsidising all the parishes in these dioceses, even though many are not in exceptional need? Should we not be putting much more of our resources into specific areas of activity, such as some of those identified in the admirable report *Youth A Part*[55] which draws attention to the cataclysmic decline in contact between the church and young adults? Not all of this work can be tackled on a parish basis. Some could be deanery-based. Much should be ecumenically community-based. Additional resources, under the banner of Churches Together, could give a huge boost to the ecumenical movement as Christians work together in fellowship and trust. This would at the same time provide a perfect counter to congregationalism in our parishes. Is it too much to hope that a resurgent church, a revitalised Christian movement, could rejuvenate the spiritual life of the nation? A note of caution is apposite. Use of resources must be carefully evaluated. Throwing money at a problem by itself is seldom the answer. To be successful, a strategy needs to be discussed and owned at every level. Ultimately, decisions can only be taken with the support of those responsible for implementing them. A prerequisite to such support is openness, trust and full accountability.

Conclusion

These then are some of the areas of concern which may find a place on the agenda of the Church of England in the twenty-first century. They cannot and must not be thought of as the financial agenda because finance is merely an instrument through which the Holy Spirit works. Finance cannot be looked at in isolation. It is a resource, in some respects an essential resource it is true, but one resource among several which God puts at the disposal of his people. How the church uses these resources affects almost every aspect of church activity, at every level.

No doubt we all have our own ideas as to where the priorities should lie and this paper does not seek to set out a shopping list of pet projects. However, if in the twenty-first century the church is to fulfil its high calling, there will have to be a fundamental review of our own deep-seated attitudes, at all levels within the church. These are the themes which have surfaced over and over again throughout this paper.

First and foremost is the need for trust: trust in God and trust in each other. Bishops can provide the lead by being prepared to trust their professional staff and even synods! Clergy can respond by trusting their bishops and their congregations, forsaking their reliance on the unrealistic security of outmoded conditions of employment which stifle flexibility and undermine the credibility of the gospel they preach. Laity need to learn to trust the church beyond the parish boundary, to trust those whose priority is the Kingdom of God rather than the church fabric, however worthy that concern may be, and to trust God himself to empower them to be his disciples. Perhaps most difficult of all, we must grow in faith at least to the point where we are prepared to acknowledge that as mere trustees of God's bounty we should freely offer to his service the first fruits of his gifts. Inevitably, this will involve us in sacrificial giving: doing without something which we value, perhaps giving up some part of our security for the future, and instead, placing our trust in God. Only then can we hope to know the full extent of that peace which is beyond our understanding.

However, it is unrealistic to expect this growth in trust unless it is matched by a willingness to be accountable in everything we do; not only accountable to God, but accountable to each other. This involves transparency in all our dealings, an openness to one another and to the Holy Spirit at work within us all. There can be no room for hiding behind a smokescreen of misleading information, no room for half-truths, for posturing and empire-building and defending what we see as 'our' position. If we genuinely seek to do God's will, we must do our best to put aside these worldly follies and concentrate solely on making the fullest use of our gifts in his service.

We must not continue to squander God's gifts on an increasingly burdensome relationship with the State. The financial consequences of an unrealistically bureaucratic, legalistic and top-heavy straitjacket in which the church tries to function, almost as a Department of State, are incalculable. The role of the Prime Minister as *de facto* head of the church, and of Parliament as spokesman for the laity, can only be defended if they choose not to act. But Prime Ministers continue to cherish their powers of appointment in the church, and Parliament still claims to speak for all church people. How long, in a multi-faith society, will the church cling to the illusion that Church and State are indivisible?

We have seen that by God's grace the church has at its disposal all the resources it needs. In purely financial terms, quite apart from our personal share of God's bounty, those assets currently entrusted to the Church Commissioners can be expected to continue to produce a substantial and growing income long after the old unfunded pensions liability has been extinguished. When responsibility for clergy pensions has been transferred to the parishes what will happen to the burgeoning income generated by our historic resources? Will this ongoing cash flow be utilised to provide essential funding for bold new initiatives reflecting the church's concern for the wider flock, the young, the homeless, the great mass of largely single-parent families struggling on State support alone, the deprived, the outcast? Or will it be frittered away to help already affluent congregations and to maintain a cumbersome bureaucracy? And, crucially, we must ask where will these decisions be taken?

Consideration of policy and resources must always go hand-in-hand, although this has seldom happened in the past – perhaps the reason for so much under-use of God's gifts. If the theology of the gracious gift as outlined in the Turnbull Report is to underpin the decision-taking processes then there is hope for the future. But resistance to change is always strong and nowhere is it more entrenched than in the Church of England. As Trevor Beeson observed, more than twenty years ago,

> Change threatens to undermine the security of many churchmen who, in a world of bewildering change, often cling to the institutional structures of the Church with the desperation of those standing under sentence of death. The Church of England's crisis has a deep psychological content and this, rather than theological inadequacy, poses the greatest threat to the recovery of its well-being.[56]

Responses to the vision set out in the Turnbull Report have done much to confirm Trevor Beeson's view. Generalisations must always be handled with care but the proposals appear to have been received with much more enthusiasm by those in the dioceses and at the grass roots who will be involved with implementing the changes 'at the coal-face', than by members of General Synod who see the creation of an Archbishops' Council as undermining their own authority and importance. Whilst most of the powerful bodies at the heart of church administration outwardly profess a cautious welcome for the new approach they have proved very effective in lobbying the Implementation Steering Group to have the proposals watered down to the point where they become almost unrecognisable. Thus the Steering Group contents itself with putting forward recommendations which represent the lowest common denominator of what is acceptable to the vested interests of the Pensions Board, the Church Commissioners and the like. Meanwhile the House of Bishops demonstrates its willingness to provide effective leadership by maintaining a deafening silence.

These failures reflect not only an innate resistance to change. They are symptomatic also of a debilitating lack of confidence which pervades the church from top to bottom. The omens are not good.

Yet in spite of itself the Church of England has come a long way, and, however reluctantly, accepted many changes since Trevor Beeson was writing a quarter of a century ago. There is a deep understanding, especially at the grass roots, that all is not well and things will have to change if the church's decline is to be reversed. At the other end of the scale the church is blessed with some bishops, including both Archbishops, Carey and Hope, who have at times demonstrated a willingness to do what they can to give the church establishment a heave in the right direction. It is just possible that the Church of England still has the will and the leadership to transform itself into a dynamic and humble servant of all God's people – the entire nation. Perhaps the omens are not quite so bad after all.

The Holy Spirit is undoubtedly at work in the world. Those who worship Mammon are becoming increasingly disenchanted with the sterility of 'consumerism' and the pursuit of the illusions of 'happiness' and self-interest at the expense of all else. The unprecedented outpouring of public grief at the tragic death of Diana, Princess of Wales, was surely a symptom of this disenchantment. At a time of extraordinary affluence Mammon's failure to deliver is obvious to all with eyes to see. The yearning to recover something of our spiritual heritage is growing. It is most visible among young adults, the ethnic minorities, those who have been left behind in the scramble to share in what has been perceived as 'the good life'. Yet these are the very people least touched by the established church. This growing awareness of the spiritual dimension in our lives is not satisfied by New Age and similar movements. Although it may not be expressed in such terms, there is a longing for the Good News. There is much for the Church to do. As the people look to the church, how will it respond? Are we in the Church of England prepared to forsake the easy road of inertia, to jettison the security of the *status quo*, and to turn to God that we may be empowered to fulfil his will, to become his true disciples?

If we are, the Church of England in the twenty-first century will be a people's church. It will be closer to the Church in the first century than perhaps ever before. It will be a committed church whose ordinary members will be a royal priesthood to carry forward the church's mission in the world. Above all it will be an open church: open to the Holy Spirit, open in its dealings with one another, transparent to the world at large, a beacon of light within which there is no room for dark corners.

Such a church is blessed with many gifts – gifts which must be properly utilised in the service of the Kingdom. Building on Saint Peter's rock we have to ensure that the church serves God and all his people instead of concentrating so much on ministry to its own members. By God's gracious gift we have all the resources which are needed. By committing ourselves to his service we offer to God that part of his bounty which is required, and in so doing we reject the values of a godless world.

At the threshold of the third millennium, the Church of England is undoubtedly facing the challenge of change on many fronts. It is at a cross-roads, but it is not in a state of crisis, save possibly a crisis of confidence, of belief in itself, in its own ability to fulfil its sacred calling within the Universal Church. It is demoralised, disheartened, almost overwhelmed by the evils which surround it. Must it die that it may be born again? Or has it already suffered a slow lingering death for so long that it is now at the point of rebirth?

Notes

1. The theology of the gracious gift, 'that God in His goodness has already given to the Church the resources it needs to be God's people, and to live and work to his praise and glory', underlies the work of the Archbishops' Commission on the Organisation of the Church of England (see note 33 below).
2. *The Operation of Pension Funds: The Church Commissioners and Church of England Pensions. The Second Report of the House of Commons Social Security Committee.* HC 354 (HMSO, London, 1995), paragraph 7.
3. T. Arnold, *The Principles of Church Reform* (1832).
4. HC 354, ibid., paragraph 100.
5. T. Beeson, *The Church of England in Crisis* (Davis Poynter, London, 1973), p. 151.
6. *The Church Commissioners Measure (No. 2)* (HMSO, London, 1947), preamble.
7. HC 354, ibid., paragraph 11.
8. L. Paul, *The Deployment and Payment of the Clergy* (CIO, Westminster, 1964), pp. 133–4.

9. *The Church's Needs and Resources: A Sixth Report* (CIO, Westminster, 1972), p. 9.
10. Sir D. Lovelock in evidence given to the House of Commons Social Security Committee on 14 December 1994 and reported in HC 354, ibid., Q. 203.
11. R. Watson & Sons, *Church Commissioners, Report on Liabilities and Investment Strategy* (London, 1994), p. 2.
12. T. Lovell, *Number One Millbank* (HarperCollins, London, 1997), pp. 147-9.
13. HC 354, ibid., paragraph 56.
14. K.V. Bladon, 'The Church Commissioners: Time for an Enquiry?' (1992) (Private circulation only).
15. J. Plender, 'Unholy Saga of the Church's Missing Millions' (*Financial Times*, London, 1992)
16. T. Lovell, *Number One Millbank*, ibid., p. 172.
17. Sir D. Lovelock in oral evidence reported in HC 354, ibid., Q. 281.
18. HC 354, ibid., paragraph 31.
19. Report to the Archbishop of Canterbury by the Lambeth Group (London, 1993), p. 15.
20. Sir M. Colman in oral evidence reported in the *Fifth Report of the House of Commons Social Security Committee: Church of England Pensions.* HC 340 (HMSO, London, 1996), Q. 12.
21. *Church Commissioners' Annual Report and Accounts, 1996* (Church Commissioners, London, 1997). Ten-year financial summary.
22. *Church Statistics, 1996* (CBF, London, 1996), based on capitalised value of other Ordinary Income of PCCs: Table 25.
23. *Church Commissioners' Annual Report and Accounts, 1996*, ibid., based on capitalised value of glebe income and other diocesan funds.
24. *Church Statistics, 1996*, ibid., Table 32.
25. *The Ordained Ministry: Numbers, Cost and Deployment* (GS 858, London, 1988), Annex IV, and *Numbers in Ministry 1996* (GS Misc. 476, London, 1996), Table D.
26. The green-backed guide issued by the Church Commissioners on the design of parsonage houses, popularly known as 'the Green Book'.
27. L. Paul, *The Deployment and Payment of the Clergy,* ibid.
28. J. Tiller, *A Strategy for the Church's Ministry*, (CIO, London, 1983).
29. M.G. Fuller (*Church Times*, London), letter published 24 October 1997.
30. The Watsons' report, ibid., Executive Summary, Section 6.
31. *The Draft Clergy Pensions Measure, Briefing Note* (Church Commissioners, 1996), paragraph 12.
32. Updated figures based on article: K.V. Bladon, 'The Cost of Providing a Vicar' (*Church Times*, London, 1993).
33. The Report of the Archbishops' Commission on the Organisation of the Church of England, *Working as One Body* (Church House Publishing, London, 1995), paragraphs 1.10, 1.16 and 1.18.
34. *Working as One Body,* ibid., paragraph 1.25.
35. *Working as One Body*, ibid., paragraph 8.12.

36. HC 354, ibid., paragraph 6.
37. HC 340, ibid., paragraph 10.
38. I acknowledge with gratitude the willingness of Sir Michael Colman and Mr Patrick Locke to devote so much time to dealing with questions raised at an interview, and subsequently, in October 1996.
39. *Working as One Body*, ibid., paragraphs 5.41, 5.42 and 5.44.
40. Millbank is a reference to the Church Commissioners' headquarters at 1 Millbank, Westminster.
41. Sir M. Colman. Letter to the author dated 21 November 1996.
42. Catherine Osgerby (*Church Times*, London), report published 4 April 1997.
43. Ruth Gledhill (*The Times*, London), report published 1 April 1997.
44. *Supporting the Ministry – Sharing the Cost, Newsletter Two* (CEPB, Church Commissioners and CBF, London, 1996), p. 2.
45. HC 340, ibid., paragraph 33.
46. HC 340, ibid., paragraph 35.
47. HC 340, ibid., paragraph 4.
48. Rt. Hon. M. Alison MP, speaking to the General Synod in the debate on 'The Turnbull Report: a Framework for Legislation'. 13 February 1996.
49. *Working as One Body,* ibid., paragraph 8.2.
50. R. Leach, 'A Nice Little Earner' (*Church of England Newspaper*, London), article published 17 November 1995.
51. R. Leach, ibid.
52. HC 354, ibid., Annex 16.
53. Dr D. Hope speaking to General Synod, 13 February 1996. *Report of Proceedings*, p. 121.
54. I am grateful to Mr Alan McLintock and Mr David Williams, Secretary of the CBF, for their time and candour in discussion of these matters.
55. *Youth A Part* (National Society/Church House Publishing, London, 1996), GS 1203.
56. *The Church of England in Crisis,* ibid., p. 69.

3

New Wine in Old Skins: an Examination of the Legal Position[1]

Lynne Leeder

Our money is spent[2]

Whilst it may take its inspiration from above, finance is as central to the Church of England as it is to any secular organisation. Although it is the established Church it receives no general financial support from the State,[3] and is thus essentially reliant upon its own resources and whatever it may receive from well-intentioned benefactors. Whilst these resources are widely considered to be substantial, and although in the past the Church of England has been the beneficiary of generous endowments, at the end of the twentieth century it faces a serious financial crisis as its liabilities multiply just as its income declines.

These financial pressures, and the nature of the church's investment portfolio, placed the issue of its finances at the top of the agenda of those seeking reform in the structure of the Church of England. Thus the Lambeth Report[4] on the Church Commissioners' investment policy was followed by the Archbishops' Commission on the Organisation of the Church of England,[5] under the chairmanship of the Bishop of Durham, Michael Turnbull. However, whilst financial concerns may have provided the impetus for establishing the Commission, its remit went beyond investment policies, directing it to recommend ways of strengthening the effectiveness of the Church's central policy-making and its resource-direction machinery.

In its recommendations the Turnbull Commission proposed a slimmed down executive, with a new Archbishops' Council at its heart. This Council would produce an overall policy for the church and provide a single entity to replace the current 'cat's cradle' of autonomous and semi-autonomous bodies with their often overlapping functions. As part of its proposals the Commission recommended that the national finance policies of the church be directed by a financial department of the new Council.

The means by which the church currently organises its finances are complex.[6] In essence it may be said that central funds are administered by the Central Board of Finance, which is the financial executive of the General Synod, or by the Church Commissioners.

The role of the Church Commissioners has never been to fund the whole work of the church, though many have erroneously come to regard their role thus. Rather they are the holders of certain historic funds,[7] the income from which goes into a General Fund, out of which the Commissioners make grants for stipends, pensions,[8] church buildings, episcopal residences and expenses, and various other purposes. Already the income generated by the Commissioners from the assets which they hold is insufficient to meet the calls made upon it. This fact has been recognised most notably in respect of pensions and has led to steps being taken to obtain the funding for future pension contributions from the dioceses.[9]

One of the functions of the proposed Archbishops' Council would be the assumption of the powers and responsibilities of the Central Board of Finance as well as the functions of the Church Commissioners as the Central Stipends Authority. The Council would also have control over the application of the Church Commissioners' income, although despite past criticism of their investment policies a reduced number of Church Commissioners[10] would be left with the task of managing their assets. In addition the Council would also take on various other financial functions, as well as overseeing the church's resources and having the power to redistribute assets. Although a uniform policy with regard to the application of central church funds may well provide significant benefits, both in terms of effective deployment of resources, and to a limited extent administrative savings, the equally important tasks of generating additional funds would appear to have been ignored.

Despite deriving its impetus from financial considerations, the recommendations of the Turnbull Commission do not appear to address the means by which effective investment of church funds can be ensured for the future. Management of the church's central assets will still be split, and greater autonomy will be given to the dioceses to manage their own financial affairs. The failure to provide a coherent policy for both the stewardship of funds already under its control and for the generation of new funds, ignores the fundamental problem facing the church: that its income is inadequate to fund its needs.

From its earliest days the Church of England was supported by endowments and gifts of the faithful, a practice that was later supplemented by the introduction of enforceable tithes, the burden of which fell upon those with property whether faithful or not. As the Turnbull Commission recognised, the abolition of tithes has left the Church of England back where it started, reliant on the gifts of the faithful, but with the present generations of churchgoers not endowing the church as past generations have done. Yet it is to the faithful that the church must now look to sustain itself into the twenty-first century.

Each diocese contributes to central funds, its contribution being calculated by reference to the actual and potential income of the diocese and its parishes. At present each diocese elects a member of its diocesan board of finance to the Central Board of Finance, thus giving each a say in the way those funds are distributed. Under the proposals of the Turnbull Commission the functions of the Board will be undertaken by the smaller Archbishops' Council and its executive. At the same time the Turnbull report proposed that each diocese take over responsibility for diocesan accounts held and administered on their behalf by the Church Commissioners.[11] Thus each diocese would gain greater control over all its own funds but have a lesser voice in the organisation and distribution of central funds.[12] The overall impact will be to reinforce the hierarchy of the church, yet at the same time place greater emphasis upon the diocese as an essential unit of the church.

To what extent dioceses might become financially autonomous is not clear. The Turnbull Commission speaks in terms of the balance between the national level and the dioceses changing over time as the dioceses' reliance on income from the central historic resources declines as a proportion of their overall expenditure. It also envisages that in time almost all national funding will come from contributions apportioned amongst the dioceses. Not only will dioceses need to be virtually self-supporting and no longer reliant upon grants from central funds, but they will become the pillars upon which the national finances themselves will be rebuilt. Accordingly the demands upon the faithful can only increase.

Already the church operates the quota system, which may be regarded as a form of voluntary taxation upon the parishes. Although the income of each of its parishes has been taken into account in assessing its contribution to central funds, each diocese has its own arrangements for determining actual parish quotas or shares from which it derives its own income. In some dioceses apportionment is based on actual income or ability to pay whilst in others it is based upon potential income determined by criteria such as numbers on the church electoral roll or the average number of adults attending services regularly. Despite the fact that the church already relies heavily upon the quota system for its income, and will need to do so to an ever greater extent in the future, the quota is not legally enforceable.[13] The church is dependent upon voluntary contributions and those contributions may be withheld by parochial church councils if they are not happy with the way in which the diocese manages its affairs. Indeed a recent well-publicised example of such a protest was the suggestion that parishes in south London refuse to pay their quota following the service in Southwark Cathedral to mark the twentieth anniversary of the Lesbian and Gay Christian Movement.

Parishes are already encouraged to set up arrangements by which those who frequently attend church commit a realistic amount of their income to the church at regular intervals. Those who do contribute in this way are likely to want an ever more significant say in the running of the church, at parish, diocesan and national levels. Over time this is likely to have a profound effect on the concept of the Church of England as an inclusive church for the nation, as the interests of the 'paid up' members who fund its operations begin to take precedence over what may be termed its nominal members.

Episcopal leadership into the twenty-first century

The Turnbull Commission was of the opinion that the tendency to encapsulate the position of the church as episcopally led but synodically governed obscured the role of the bishops in synodical government itself. The Commission's report emphasises the importance of episcopacy and of the House of Bishops of the General Synod in its role as a chief college of pastors. In their episcopal role as overseers the bishops have the most general knowledge of their dioceses and thus collegially of the whole church, and as its chief pastors the House of Bishops will continue to issue papers on matters of importance to the church. At the same time, because of this conviction about the importance of the episcopate, the recommendations of the Turnbull Commission regarding the new centralised structure are based upon the model of the bishop in synod.

The aim of the new Archbishops' Council is to enhance both episcopal leadership and synodical government, providing an executive body for the church. The intention here is to develop a clearer sense of direction by drawing upon the guidance of the House of Bishops, with the Council taking responsibility for the overall resource needs of the church, both human and financial.

Current General Synod legislation envisages that the Council will consist of the Archbishops of Canterbury and York as Joint Presidents, together with representatives of the three houses of the General Synod,[14] a Church Estates Commissioner and up to six additional members appointed by the Archbishops of Canterbury and York with the approval of the General Synod and following consultation with the Council and a new Appointments Committee, bringing the total possible membership to nineteen.

The intention is to produce a slimmer executive with fewer committees. In addition to taking over the various financial functions already discussed, the Council will assume the main functions of the General Synod's Standing and Policy Committees and the Advisory Board of Ministry, all of which will cease to exist. The work of the other Boards and Committees of the General Synod will also come under the control of the Council, whilst the business of the General Synod itself will be prepared by a new Business Committee.

The role of the Council will be to oversee the direction of staff and resources at a national level. Executive bodies concerned with the church's heritage[15] which will continue to serve the church at national level will interrelate through the Council via a Church Heritage Forum. The close link between the Council and the House of Bishops will be emphasised by their sharing a central secretariat whilst the Council will support the dioceses and co-ordinate their work.

The Council will report and be accountable to the General Synod,[16] but not subordinate to it. Synod will have the right to reject policy proposals and legislation introduced by the Council and to reject the national budget which will be prepared by the Council. Synod will also have the right to question the Council on any matter for which it is responsible.

That the proposals will bring a fundamental change to the current administrative structure of the church cannot be doubted. The balance of power within the church is swinging ever more towards her bishops; a trend which is evident if one looks beyond the new centralised structure. For example, clergy are increasingly suffering insecurity of tenure, and, lacking a freehold, are subject to the removal of their licences by their bishop. Furthermore, the visitatorial powers of the bishop in regard to cathedrals are likely to be increased, and his discretion regarding the disciplining of clergy is also likely to be extended.[17]

As the Church looks towards the twenty-first century it appears to be reversing the moves towards democratisation seen during the twentieth century. The 'Enabling Act' of 1919[18] and the subsequent introduction of synodical government[19] ensured that for the first time in its history the laity was given a significant voice in the affairs of the church as a whole. Now, at a time when they are being asked to contribute more to the church, especially in terms of the financial demands which will be made upon them, the laity's role in the decision-making process will inevitably be decreased.

A church for the nation?

As the public or state-recognised form of religion within England,[20] being established by law,[21] the Church of England occupies a unique position. The report of the Turnbull Commission speaks of the church's nation-wide mission and of the church's structures serving all the people of the nation. However, given the present multi-cultural society, in which a significant percentage of the population are not Christians, or are members of other Christian denominations, the question of disestablishment cannot be ignored.

The debate over multi-culturalism has been given a fresh impetus in the last few years by a number of statements from His Royal Highness the Prince of Wales. In his proposed abandonment of the traditional formula that saw the Sovereign as the Defender of the Faith in favour of a new definition that sees the Sovereign as Defender of Faith, he would seem to be intending more than a severing of the link between Monarch and Church, and indeed his position would appear to strike at the very heart of the unique claim of the Church of England to be the spiritual expression of the nation. Whilst the criticism which followed his statements may have led the heir to the throne to make a tactical retreat, the Reformation Settlement that saw the Sovereign as head of both Church and State may well continue to come under pressure as a result of the differing aspirations of each party.

What constitutes membership of the Church of England varies considerably depending upon the context in which the question is asked, but in one sense its membership includes all those who do not actively exclude themselves from being members. All those who reside in a parish whether or not they are Christian are entitled to the basic ministrations of the church.[22] Thus they have a right to attend divine services,[23] to have their children baptised,[24] and to be married in church if they fulfil legal requirements;[25] whilst all parishioners, and those dying within the parish, have a common law right of burial in the churchyard provided there is space.

If the Church of England is to remain the established church then

logically it must see its role as one of ministering to the whole nation.
Yet it is highly debatable as to whether the church does still see itself
in this way.[26]

The debate within the church[27] and the reluctance of many clergy
to administer the sacrament of baptism to infants whom they believe
have no reasonable prospect of being brought up as Christians is one,
albeit highly significant, example of an increasing tendency to regard
the Church of England as a sect, membership of which requires
demonstrable commitment. At present ministers of the Church of
England cannot lawfully refuse to baptise an infant within their cure,
although, provided the child is not weak or in danger of death, there
is some discretion to delay in order to prepare or instruct the parents
or godparents as to the meaning of the sacrament.

Similarly there is no discretion to refuse marriage to persons
lawfully entitled to marry in the parish church whatever faith they
profess or none. Although many clergy are reluctant to solemnise the
marriages of such persons, at present a direct refusal would bring
them into conflict with the State whose marriage officers they are.

If the church wishes to restrict the administration of its rites of
passage to those with a proven commitment to membership rather than
to all who seek its ministrations, an exclusion which could only be
effected by a change in the law, then in a fundamental way it has
ceased to be a church for the nation.

Sensing that the church is in danger of becoming an exclusive
organisation some are seeking to make its rites as open to all as possible. Although they did not finally gain approval, some members of
General Synod suggested[28] that the new revised form of service for
the baptism of infants should dispense with the need for either parents
or godparents to make a specifically Christian profession of faith.[29]

The tide may turn back from a church which had started to become
exclusive to one that becomes inclusive, but at what cost? The church
cannot rediscover its universal mission by evacuating all content from
its traditional formularies and expressions of faith. Or rather it may
legally be so able,[30] but should it choose this route it will abandon all
moral and spiritual authority. For to believe is to believe in something
and the weaker the definition the weaker the belief.

Another interesting alteration to the implicit pact between church
and nation is the curtailment of rights of patronage. Advowsons or
rights of patronage, that is, the right to present a priest to a benefice,
are secular property rights and remedies for interference with them
are available from both the secular and ecclesiastical courts.[31]
Although advowsons are no longer of financial value since they cannot
be sold[32] they remain an important property right.

The Patronage (Benefices) Measure 1986 introduced significant reforms to the system of patronage involving curtailment of the rights of the patrons themselves. Any patrons who are unable to declare themselves as being actual communicant members of the Church of England must now exercise their rights through a representative who is such a communicant,[33] whilst presentation itself is now subject to approval by parish representatives and (unless he is the patron) the diocesan bishop, subject to review by the relevant archbishop.[34]

The traditional link between the church and prominent individuals, institutions and other bodies has been further weakened by pastoral reorganisation, which may in some cases lead to the complete loss of all rights of patronage,[35] and by the ability of the diocesan bishop to suspend presentation to a benefice.[36] The entire system of patronage is now in danger of disappearing entirely in the twenty-first century as bishops and congregations increasingly usurp the functions of the patron with regard to the selection of a suitable candidate, and rights of presentation are removed either for a specified period of time or forever.

Conformity of worship – a broad principle

Today many active members of the Church of England choose to attend a church other than their parish church, 'shopping around' for a church whose style of worship suits them. Until the late nineteenth century no deviation whatsoever from the forms of service set forth in the Book of Common Prayer was permitted. However, it was not until the latter half of this century,[37] that the principle of uniformity of worship truly gave way to that of conformity. Now in addition to the Book of Common Prayer (the use of which is still protected) there is the Alternative Service Book and other forms of approved services. The existence of these alternatives, together with the possibility of the minister introducing variations to them which are not of 'substantial importance', the addition or interpolation of hymns, the inclusion of forms of worship such as liturgical dance, and the type of music selected by the minister, means that the style of worship in a particular parish may be highly individual. In addition ministers having the cure of souls are permitted to devise services themselves for occasions where no provision already exists.[38] A century ago someone could have gone from one parish to another knowing precisely what form of liturgy to expect; today it is probable that no two parishes offer an identical form of worship.

The breakdown of the traditional parish structure

Traditionally only those who were parishioners, in the sense of being resident within the geographical confines of the parish, were able to take an active role in the affairs of the local parish church. However, the concept of the 'habitual worshipper' has been developed to take account of modern circumstances, where people choose the church at which they worship, giving such persons essentially the same rights as the traditional parishioner. Thus, for example, all those on the church electoral roll have a statutory right to burial in the churchyard provided there is space.[39]

Today the church electoral roll, which each parish must keep, is open to all lay persons aged 16 years of age upwards who are baptised and prepared to declare themselves to be members of the Church of England,[40] and are either resident in the parish or have habitually attended worship in the parish during a period of six months prior to enrolment.[41] For the purpose of enrolment upon the church roll 'membership' of the Church of England is not defined; thus any resident within the parish prepared to declare themselves as such is taken as a member, baptism[42] being the only qualification.

The churchwardens for each parish church are chosen at a joint meeting of parishioners, parishioners here meaning those on the church roll and those on the local government electoral roll. The fact that this second group, who may not be members of the church nor indeed even Christian, is entitled to elect churchwardens is the final vestige of the churchwardens' historic role as representatives of the general body of parishioners. And at present the churchwardens may be chosen from those either resident in the parish or whose names are on the church roll, but new proposals will mean that residence alone will not suffice.[43]

The annual parochial church meeting is already open only to those members of the laity entered on the church roll. It is this meeting which elects the parochial representatives of the laity to the parochial church council (PCC), from amongst those persons on the church roll who are 'actual communicants'.[44] It also discusses various reports made by the PCC relating to the financial affairs of the parish and parish matters generally, and any person entitled to attend this meeting may ask any question about parochial church matters or bring about a discussion of any matter of parochial or general church interest.

In many parishes the habitual worshippers who do not reside within the parish far outnumber those who worship at their local church. If these habitual worshippers also form a majority on the church roll, at the annual parochial church meeting and on the PCC they will have a profound influence in dictating both the form of worship within the parish and, as new clergy are appointed to the parish, the appointment of the clergy themselves. If one adds to this the increasing reliance that the parish will have to place upon the voluntary gifts of its regular congregation, then the need to attract and maintain a body of worshippers and thus to focus on the requirements of these rather than upon the church's mission to those resident within the parish who are not regular churchgoers, becomes all too apparent.

Ordination of women priests

Following the ordination of women to the priesthood the Church of England now consists of what many consider to be a two-tier church, with those opposed to such ordination facing increasing marginalisation. This again has a serious impact both upon the breakdown of the traditional parish structure and upon the functioning of the diocese as a cohesive unit.

In order to avert schism, arrangements were made which sought to ensure that the consciences of those opposed to the ordination of women were respected and that suitable pastoral provision was made for them. However, the manner in which this avowed aim was carried out was far from satisfactory, with the protection afforded to opponents being dependent upon a system which is largely voluntary, and reliant upon goodwill rather than solid legal foundations.

The Priests (Ordination of Women) Measure 1993 must be read in conjunction with both the Episcopal Ministry Act of Synod 1993, and the Code of Practice issued by the House of Bishops of the General Synod.[45] Neither the Act of Synod (despite its title) nor the Code has statutory force; rather they have moral force and may give rise to legitimate expectations as to the manner in which opponents can expect to be treated. The difficulties which all such Acts of Synod and Codes have caused within the church's legal structure as a whole are considered further below.

The Measure itself enabled diocesan bishops in office when it came into force[46] to make declarations stating that a woman is not to be ordained to the office of priest, or to be instituted or licensed to the offices of incumbent, priest-in-charge or team vicar, or to be given a licence or permission to officiate, within the diocese. A diocesan bishop taking office subsequently is not able to make any declarations, although he is afforded some limited protection by the Act of Synod, so that he need not ordain, license or institute women priests himself if opposed to their ordination.[47] However, this limited protection may not be sufficient to enable opponents to accept episcopal appointments in the future. An opponent would be in considerable difficulty, for example, in accepting pastoral responsibility for women priests. Consequently, in a relatively short space of time opponents are likely to be under-represented in the church hierarchy and to lack a significant voice in the future development of the church. The Turnbull Commission emphasised the role of the bishops in directing the church in the twenty-first century. If the episcopacy does not itself reflect the differing convictions of those within the church, then this will have significant implications for the development and direction of the church in the future.

The 1993 Measure also provides for parishes to make one or both of two resolutions, stating first that they will not accept a woman as the minister who presides at or celebrates Holy Communion or pronounces the Absolution in the parish, or secondly as the incumbent, priest-in-charge or team vicar of the benefice. Unlike the declarations which may be made by a diocesan bishop, a parish may, with certain exceptions once a woman is instituted or holds certain offices within the benefice, pass such a resolution at any time.[48]

Parishes which have passed either or both resolutions may then petition the diocesan bishop that appropriate episcopal duties in the parish be carried out in accordance with the Episcopal Ministry Act of Synod 1993, under an arrangement known as extended episcopal care. The arrangements may be either diocesan,[49] regional[50] or provincial; the latter being the most publicised with the appointments by the Archbishops of Canterbury and York of additional suffragan bishops[51] who act as provincial episcopal visitors and have acquired the appellation of 'flying bishops'. These bishops are to carry out, or cause to be carried out, for any parish in the province such episcopal duties as the diocesan bishop may request.

That the diocesan bishop must request that such duties be carried out is important, and is true of all the arrangements for extended episcopal care. No bishop can exercise his ministry in another bishop's diocese without that diocesan's consent, and all suffragan bishops only have such authority as is delegated to them by the diocesan bishop. When the bishops met in Manchester in 1993 to draw up the scheme they recognised that a diocesan bishop would continue to accept full responsibility for the episcopal oversight and pastoral care of those in his diocese, and hence they spoke of extended care rather than alternative episcopal oversight.

Many clergy and parishioners may, as the result of the position adopted by their diocesan bishop with regard to the ordination of women, consider themselves to be in impaired communion with him. Yet the diocesan bishop remains legally and administratively the chief pastor and incumbent paramount of the diocese, and all clergy who are ordained, instituted or licensed in the diocese take an oath of allegiance to him.

Were the church to permit the consecration of women bishops the position of opponents would become impossible under the current arrangements. Yet any scheme which cut across the authority of the diocesan bishop, enabling another bishop to have full and direct oversight of those within identified parishes, will bring about a fundamental change to the historic structure of the Church of England with wide-reaching implications.

A further difficulty arises from the present arrangements because extended episcopal care is only available to a parish acting as a whole. No individual may petition the diocesan bishop, thus in effect forcing such an individual unable to accept the full ministry of their diocesan bishop to ensure that they worship at a parish which has passed resolutions pursuant to the 1993 Measure. This overrides the traditional concept of the local parish church as the focus of worship and encourages 'shopping around' for a suitable parish, which in a rural area may entail travelling considerable distances.

Nor do the arrangements seek to ensure that the opponents of women priests are adequately represented within the structure of synodical government. Not merely will this group be under-represented at episcopal level but it is likely that they will be significantly under-represented at diocesan synods and in the Houses of Clergy and Laity in the General Synod. Whilst elections to these bodies are conducted by reference to whole dioceses or areas, the voice of a significant minority, but one which is spread across the country rather than predominating in any particular dioceses, will not be heard.

When legislation was passed enabling women to be made deacons steps were taken to ensure the representation of women deacons in the House of Clergy of the General Synod.[52] Once women were ordained no similar steps were taken to ensure that the opponents of women's ordination were similarly represented. Legislation to enable the 'flying bishops' to sit as *ex officio* members of the House of Bishops would be one means of so doing, together with representatives of the clergy and laity elected from and by all those parishes which have petitioned for extended episcopal care to the Houses of Clergy and Laity respectively.

Although the Code of Practice enjoins that great sensitivity be exercised, so that those of differing convictions remain in the highest possible degree of communion, tensions will inevitably arise.

Furthermore, the fact remains that many opponents no longer feel able to participate fully in every aspect of the church's life and consider themselves to be members of a two-tier church in which they find themselves increasingly marginalised as the number of women priests grows. The possibility of schism cannot be regarded as having finally receded until those of all convictions feel themselves to have equal status within the church.

The clergy's changing status

Security of tenure for most clergy may well become a thing of the past. An incumbent of a benefice is the holder of a freehold office, but incumbents' rights are already so curtailed that to describe them as being in possession of a freehold living is something of a misnomer. The requirement to retire at 70[53] introduced by the Ecclesiastical Offices Age Limit Measure 1975 has already reduced this, and other ecclesiastical offices, to what is in effect an appointment for a term of years, whilst the Incumbents (Vacation of Benefices) Measure 1977[54] introduced a procedure by which incumbents can be removed from office because they are unable to perform the duties of the benefice due to age or infirmity of mind or body, or as the result of a pastoral breakdown.[55]

Neither of these Measures may be undesirable in principle. It is increasingly common to impose retiring ages upon various office holders.[56] However, in an era of declining numbers of clergy, what may be undesirable is the lack of flexibility to extend the retiring age beyond 72 years of age in any circumstance. The 1977 Measure is clearly desirable in circumstances where incumbents become unfit and do not resign as a consequence, there being no other direct way of removing them from office.[57] The Measure requires an enquiry on grounds of disability to consider whether the incumbent should be given assistance, and gives the bishop discretion to appoint an assistant curate (to which the incumbent must agree if he or she is to remain in office), or to give the incumbent leave of absence for up to two years.[58]

In regard to situations of pastoral breakdown the 1977 Measure has some welcome features, and is not a completely one-sided weapon by which parishioners may seek to remove their incumbent. A request for an enquiry may be made by the incumbent himself as well as the archdeacon or by a majority of two-thirds of the lay members of the parochial church council.[59] And where a tribunal which has enquired into the situation reports that the breakdown has been contributed to by the conduct of the parishioners over a substantial period of time the bishop may rebuke any parishioners involved and disqualify them from being churchwardens or members or officers of the parochial church council of both the parish involved and any other parish within the diocese.[60]

No enquiry may be instituted until attempts have been made to resolve the situation.[61] To this end the House of Bishops of the General Synod has produced a Code of Practice containing rules of guidance drawn up to promote better relations between incumbent and parishioners and to remove the cause of their estrangement.[62] As well as setting forth conciliation procedures the Code makes it clear that proceedings pursuant to the 1977 Measure are not an alternative to disciplinary proceedings under the Ecclesiastical Jurisdiction Measure 1963, nor are they to be used as a substitute for pastoral reorganisation. That the church should have direct[63] legal means of separating incumbent and parish where a total breakdown in relations has occurred is to be welcomed. However, the 1977 Measure gives considerable discretion to the diocesan bishop since he must decide, after an initial report has been prepared, whether an enquiry is to be instituted at all.[64] Increasingly when a vacancy in a benefice arises the diocesan bishop exercises his rights under the Pastoral Measure 1993 to suspend presentation to the living.[65] Once a suspension period is in force it is still necessary for the ecclesiastical duties of the benefice to be performed, and this is generally done by means of the appointment by the bishop of a priest-in-charge.[66] A priest-in-charge is simply licensed by the bishop for the duration of the period of suspension,[67] and has the same rights and duties in respect of the cure of souls and the provision of church services as an incumbent, but with no security of tenure. The concept of the priest-in-charge is a modern-day one, and one which has come to be specifically recognised in legislation relating to the Church of England. Like all clergy licensed by the bishop, that licence may be revoked at will, and this is yet another example of the increasing power of the bishops in regard to parochial clergy.

Save in very limited circumstances all unbeneficed clergy require the permission of the diocesan bishop in order to officiate, permission being given either in writing or in the form of a licence. The bishop's discretion is absolute; he need not give permission nor any reason for refusal, even if the minister is licensed or beneficed in another diocese.[68] Written permission may simply be withdrawn, but a licence may also be revoked summarily by the bishop for any cause which appears to him to be good and reasonable.[69] The minister in such a case must be given the opportunity to show good reason to the contrary and has a right of appeal to the archbishop against the revocation.[70] However where the licence is not revoked summarily but on reasonable notice, it would appear that the bishop need give no reasons at all, nor is there any right of appeal.[71]

Although under ecclesiastical law unbeneficed clergy have no security of tenure, increasingly they are gaining the protection of secular employment law. The Employment Protection (Consolidation) Act 1978 sets out various rights of employees, including a right not to be dismissed unfairly.

Those clergy engaged in sector ministries such as education or industry or in extra-parochial ministry in institutions such as schools and hospitals are generally employees.[72] The position of those engaged in parochial work is more difficult. Although the Courts have so far accepted that these are holders of an ecclesiastical office, whose rights are not defined by contract,[73] recent decisions by employment and industrial tribunals have called into doubt,[74] and in one instance declined to follow,[75] this line, with the consequence that such a minister may in fact be held to be employed. Given the way that employment law is developing it is probable that by early in the twenty-first century only those who are incumbents and senior clerics will not be held to be employed for the purposes of secular law.

It is already a common arrangement for a minister to hold both an ecclesiastical office and to be involved in a sector ministry, and thus, for example, to hold both a parochial and a diocesan post. Some receive a part-time stipend and part-time salary, but there is an increasing trend to one source of income from the diocese, with the consequence that the question of whether or not there was an intention to confer an office or an employment upon them is increasingly likely to be answered in favour of a contract of employment.

That said, increasingly contracts of employment for clergy are for fixed-term appointments of relatively short duration. In general the umbrella of employment law provides no guarantee of future re-employment in such situations.[76] The clergy in common with the rest of society are increasingly subject to uncertainty regarding their prospects of employment.

Many employees of the Church of England are members of the laity, employed by the church not merely in administrative posts but also as licensed lay workers and readers involved in parochial ministry.[77] In England, at least since the Reformation,[78] the clergy have been regarded as persons set apart from the rest of the *laos* or God's people. Most secular occupations have been regarded as unsuitable for them and restrictions are placed upon the clerics' way of life and their involvement in occupations or activities unsuitable to their calling.[79] Now with the recent trend to ordain non-stipendiary ministers who remain in their secular occupations, whilst, at the same time, licensing full time lay parochial workers, the distinctions between clergy and laity are becoming increasingly blurred.

This is most evident in the case of deacons. Although entitled to be present or represented as members of the clergy within the system of synodical government, their liturgical and sacramental functions are now virtually indistinguishable from those of lay persons. The only exception relates to the solemnisation of matrimony, which a deacon may lawfully perform but with the caveat that this should normally be solemnised by a priest.[80]

The likelihood is that in the twenty-first century the distinction between clergy and laity will become even more blurred. Team ministries provide a formal legal structure for collaborative ministry in which all those licensed to serve in the area as members of the team, whether clergy or laity, have an active role.[81] However, in many parishes an informal structure for collaboration exists. Whilst the incumbent or priest-in-charge has an identifiable role of leadership the distinction between assistant clergy and laity licensed to serve in a parish becomes less clear, with the consequence in many parishes that the theology of a separate priesthood and its sacramental role within the church will itself be undermined. Furthermore, as parishes are increasingly asked to contribute more and more to church funds, the costs of additional clergy will increasingly be questioned.

Collaborative ministry

As we have already noted collaborative ministry exists both formally, in team and in group ministry, and informally, within the Church of England. In the latter part of the twentieth century great ecumenical strides have been taken resulting in a collaborative ministry between the Church of England and other churches. This collaborative ministry is most striking in schemes for the sharing of church buildings which may extend to schemes for joint worship[82] and in local ecumenical projects.[83] The ability of clergy and laity of the Church of England and other churches to participate in public worship in accordance with the forms of service and practice of each others' churches, and for places of worship of the Church of England to be used for worship in accordance with the forms of service and practice of those other churches have produced a widespread ecumenical collaborative ministry.

Whilst the development of a widespread ecumenical ministry is to be welcomed it nonetheless raises profound questions regarding the future of the Church of England as the established church. That it should continue to enjoy special status and privileges will become increasingly difficult to justify in an environment where, in practice, it is no more than one of a number of Christian denominations.

A new direction for the new millennium?

The Church of England is enjoined by Canon[84] to seek reconciliation with other Christian denominations, and its desire to do so is apparent in its attempts to restore relations with other churches both at home and abroad. The recent Porvoo and Meissen Declarations are examples of this desire to restore communion with Churches abroad, whilst at home the possibility of uniting with the Methodist Church, rejected in 1972, may become a reality early in the twenty-first century.

Should this occur the union will have a decisive influence upon the theology of the church in the new millennium. The Church of England is at liberty to develop its theology, indeed it may, subject to Parliamentary sanction, alter its doctrines.[85] Thus according to the laws of England the Church of England may alter its fundamental doctrines, provided the correct procedures are followed.[86] The Courts will not enquire whether in so doing the church has breached divine or natural law,[87] nor whether in so altering its doctrine it has ceased to be part of the Western Catholic Church.

The tension between secular and ecclesiastical law

The laws of England are one, secular and ecclesiastical law being branches of one unitary system, each having its own sphere of jurisdiction.[88] The history of their respective jurisdictions is a long one, dating from their separation following the Norman conquest, and did not always divide along subject lines necessarily appropriate to each.[89] Today the jurisdiction of the ecclesiastical courts is limited to the protection of consecrated land, disciplinary proceedings against the clergy, and adjudicating and enforcing certain civil rights in connection with ecclesiastical matters and property. However, despite this broad demarcation, which appears to leave church affairs in the hands of the ecclesiastical courts,[90] there is an increasing trend towards greater intervention in such matters by the secular courts.

The ecclesiastical courts are, within their own sphere of jurisdiction, as unfettered as the High Court is in secular causes.[91] Nonetheless it is the High Court which exercises control over the proper exercise of that jurisdiction, in other words ensuring that the ecclesiastical courts do not exceed their jurisdiction, the Queen's Bench Division of the High Court having the power to issue a writ of prohibition to the ecclesiastical courts: a power pre-dating the Reformation.[92]

The rules[93] pursuant to which a writ of prohibition is now issued by the High Court belong to a branch of administrative law which is known as judicial review. At present it is not clear whether, under the current rules of procedure, the powers of the High Court also extend to the issue of writs to correct or quash proceedings in the ecclesiastical courts,[94] although it is likely that this will be established at some point in the near future. That the secular courts may soon be in a position not merely to prevent the ecclesiastical courts exceeding their jurisdiction but may also correct and control them, is a significant step in the decline in power of the ecclesiastical courts.

The secular courts are also becoming involved in a variety of ecclesiastical matters with the increasing availability of judicial review of administrative actions and of what may be termed quasi-judicial decisions. The availability of judicial review depends upon two factors: first, that the function of the body or officer complained of is a public one, and secondly, that no other remedy is available. Bodies established and regulated by statute are subject to review and this will include many church bodies. The question of whether ethical considerations should influence the investment policy of the Church Commissioners (a body established by statute) has already been the subject of judicial review.[95] The administrative acts of bishops may also be subject to review[96] as may the actions and decisions of tribunals, such as those established to hear an enquiry under the Incumbents (Vacation of Benefices) Measure. The law relating to judicial review is still in its infancy and is developing on a case by case basis. Whilst it is difficult to generalise as to the bodies which may in future be held subject to review, the indications are that its scope is continuing to grow.[97]

As we have already seen in the context of the ordination of women to the priesthood, Acts of Synod and Codes of Practice have only moral as opposed to statutory force.[98] Notwithstanding this fact, the weight which the ecclesiastical courts have been prepared to attach to guidelines or statements issued by the House of Bishops of the General Synod is demonstrated by a recent case in which such a statement was followed despite it being inconsistent with a Canon.[99]

Increasingly the Church of England is supplementing ecclesiastical law with a plethora of Codes of Practice, guidelines and other material. The extent to which these forms of what is sometimes termed 'quasi' or 'tertiary legislation' give rise to enforceable legal rights is far from clear, but the trend in recent years has been towards increased judicial intervention.[100] Such quasi-legislation may also give rise to a 'legitimate expectation' that it will be applied properly and fairly,[101] an expectation enforceable by means of judicial review in the secular courts.

As the Church of England comes to depend more and more upon quasi-legislation to set out the rights of its members, so increasingly does it subject itself to the scrutiny of the secular courts and thus to weaken the jurisdiction of the ecclesiastical courts. The broad subject-based division between the secular and ecclesiastical jurisdictions which had been achieved by the twentieth century will, unless efforts are made to reverse the trend, be replaced by an increasing ability on the part of the secular courts to review the administration of ecclesiastical law.

Divergence of ecclesiastical and secular law – a question of divorce?

As we have seen, ecclesiastical and secular law are branches of one legal system. Accordingly it is said that Church and State cannot be at variance on issues of law, yet the two have now diverged over the question of second marriages, where a former spouse is still living.[102] Until the State's introduction of divorce in the modern sense of that term both Church and State held the view of western Catholic canon law, that marriage not merely sprang from a contract but was an indissoluble union. Although the Church has recognised the right of the State to terminate the legal consequences of marriage it has adhered to the view that the parties remain husband and wife even though the legal nexus is broken.[103]

Ministers of the Church of England are marriage officers of the State. Accordingly they are generally under an obligation to marry persons who are legally qualified to intermarry[104] according to the rites of the Church if one of them possesses the legal qualification of residence for the relevant parish church or centre of worship, whether or not they are members of the Church of England.[105]

The Church has come under some pressure to reappraise its theology of marriage and to bring ecclesiastical law into line with the secular law.[106] However, at present an uneasy compromise exists. Secular law recognises the right of a minister of the Church of

England to decline to marry, or to permit the marriage in a church or chapel of which they are the minister, those otherwise entitled to marry who have a former spouse still living.[107]

Perhaps of greater significance than the theological debate regarding the nature of divorce and remarriage is the divorce between secular and ecclesiastical law. Although divergence is clearly possible two problems emerge. First, the pressure upon the church to fall in line with secular trends, and the remarriage of divorced persons is not the only example where such pressure is being brought to bear. Secondly, if State and Church cease to be in agreement on various issues, the close principle of establishment itself is called into question.

In my father's house there are many mansions[108]

In the light of this examination of various aspects of current legislation and some of the proposed changes to the church's legal structure, where can the church be said to be heading as it faces the next millennium?

First, it is clear that the twenty-first century Church of England will be an altogether smaller and less ambitious project. Just as in the 1960s and 1970s large rectories were sold and the rector re-housed in a utilitarian four-bedroomed 'box', so the church is gradually giving up its pretensions to a wider ministry, and cutting its cloth to suit its reduced circumstances. As with the old rectories, there may be practical gains in such a policy but there may also be other less tangible losses.

The trend is towards an enhanced role for the diocesan bishops, whose power both at local and national levels will effectively be greater than ever before, since there is no longer the same interest on the part of secular authorities in the affairs of the church as there was at the beginning of the twentieth century. During this century as secular power retreated its role was effectively given to the new democratic structures which became the counterweight, balancing the bishops' powers and ambitions. Now that the retreat of secular power has been accelerated – and how long will it be before another tranche of self-rule is granted? – and the democratic powers of the church reduced, the scales are in danger of becoming unbalanced.

A further trend is towards an increasingly 'secular' church, with the jurisdiction of the secular courts gradually sweeping away the idiosyncrasies of the church's own legal structure. How long can the church hold on to its rights of ecclesiastical exemption from planning controls ordinarily applicable to listed buildings,[109] particularly if, as seems likely, it obtains considerable resources from the Millennium and Heritage Funds derived from the national lottery? And how long before its treatment of its clergy and lay employees must be changed to comply with United Kingdom and for that matter European legal practices?[110] Whilst the new house may be easier to run, little of the character of the old building will remain.

What then of the parish itself, the focus of the church life of most ordinary churchgoers? First, 'our parish' is no longer necessarily the parish in which we reside. We may prefer to travel some distance to find a church whose liturgy or clergy we prefer. Back in our 'home parish' new churches may have been planted[111] from elsewhere – maybe even from another diocese – or the building may be shared with communicants from other denominations. And how burdensome the churchgoers of the next millennium will find the financial requirements of the church in comparison with those living in this century. Not only is the house smaller, but it seems to cost more to run as well.

Yet whilst it may prove a struggle, it is perhaps in the changes to the financial provisions for the church that the most positive elements of the picture may be found. For history has shown us that there cannot for long be taxation without representation, and the newly responsible and financially burdened churchgoers are unlikely to allow control of 'their church' to pass entirely from their grasp.

Then also, the financial necessities may lead to changes in parish boundaries – and for that matter diocesan boundaries – which should perhaps have been made some time before. Every garden calls for the occasional use of the secateurs if it is to retain its beauty, yet if instead a scythe is used too vigorously, much of its charm will pass away also.

In common with all the great institutions of this country the Church of England now stands at the gateway of the next century, and indeed of the next millennium, in a considerably weaker position than was the case at the end of the nineteenth century.

A collapse in its authority and doubts amongst certain of its office holders as to the distinctive nature of its collective mission has bought the Church of England to its present position. Its strengths can be rebuilt by drawing on the considerable resources of goodwill, by even greater democratisation of its structures, and a restatement of those values and beliefs which have hitherto given the Church of England its identity. If these elements are present, who is to say that the church will not withstand the trials and tribulations of its next hundred years as well as it has withstood those of the previous century. If they are missing, all the 'management initiatives' and 'special commissions' will not prevent its headlong decline into anachronism and irrelevance.

Notes

1. This article was conceived before the publication of *Synodical Government in the Church of England,* being the report of the review group appointed by the Standing Committee of the General Synod (GS 1252), (Church House Publishing, London, 1997), under the chairmanship of Lord Bridge of Harwich. Whilst there is not space here to discuss this report in detail, it is worth considering briefly three elements which would seem to confirm points made in this article.

   First, the Bridge report is, as it itself acknowledges, a logical extension of the proposals of the Turnbull Commission. The effect of the changes to the representative structure which it proposes (abolition of the statutory basis deanery synods, substantial reductions in the number of members of General Synod from the Houses of Clergy and Laity and the abolition of the Convocations) would leave the bishops with more power than at any time since the creation of the Church Assembly in 1919.

   Secondly, whilst the proposals may lead to a more streamlined administration they represent an abandonment of the principle of minority rights through guaranteed representation. It is interesting to note, for example, that whilst cathedrals have been thought to be of sufficient importance to merit one of the largest recent church reports, their deans and provosts would no longer have an automatic right of representation and would have to seek election to the House of Clergy alongside other clerics in the diocese.

   Finally, the response which the Bridge report received at the November 1997 sessions of the General Synod is perhaps indicative of the fact that representatives of the church's grassroots are not prepared to accept any diminution in their role. As the financial burden upon them increases, far from accepting such proposals, they are likely to demand a greater role in the running of the church of the twenty-first century.

2. Genesis 47.18.

3. Limited support is received, for example, in the form of grants in respect of redundant churches and towards the repair of historic houses, and the salaries of chaplains to the armed services, prisons and hospitals which are normally met by the State.

4. Report to the Archbishop of Canterbury by the Lambeth Group and Coopers & Lybrand, dated 19 July 1993.

5. *Working as One Body*, The Report of the Archbishops' Commission on the Organisation of the Church of England (Church House Publishing, London, 1995) and *Working as One Body: The Framework for Legislation*, GS 1188, (Church House Publishing, London, 1996).

6. For a summary see L. Leeder, *Ecclesiastical Law Handbook* (Sweet & Maxwell, London, 1997), Ch. 8.

7. The Commissioners are the successors to the corporations of Queen Anne's Bounty and the Ecclesiastical Commissioners. The funds of

Queen Anne's Bounty, established in 1704 to assist poor clergy, derive from the First Fruits and Tithes payable to the Crown following the Reformation, whilst the Ecclesiastical Commissioners were established in 1836 to carry out the recommendations of two Royal Commissions in regard to the raising and distribution of revenues from episcopal duties and the estates of cathedral and collegiate churches. The Commissioners also hold assets, transferred to them pursuant to the Episcopal Endowments and Stipends Measure 1943, which originally belonged to the bishops.

8. *Financing Clergy Pensions*, GS 1172, (The General Synod of the Church of England, London, 1991). See also *Working as One Body*, The Report of the Archbishops' Commission on the Organisation of the Church of England (Church House Publishing, London, 1995), Ch.9.

9. *Pensions Measure 1997*.

10. The attempt to reduce the number of Church Commissioners from 95 to 30 may prove a stumbling block to the passage of the proposed Measure intended to implement the proposals of the Turnbull Commission. Whilst the intention is to retain the broad balance of Commissioners the proposals are seen by some as weakening the links between Church and State and an attempt to reduce Parliamentary control of assets in which the State has a significant interest.

11. These being a pastoral account for the purposes of the Pastoral Measure 1983, a parsonage buildings fund, and capital and income accounts for the stipends funds. Although the report did not refer to the income account it is difficult to see how dioceses could take responsibility for the capital account without also taking responsibility for the income account.

12. At the moment the legislation following the report of the Turnbull Commission proposes that the Finance Committee of the new Council will include representatives of the General Synod and Diocesan Boards of Finance. In addition there are plans to establish a new consultative body to be known as the Diocesan Finance Forum. Its membership will include two Diocesan Board of Finance representatives (normally the Chairman and Secretary) plus one of each diocese's representatives on General Synod.

13. See N. Doe, *The Legal Framework of the Church of England* (Clarendon Press, Oxford, 1996), pp. 479–82. There is one limited exception in some dioceses where the quota takes into account the contribution of the parish to repairs to the parsonage house of the parish: that element of the demand is legally enforceable.

14. It is proposed that the Prolocutors of the Convocations of Canterbury and York (who lead the House of Clergy in the General Synod), the chairman and vice-chairman of the House of Laity of the General Synod, together with two elected representatives of each of the three Houses of General Synod would be members of the Council.

15. These include the Council for the Care of Churches, the Cathedrals' Fabric Commission, the Advisory Board for Redundant Churches, the

Redundant Churches Committee and the Churches Conservation Trust.

16. Any members of the Council who were not members of the General Synod would be *ex officio* members so that they could present the Council's business to the Synod.

17. As to which see *Under Authority*, The Report of the General Synod Working Party reviewing Clergy Discipline and the Working of the Ecclesiastical Courts, GS 1217, (Church House Publishing, London, 1996).

18. i.e., The Church of England Assembly (Powers) Act 1919. This gave statutory recognition to the National Assembly of the Church of England and gave that body the right to pass Measures which, subject to Parliamentary scrutiny and approval, would have the force and effect of an Act of Parliament. This Act also gave legal recognition to parochial church councils.

19. By the Synodical Government Measure 1969. The Measure transferred the powers of the National Assembly of the Church of England to the General Synod and introduced diocesan and deanery synods in place of the diocesan and, where they existed, ruridecanal conferences.

20. *Halsbury's Laws of England* (4th edn, Butterworth, London), vol. 14, paragraph 334.

21. *Re Barnes and Simpson v. Barnes* [1930] 2 Ch. 80 at 81.

22. *William Case* (1592) 5 Co Rep 72b; *Bannister v. Thompson* [1908] P 362; *R. v. Dibden* [1910] P 57 CA affd. sub nom. *Thompson v. Dibdin* [1912] AC 533 HL The right to such basic ministrations would depend upon the religion, if any, which the person professed. Thus anyone within the parish could be visited if sick, but only baptised persons could receive Holy Communion of the Sick.

23. *Cole v. Police Constable 443A* [1937] 1 KB 316.

24. Provided the legal formalities regarding notice have been complied with and the child is to have two baptised and (unless the minister dispenses with the requirement) confirmed godparents: Canons B 22, paragraphs, 1, 4, B 423, paragraphs, 1, 2, 4: *Bland v. Archdeacon of Cheltenham* [1972] Fam.157. Different consideration apply when the child is weak or in danger or death: Canon B 22, paragraph 6.

25. *Agar v. Holdsworth* (1758) 2 Lee 515; *R.v. James* (1850) 3 Car & Kir. 167 at 172, 173, 175.

26. N. Warren, ed., *A Church for the Nation* (Gracewing, Leominster, 1992).

27. As to which see M. Reardon, *Christian Initiation: A Policy for the Church of England* (Church House Publishing, London, 1991).

28. In the November 1996 sessions of the General Synod.

29. At present there is a requirement that a child must have at least two and normally three godparents who must be baptised and, unless the minister dispenses with the requirement, also confirmed: Canon B 22, paragraphs, 1, 3; Book of Common Prayer, introductory rubric to the Publick Baptism of Children. Presumably these requirements would also be dispensed with.

30. The Church of England may, provided the correct procedures are followed, alter both its doctrines (cf. note 84 below) and its forms of service pursuant to the Church of England (Worship and Doctrine) Measure 1974.

31. There are four remedies available depending upon the circumstances of the case, these being an action of *quare impedit* in the secular courts, a suit of *duplex querela* or a *jus patronus* in the ecclesiastical courts or an appeal to the relevant archbishop and the Dean of Arches and Auditor.

32. Nor transferred for any valuable consideration. Restrictions upon their sale were imposed early in the twentieth century but the absolute prohibition came into force following the enactment of the Patronage (Benefices) Measure 1986, section 3. Even transfers which are not for valuable consideration are subject to special provisions: ibid.

33. Patronage (Benefices) Measure 1986, section 8. Actual communicant is defined by ibid., section 36; the definition is essentially the same as that set out at note 43 below.

34. ibid., section 13. The 1986 Measure does not affect the ability of the diocesan bishop to refuse to institute or admit a patron's presentee on grounds of unfitness or disqualification sufficient in law to justify such a refusal: Benefices Act 1898, sections 3, 11; Benefices Measure 1972, section 1.

35. A pastoral scheme pursuant to the Pastoral Measure 1983 may provide for the vesting of rights of patronage in respect of a benefice in a new patron or patrons. Although regard must be had to the interests of those whose rights of patronage may cease to exist by virtue of the scheme and to the interests of patrons whose benefices are to be held in plurality, where there are pastoral or practical objections a scheme need not provide for new rights of patronage to be conferred on any or all such patrons nor for the sharing of their rights: Pastoral Measure 1983, section 32.

36. Pastoral Measure 1983, section 67. Before doing so the bishop is required to consult the diocesan pastoral committee. It would appear that suspension can only occur pending the possible making of a pastoral scheme or order, although the point remains unclear. The question was raised following the suspension of the presentation to St Luke's, Kingston by the Bishop of Southwark, but although leave for judicial review of the bishop's action was granted in 1996 the matter was settled before the case came on for hearing. Suspension is for a period not exceeding five years, but this may be extended by further periods each not exceeding five years. Suspension ends if the pastoral committee and bishop give consent to present to the living, or the bishop terminates the period, or a pastoral scheme or order is made: Pastoral Measure 1983, section 67.

37. With the introduction of the Prayer Book (Alternative and Other Services) Measure 1965, now repealed and replaced by the Church of England (Worship and Doctrine) Measure 1974.

38. For an analysis of the current legal position see R. Bursell, *Liturgy, Order and the Law* (Clarendon Press, Oxford, 1996).

39. Church of England (Miscellaneous Provisions) Measure 1992, section 3 (1).
40. Or of a Church in communion with it. For a list of those churches with which the Church of England is in communion see *The Church of England Year Book* (published annually by Church House Publishing). In addition to the churches of the Anglican Communion these include the Church of South India, the Old Catholic Churches in the Netherlands, Austria, the former Czechoslovakia, Germany, Poland and Switzerland, Croatia and the USA. The churches with which the Church of England is in communion are not to be confused with those churches with which it is in intercommunion; this second group comprising churches which have maintained the historic three-fold ministry and which subscribe to the doctrine of the Holy Trinity.
41. Church Representation Rules set out in the Synodical Government Measure 1969, Schedule 3, rule 1 (2). A further category of persons who may also be enrolled are those who are in good standing with a church not in communion with the Church of England but which subscribes to the doctrine of the Holy Trinity, who are also prepared to declare themselves members of the Church of England and to have habitually attended worship in the parish over a period of six months prior to enrolment: ibid.
42. Whether in the Church of England or otherwise: *Kemp v. Wickes* (1809) 3 Phil Ecc R 264 at 275.
43. A new draft Churchwardens Measure has been prepared and is likely to come into force by the date of publication of this volume.
44. Synodical Government Measure 1969, Schedule 3, Church Representation Rules, rule 10. Actual communicants being those who have received communion according to the use of the Church of England or of a Church in communion with it at least three times during the preceding twelve months, and who are confirmed, ready and desirous of being confirmed or entitled to and actually receiving Holy Communion: ibid., rule 54.
45. On 12 January 1994. The Code provides for matters not 'easily or appropriately provided for in the legislation'.
46. On 22 February 1994.
47. Instead this is to be carried out by the archbishop or his commissary. These provisions of the Act of Synod extend to a bishop who could have made any of the declarations pursuant to the 1993 Measure but who was unwilling to do so.
48. Where a woman holds the office of incumbent, priest-in-charge or team vicar within the benefice the parish is precluded from passing the first resolution regarding the sacraments, but not it would appear from passing the second. A woman incumbent and, to a lesser extent, woman team vicar, has security of tenure and it is far from clear what might occur were the second resolution passed in such circumstances.
49. These are arrangements made as far as possible by the diocesan bishop within his own diocese for appropriate care of clergy and parishes.

50. A region consists of two or more dioceses in a province which are designated as such by the archbishop for the purposes of the Act of Synod, the arrangements being made by the diocesan bishops of that region acting together who nominate one or more of the bishops within the region opposed to the ordination of women to carry out any episcopal duties for a parish in the region as requested by one of the diocesan bishops.

51. In Canterbury there are two appointments to the sees of Ebbsfleet and Richborough, and in York one to the see of Beverley.

52. Canon H 2 as amended by Canon promulged on 26 February 1986. With the subsequent ordination of women to the priesthood this provision was repealed.

53. In certain cases it is possible to extend retiring age to 72 years and the Measure does not apply to those already in office on 1 January 1976.

54. As amended by the Incumbents (Vacation of Benefices) Measure 1993.

55. In all cases where, as the result of procedures under the 1977 Measure, the incumbent resigns or the benefice is declared vacant as the result of a pastoral breakdown, they are entitled to apply for compensation for loss of office, whilst those found to be incapacitated will be entitled to an immediate pension if they have not already reached retirement age: Incumbents (Vacation of Benefices) Measure 1977, sections 13, 14. Those who are incapacitated are treated as permanently so incapacitated for the purposes of the Church of England (Pensions) Measures and Regulations: ibid.

56. High Court judges are but one example.

57. Even if disciplinary proceedings for neglect of duty were commenced in regard to the failure to perform the duties of the office the incapacity may prove to be a defence. Assuming it did not, only a sentence of deprivation could permanently remove the incumbent from office, but the Court might be in some difficulty pronouncing this, given that the sentence must relate to the gravity of the offence and not be imposed for the purposes of separating the incumbent from his or her benefice, however desirable that may appear to be: *Bland v. Archdeacon of Cheltenham* [1972] Fam. 157.

58. Incumbents (Vacation of Benefices) Measure 1977, sections 6, 11.

59. ibid., section 1A.

60. ibid., section 10.

61. ibid., Section 1A

62. The Incumbents (Vacation of Benefices) Measures 1977 and 1993 Code of Practice issued in January 1994 which was issued in fulfilment of a duty imposed upon them by the 1977 Measure (as amended) itself.

63. Disciplinary proceedings of themselves might not lead to a separation of the incumbent and parish: see note 57 above.

64. The Incumbents (Vacation of Benefices) Measure 1977, section 3.

65. See note 36 above.

66. Before making such an appointment the bishop must consult with the parochial church council of any parish concerned and, so far as practicable, with the patron: section 68 (2), (3).

67. Pursuant to the Pluralities Act 1838, section 99. The appointment under this Act is in respect of a curate in all cases where a benefice is sequestered. Sequestration, which concerns the profits of the benefice and the obligation to provide for the ecclesiastical duties of the benefice to be performed, follows once a living becomes vacant, whether because of the suspension of presentation or for any other reason.
68. *Bishop of Down v. Miller* 11 I, Ch R 1 at 9.
69. Church of England (Legal Aid and Miscellaneous Provisions) Measure 1988, section 7; Canon C 12, paragraph 5.
70. ibid.
71. *Legal Opinions Concerning the Church of England* (7th edn, Church House Publishing, London, 1994), p. 230. However, the bishop's action in such cases may be liable to judicial review.
72. ibid., pp. 122–4.
73. *Re National Insurance Act 1911: Re Employment of Church of England Curates* [1911] 2 Ch 563. The decision was followed in *Methodist Conference President v. Parfitt* [1984] QB 368, CA (where Dillon LJ expressed the view that the spiritual nature of the work might not exclude the possibility of a contractual relationship: ibid., p. 376) and *Davies v. Presbyterian Church of Wales* [1986] 1 WLR 323 HL.
74. *Barthorpe v. Exeter Diocesan Board of Finance* [1979] ICR 900 EAT; *Turns v. Smart, Carey and Bath and Wells Diocesan Board of Finance* (Employment Appeal Tribunal No. EAT 510-90); *Fane v. Bishop of Manchester* (Industrial Tribunal No. 8-229-232, 27 February 1990).
75. *Coker v. Diocese of Southwark* [1995] ICR 563. In this case the industrial tribunal accepted jurisdiction to hear a claim for unfair dismissal by an assistant curate, thus accepting that a contract of employment was in existence.
76. In such cases the employee is usually required to enter into an agreement pursuant to the Employment Protection (Consolidation) Act 1978, section 142, to the effect that, where such a contract is not renewed, claims for unfair dismissal or for redundancy are not maintainable.
77. Their position, and that of deaconesses, is not entirely clear, but if in receipt of a salary it would appear that they are employed: *Barthorpe v. Exeter Diocesan Board of Finance* [1979] ICR 900 EAT. To exercise their ministry these persons must be licensed by the diocesan bishop and are subject, in the same way as the unbeneficed clergy discussed above in the main text, to revocation of that licence. Any such revocation would almost certainly result in the termination of the contract of employment, it being likely that dismissal in such circumstances would be fair: see *Legal Opinions Concerning the Church of England* (7th edn, Church House Publishing, London, 1994).
78. Prior to the Reformation there was some blurring of distinctions with the existence of minor orders such as readers and acolytes and male members of religious orders, who might or might not be ordained.
79. The present day Canons set out requirements as to the way of life to be followed by ministers; Canon C 26. Further there are statutory

prohibitions against their involvement in farming, trade and other activities without the consent of the bishop: Pluralities Act 1838, sections 28–31.

80.   See the guidelines issued jointly by the Archbishops of Canterbury and York entitled 'Solemnisation of Matrimony by Deacons'.

81.   Pastoral Measure 1983, section 20.

82.   Pursuant to the Sharing of Church Buildings Act 1969. The Act applies to church buildings used as places of worship, church halls or centres, youth clubs or hostels, and residences for ordained ministers or lay workers: ibid., section 12. The Act applies to the Roman Catholic, Methodist and United Reformed Churches, the Church in Wales, the Presbyterian Church of England, any church of the Baptist or Congregational denomination, any congregation of the Association of Churches of Christ in Great Britain and Ireland and may also apply to any church represented on the general council of the British Council of Churches or the governing body of the Evangelical Alliance or the British Evangelical Council if such a church gives notice that the Act should apply to it: ibid., section 11.

83.   Pursuant to the Church of England (Ecumenical Relations) Measure 1988. The Measure, and Canons B 33 and B 44 made pursuant to it, apply to all Churches designated by the Archbishops of Canterbury and York. These Churches must subscribe to the doctrine of the Holy Trinity (which excludes the Unitarians) and administer the sacraments of Baptism and Holy Communion (which excludes the Salvation Army and the Society of Friends, or Quakers as they are generally known) and be churches to which the Sharing of Church Buildings Act 1969 applies: ibid., section 5. For designated churches see *The Church of England Yearbook* (published annually by Church House Publishing).

84.   Canon A 8.

85.   In this the Church of England has more freedom than the unestablished Churches which are generally so fettered by the manner in which they came into being that they cannot seek to alter their doctrines, as was demonstrated in the case of the Free Church of Scotland: see *General Assembly of the Free Church of Scotland v. Lord Overtoun* [1904] AC 515.

86.   *R. v. Ecclesiastical Committee of Both Houses of Parliament, ex parte the Church Society, The Times,* November 4 1993.

87.   Divine law being that law which is revealed or is made explicit in the Scriptures and natural law being that law which is unrevealed but implicit in the natural order.

88.   *Attorney-General v. Dean and Chapter of Ripon Cathedral* [1945] 1 Ch 239 at 245.

89.   For example, until the mid nineteenth century the ecclesiastical courts enjoyed jurisdiction over testamentary and matrimonial causes.

90.   A few church matters remain in the hands of the secular courts, such as appeals relating to clergy pensions and proceedings to enforce an order relating to the deposit of parochial registers and records.

91. *R. v. Chancellor of St Edmundsbury and Ipswich Diocese, ex parte White* [1947] K.B. 263.
92. *Mackonochie v. Lord Penzance* (1881) 6 App. Cas. 424
93. Rules of the Supreme Court, Order 53.
94. It has been accepted that, where an ecclesiastical court declines juris-diction of a matter within its sphere, it may be compelled by *mandamus* to take cognisance of the matter: *R. v. Archbishop of Canterbury* (1856) 6 E & B 546: *Allcroft & Lighton v. Lord Bishop of London* [1891] AC 666 HL But in *R. v. Chancellor of St Edmundsbury and Ipswich Diocese, ex parte White* [1948] KB 195 the Court of Appeal held that a writ of *certiorari* (to quash proceedings) could not be issued. Judicial review pursuant to Rules of the Supreme Court Order 53, under which writs of prohibition are now issued, applies to an 'inferior court', and it is doubtful that an ecclesiastical court is an 'inferior court' for these purposes. However, it is difficult to draw a distinction between a writ of prohibition issued pursuant to this Order and a writ of *certiorari* or *mandamus*. In the case of *R. v. Chancellor of Chichester Consistory Court, ex parte News Group Newspapers Ltd & Others* [1992] COD. 48, the Divisional Court felt bound to follow the decision in *ex parte White* but nonetheless questioned its reasoning, describing the distinc-tion between the differing writs as 'devoid of logic'.
95. *Harries v. Church Commissioners* [1992] 1 WLR 1241.
96. For example, in the recent case concerning St Luke's, Kingston: cf. note 36.
97. See further N. Doe, *The Legal Framework of the Church of England* (Clarendon Press, Oxford 1996), pp. 128–9, 139–41.
98. As to Acts of Synod see *Bland v. Archdeacon of Cheltenham* [1972] Fam. 157 at 166.
99. *Re St James, Shirley* [1994] Fam 134. The case was concerned with the issue of the repositioning of fonts; the court following the *Response by the House of Bishops to Questions raised by Diocesan Chancellors* dated June 1992, the content of which is reproduced in the court's decision. Once such a statement is incorporated within the *ratio decidendi* of the court's decision it acquires the force of law.
100. See in Doe, *The Legal Framework of the Church of England* (Oxford, 1996), pp. 19–22.
101. *R. v. Criminal Injuries Compensation Board, ex parte Lain* [1967] 2 QB 864.
102. The difficulties only arise of course in the case of a divorce where marriage has been dissolved by a decree of divorce. In regard to a decree of nullity, that is a declaration that what appears to be a marriage is not in fact so (in other words an annulment), Church and State are essentially in agreement. Even here there is one area of disagreement since the State regards a wilful refusal to consummate a marriage as grounds for declaring a marriage void, whereas the Church does not accept a ground of nullity which did not exist at the time of the marriage ceremony.

103. Acts of the Convocations of Canterbury and York state that remarriage after divorce during the lifetime of a former spouse always involves a departure from the true principle of marriage so that the church should not permit the use of the marriage service in respect of anyone who has a former partner still living. The resolutions, which were declared Acts of Convocation, were passed by Canterbury in 1937 and (in a similar form) by York in the same year. The Canterbury resolutions were reaffirmed with modifications in 1957 and are published as an annexure to *The Canons of the Church of England* (5th edn, Church House Publishing, London, 1993). Those Acts remain in force notwithstanding that the House of Bishops issued guidelines in 1985, *Marriage Discipline*, being a report issued by the House of Bishops of the General Synod, GS 669, (13 February 1993), regarding the possible remarriage in church in certain cases where the previous marriage failed, either in its intention or development, to acquire the nature or purpose of marriage taught by Christ. The consequence of this is that, whilst some dioceses adhere strictly to the Acts of Convocation, most follow the Bishops' guidelines, which impose a duty to consult the diocesan bishop but leave the final decision on remarriage to the conscience of the individual minister. The resultant confusion and difference in the treatment of divorced persons wishing to remarry from parish to parish as well as diocese to diocese is far from desirable.

104. In other words, such persons fulfil the legal requirements as to age (and, if under eighteen years of age, to parental or equivalent consent), degrees of affinity, and are not of the same sex. In certain limited cases a minister of the Church of England is not obliged to solemnise a marriage, nor permit it to be solemnised in the church or chapel of which he or she is the minister, on grounds of affinity. The first is where but for the provisions of the Marriage (Prohibited Degrees of Relationship) Act 1986 any marriage would be void by reason of the degree of affinity between the parties, and the second where a man seeks to marry his deceased wife's sister or deceased brother's widow or where a person seeks to marry either his or her niece or nephew by marriage. As to both of which see L. Leeder, *Ecclesiastical Law Handbook* (Sweet and Maxwell, London, 1997), Ch. 10. However, in none of these cases does the Church deny the validity of such marriages.

105. cf., note 24.

106. One argument is that, since Church and State cannot be at variance, legislation which recognises divorce and the possibility of remarriage whilst a former spouse is still alive is to be understood as part of the overall process arising from the Reformation. The counter argument being that the Church's authority to legislate, unlike the State's, is restricted by its inability to alter the framework of divine law which dictates the indissoluble nature of marriage.

107. Matrimonial Causes Act 1965, section 8 (2).

108. John 14.2.

109. Planning (Listed Buildings and Conservation Areas) Act 1990, section

60. The exemption is now restricted to those buildings of the Church of England subject to the faculty jurisdiction or to the procedure under the Care of Cathedrals Measures 1990 and 1994: Ecclesiastical Exemption (Listed Buildings and Conservation Areas) Order SI 1994 No. 1771.

110. The Church of England may already be in breach of European Community Directive No.76/207 (Equal Treatment for Men and Women as regards Access to Employment, Vocational Training and Promotion and Working Conditions) in regard to the current legislation and practices surrounding the employment of women priests. Insofar as such women priests are held to be employees, the church would presumably seek to rely upon the Sex Discrimination Act 1975, section 19. However, that provision only excludes from the scope of the 1975 Act employment for the purposes of an organised religion where the employment is limited to one sex, and the church could therefore only gain protection if 'the employment' refers to the specific job, not to employment within the church as a whole. Further it is highly debatable that the powers of derogation under the EC Directive 76/207 extend to section 19 of the 1975 Act in any event, thus bringing the church into conflict with European Community Law.

111. See *Breaking New Grounds: Church Planting in the Church of England*, GS 1099, (Church House Publishing, London, 1994), a report commissioned by the House of Bishops.

Part Two:
Leadership, Mission and Ministry

4

Spiritual Authority and Leadership in Society and Church

Paul Avis

In search of spiritual authority

The centurion who appealed to Jesus to use his word of authority to heal his servant (Matt. 8.5–13) well understood the paradox that only those who are under authority can exercise authority. 'Lord, I am not worthy to have you come under my roof; but only speak the word and my servant will be healed. For I also am a man under authority, with soldiers under me; and I say to one, "Go," and he goes, and to another, "Come," and he comes, and to my slave, "Do this," and he does it.' The centurion's insight into the authority of Jesus is rewarded with the accolade, 'Truly I tell you, in no one in Israel have I found such faith.' We discover the meaning of authority not by exercising it but by obeying it. Only those who acknowledge authority can possess authority. As Paul Tillich said in his telling sermon 'By What Authority?', 'He who tries to be without authority tries to be like God'.[1]

We might respond immediately to the point that only those who acknowledge authority can possess authority by saying, Yes, of course, that is just how it is in the Church: the laity are under the authority of the clergy, the clergy are under the authority of the bishops and the bishops are under the authority of Christ. That is why laity, clergy and bishops, in their turn, have authority to exercise the ministry and service appropriate to them. The bishops lead the clergy, the clergy lead the laity and the laity – well, they provide a witness and example to non-Christians.

115

That hierarchical answer to the question of authority forgets that *all* authority in the Church – not just the authority exercised by bishops, or even by priests – must be the authority of Christ. There is no authority other than the authority that resides in God. Therefore, the authority that belongs to the laity is the authority of God, the authority that belongs to the clergy is the authority of God, and the authority that belongs to the bishops is the authority of God. They are not three degrees of authority, or three levels of authority, or three kinds of authority. They are one and the same authority, the identical authority, embodied, mediated, dispersed throughout the whole Church.

This – and nothing less than this – has to be said on the basis of the Christological nature of the Church, which is the body of Christ. Christ has willed to be identified with his Church. As Bonhoeffer claims, 'Christ exists as the Church'.[2] The Church is to be identified with Christ in a tension (inherent in all forms of identity) between sameness and difference. This is, of course, the doctrine of the mystical body which is common to the patristic theology of East and West. Hilary says, 'He is himself the Church, comprehending it all in himself through the mystery of his body.' Augustine writes: 'There are many Christians but only one Christ. The Christians, along with their Head ... form one Christ.' Again: 'The whole Christ is the head and the body.' Christ and his members constitute one person.[3]

There is, then, one authority which is the property of Jesus Christ. He is both the source of all authority and the Lord over all authority (Col. 1.16; 2.15; Eph. 1.20ff). We should say, therefore, not only that Christ *has* the one authority but that Christ *is* the one authority. In this respect he is the embodiment and plenipotentiary of God (the Father). There is no true authority in the Church except the one authority that is God. Laity, clergy and bishops participate in this one authority according to their particular calling and in proportion to their proper responsibilities. Each acknowledges an authority that belongs to others and to all. Each points to an authority that transcends any and every manifestation of it.

> When the bishop exercises the authority that is entrusted to him, especially in ordination and confirmation and in the oversight of the clergy and churchwardens, he does so in the full recognition that the clergy and laity are endowed with authority according to their callings and in proportion to their tasks because they also participate in the same source of authority as he does himself.
>
> When the clergy exercise the authority that is entrusted to them, in the ministry of word and sacrament and in pastoral oversight in their parishes, they do so in full recognition that Christ has given

his authority also to the laity and to the bishop according to their calling and in proportion to their tasks.

When the laity exercise the authority that is entrusted to them, especially in the care of their parish church, in the oversight of all its activities, and in service and witness in the wider community, they do so in full acknowledgement that Christ has also imparted his authority to the clergy and to the bishop to enable them to fulfil the vocation that is peculiarly theirs.

These diverse expressions of authority in the Church manifest the one God-given economy (*oikonomia*) of authority in the body of Christ. One instance of authority should neither detract nor subtract from the sum total of the plenary authority that is constituted by Christ's embodiment as the Church. That is why the New Testament, in reinforcing the respect that is due to particular authorities within the Church, grounds it in the principle of mutual submission: 'Be subject to one another out of reverence for Christ' (Eph. 5.21).

On the basis of the principle of mutual submission, and on that alone, there is a proper place for hierarchy in the Church – not in the oppressive and improper sense of 'the rule of the clergy', but in the acceptable and etymologically correct sense of 'sacred authority' where we give to every order in the Church (laity, clergy, bishops) the respect and acknowledgement that is their due. As Brian Horne suggests, there is a coinherence of community and hierarchy in the Church.[4]

In the area of hierarchy (in the sense of sacred authority), however – and here my emphasis is rather different from that of Brian Horne – the role of obedience is minimal, being almost entirely limited to canonical obedience to the bishop in all things lawful and honest on the part of the clergy. For the Church is a voluntary society where the constraints lie in the realm of the motivation of its members and the non-material reward that they receive through being affirmed, encouraged and supported in their proper work of worship, ministry and mission. This is obviously true of the laity, who do not have to do as they are asked unless they want to, but is also to a large extent applicable to the clergy, who are not in the job for material reward or social advancement, but purely to fulfil a calling which lies in the realm of moral obligation, and in fulfilment of that calling are constrained to consecrate their whole life and lifestyle to their vocation.

Comparisons are often made between the church and the armed services and experience as, say, an army officer is regarded as commending a person for leadership in the church. But the church and the armed services are at diametrically opposed ends of the spectrum of authority in terms of the sanctions and powers of coercion that are available to reinforce leadership. Holding the Queen's commission may draw out many valuable qualities in a person, but it cannot, in itself, teach a person how to exercise authority in the modern church. I do not believe that the reality that the church is dominantly a voluntary organisation in a pluralist society is fully reckoned with by many in positions of leadership and influence in the church.[5]

Even Jesus himself points to the authority that comes from God. In answer to the question of the chief priests, the scribes and the elders, 'Tell us, by what authority are you doing these things? Who is it who gave you this authority?', Jesus asks a question in return: 'Did the baptism of John come from heaven, or was it of human origin?' But his interlocutors could not answer, for if they said that John's authority was from God, they would condemn themselves for not believing him, but if they said that it was of human origin, the people would stone them for blasphemy, for they recognised the action of the Spirit of God in John. Because they refuse to answer Jesus' question, he refuses to answer theirs (Luke 20.1-8). As Tillich comments, 'An answer to the question of authority is refused by Jesus, but the way in which he refuses the answer *is* the answer.' There is an authority beyond the sanctity of the priest, the learning of the scribe and the paternalism of the elder. It is the authority of the transcendent, of the Spirit that blows where it wills, before whom all human pretensions are less than nothing and mere vanity.[6]

The cultural context of spiritual authority in modernity and postmodernity

Authority and leadership in the church at the turn of the twentieth century is exercised in the context of both modernity and postmodernity. These are best understood not as two separate eras but as two interrelated moments in contemporary culture.[7]

Modernity represents the impetus of the Enlightenment which, from one point of view, can be understood as a radical challenge to all forms of assumed authority, whether of the state (the *ancien régime*), the church (mainly the Roman Catholic Church – Anglicanism and Lutheranism were more hospitable to critical ideas), or of received philosophical paradigms (Descartes and Locke, in different ways, wanted to start with a clean slate). The ideal of the Enlightenment is that of the individual reason and conscience, embodying universal canons of truth and justice, as the arbiter of all claims made by traditional authority. After the Enlightenment there is no self-validating authority, no form of authority that is not open to question and challenge. The legacy for religious authority is that every kind of claim to the allegiance of children of the Enlightenment must win their free assent by reasoned conviction.

If it wants to receive a hearing, religious authority today, in the shadow of the Enlightenment, must therefore be a liberating authority – one that is enabling, not domineering, that encourages believers to take responsibility for their faith and their church, that commends itself by a spiritual and theological competence, that invites voluntary co-operation rather than expecting obedient acquiescence, that challenges its people supportively, and provides a framework for Christians to grow in spiritual maturity, and even to make mistakes, knowing that there is an unconditional acceptance and support behind them. This is what Charles Handy calls 'post-heroic leadership' – a leadership that does not pretend to have all the answers nor attempt to solve all the problems, but which gives the impetus, support, advice, encouragement and resources that enable people at the sharp end of the problems to tackle them constructively.[8]

Postmodernity, on the other hand, stands for an intensification of the critical thrust of modernity, where it is turned back reflexively upon itself, thus continually undermining all that it holds dear. Authority in postmodernity is confronted by a corrosive scepticism that attacks even the Enlightenment's faith in critical reason. Postmodernity does not believe that there is a truth that is universally valid. It assumes a world of fleeting images that compete for our interest or amusement. The culture of postmodernity lends itself to psychological manipulation. This connects with the innate human thirst for authority and creates mindless devotion – a reaction to the Enlightenment's model of cool, rational discernment. Studies of leadership in small groups and mass movements has alerted us to the ease with which emotional identification can be established between leader and led – a pathological sense of dependence which is a reversion to immature, infantile passivity.[9] It is an ever-present temptation to all, especially priests and bishops, who influence others at the deepest level of their values and commitments to collude with this readiness for self-abandonment. But it is the antithesis of responsible discipleship and leads inevitably to bitter disillusionment when devotees discover that their adored leaders are as human as they are and have feet of clay. The Sheffield 'Nine O'Clock Service' scandal is only an extreme example of a widespread phenomenon.

Religious authority today, in the culture of postmodernity with its market-place of competing images, must be sensitive to its symbolic function. The words and deeds of Christian leaders that impact on public consciousness will be few. They must, therefore, be designed to stand for and represent much more that could be said and done. Our words and deeds will touch, for good or ill, the unconscious, unarticulated emotional and intuitive needs and expectations of many people with whom we have no direct personal contact. Religious leaders, at whatever level, are bearers of values and perform a role in articulating the identity, ideals and goals of individuals, groups and whole societies. Religious leadership should, then, be such as to resonate symbolically with the inchoate and unarticulated religious and moral aspirations – the sense of the sacred – of a broadly diffused audience. The symbolic import of the interventions that spiritual leaders make, either of word or of action, need to be calculated carefully.

This approach to leadership and authority in the Church seems to me to have a special affinity with the Anglican tradition. Anglicanism attempts to give due weight to the evidence of scripture, reason and tradition. It welcomes the contribution of sound learning and allows its scholars considerable latitude to explore and to question. Anglicanism is characterised by a dispersed distribution of the sources of authority, operating as a system of checks and balances. The notion of dispersed authority received its classical expression at the Lambeth Conference of 1948 which suggested that right judgement and correct teaching can only be attained by first gleaning clues from the diverse sources where they have been distributed in the wisdom of God: 'Scripture, tradition, creeds, the ministry of the Word and sacraments, the witness of saints, and the *consensus fidelium* which is the continuing experience of the Holy Spirit through his faithful people in the Church.' This emphasis suggests that a prolonged process of learning and discernment is required in which the whole Church is involved. The statement goes on to suggest that there is a God-given purpose in the dispersal of authority in the Church:

> It is thus a dispersed rather than a centralised authority, having many elements which combine, interact with, and check each other; these elements together contributing by a process of mutual support, mutual checking, and redressing of errors or exaggerations to the many-sided fullness of the authority which Christ has committed to his Church. Where this authority of Christ is to be found mediated not in one mode but in several, we recognise in this multiplicity God's loving provision against the temptations to tyranny and the dangers of unchecked power.

This prevents us, in Anglicanism, from taking snap decisions and entails consulting the faithful through the various levels of our synodical system. It serves as a safeguard against hasty innovation and ensures that, when a major step in the continuing reformation and renewal of the Church is called for (such as the ordination of women), it carries the great majority of laity and clergy along with it. Anglicanism does not pretend to have an answer to every question readily available and does not legislate for all aspects of the faith and morals of its people. It leaves much to the reason and conscience of the individual. It encourages its members to think for themselves and provides ample resources – biblical, traditional and contemporary – for them to do so. Anglicanism bears the scars of the Enlightenment and is sufficiently stripped down and flexible to respond to the challenge of postmodernity.

If the pluralistic approach to authority in Anglicanism resonates with our postmodern society, it also has implications for the exercise of authority in the church, as we shall see. We now pursue the theme of spiritual authority and leadership in two spheres: those of society and the Church.

Spiritual Leadership and Authority in Society

Spiritual leadership in contemporary English society is constrained by secularisation and pluralism. These should be carefully distinguished.

Secularisation

First of all we should dispatch the glib assertion that we live in a secular society. While religious practice, according to various traditions, is still significant and a majority of the population accepts the central beliefs of Christianity and many others hold dear certain 'sacred' values, we cannot be said to live in a secular society. It is true, however, that there are strong forces of secularisation at work in our midst. Secularisation has made powerful inroads into our society. What is meant by this statement?

First, we should note that 'secularisation', which is a value-neutral, sociological term, should be distinguished from 'secularism', which is a militant godless ideology. 'Secularisation' is best used to refer to the diminishing social significance of religion, its reducing effect on public policy and social mores, its declining influence and impact on our common life. It does not imply the demise of religion, which evidently continues to flourish, though increasingly in the private sphere, in voluntary groups, in the home and in the heart, rather than as a plank of public policy and as the cement of social cohesion.[10]

Let me say at once, however, that it does not follow that the churches and their leaders should immediately abandon the public nature of religious profession, give up their remaining public role and throw in the towel as far as public doctrine is concerned. That, in my opinion, would be to collude uncritically with some of the more subversive tendencies in postmodern culture. As we shall see, there are alternative strategies open to us.

Secularisation, to the extent that it has shaped today's world, is the product of several socio-economic factors in urban and industrial societies.[11]

(a)   The diversification of the institutions that service and regulate our lives. In the past, the Christian Church was responsible for forms of community service and social control – such as education, medicine, poor relief, moral discipline and leadership in the community – which have since become spread through various social institutions, leaving the church largely to its more immediately spiritual functions. That is not to suggest that the churches have withdrawn from community service, ministry to the poor, etc, but only that statutory provision – inadequate though it may often be – is the ordinary means by which society administers such areas, the churches operating as the junior partner in the form of voluntary effort. This marginalisation of the church's ministry in the mundane sphere offers the dangerous temptation of a purely 'spiritual' message and a disembodied existence for Christian witness.

(b)   The society-wide organisation of human life. In the not too distant past, life was organised, to all major intents and purposes, at the local rather than at the regional or national level. Local units, based on the parish, had the church at their centre. The church understands locality and relates to people as individuals, families, congregations or parishes. Education, health care, work, leisure were locally circumscribed. Now they are structured nationally and regionally. Here the church is not as strong or as well-organised as it is at the local level and consequently finds it difficult to make its influence felt on policy. Many people are employed by national or international corporations and the decisions that affect their well-being are made at a distance. Vast numbers of commuters travel far from their homes to work. These factors take people out of the immediate sphere of the church's influence for some of the most crucial aspects of their lives. How can the church make contact with them outside of home and community?

(c)   Modern technology and postmodern systems of communication are impersonal. An industrial society subsumes the individual into the

requirements of its macro-structures. He or she becomes merely a cog in a complex machine of production, distribution and exchange. Our present increasingly post-industrial society – which seemed to hold the key to greater freedom and scope for the individual – is proving to be equally hostile to the well-being of individuals. Where electronic communication is the dominant mode of transmission of information, the personal factor is again at a premium. Both modernity and post-modernity, then, militate against the interdependent nature of traditional, pre-industrial patterns of work and sociality centred on the local community. But the Church addresses people as persons at the deepest level of their being. Its ministry is conducted in the dimensions of beauty, truth and goodness – the beauty of liturgy, sacraments and architecture; the truth of divine revelation and adequate human interpretation; the goodness of moral discipleship in the Christian community. Clearly, Christianity stands for a radical alternative to the impersonal forces that are now dominant.

These three socio-economic developments have brought about a changed situation for spiritual leadership in society. They have – in a nutshell – contributed to the fragmentation of human life and the loss of integration and well-being, the breakup of communities with their traditions of belief and practice, and the consequent privatisation of values, including religious values. Thus the first casualty of secularisation is community; the second is religion in its public manifestation. Religious and ethical values depend on moral communities which generate, legitimate and sustain those values. When communities lose their cohesion and break down, due to economic and social pressures, corporate life – infused by shared values – suffers accordingly.

How should religious leadership respond to secularisation which marginalises religion in the public forum? The challenge has been put astringently by Bryan Wilson, the doyen of secularisation theorists:

> The secularisation thesis implies the privatisation of religion; its continuing operation in the public domain becomes confined to a lingering rhetorical invocation in support of conventional morality and human decency and dignity – a cry of despair in the face of moral panic.[12]

Should the church and its leaders accept this despondent conclusion? Certainly not! There are three things the church does and should continue to do even better, in which its chosen leaders may play their allotted part.

Throw its weight behind the support of community structures

Bearing in mind that community is the first casualty of secularisation and religion is the second, and that where community succumbs, the fate of religion is almost decided, the church must be committed to building community. The churches can act (ecumenically) to show in well-researched and rigorously thought-out reports that resources put into local facilities, such as schools, health-centres, recreational facilities and locally identifiable policing are actually cost-effective in reducing delinquency, crime, vandalism, truancy, vagrancy and various forms of substance abuse by creating a climate of mutual responsibility and collective security in which people are encouraged to be true neighbours and to take responsibility for one another's well being. Governments desperately seeking short-term economies must be made to see that the maintenance of the social fabric must be costed too and repays the investment put into it.

Of course, the churches must also influence by example – by their own commitment to structures of community (as in the case of the Church Urban Fund, following on from the Archbishop's report *Faith in the City*). The most effective example that a territorial church like the Church of England can give is to make the maintenance of its parochial structure – whereby the church is profoundly and inextricably involved in the community – a major priority and to give attention to the theology of the church at parish level where the word of God is preached and the sacraments are administered. The parishes are the building blocks of the church and the power-base of religious leadership. The Church of England has more reason than most to 'love the local'.

Address issues of public policy from a theological standpoint

The influence of such theological reflection will be, at least in part, a function of its quality. This contribution can be (and is) channelled through the appropriate forums (the General Synod, the House of Lords) and more directly through the mass media in the form of high-profile statements and prepared briefings by the archbishops. (It is a reflection on the extent of secularisation that the general influence of diocesan bishops has been eroded to such a degree that only archbishops can gain sufficient attention to make this sort of bid viable.) Where ecumenical and even inter-faith co-operation on ethical and social issues is possible it strengthens the case. This suggestion raises questions concerned with pluralism and we will come back to these in a moment.

Build on the persistence of the sense of the sacred

Reflection on spiritual authority and leadership in a society undergoing secularisation has to confront the paradox of the vitality of the sense of the sacred in a period of the declining influence of institutional religion. The persistence of the sacred is evident in several ways.

(i) There is a strong sense of the sacred to be found in the widespread phenomenon of 'common religion' – the often unarticulated religious beliefs and values of those who do not regularly attend church, so familiar to the parochial clergy in rural and semi-rural areas, particularly in the ministration of 'rites of passage' which provide the Church of England with irreplaceable pastoral opportunities.[13]

(ii) The sense of the sacred is finding fresh expression in the New Age phenomenon with its twin emphases: ecological and therapeutic – concern for the integrity of the environment and for the wholeness of human being. The Church can approach the New Age movement with discrimination, approving the resurgence of the sense of the sacred while criticising some of the ways in which it is manifested. The Christian Church holds out the possibility and promise of a healing and wholeness of personhood, society and creation in Christ.

(iii) The sense of the sacred is still powerful in many expressions of voluntary work, whether organised or informal – concern for the suffering, care of the sick, the infirm and the handicapped; generous giving to charities; neighbourly action and selfless service in innumerable ways. These would not happen unless people were motivated by the sense that human life – particularly in the very young and the suffering – is sacred, bearing a value that has been placed upon it by a power greater than ourselves.

(iv) The sense of the sacred is testified to by the significant instances of religious experiences that have been researched by the Sir Alister Hardy Institute. It enables us to see our supposedly secular society in a new light when we learn that between a quarter and a third of all people claim that they have had an experience of a transcendent reality of surpassing value.[14]

(v)   The enormous popularity of cathedrals and parish churches as places of (motorised) pilgrimage testifies to the persistence of the sense of the sacred, identified with holy places, places where prayer has been valid for previous generations and where sacred truths are embodied in architecture, art and music.

Thus the persistence of the sense of the sacred is evidenced in our so-called secular society in the tenacity of religious belief even among those who do not regularly participate in the life of the Church, in new forms of ecological and therapeutic concern, in the incomparable value generally placed on the human person, human dignity, and new human life, in compassionate action for the suffering, in the extent of private religious experience and in the role of historic places of worship in evoking a sense of the beyond.[15] Though all these have their effect on public policy through the weight of public opinion on legislators and the executive, their motive force is in the heart of the individual and where two or three are gathered together – in the home, the house group, the congregation or the voluntary society. We could well ask: Is there anyone for whom nothing is sacred? Surely few or none. Christianity (though not only Christianity) sees this as a reflection of the divine image in humanity and a sign of the grace of God at work far and wide in the world through the Holy Spirit.

So Christian leaders in a society undergoing secularisation need to take the persistence, or even the resurgence of the sense of the sacred seriously. They need to address not only the public forum of social policy but also the private forum of individual conviction and personal religious experience. They should demonstrate that they value, nay prize the ordinary parochial way of being a Christian and that they do not restrict their appreciation of religious experience to their own particular fold, but recognise the grace of God and the presence of the Holy Spirit working beyond the approved structures of the Church with its ministry and sacraments, so enabling individuals to make the essential connection between their most deeply cherished moments and the specific gospel of the Christian Church. Thus religious leadership in a society that is being secularised should speak to the conscience of the nation by enunciating moral and religious principles that are in danger of being overlooked or eclipsed and should speak at the same time to the heart of the individual who has an awareness of a sacred realm and experiences intimations of the reality of God, but who has not yet identified these glimmerings with the gospel of Christ.

Pluralism

If our society is not (yet) thoroughly secularised, it is certainly pluralist. Christianity is only one (though still numerically the strongest) of a number of religions, movements or causes to which people are free to give or withold their allegiance. The pluralism of English society, as it affects the Church of England, is the result of a series of political measures, between the mid seventeenth century and the mid twentieth century, which had the effect of creating a space between the Church of England and other central institutions of national life, principally the Crown, Parliament, the law and education. Though the Church of England aspires to serve the whole community, it cannot claim to be the national church. The anomaly between being the established but not *the* national church can be traced back to the decision in 1689 to opt for political toleration, which opened up civil offices to non-Anglicans, rather than ecclesiastical comprehension which would have brought dissenters within the national church.[16] The Church of England still enjoys the vestiges of establishment, which bring innumerable pastoral opportunities, and probably still holds the lion's share of the religious activity of the nation, but it has to win support and gain allegiance, just like any other religious organisation, in a competitive situation.

In a pluralist society church leaders have no God-given right to be heard and cannot expect necessarily to be heeded. Like everyone else who thinks that he or she has something to say, Christian leaders have to earn a hearing on their merits. Only skill in interpreting and communicating the faith in a way that meets modern needs will win them an audience, both in the church and in the wider society. Without this basic competence in interpretation and communication, bishops will be denied their vital role in the community.

Much ado is made of communication in the church today: every bishop and diocese expects to have its communications officer. The fundamental question, What are they to communicate?, is not so frequently addressed. Are we to communicate our conflicts, confusions and mistakes? Obviously not. Sound, informed, perceptive interpretation of Christian theology from the heart of the tradition is what should be communicated. Communication is an abstraction like democracy or freedom, that everyone believes to be a good thing in theory, yet is extremely difficult to implement in practice. Communication on behalf of the church cannot be handled by means of technical proficiency alone. It requires both theological judgement and the authority to utter it. When we hear through the media that 'a spokesperson for the archbishop/bishop said ...' we remain totally

unimpressed. A spokesperson or communications officer lacks authority and has not had the opportunity to win our trust by demonstrating,
over a period of time, his or her theological competence and sound
judgement. Communications officers may be extremely valuable in an
advisory capacity, but they cannot do the bishops' work for them.
That is why I stress interpretation before communication.

Skill in interpretation and communication is the *sine qua non* for the
bishop's authority and leadership role in the community. I will discuss
the community context under three aspects. Church leaders have a
power-base, an audience, and a rapport between the power-base and
the audience. The bishop's power-base is the church, comprising
above all the parishes and their activities, and secondarily the synods
and councils of the church above parish level. The audience extends
beyond the Christian community in the parishes and synods to the
environing society. The rapport that the bishop needs to establish
connects the two and stimulates interaction between church and world.
To put it another way, the bishop speaks from the midst of a community – and thus as a representative person; the bishop speaks to the
wider community in the name of the church, not as a private individual; the bishop seeks to build up an understanding with the audience,
creating confidence and trust, and to establish a framework of recep-
tivity to the message. Let me now try to expand these propositions.

The bishop speaks from the midst of community

Alastair MacIntyre has reminded us in *After Virtue* and subsequent
writings of a truth that the Christian Church ought never to have forgotten: beliefs and values have their true home in communities. It is moral
communities, with their rich resources of tradition and their strong
creative interaction between members, that generate and sustain a
worldview. The Christian worldview, therefore, with its distinctive
beliefs and values, is not free-standing, but belongs only within the
Christian Church as a moral community – probably the greatest of all
moral communities. A bishop is a leader of a moral community and
draws from it the values and beliefs which he is called to articulate in an
authoritative way. The authority comes from the community, not from
the pluralist society. It is the community that legitimates (sociologically
speaking) the calling, though (theologically speaking) the calling comes
from God through the Church. The bishop can, then, never behave as a
sort of freelance theological pundit, who is not accountable – a sort of
roaming prophet who writes his own script. Karl Rahner calls theology
the 'science of faith in the bosom of the Church'.[17]

In his study *The Authority of a Bishop*, John Halliburton points out that St Athanasius was elected bishop at a crucial moment in the history of the Church because he was 'not the man of contrary opinions, but the man of the same faith' as the people of God. 'He taught the faith of the people, they could trust him to speak for them. For no one will trust a bishop without a Church; God after all speaks through the Church, not just through the bishop, and an unseated bishop, however validly ordained, has nothing to bring with him from the people of God.' But (Halliburton goes on), if it is true that the bishop embodies, so to speak, the faith convictions of the local church, he or she will give high priority to consulting with the whole body of Christian people in the diocese, ordained and lay, in order to discern with them what the Spirit is saying to the Church.[18]

The Church of England report *Episcopal Ministry* suggests that, by virtue of prayer, study and reflection, the bishop should be 'the still centre of the spiritual life of his diocese'.[19] I cannot believe that the authors of this report, several bishops among them, were unaware how far from the reality of a bishop's hectic life the description 'the still centre' is! It sounds frankly romantic, dripping with pathos, but it points to an important truth: a bishop must be attuned both to God and to the Church. With a mind open to Christian truth and a heart open to the needs of Christian people, the bishop occupies the pivotal point in the life of the diocese. This ministry can be damaged by frenetic activity and rushing about; it can be enhanced by disciplined study and prayerful reflection. That is why it is, paradoxically, vital to anchor the role that the bishop has in a pluralist society firmly in the life of the Christian community.

The bishop speaks to the wider community

In his recent book *A Church Without Walls: Being Anglican in Australia*, Bruce Kaye has asked what particularly distinguishes Anglicanism throughout the Communion and throughout its centuries of tradition. Kaye finds this distinctive character in Anglicanism's incarnational, 'Church-in-society' model of ecclesiology.[20] In this commitment to the community, involvement in it, and service and witness to it the bishop has a crucial role. The bishop's task is to reach an audience beyond the committed and half-committed. He aims to make contact – to establish a rapport – with many outside the fold: lapsed Christians, enquirers and seekers, open-minded agnostics, public-spirited folk of goodwill towards the Church, even receptive persons of other faiths. He or she aspires to do this as an evangelist, to proclaim the gospel, the *kerygma*, the call to repentance and faith. But the bishop also aspires to do this as a prophet and teacher, seeking to put across Christian moral principles and to bring the Christian theological world-view to bear on currrent issues. Let me dwell for a moment on this teaching and prophetic role.

Here the bishop will be addressing issues of public policy, social questions with an ethical dimension. The bishop's contribution will inevitably be of broad generality – but without being nebulous. He will be wise to stick to principles and should not be afraid of stating the obvious. People long for fundamental truths to be publicly stated and not to go by default. We should overcome the scruples that jib at stating so-called platitudes.

Only exceptionally will it be appropriate for bishops or archbishops to comment on particular political programmes. There is a pastoral reason for this: specific political judgements will inevitably lose a bishop support in his constituency among those people of goodwill who agree with the bishop about the ends of social policy but disagree about the means. It may be that some of those people also know more about the subject than does the bishop. Lay people often have greater expertise than clergy about how social and economic constraints operate. John Macquarrie suggests that politics is a lay ministry:

> Bishops and other clerics are politically too naive, for most of them have no first-hand acquaintance with industry or commerce or government. They suffer from the further weakness of cherishing ethical absolutes which they apply without regard to the relativities of particular situations ... A few active and intelligent lay Christians involved in the political process are worth a thousand sententious utterances by bishops and synods.[21]

Macquarrie is broadly following the tradition of Christian social thought crystallised in Archbishop William Temple's classic work *Christianity and Social Order* (1942). Temple warned against the Church pronouncing on political policies:

> It is of crucial importance that the Church acting corporately should not commit itself to any particular policy. A policy always depends on technical decisions concerning the actual relations of cause and effect in the political and economic world; about these a Christian as such has no more reliable judgement than an atheist, except so far as he should be more immune to the temptations of self-interest.

Temple continues: 'The Church is committed to the everlasting Gospel and to the Creeds which formulate it; it must never commit itself to an ephemeral programme of detailed action.' It is for the Church corporately to enunciate Christian principles and to point out where society is departing from them, he argues. But it is for Christian citizens, the laity, acting in their civic capacity, to attempt the task of reshaping the social order in closer conformity to those principles.[22]

Temple was, in fact, prepared to comment in that book on aspects of actual policy in general terms, but he made it abundantly clear that he was doing this as a private individual and not as Archbishop of Canterbury – and we need to remember that there was a National Government at the time. When he spoke with the authority of his office, Temple confined himself to fundamental principles and broad objectives. He began with the basic Christian worldview: God as creator and redeemer, humanity as the child of God, destined for a life of eternal fellowship with God. He affirmed as axiomatic that love should be the dominant Christian motive and that the primary form of love in social organisation is justice. From these principles, Temple derived certain fundamental human rights: adequate housing, education and employment; times of recreation; liberty of worship, speech, assembly and association; and a say in the way one's labour is used.[23] The Church's role, Temple believed, was in the articulation of 'middle axioms' – somewhere between general principles and practical programmes. The notion of 'middle axioms' is not beyond criticism: it suggests that they can be derived from theological anthropology in isolation from empirical input from social sciences such as economics.[24] But Temple was certainly right to warn Christian leaders away from becoming embroiled in political debate.

The bishop constitutes a link between the Church and society

Bishops have a vital role in giving the Church a public profile. As recipients of the projections of those outside the Church, as well as of those within, they have a bridging function. They make contact, symbolically, between the inchoate spiritual aspirations of people outside the Church, on the one hand, and the teaching and sacraments – the symbol system – of the Church, on the other. These projections can be positive or negative.

If he is to be effective in offering leadership as a minister of the Gospel and a spokesman for the Church, he needs to be the focus

for positive projections, for the hopes and longings of the population for a peaceful and just society and the promise for the future.
This aspect of the leadership role is offered publicly by the bishop
in his participation in government and civic functions and in his
association with prominent citizens.[25]

On the other hand, those who will never be prominent, those who are
poor, marginalised and dispossessed must be able to look to the bishop
as someone who can speak for them. The bishop clearly needs to
develop St Paul's ability to be 'all things to all men' if he is to be in
the swim of civic life while taking a stand in solidarity with the poor!
I doubt whether it can be done without becoming the target of misun-
derstandings and resentments from both sides. But that experience is
not unknown both to bishops and to the parochial clergy, both of
whom are on the receiving end of the familiar syndrome which
projects parental images, suffused with feelings of infantile dependence and adoration, on to persons who have a caring and nurturing
role, in explosive combination with numinous authority. In the bishop,
whose authority is greater, this phenomenon is magnified and a bishop
is the recipient of a host of negative projections. Because we are
dealing here with what is irrational and repressed, and because of the
emotional investment that is entailed, the bishop can become the target
of disproportionate negative feelings when he inevitably fails to live
up to the unreasonable expectations of the flock. How can Christian
leaders cope with this double bind?

St Paul cries, 'Who is sufficient for these things?'. It is beyond
what flesh and blood can stand to remain unscathed in the crossfire of
positive and negative projections. Whatever we do will alienate some
and if we try to please everyone we will never achieve anything. On
the other hand, however, it is fatal to get into the frame of mind which
does not care what anyone thinks: we have to carry our people with
us. We need to develop sensitive antennae and take people's perceptions seriously. Because a bishop is inevitably distanced from the
people – much more so than a parish priest – this realm of projection
is where much of his work lies. It may be an unpalatable fact that our
interaction with people lies in the realm of conflicting projections.
How do we handle this? By bearing the cross, yet going steadily
forward; by self-giving which never unfits us for our task; by holding
out that unconditional acceptance that belongs to the gospel; by
affirming our people in the discharge of the responsibilities that are
properly theirs; by putting ourselves in their shoes, while never
forgetting that no one else can wear ours; by never evading a challenge but without pretending to be invulnerable.

Leadership in contemporary society stands under the shadow of the

Enlightenment with its challenge to all privileged and unquestioned authority. All manifestations of authority today – whether popes or presidents, monarchs or prime ministers – have to justify their existence. They are required to have a role and function in the service of the community and are held accountable by the community for how they discharge it. They stand permanently open to challenge and question. They cannot expect unreasoning obedience or uncomprehending compliance. Sacred status cuts little ice any more. Leaders today obtain a following through free assent. They win that free assent through rational persuasion – convincing one's constituency, fostering conviction, demonstrating competence – and that, in the modern world, is what gives one the right to speak and lead. As Edmund Burke said, it is through the use of words (both spoken and written) that we govern men.

Leadership and Authority in the Church

The New Testament word for leadership and authority in the Church is *episcope*, oversight. The World Council of Churches' Lima statement *Baptism, Eucharist, Ministry* of 1982 suggests that oversight takes three fundamental forms: personal, collegial and communal. It actually refers this to the ordained ministry, but the application of the threefold scheme has subsequently become wider, to include the range of forms of oversight in the Church, in which both the ordained and the not ordained play their part.

> It should be *personal* because the presence of Christ among his people can most effectively be pointed to by the person ordained to proclaim the Gospel and to call the community to serve the Lord in unity of life and witness. It should also be *collegial*, for there is a need for a college of ordained ministers sharing in the common task of representing the concerns of the community. Finally, the intimate relationship between the ordained ministry and the community should find expression in a *communal* dimension where the exercise of the ordained ministry is rooted in the life of the community and requires the community's effective participation in the discovery of God's will and the guidance of the Spirit.[26]

This threefold pattern has been accepted into the ecumenical consensus and provides a convenient structure for our discussion now. But we would do well, I believe, to reverse the order, in order to bring out the principle that in the New Testament *episcope* is corporate rather than hierarchical. Episcope begins with bearing one another's burdens. It would not be true to the New Testament to suggest that there are the few who have oversight of others, and the many who have oversight of no one. In the kingdom of God there is a wonderful role-reversal and exchange of responsibilities. It is not that some are (under) shepherds while the rest are merely sheep, but rather that all the sheep have been promoted to be shepherds in the sense that they are involved in pastoral care for one another, just as the Good Shepherd has taken on the role of a lamb led to the slaughter and a sheep dumb before her shearers. Similarly, those who are known as the principal (under) shepherds remain, at the same time, sheep under the watchful oversight of the Good Shepherd – and as such they are the subjects of pastoral concern on the part of the whole flock.

Communal authority

The traditional term for the communal or corporate authority of the church is *conciliarity*. Conciliarity means the whole church sharing in responsibility for its life, leadership and policy. The whole body is activated to play its part. Conciliarity is concerned with involvement. In conciliarity, authority is not centralised but dispersed, not hierarchical but corporate. Decisions are taken by the church in a representative, constitutional way, through synods and councils, where bishops (who have a special, but not exclusive concern for doctrine and worship) are assisted by presbyters, deacons and lay people.

It could be claimed that the conciliar principle, the communal expression of authority, goes back to St Paul's theology of the body of Christ and that its first opportunity came with the Council of Jerusalem (Acts 15). Conciliar catholicism emerged in the late medieval church to counter monarchical catholicism which had oppressed Christendom, fragmented the papacy and split the church. The conciliar principle was developed in the two centuries before the Reformation by canon lawyers and such theologians as Ockham, Marsilius, Gerson and Cusanus. It was defined and implemented by the Council of Pisa and the General Councils of Constance and Basel in the first half of the fifteenth century. Conciliar thought located plenary authority in the whole Church, of which councils (local, provincial, national or ecumenical) were the executive expression. The conciliar movement recognised national identities and aspirations, accepted subsidiarity, welcomed academic contributions and gave a role – albeit limited – to the laity. The Reformation was a violent explosion of dammed up and frustrated conciliar forces. Continental and Anglican Reformers alike appealed to conciliar principles and called for a free General Council which would not be dominated by the pope.

Ironically, the reformed English church, subordinate to the crown, was more monarchical than conciliar. But during the past century or so, with the emergence of the Anglican Communion, the restoration of the Convocations of the clergy and the development of representative church government, the monarchical element has rapidly diminished and Anglicanism has become truly conciliar. The Anglican ideal of dispersed authority, articulated through synodical bodies at various levels, is an estimable expression of conciliar authority, that is to say, of communal *episcope.*

Conciliarity appeals to the corporate nature of the Church as the priestly body into which believers are incorporated by baptism. As sharers in Christ's threefold messianic office as Prophet, Priest and King, all the baptised have a prophetic, priestly and royal ministry. That principle provides the biblical and theological mandate, grounded primarily in Christology and baptism, for the involvement of all the faithful in the affairs of the church. A conciliar ecclesiology is inimical to hierarchy and therefore to patriarchy. It is conducive to egalitarian images of the Church as the body of Christ and the people of God. It is opposed to any dichotomy between leaders and led, governors and governed, teachers and taught, active élite and passive majority. It places a high value on mutual understanding and consultation and enables extensive participation of laity and clergy, as well as bishops, in policy-making. Conciliarity places responsibility where it belongs – in the body or *laos* which consists of the not-ordained more than it consists of the ordained.

The principle of conciliarity is particularly receptive to the distinctive Anglican idea of dispersed authority. Conciliarity arose in the centuries immediately preceding the Reformation in response to a sense of the frailty and fallibility of the human instruments of authority in the Church. A centralised, monarchical authority lacked the power of self-criticism and self-correction. It will always be the case that if power is concentrated at the centre and the centre makes a serious error of judgement in teaching or policy, the whole body will be set on the wrong course and – like a great ocean liner – will not easily be able to change direction. But conciliar authority reflects the deep wisdom of Christian experience. It recognises that there is a limit to the amount of responsibility that one person or small group of people can be expected to bear for the spiritual well-being of many others. It lightens the burdens of Christian leaders by placing their distinctive ministry within the economy of the whole body.

The conciliar (synodical) structures of their church sometimes cause grief and frustration to Anglicans, but they stand for the vital principle of communal oversight. They are an implication of the Gospel; they are founded on a major strand of pre-Reformation ecclesiology; and they consort admirably with the ecumenical consensus.

Collegial authority

Once we have done justice to communal authority and so spoken about the Church as a whole, then – and only then – we can appropriately move on to consider collegial authority. Conciliarity is prior to collegiality and is its theological presupposition. Once we have secured the role of all the baptised in taking their share of responsibility for the Church, we can go on to ask how the contribution of all Christian people can be enhanced by those who share particular responsibilities working together. If conciliarity is about involvement, collegiality is about partnership – partnership in ministry, in oversight, in mission. The Anglican–Reformed dialogue *God's Reign and our Unity* of 1984 says: 'As God calls us into a reconciled fellowship, so all ministry must have a *collegial* character – exercised not by one person alone but in shared responsibility with colleagues.'[27]

The idea of the episcopal college stems from St Cyprian of Carthage (martyred AD 258) who, in his work *On the Unity of the Catholic Church* claimed that the episcopate constituted a unity of which each bishop holds his part in the totality (*Episcopatus unus est cuius a singulis in solidum pars tenetur*).[28] In the Roman Catholic Church collegiality concerns the vexed question of the relationship between the episcopate and the papacy. The term 'the college of bishops' belongs originally within Roman Catholic ecclesiology. Vatican II affirmed the bishop as the chief pastor and principal sacramental minister in the local church or diocese but severely curtailed the authority of the college of bishops by making it clear that this only exists in communion with the pope who is its president.[29] In Anglicanism (and Orthodoxy, episcopal Lutheranism, and the Old Catholic Church), on the other hand, there is no higher authority than that of the bishops working collectively, except an ecumenical council.

If the bishops are to act collegially in giving a lead to the Church on contentious theological matters – as the House of Bishops of the Church of England has attempted to do in recent years over 'the Durham affair', homosexuality and the ordination of women – it needs to have in its midst the theological resources, skills and competence that are commensurate with the role that is being claimed. In more than one of the above instances, it has to be said, this has not entirely been the case. While the House of Bishops report *Issues in Human Sexuality* (1991) could not fail to leave some constituencies dissatisfied, it was a coherent and informed statement, worthy of serious attention.[30] *The Nature of Christian Belief* (1986), on the other hand, was contorted in style and casuistical in argument, when it affirmed, not the truth of the Virginal Conception and the empty tomb as such, but the belief that Christians had traditionally held that these things were true. As a result, the statement left both liberals and conservatives dissatisfied.[31] With regard to the ordination of women to the priesthood, the House of Bishops produced a couple of useful reports, but then jeopardised the vote in General Synod by provocatively claiming, in their presentation of the legislation, that this step was required by tradition, instead of relativising tradition in the light of Scripture and reason (which would have been the authentic Anglican approach) and then commending the proposal as an instance of theological development within tradition (which would have drawn on Roman Catholic insights).

It would be retrograde if the development of collegiality among the bishops resulted merely in a strengthening of the executive at the expense of the rightful responsibilities of presbyters and laity, thus increasing the distance between the episcopate and the rest of the body. At a time when the Church of England is becoming more centralised, there is a need to affirm the communal or conciliar modes of *episcope*. The bishops collectively can exercise their proper oversight in accordance with the principles of conciliarity by taking seriously the notes of encouragement or warning that emerge from synodical discussion, by seeking to carry the whole church with them by patient education and steadfast example when controversial issues have to be resolved, and by maintaining an openness to sources of inspiration, insight and guidance that arise from outside the episcopate. By so doing they will strengthen the morale, cohesion and sense of purpose of the whole church and win the support and loyalty of all Christians of goodwill (the two are not, alas, synonymous!).

As well as collegiality between bishops, we can speak about collegiality between presbyters, between presbyters and their bishop and between both and the laity. In a synod there is a college of presbyters and a college of lay people as well as a college of bishops. In a cathedral, the Dean and Chapter constitute a college and this is also true of the Greater Chapter when honorary canons and prebendaries are included.

The notion of a college suggests a corporate existence in which decisions are agreed and actions are undertaken *as one*. Collegiality has to do with common loyalty, collective responsibility and the sharing of burdens. It is opposed to maverick behaviour, flamboyant gestures, flaunting the ego, *amour-propre* and stealing the limelight. It enables us to present a common front to threats and to develop a common strategy in order to rise to challenges. When broadly applied in this way, collegiality can strengthen the system of checks and balances that has traditionally secured spiritual liberty in the Church of England.

Personal authority

Once we have affirmed the communal (conciliar) and collegial aspects of authority, then – and only then – we can go on to speak of the personal aspect. The authority that is entrusted to an individual belongs primarily in the context of the authority that is entrusted to the whole body and secondarily in the context of the authority that is entrusted to persons working together collectively within the body. If conciliarity is about involvement and collegiality is about partnership, the personal dimension of authority is about *primacy*.

The New Testament speaks not of primacy – on the contrary, it insists that the first shall be last and the last first – but of 'pre-eminence'. Some are 'led into prominence as servants of Christ with gifts of discernment and boldness'.[32] The New Testament is not without its hierarchical elements (in our proper sense of sacred authority) but it is a hierarchy that is transfigured in the light of the Servanthood of Christ. If the apostolic Church recognised pre-eminence, we may legitimately speak today of primacy or the authority of personal office.

Like conciliarity and collegiality, primacy has entered the Anglican vocabulary from Roman Catholic ecclesiology via ecumenical dialogue. Rome has a full-blooded primacy in the pope that involves the claims of universal immediate jurisdiction over all local churches and their bishops, unchallengeable authority for the 'ordinary magisterium' or teaching office of the Church and the potential for infallible statements on faith and morals.

Anglicans have a pale shadow of primacy in the office of the Archbishop of Canterbury who is both Primate of All England and president of the Lambeth Conference. It is a primacy of consent, expressed in moral authority and pastoral solidarity. Without judicial authority, except in visitations and appeals, the primacy of the

Archbishop of Canterbury in the Anglican Communion could be called a primacy without teeth, but Anglicans believe that it is all the stronger for having to win its authority by example, affection and fellowship, rather than being able to pull rank.

A diocesan bishop has primacy in his diocese. He has enormous influence – partly thanks to generally deferential clergy and frequently obsequious laity – but limited direct power. He makes his mark on the complexion of the diocese through appointments (suffragan and area bishops, archdeacons, cathedral canons and honorary canons and prebendaries, rural deans in most dioceses, the Diocesan Director of Ordinands, certain important lay posts), his say in the appointment of a dean or provost, and through his involvement in patronage. Let us dwell on the latter for a moment.

The bishop is sole patron of a proportion of parishes; he is consulted by patrons of livings where he is not the patron and has a veto by virtue of his power to license; he is a member of the Diocesan Board of Patronage; he appoints team vicars jointly with the team rector; he controls ordinations and the placing of deacons. For some bishops, evidently, this is not enough. Some diocesans regard the involvement of laity and presbyters in patronage as a hindrance. They believe that they would make the best appointments if left to their own devices. The bishop, they believe, knows both the needs of the diocese as a whole and the needs of the individual parish(es). Fundamentally, they do not naturally think in conciliar or even collegial terms. They are resistant to the idea that senior presbyters or lay people with extensive local knowledge could be trusted to contribute to decisions. Any exercise of the authority of personal office that marginalises or bypasses the conciliar and collegial embodiments of authority weakens the body of Christ and does much to confirm non-episcopal Christians in the prejudice that they are better off without bishops.

As local, dispersed authority – embodied in private patronage, the freehold and the sole cure – is weakened through lack of money and personnel, the power of the executive becomes magnified to fill the vacuum. While the number of stipendiary parochial clergy is steadily reducing, the number of 'dignitaries' (so called) has steadily increased in recent decades and now is probably static, resisting the trend to retrenchment and economy. It is said that the proportion of bishops to parochial clergy has increased eightfold in the past century or so. Some diocesans have been frustrated in their desire to reduce senior posts. The burden of administrative work is such that to concentrate it more intensively would be crushing for the individuals concerned. Perhaps that is because the institution as a whole has not promoted

delegation, subsidiarity, involvement and shared responsibility sufficiently to create the conditions for reducing the executive. The
episcopate will be the last to feel the draught of depleted finances and
shortage of personnel.

The Church of England is so constituted and structured that the
diocesan bishop exercises his primacy of *episcope* in both a conciliar
and a collegial manner. As far as conciliarity is concerned, the bishop
presides in the diocesan synod and neither he nor it can get very far
without agreement as each house of the synod has, in effect, a veto in
important matters. But the bishop will not see the synod merely as a
piece of legislative machinery for approving the budget and diocesan
policy decisions, but will regard its elected lay and clerical members
as colleagues to be consulted, encouraged and affirmed in their
responsibilities – for in a representative manner (as the conciliar tradition insisted) they are the church. This is even more true in the case
of the Bishop's Council for this is indeed an expression of conciliarity (it belongs within the synodical structure, being the standing
committee of the diocesan synod) but it is an expression of conciliarity elevated to the level of collegiality. The bishop and his council are
a team taking counsel together and sharing responsibility for the
welfare of the local church, the diocese. The bishop's staff meeting is
a signal example of collegiality and is more appropriately called a
team meeting, for its members – bishops, dean or provost, archdeacons – are there to give mutual support so that each may fulfil more
perfectly his particular responsibilities in the life of the local church.
At the parish level, the bishop enters into solidarity with the people
of God, with their pastors with whom the bishop shares the cure of
souls, and particularly with the churchwardens who are the bishop's
officers, his eyes and ears.

St Ignatius of Antioch (martyred AD 107) calls the presbyters and
deacons the bishop's 'precious spiritual crown'.[33] If the clergy are the
crown then surely lay people are the jewels in the crown. Bishops can
exercise *episcope* in their dioceses, in accordance with the principles
of conciliarity and collegiality, by sharing their responsibilities, as far
as is appropriate, with senior presbyters (other than archdeacons) and
elected lay people, consulting through synodical and other channels,
leading by reasoned persuasion, and encouraging the local church as
a whole to take responsibility for its life. In this way, they will
encourage the body of Christ to realise progressively its true nature
and help to release its energies for its mission to the world around.

A vicar or rector has primacy in his or her parish, a dean or provost
has primacy in the governing body of a cathedral, and a rural dean
has primacy in the deanery, as does the lay chairperson, and church-

wardens have primacy in a parish. The same principles apply. By virtue of that primacy they carry a weight of authority. What this means in practice is that the church has entrusted them with special responsibilities which are greater than those borne by others. In consequence they have to work harder, bear more stress and 'carry the can' when things go wrong. All these various office-holders in the church, from churchwardens to the archbishop, enjoy a degree of primacy that is entailed in personal oversight. The greatest responsibility and privilege that primacy brings is the calling to offer leadership. In conclusion, let us reflect a little further on spiritual leadership in the Church. I suggest that it has three facets.[34]

> *Liberating authority* is a conception and style of authority which brings out its root meaning of enabling, generating and augmenting, rather than dominating, controlling or inhibiting; an authority that is justified by a pastoral and theological competence that invites voluntary acknowledgement from others rather than making hierarchical demands upon them or manipulating them by psychological tricks in order to obtain their compliance.

> *Therapeutic leadership* is a quality of leadership that transcends mere management (the efficient control and deployment of resources, human, financial and of plant) though it does not either despise or neglect that; a leadership that rejects the temptation to play on people's vulnerability or dependence; that enables individuals and communities to take responsibility for themselves by affirming, sustaining and guiding them in their proper callings and enabling them to give of their best.

> *Constructive conflict* is an approach to conflict in the Church which, while not of course seeking to promote it, recognises that argument over the interpretation of the gospel and the aims of the Church has been endemic since the days of the Apostles, and that argument is a sign of the vitality of the Church; that seeks ways of channelling this into contructive courses, so releasing vital energy, rather than merely playing safe and attempting to contain conflict through managerial techniques.

In what Anthony Giddens has called our 'post-traditional society',[35] spiritual leadership cannot count on sacred status for its authority, but needs to win that authority through evident spirituality, pastoral proficiency and theological expertise. Under modern conditions authority is conceded cautiously, tentatively, provisionally and above all voluntarily. Neither clergy nor lay people respond to unargued exhortations or to policy decisions in which they have not been involved, but they will respond to reasoned persuasion backed by committed service and proper example. Adopting the path of reasoned persuasion means practising open leadership and involves decision-making, not consulting merely one's own conscience, and not playing the hero who must carry the burden alone; but instead arriving at decisions through genuine consultation that is not a façade for autocracy, subjecting policy to rigorous analysis and availing oneself of the best-informed advice. It means being steady, clear, consistent, patient and intellectually credible. That is the quality of leadership that, I am convinced, will evoke a response in the Church and beyond.

Notes

1. P. Tillich, *The New Being* (SCM, London, 1956), p. 85.
2. D. Bonhoeffer, *Communio Sanctorum* (Collins, London, 1963).
3. J.N.D. Kelly, *Early Christian Doctrines*, 3rd edn. (Black, London, 1965), pp. 409, 413. R.F. Evans, *One and Holy: The Church in Latin Patristic Thought* (SPCK, London, 1972), p. 84.
4. B. Horne, 'The Republic, the Hierarchy, and the Trinity: A Theology of Order' in C. Hall and R. Hannaford, eds., *Order and Ministry* (Gracewing, Leominster, 1996), pp. 1–19.
5. P. Avis, *Authority, Leadership and Conflict in the Church* (Mowbray, London, 1992).
6. P. Tillich, op. cit., p. 80.
7. See A.C. Thiselton, *Interpreting God and the Postmodern Self* (T & T Clark, Edinburgh, 1995) for a digest of views.
8. C. Handy, *The Age of Unreason* (Business Books, London, 1989).
9. cf., W. Reich, *The Mass Psychology of Fascism* (Penguin, Harmondsworth, 1975). W.R. Bion, *Experiences in Groups and Other Papers* (Tavistock Press, London, 1961).
10. S. Bruce, ed., *Religion and Modernization: Sociologists and Historians Debate the Secularization Thesis* (Clarendon Press, Oxford, 1992).
11. ibid., pp. 8ff. J. Beckford, *Religion and Advanced Industrial Society* (Unwin Hyman, London, 1989).
12. B. Wilson in P.E. Hammond, ed., *The Sacred in a Secular Age*, (University of California Press, Berkeley, Los Angeles, London, 1985), p. 19.
13. G. Davie, *Religion in Britain since 1945: Believing without Belonging* (Blackwell, Oxford, 1994).
14. D. Hay, *Religious Experience Today* (Mowbray, London, 1990).
15. J. Sacks, *The Persistence of Faith* (Weidenfeld and Nicolson, London, 1991).
16. J. Spurr, *The Restoration Church of England 1646–1689* (Yale University Press, New Haven and London, 1991), pp. 119ff.
17. K. Rahner, *Theological Investigations*, vol. 21 (Darton, Longman and

Todd, London, 1988), p. 101. A. MacIntyre, *After Virtue* (Duckworth, London, 1985). R. Gill, *Moral Communities* (University of Exeter Press, 1992).

18. J. Halliburton, *The Authority of a Bishop* (SPCK, London, 1987), pp. 25f.
19. Archbishops' Group on the Episcopate, *Episcopal Ministry* (Church House Publishing, London, 1990), p. 173.
20. B. Kaye, *A Church Without Walls: Being Anglican in Australia* (Dove, Victoria, 1995).
21. J. Macquarrie, *Theology, Church and Ministry* (SCM, London, 1986), pp. 210ff.
22. W. Temple, *Christianity and Social Order* (Penguin, Harmondsworth, 1942), pp. 18ff, 35.
23. ibid., pp. 19, 54ff, 73ff.
24. A. Suggate, *William Temple and Christian Social Ethics Today* (T & T Clark, Edinburgh, 1987), pp. 35ff, 69, 146, 148–50.
25. G. Ecclestone, *The Parish Church* (Mowbray, London, 1988), p. 15.
26. World Council of Churches (Faith and Order), *Baptism, Eucharist and Ministry* (WCC, Geneva, 1982), p. 26 (M:26).
27. Anglican–Reformed International Commission, *God's Reign and Our Unity* (SPCK, London; St Andrew Press, Edinburgh, 1984), p. 59.
28. Cyprian, *De Lapsis and De Catholicae Ecclesiae Unitate*, ed. M. Bevenot SJ (Clarendon Press, Oxford, 1971), p. 65. cf. M. Chapman, 'Cyprianus Anglicus: St Cyprian and the Future of Anglicanism' in R. Hannaford, ed., *The Future of Anglicanism* (Gracewing, Leominster, 1996), pp. 104–17.
29. W.M. Abbott, ed., *The Documents of Vatican II* (Geoffrey Chapman, London and Dublin, 1966), pp. 98ff.
30. House of Bishops, *Issues in Human Sexuality* (Church House Publishing, London, 1991).
31. House of Bishops, *The Nature of Christian Belief* (Church House Publishing, London, 1986).
32. J. Koenig, 'Hierarchy Transfigured: Perspectives on Leadership in the New Testament', *Word and World* 13:1 (1993), pp. 26-33.
33. Ignatius of Antioch, *Epistle to the Magnesians*, 13.
34. See further, P. Avis, op. cit.
35. A. Giddens, *The Consequences of Modernity* (Polity Press, Cambridge, 1990).

5

The Church's Mission in Society

Margaret Selby and Christopher Smith

'If we belong to the Church ..., we are obliged to ask concerning every field of human activity what is the purpose of God for it?'[1]

Archbishop William Temple's statement in the first chapter of his book, *Christianity and the Social Order*, has a ring of certitude and clarity of purpose which epitomises the overall tone of his work. He was, of course, addressing a very different church and nation in 1942 from that which now exists. The Church of England was easily the most dominant and well-attended ecclesiastical community south of the border; establishment, that intimate political link between Church and State, was a legal and political reality (Edward VIII had not long abdicated because of his love for a divorced woman); and when archbishops spoke or wrote they commanded a more than respectful hearing. The nation, too, was more easily defined. At the time of the book's publication there was a powerful sense of self-identification, a unity forged by the vicissitudes and sacrifices of global war and a common enemy. The United Kingdom was still a great military and industrial power, and the British Empire was very much a seemingly constant reality.

When, therefore, the Archbishop of Canterbury set out a visionary agenda for a new social order in the land, a vision which influenced profoundly the ideas of Beveridge and the radical Labour administration of 1945, he could do so with a confidence which is not so easily expressed in the last decade of the twentieth century. There is no doubt that we are still 'obliged to ask concerning every field of human activity what is the purpose of God for it'; that the church has a unique mission to any society to which it belongs, and that the Church of England has a distinctive contribution to make to English society in the twenty-first century. However, in order to discern what our mission should be, it is important that the 'field of human activity' we address is one rooted in reality; in what, as far as we can tell, is the case and not in what is located in nostalgic reveries or utopian dreams. We are also aware that the reality of 1997 – from which we must predicate that of 2027 – is capable of change which we cannot predict. Who in 1987, for instance, would have foreseen the tragedy of Bosnia? At the time of writing it is not known whether the recent change of Government in this country will lead to any radical change in the ordering of our society.

This chapter attempts to look at overall trends, both nationally and globally, which seem to be permanent features of life in *this land* and in the light of them to explore how the church should engage in her mission.

A new revolution

The England of William Temple still sat fairly comfortably upon the benefits derived from being the pioneer of the Industrial Revolution. In the last half-century we have witnessed and experienced a new revolution which has irreversibly altered that society. We are living through a period of intense and accelerating technological change. This influences and will continue to affect the way human beings live. How does this technological revolution express itself, and what effects does it have upon the way people live? It is possible to identify various aspects of this revolution: communications, robotics and biotechnics.

The exploration of space has led to an explosion in the possibilities of satellite communication. This, allied to the development of an ever more sophisticated use of computer technology – the Internet being its most recent manifestation – has led to humanity sharing in an unprecedentedly speedy means of access to information of all kinds. We now live in a 'globalised society'. Consequently, what happens in Japan is almost instantly accessible in Jerusalem.

At the same time, the practical applications of automation, which was the technological engine driving the industrial revolution, have led through the development of the microchip to the most sophisticated use of robotics in the means of the production of most manufactured goods. A new breed of serfs, (the Czech word *robotnik* means just that), is replacing the need for much unskilled human labour.

Just as the frontiers of communication and automation are being pushed ever outward, so the possibilities of change in the field of animal and plant biology have increased. Genetic engineering can already produce disease-resistant strains of grain and leaner meat. It also has the potential for engineering human life. 'Disease–resistant people' is not a futurologists' pipe dream any more, but a theoretically viable actuality. When such genetic knowledge is allied with advanced medical and surgical technology, then advances such as organ transplants and *in vitro* fertilisation may be seen as merely the first and probably rather crude applications of a biotechnological revolution.

The effects of the new revolution have already become evident in our society. The globalisation of information, for instance, has led not only to the possibility of individual and free access to an international bank of knowledge, but also to a globalisation of the use of that knowledge. In terms of news, this has meant that people throughout the world could observe, almost as it was happening, the bombing of Baghdad and the crushing of the Chinese democracy movement in Tiananmen Square. It has also, probably most significantly, led to the globalisation of the money markets. Massive shifts of capital will occur in minutes. Resources can be switched with extraordinary speed from one part of the world to another by bankers and stock exchange dealers. 'Market forces', which transcend national boundaries, and which as a result have no rooted allegiance to any local interest, dominate the world economy. Economic isolationism is no longer a realistic option for any one country.

Added to this development, and to the expansion of robotic technology, has been the growth of the multinational corporation. Such bodies, which are transnational and which serve their own interests before those of others, are able to locate and re-locate their operations wherever in the world they deem to be most advantageous to themselves. Along with the robotics revolution goes the redundancy of many millions of human beings, replaced by mechanical serfs. The effect of this on global patterns of work has been dramatic. People no longer expect jobs for life; 'downsizing' and 'delayering' are not temporary phenomena but permanent features of the new revolution. The drive for maximum profitability often means that 'human' factors and needs come much lower on any scale of decision-making of those in control of financial and industrial resources. A pattern is emerging both internationally and nationally of those who have the wealth becoming wealthier, and those who do not becoming poorer.

One of the most significant effects of these shifts in power has been the diminution of the potency of the nation-state and its institutions. This trend which was discernible over sixty years ago has now become normative. In October 1930 *The Economist* concluded:

The supreme difficulty of our generation ... [is that] our achievements on the economic plane of life have outstripped our progress
on the political plane to such an extent that our economics and our
politics are perpetually falling out of gear with one another. On the
economic plane, the world has been organised into a single, all-
embracing unit of activity. On the political plane, it has not only
remained partitioned into sixty or seventy sovereign national states,
but the national units have been growing smaller and more numerous and the national consciousnesses more acute. The tension
between these two antithetical tendencies has been producing a
series of jolts and jars and smashes in the social life of humanity.[2]

There are now not 'sixty or seventy sovereign states', but one hundred
and ninety-seven. None of them, however, can claim to be truly
sovereign, for all are subject to the influences of global finance and
the market economy. This being the case, any claims by those in positions of authority within these nation-states to be in absolute control
of the destiny of their national community is an illusion, and one
which their citizens see through very quickly. The only option for
total self-sufficiency on a national level is the horrific one of Pol Pot's
'Year Zero' in Cambodia. The growing internationalisation of world
society can and does lead to a sense of impotence in local communities. Hence a continuing antithetical trend is developing, of people
needing and wanting to gain a sense of significance in the face of
impersonal global and international forces. As a result, demands for
regional autonomy and 'national' identity grow and are focused in
separatist and nationalist ideologies which are often linked to religious
identity.

In the world of work, a commentator such as Charles Handy says
'much of life now looks like a doughnut. Organisations as well as
individuals come to realise that they have their essential core, a core
of necessary jobs and necessary people, a core which is surrounded
by an open flexible space which they fill with flexible workers and
flexible supply contracts'.[3] Such 'flexibility' means that there is a need
for mobility in the workforce. It is needed mentally in the form of
retraining for new jobs, and physically in that, as places of work relo-
cate, people have either to follow the diminishing number of 'core'
jobs or, if they do not possess such a means of employment, to offer
their specialist services as subcontractors/consultants. This latter
method, often reliant on a domestically-sited PC, is becoming a much
more significant mode of occupation in the 1990s. There is no
evidence that such a trend – home-based work – is going to diminish
in the twenty-first century century. Rather, the reverse is likely to be

true. These developments in patterns of work are not unique to the British Isles. Globalisation has global effects. However, where our society is unusual is that the last two decades have witnessed a seemingly uncritical and over-enthusiastic embracing of some of the implications of market forces and consumerism. Recent reports produced by the United Nations Development Programme and the Organisation for Economic Development and Co-operation (quoted in *The Independent* 21 July 1996) indicate that such policies have had the effect of magnifying these trends which are manifest throughout the world. The UNDP's report states that 'Britain is now the most unequal country in the western world with the poorest two-fifths of its people sharing less of the national wealth than in any industrial country apart from Russia. The gap between the richest and the poorest fifths is exactly the same as in Nigeria and far worse than in such countries as Jamaica, Sri Lanka or Ethiopia.' The OECD reports, 'wage inequality in Britain ... has increased more than anywhere else over the last decade'. And, it adds, 'rising inequality is extremely worrying. For a start, greater inequality in many countries has not improved the lot of the poor at all. The "trickle-down" just did not happen.'[4]

In a gloomy assessment of the situation, *The State We're In*, written in 1995, and which these most recent international reports underline, Will Hutton states:

> The extension of the market principle deep into society has destabilised many areas of national life ... Herein lie the origins of family stress, the crises of parenting and the general communal decay which are at the root of so many of Britain's problems. Altruism and the civilising values of an inclusive society have been sacrificed on the altar of self-interest, of choice, of opting out and of individualism.[5]

Whatever may happen electorally, it would appear that Britain, along with many other nations, is gripped by a social and economic malaise which is set to extend well into the next century.

A changed culture

Alongside the massive social and economic changes we are experiencing as a nation, other new permanent features of life in Britain have emerged since 1942. We are now a multi-cultural society. The significant immigrations into the United Kingdom of many Afro-Caribbean people in the 1940s and 1950s, of Kenyan and Ugandan

Asians in the 1960s and 1970s, and of the inhabitants of the Indian sub-continent in the 1970s and 1980s mean that some 5.9 per cent of the British population now have their roots in a different culture. This has led to some obvious and natural developments, such as the visibility of Hindu, Sikh and Muslim places of worship and the growth of the Black-led Churches. The complexion of British sporting life has changed, and people wherever they live cannot but be aware that our society is multi-cultural, multi-ethnic, and multi-religious. This rich diversity of peoples sharing the same citizenship is much to be welcomed. However it would also be true to say that the welcome has not been universal throughout British society, and when the effects of poverty and injustice – which are endemic throughout all of British society – are even more disproportionately felt by some sections of the black community, then stresses and tensions are the unfortunate outcome.

Perhaps the most significant cultural change of all has to do with the position and self-perception of women. Some commentators are suggesting that 'the future is feminine'. They see the potential effects of women's liberation from the necessity of unwanted childbearing, of Equal Opportunities legislation, and of the co-operative and team-building skills at which, at the moment, women seem to be more adept than men (and which are in great demand in modern economic life), as being radical and far-reaching. There are suggestions that the next century will witness an increasing marginalisation of many men both in the workplace and in the home. What is certain is that the clock cannot be turned back to the time when a woman's place was deemed firmly to be in the home. Nor will there be a return to a simplistic view of the nuclear family, extolled by advertising agencies in the 1950s. Women have claimed equality of opportunity both in the home and in the workplace. The fact that many women have not yet achieved their goals does not mean that their aspirations are going to change, nor that the move towards full equality between the sexes will be halted.

Along with the shift in the perception and position of women there is a discernible change in the ways in which we view our own humanity. This has been partly due to the rapid advances in biotechnology and medical science. Some genetic research for instance holds out, tantalisingly, the idea that the isolation of specific genes will provide doctors with the information necessary to solve some long-standing human health problems. Already, this can be done with certain conditions such as Down's syndrome and cystic fibrosis. At the moment the result of such genetic pinpointing is the offering of the termination of pregnancy. However 'genetic engineering' holds out the possibility of

changing genetic components at source and thus eradicating the condition. The interesting idea is that it is 'engineering', implying by the
very use of the word that when treating a human being we are treating primarily a biological mechanism. A similar underlying
assumption may be seen in the use of 'mind-changing' drugs such as
Prozac to treat depressives. In a commentary upon a recent American
court case in which Joseph T. Wesbecker, who was being treated with
Prozac, shot twenty of his co-workers, killing and injuring twelve,
John Cornwell says,

> The past ten years have seen the development and marketing of new
> pharmaceutical products that claim to offer antidotes not only for
> clinical depression but for individual unhappiness and general
> discontent. The philosophy that underpins this notion is based on a
> belief that our happiness and misery, our joys and sorrows, our
> vices and virtues, are to be found not in the way we habitually live
> and work as members of families and communities, but exclusively
> in the state of our brain molecules. If this philosophy prevails, it
> follows that we shall increasingly turn from social and communi-
> tarian solutions to pharmacological ones with inevitable and
> far-reaching consequences.[6]

The concept of the human being as primarily a biological machine is
accompanied by what seems to be an all-pervading notion that humanity's prime purpose is that of consumption. 'Consumer' language
proliferates – along with shopping malls such as Meadowhall near
Sheffield and the Metro Centre in the north-east of England. Unlike
city centres, which attract people to them for a wide variety of
reasons, of which the purchase and consumption of material goods is
only one (there are parks, art galleries, churches, mosques, concert
halls and museums, for instance) the overriding philosophy of such
places is that of the market. In this country, the market-driven model
of humankind as consumer has been translated into other areas of life;
health, education, and transportation to name but three examples.
Thomas Merton's words of the early 1970s concerning the problems
faced by young novices have, not untypically, a prophetic ring:

> Man is a consumer who exists in order to keep business going by
> consuming its products whether he wants them or not, needs them
> or not, likes them or not. But in order to fulfil his role he must
> come to believe in it. Hence his role as consumer takes the place
> of his identity (if any). He is then reduced to a state of permanent
> nonentity and tutelage in which his more or less abstract presence
> in society is tolerated only if he conforms, remains a smoothly

functioning automaton, an uncomplaining and anonymous element in the great reality of the market.[7]

He continues, 'It is characteristic of this affluent marketing society to generate at the same time unrealistic expectations and superficial optimism overlaying an undercurrent of suspicion, compounded by self-doubt, inferiority feelings, resentment, cynicism and despair.' 'Unrealistic expectations and superficial optimism' have, not surprisingly, been harnessed by the marketing society in its leisure provision. The development of video technology, computer games, and the new 'virtual reality' concepts have made it possible for more and more people to conduct their leisure-time recreation in isolation. This is a natural development of the principle of the stage and the cinema where people are 'entertained' rather than creating their own amusements. Fr Belton in his *Manual for Confessors*, whilst seeming to the modern reader very 'Victorian' in a prudish sort of way, makes an important point when considering the dangers of the music hall and the cinema in his chapter on 'Confessions of Youths and Girls': 'Our condemnation of the music hall and the cinema, therefore, is the condemnation of an excessive indulgence in a form of entertainment which does little or nothing to recreate and educate the mind.'[8] Belton's fundamental objection to the entertainments of his time was that those being entertained were in a passive mode. With the advent of 'virtual reality' entertainment the logic of passive amusement of a consumer is further developed, and it would be true to say as Hey does that 'for a very large number of people, life is lived at second hand'.[9] This could be said not only about the video technologies, but also about the whole 'nostalgia and heritage' industry which is burgeoning in this country.

As it approaches the twenty-first century Britain is experiencing the same phenomena as the rest of the world. However, these are more marked than in many other 'developed' nations: the globalisation of finance, the market economy, a biotechnical revolution, and their effects have resulted in increased mobility of labour for those 'in work', a growing underclass of deprived people, a society heavily influenced by materialist, consumerist values, and one which is grappling with a range of concepts concerning what it is to be human. Everyday life is increasingly becoming divorced from local, geographical communities due to changing patterns of work and leisure.

Culturally, the country has become much more diverse, largely due to the inheritance of its imperial past, and, because it is felt by many that the nation state has only a marginal ability to influence global activity, people's confidence in the institutions of the State, Crown, Parliament, the Law, and the Church is low. A gloomy summing up of the situation is provided by Will Hutton: 'Britain in the 1990s has lost its sense of direction and its people are at odds with themselves'; and 'what binds together the disorders of the British system is a fundamental amorality'.[10]

Kennedy, who is only slightly less pessimistic than Hutton, when reviewing the world scene says this: 'As the twenty-first century approaches, therefore, the peoples of the earth seem to be discerning that their lives are ever more affected by forces which are, in the full meaning of the word, irresponsible.'[11]

It is in this milieu that the Church of England is called to exercise her mission in the next century. As is apparent in David Bosch's work, *Transforming Mission*, the twentieth century has seen many attempts by Christian thinkers to define the nature of the mission of the Church. However that mission has been defined, it is beyond question that one of the normative elements in the Church's life is the *Missio Dei*, and that engagement in this task has the potential continually to reform and purify an ecclesial institution. 'Mission is ... the participation of Christians in the liberating mission of Jesus, wagering on a future that verifiable experience seems to belie. It is the good news of God's love incarnated in the witness of a community for the sake of the world.'[12] Temple's phrase that the Church is obliged to ask 'concerning every field of human activity what is the purpose of God for it' complements Bosch's words, and both Bosch and Temple provide an appropriate starting point from which to consider the mission of the Church of England to society in the coming century. If, however, society is truly experiencing 'profound and accelerated changes', and if 'the world is re-conceiving itself', then any attempts to analyse, and predict a precise model of the Church's mission are bound to be at best only marginally successful and, at worst, irrelevant. What is certain is that the Church of England, along with other Christian and world-faith communities, is facing great problems and great opportunities.

It would be true to say that what is startling and novel about the societal change presently being experienced is not the change itself. Life for individuals and for society is to some degree or other defined and expressed by change, and by human beings' reactions to it. Some, in every generation will wish to claim that the change which they experience is qualitatively different to that which has preceded it. This has always been the case. Others will disagree. What few would deny is that there is a quantitive difference in society's development at the end of the twentieth century. Because of the rapid technological advances of the last few decades and the 'revolution' which has been described in the first part of this chapter, that feeling is not misplaced. There has been a marked acceleration in the pace at which society is changing. It would also be true to say that no observer of movements in society can be detached from what is observed. Indeed, the very act of observation, and even more so its articulation, contribute to the process of change itself.

Because of these considerations, the present changes in our society seem to demand speedy responses. The problem with acceding to such demands is that they are almost instantly dated. This is a problem which is not unique to the Church. Any group of people attempting to engage with contemporary society, whether politicians, Christian thinkers or caring professionals, find that arriving at seemingly appropriate solutions to perceived problems is an exercise fraught with difficulty and frustration. Youth workers, for instance, say that the cultural fashions and group behaviour of young people change so quickly that policy-making in this area is very difficult indeed. Not surprisingly, the Church, set as it is in such a society, can soon discover that it has been left behind in its thinking.

One solution to this problem is to approach the mission of the Church in a 'modular' manner. This has its attractions. With the increasing globalisation of markets and information networks, and with the increasing sense of individual and corporate impotence which often accompanies such change, it can be reassuring to concentrate upon limited and specific areas of human activity. The growth of nationalist/separatist movements has already been cited as evidence of such a feeling on a societal level; the concentration upon specific and well defined individual issues, sexuality for example, would be a response at a personal level. Philosophically, such an approach to the experience of change is aptly described as 'post-modernist'. For post-modernists, the 'meta-narrative', that is, any overarching world view such as Christianity or Marxism, is dead. Therefore, any attempt to discern universal values for humanity as a whole is held to be a fruitless exercise. As a result, all that people can attempt to do is to create some significance for their own lives by concentrating upon issues or problems which directly affect them. Hence the rise of a modular approach to issues. Since the Church exists in a localised, incarnated, environment it is not surprising that it experiences great pressure to respond very specifically to the immediate issues with which it is faced. Thus, for example, many Orthodox Christians in the former Yugoslavia have seen the primary role of their church as that of supporting Serbian nationalism, and many Catholic Christians have adopted a similar stance towards Croatian aspirations. In this country the Church of England is being pressurised into grappling with the issues surrounding sexual politics. Such matters, like many others, tend to be perceived and discussed as if they were self-contained. Consequently, there is a tendency within the Church to look for immediate solutions and to see this as a form of meaningful engagement with society.

Such a methodology, however, does not adequately take into account one fundamental aspect of the nature of the Church. As the body of Christ, the Church is called to be a particular, specific, sign of Christ's presence in the world, but also it bears witness to the universal scope of God's love for the whole of creation. The Church is always a particular community; but it confesses a universal message. This universalist imperative means that the Church Catholic with its Christian 'meta-narrative' has to address not only the specifics of human life, but also the universals. Biblical language in both the Old Testament and the New insists that the revelation of God, whilst earthed in the specific salvation history of the Jewish people and shown forth in the incarnate Christ, is not simply for those particular communities but for the whole world. Isaiah sees the temple at Jerusalem as 'a house of prayer for all peoples' (Isa. 56.7) and the writer of the Gospel of John is clear that it was for love of the world that God gave his only Son (John 3.16). Maintaining a Catholic vision, therefore is an important exercise at this present time, for alongside the thrust to particularise many human concerns, there is a growing desire to discover and express values which are applicable to all people. One example of this would be the United Nations' declaration on the rights of children. The attempt to formulate a moral code which will be taught to all young people in our national schools is another. Nor has the belief in other universal meta-narratives disappeared. Whilst theological and ideological overviews may be considered unfashionable in some quarters, much of the fragmentation and polarisation of society is a result of the globalisation of the world economy. This springs out of a world view which asserts the unassailability of market forces. It is very difficult to challenge a world view if there is not a contrasting one to offer. Consequently, Christians, Marxists and others with a universal aspect to their thinking cannot afford to jettison their meta-narratives, for without them no effective critique of the present received wisdom will be possible. The Church of England, as part of the Church Catholic, is therefore called to witness not only to specific situations but also to the need for a universal perspective on issues in society. It is self-evident that the English church in 1997 cannot in any way claim that it speaks for the majority of Christian believers in this country in the way that it did half a century ago. Nonetheless, there is still a sense in which the 'Church by Law Established' can be used to articulate the concerns of faith-communities in this land. A striking example of this was the production of the report, *Faith in the City,* by the Archbishop of Canterbury's Commission on Urban Priority Areas (1985). The 'Established Church' in this instance was convinced that there were matters of national concern to do with the state of society. The national dimension is one which should not be abandoned lightly. William Temple's opinion still holds good that whilst 'it is of crucial importance that the Church acting corporately should not commit itself to any particular policy', and as such 'must not commit itself to an ephemeral programme of detailed action', because it is also 'committed to the everlasting Gospel and to the Creeds that formulate it' it is still incumbent that it goes on asking about 'every field of human activity what is the purpose of God for it'.[13]

If, then, there continues to be a Catholic vision which insists that the mission of the Church is to the whole of society, the next question concerns the means by which it is able to relate to that society. As all action springs from being, it is important to consider afresh what the Church is called to be. Three models of the nature of the Church, two of long-standing, and one which is more recent, may be useful in such a consideration. These are the models of the Church as the Body of Christ, the People of God, and as the Base Sacrament.

St Paul's evocative image of the Church as the body of Christ (Rom. 12.4–8; 1 Cor. 12) is one which needs to be rediscovered by Christians in every generation. And as the writer of the First Epistle of Peter states, Christians are a 'chosen race, a royal priesthood, a holy nation, God's own people that you may declare the wonderful deeds of him who called you out of darkness into his own marvellous light. Once you were no people, but now you are God's people.' (1 Pet. 2.9–10a). Both these writers also imply that the Church is a sign to those amongst whom it is set. The Pauline language of the body indicates one fundamental characteristic of the Church: that of a basic unity in which each member knows itself to be in mutual interdependence with all other members. This image in itself mirrors the life of the Trinity in which the divine persons of the Godhead live in perpetual perichoresis, in mutuality and self-giving. Thus the Church as the body of Christ points to a vision of the fundamental unity of all people under God. The Petrine images of race, priesthood, nation and people stress that membership of the Church involves belonging to a community which transcends normal racial categories, national identifications and sacerdotal hierarchies. The Church as the people of God can, therefore, challenge creatively those very factors which so often lead to destruction and division in human life. Furthermore, both images assume that the Church, by its very being, will continue to further in the world the work of God in Christ.

The model of the Church as sacrament develops further the understanding of the Church as a universal sign of God's saving love. The Dogmatic Constitution on the Church of Vatican II likens the Church to 'as it were a sacrament'. Writers like Kenan Osborne have explored the implications of such an idea, and stress that if the Church is to be true to its vocation then in all that it does, and especially in its sacramental life, it must reflect Jesus who is the primordial sacrament. Thus he says,

> In scholastic theology of the sacrament, the matter and form often described the sacrament. In this contemporary approach when one hears the word 'baptism' one should think of Jesus, when one hears the word 'confirmation' one should think of Jesus, when one hears the word 'Eucharist' one should think of Jesus and so on. If Jesus is the primordial, fundamental, basic, root sacrament, then it is only because he is sacrament that these others can be sacrament.[14]

This renewed exploration of the range of meaning appropriate in sacramental theology arises from the contemporary mismatch between the ordered thought of a Thomist universe, where sacraments can be said simply to reflect the nature of reality, and the prevailing disbelief in the very possibility of a sacramental universe, characteristic of the late twentieth century. In Thomas Aquinas himself, for whom the sacramentality of matter was an immediate reality, we note a special attention to the relation between the thing signified and the signifier – something of the microscopic approach. In a post-Vatican II context, there is serious need to avoid any sense of God being somehow 'trapped' within the sacraments of the Church: a need to focus again on the larger questions of sacramentality, in order to discover in the particular sacraments the means by which Jesus, the primordial sacrament, makes himself known. To the scholastic concern to elucidate the connection between the matter of the sacrament and its meaning in a way that heightens our awareness that all is dependent on God's grace, needs to be added a broader concept of 'signification' that we may be open to the ways in which the sacraments reveal and transform our whole relation with God.

Such ideas about the nature of the Church stand over and against post-modern views of the world, which assert that the mental and the material are two quite different modes of being; that there is no way in which God can influence the material world; and that there is a divorce between objective and subjective truth. As a result, religious experience is relegated to the sphere of personal consumer choice, and any idea of an overall purpose for society becomes irrelevant. These ideas also challenge another prevalent model of the Church, which is that of the 'Company of the Elect'. In a curious way, this model fits well with a post-modernist view of organised religion, for it sees the Church as set very firmly over against society and its life and mores. Holders of such a view of the Church will often define it as 'The Ark of Salvation', and see it as set in a world deemed to be intrinsically depraved and incapable of redemption. Only within the 'safe stronghold' of the Church can the individual believer be assured of personal salvation, and the lifestyle of believers is expected to stand in sharp contradistinction to the rest of society.

Both these contrasting views of the Church have a significant following within the Church of England. It could be said that a struggle for the soul of the church is being fought out in the synods, deaneries and parishes of the land. There is no doubt that the forces of secularism and materialism are at the moment both prevalent and strong. Because of this, the temptation to see the church as a place of safety in a potentially hostile environment is also very strong. Charles Davis, in *The Temptations of Religion,* writes that a ghetto is 'a cultural enclave resistant to secularism, close and exclusive enough to create a sufficient network of relations for cultural purposes – a counter-community with its own knowledge, language, symbols, attitudes and emotional responses'.[15] Davis was speaking from a Roman Catholic context, and arguably the pre-Second Vatican Council Roman Church was the most effective proponent of the 'Ark of Salvation' model, maintaining an illusion of Catholicity because its own ghetto was so large, and sometimes seemed to be coterminous with whole nations. The fathers of Vatican II acknowledged that such a model of the Church was defective, and from that acknowledgement emerged a renewed vision of the Church as the body of Christ in the world. The result of the Roman ecclesiological shift is that the debate about the nature of the Church has shifted to the ecclesial communities of the Reformed tradition. For some, especially many Baptist and Pentecostal churches, there has never been much argument; the Church is the company of the elect. The Church of England, on the other hand, could be said to be undergoing a crisis of identity. This can best be seen at a local level where a significant number of churches have adopted a 'ghetto' approach to their mission, and some are being successful in increasing their membership as a result. Some of the distinguishing marks of such an approach can be described as follows: congregations tend to be eclectic, the members being united by a common view of sound doctrine rather than by parochial resi-

dence; strict baptism policies are enforced, establishing a clear demarcation between those who are Christian and those who are not; the
church part of any plant is often closed when not being used by the
congregation for worship, and the minister is seen primarily as the
chaplain to the believing community. Protagonists of such a model
will often see the mission of the churches as being synonymous with
evangelism, the basic purpose of which is to increase the membership.
It must also be said that such a model, because it is attractive in the
present climate, and because it does have some scriptural warranty,
can be found in Anglican churches of all traditions. If this model were
to become the prevailing one for the Church of England in the coming
century, the resultant body would be increasingly congregational.
Current concern for 'sound doctrine' and 'orthodoxy' with its threat
of internal schism, could all too easily become a reality. Furthermore,
a church which withdraws into its own life is less able to engage with
the society in which it is set. It would not be long before such a
congregational Church of England would find itself abandoning the
poorer parts of the country, once there is no longer an overview of
the needs of the whole country. This assessment is based upon the
actual pattern of ministerial and building priorities in other churches
in England which have a congregationally-defined identity. Churches
close when they can no longer sustain their plant and the salary of
their minister. Such developments might well result from current re-
evaluations of the mission and role of the Church of England. It is,
therefore, essential that a strong case should be made for a more
genuinely Catholic, and hence all-embracing, view of the Church in
mission. This chapter is concieved as a contribution to such an exercise.

The Church as the body of Christ

As part of the world-wide body of Christ, the Church of England is
called to engage in the ongoing process of discerning what '*oikoumene*'
means. This has two ecclesial foci. One is that of promoting unity
within Anglicanism; the other is that of furthering the wider unity of all
Christian people. Since the decision by General Synod in 1993 to
ordain women to the priesthood, a new phrase, 'two integrities' has
been added to the vocabulary of the Church of England. In a church
which has always acknowledged the existence of very distinct traditions
within itself, such language fits a little more comfortably than it might
in other Christian churches. Most members of the Church of England,
whatever their own position on the ordination of women, would no

doubt prefer to live without the reality to which the language of two integrities points. There is, however, no sign that divisions on this issue will disappear in the foreseeable future. This being the case, it is better for the church to deal with the problem positively rather than negatively.

The common life of all Christian people is based upon the unity which they share 'in Christ' through their common baptism. Acceptance of a basic baptismal unity demands of Christian people that they profoundly honour other Christians whose opinions differ radically from their own. Such a demand is one which calls for a mode of Christian living which reflects the diversity in unity of the Blessed Trinity, and which holds the key to the prime obligation placed upon all the baptised to further a wider unity. It is, therefore, possible that, if the Church of England manages to live positively with the reality of two integrities, this may in turn be a witness to other Christian communities in their own search for unity.

Bernard Häring writes: 'the ecumenical movement is an unrenounceable part ... of evangelism. Ecumenism signifies experiences of the gratuity of reconciliation which comes from God.'[16] Ecumenism is unrenounceable not simply because it is a desirable end in itself, but also because it is only as the Church attempts to live out its call to be the body of Christ in the world and thus to be a sign to humanity as a whole, that it can take an active part in promoting unity amongst all people. The great High-priestly prayer of John 17 has a wider remit than simply that of promoting unity amongst the followers of Christ. Their unity is needed for a greater good 'that the world may know that you have sent me ...'(John 17.23). In a society which is becoming increasingly mobile and more fragmented, which is tending towards privatisation of action and which is in danger of losing sight of its common humanity, the promotion of such a model of unity is very important.

The Church of England is still uniquely placed to act in such a way as a sign to British society. It has refused to abandon the poorest parts of the land and its resources are still sacrificially allocated to ensure that Urban Priority Areas are decently served by clergy and buildings. It has also weathered the financial crisis of the late eighties and early nineties without compromising the fundamental vision of maintaining a workable parish system. As a result, it can still affirm credibly that it sees itself as having a mission to the whole nation. The maintenance of the ancient concept of the whole country being divided up into geographical parishes points to this vision, gives a localised expression to the two integrities (in that neighbouring parishes may be of differing 'integrity' but still be part of the same organisational structure), and provides a base through the setting up of Local Ecumenical Projects for the exploration of a wider Christian unity.

Nonetheless, the parish system has its own intrinsic problems. It would be true to say that no geographical parish in the land is in any sense coterminous with any given community. This has been the case in most parts of England for at least a century, and the accelerating changes in work patterns and social organisation mean that any direct connection between a geographical parochial locus and those who live within it is becoming increasingly tenuous. It is also true that it is impossible to find a place in this country where 'those who live in a community have overriding economic interests which are the same or complementary'.[17] It is also evident that for many people their experience of community is often primarily located within places associated with their work, family or leisure. Despite these obvious drawbacks, the continued existence of the parish system has many potential strengths, one of the most important of which is the modelling of a common life which is not based upon occupation, class, wealth or domestic circumstances. The local parish church still has the potential to signify to society the desirability of a fundamental human unity which transcends all other categories of living. Shorter writes, 'a new model of the Church must be born ... in which the experience of community is basic',[18] and Warren echoes this when he says, 'what the Church needs to find today is ways of relating, of establishing community in a way appropriate to its setting.'[19] Given the current debasement of the word 'community' (which, because it is deemed to be almost universally acceptable, is used indiscriminately as a prefix for virtually any desirable occupation or activity), a better phrase might be 'committed networks of people'. This phrase would accord well with Charles Handy's vision of the future:

> We need our village and our city ... our cities will not change fast enough. We must create our own virtual villages and cities ... the virtual organisation can be glimpsed in the new 'clubs' for the independent portfolio workers ... opportunities to meet and be challenged by strangers. Micky Kaus advocates more use of what he calls 'Third Places', places like cinemas, churches, shopping malls and other common meeting arenas. More could be done to make these Third Places into opportunities for connecting up with strangers. Too often, however, they are made up of lonely crowds ... In the world ahead we shall increasingly have to make our own connections, our virtual city, our own virtual village.[20]

If Handy's vision of the coming shape of British society is correct then it becomes clear that churches in general and the Church of

England in particular have a significant advantage over most other organisations. With their existing buildings and 'committed networks of people' located in every part of the country the churches, as visible expressions of the body of Christ, are already acting as signs of *oikoumene* to those amongst whom they are set. In order to further this signification, a local church will need to be prepared to go on reconceiving its contribution to the coming world from its geographical base, and to continue to take seriously its task to provide what Warren calls a 'prophetic word to our culture'. That word will be as much located in the life of the local church as in its utterances.

Such a reconceiving will involve organisational change. This is not precluded by the retention of the parish system. Handy speaks of the 'growing phenomenon of federalism' which renders unnecessary much previous emphasis on central administration. He writes:

> Organisations everywhere are being 're-invented' or 're-engineered ... They are breaking down, or rather blowing up their old functions and their old ways of working and are regrouping people, equipment and systems round a particular task ... They are creating work doughnuts, groups with complete responsibility for discharging the task, with specified rules and duties – the core – and a lot of discretionary space to do what they think best ... The goals of the parts have to adjust to the requirements of the whole and vice-versa ... No longer do people believe that people at the top know best; no longer can leaders do all the thinking for the rest; no longer do people want them to ... The information revolution which has overtaken us means that the centre can now be well-informed but small, it can be strong but dispersed. Power can be more balanced ... The information has made federalism possible.[21]

Whilst Handy is writing about the structures of industry and commerce, his message is also applicable to the church. More than ever before the 'concerned networks' are the places where the *koinonia* of a common Christian life is to be lived out. It is there that people can go on discovering what it can mean to belong to each other in their common humanity. The outworking of some of Handy's points can already be seen within the life of the church: 'No longer can leaders do all the thinking for the rest; no longer do the people want them to.' The New Testament clearly teaches that, in the body of Christ, status and hierarchy have no place. The Church of England, in its history, has not always reflected such biblical teaching. Status, hierarchy and clericalism have been, and in many ways still are, very much a part of its life. This is gradually changing due to various factors. The significant reduction in the number of candidates offering themselves for ordination, for instance, has already had a dramatic effect upon the life of the church in rural areas where few parishes can now expect to have their own priest as they did in the past. It does not seem likely that there will be a dramatic increase in the numbers of ordained ministers in the near future. One of the positive effects of this development has been the flourishing of an ecclesiology which speaks of the whole people of God, and in which clericalism as opposed to sacred order has little place. The church is being recalled to a renewed understanding of the proper relationship of bishop, priest and deacon to the whole *laos*, the people of God. Such an understanding does not undermine the appropriate function of the sacred ministry; rather, it places such ministries within a different perspective, one which is freed from the unnecessary baggage of status and hierarchy. Ordained ministers, instead of 'leading from the top' are beginning to be used to underpin and express the organic unity of the *laos*. By so doing, they are rediscovering the pattern of Christ the great high priest whose authority was that of a servant. Such a realignment of perceptions and roles will continue to be painful and disturbing for the church, and especially for the clergy. Nonetheless, without it much of the potential vitality and imagination of the whole church will be stifled and frustrated. Similarly, the slimming down of the central functions of the church, which has already commenced in the modest reforms of General Synod, should be accepted and welcomed in the years to come. The re-alignment of the way in which the church organises its life is beginning to reflect the picture painted by Handy. For both pragmatic and ecclesiological reasons, such organisational shifts are to be welcomed, for they have the potential of positively expressing a model of common life which is both rooted in tradition and in touch with the way other organisations function in the wider society.

The Church as the people of God

As the Church of England grapples with what it means to be the body of Christ so the vision of being a 'chosen race, a royal priesthood, a holy nation, God's own people,' can enable it to relate in a fresh way to our multi-cultural society. In his message of the inbreaking of the Kingdom of God Jesus saw his mission as universal in scope. The language of 1 Peter indicates that allegiance to Christ transcends normal categories of race and nationhood and priesthood, and so it is desirable that the Church of England reorientates itself much more radically towards the realities of England in the twenty-first century. There are, and will continue to be, a plethora of different faith narratives jostling for people's attention. Without the church abandoning its understanding that it is the heir and custodian of the belief that Jesus Christ is the unique divine *Logos* who enlightens everyone who comes into the world, it can still free itself from any remaining vestige of exclusivity.

According to Bernard Häring, the key to such a reorientation lies in the notion of 'walking with' people, especially those of other faith traditions and ideologies. Writing of the Church's call to evangelisation in a world where the centres of influence are passing from the first and second worlds to the third world, he says:

> In this exodus, there is great hope in the encounter between Christianity and the deeply religious character of the Africans, and the great oriental contemplative religions and moral cultures – Confucianism, for example, or the newer forms of Buddhism which look for a synthesis between detachment and presence, between moral–social religion and contemplation. The encounter with the great contemplative religions such as Buddhism, Hinduism and some parts of Islam could be of even greater importance ... The question put to the Church ... is: does she truly walk with the whole human race in such a way as to testify that she accompanies the Lord of History and to give a serene orientation to humanity in this epoch of a gigantic exodus.[22]

His vision is of a future in which the Christian conception of truth is expanded beyond its current, rather narrow, confines. He acknowledges that this is likely to cause anxiety, but he suggests that religion can only continue to be vital and effective if it incarnates itself 'in a new way in the whole project of actual cultures, accepting the state of exodus and the possibility of meeting and proposing a new synthesis'. To speak in such a way does not dilute the truth of Christ, but rather deepens it in order to face the challenge that awaits the church in this country. Such an exercise will need what Häring, in the same passage, calls discernment and the embracing of the evangelical spirit of poverty and contemplation.

An encounter in such a manner with people of other faiths points also to the need to 'walk with' all those who share some common idea of the spiritual dimension of human experience. Grace Davie gives her book *Religion in Britain since 1945* the sub-title *Believing without Belonging*. In it she points out that many in society want to believe but do not want to involve themselves in established religious practice.[23] David Hey's statistics make clear that 76 per cent of people in the Leeds study by Ahern and Davie reported a belief in God.[24] As the people of God the Church is called to 'walk with' all those who are searching for him, and all those who take seriously the rumour of God, from those who are seeking meaning within the varied expressions of what is commonly called 'New Age' religion to those whose Christian faith survives in a vestigial form from an earlier age. The challenge for the Church is how to be transparently open to others in their spiritual search whilst at the same time making accessible to them the treasures of its traditional resources of contemplative prayer, Christian insight, and a common liturgy, all in a way which will engage with people's real intuitions of the divine. The alternative is one of retreat, dismissing the reality of other faiths and other religious expressions as at best defective or at worst demonic. Missiological thinking and practice from around the world indicate that such an approach is ultimately self-defeating.

The 'walking with' model offers other possibilities for the Church. The Church of England has a long tradition of 'walking with' others in society, whether they be religious or not, for what is deemed to be the common good. One of the prime tasks of the people of God is to be conformed to and to further the mission of the Kingdom. The good news proclaimed by the Church is that all are called to be God's children and that as his children are reliably loved by him. As a result of experiencing such reliable love from their heavenly Father, they too are called to love reliably in their relationships. Consequently the Church has a mandate to speak out and work for the realisation of the values of the Kingdom in society, and to draw attention to situations where they can be discerned. The implications of such an obligation, are that the Church will continue to stand for the furthering of justice and peace especially on behalf of the poor.

Will Hutton writes, in *The State We're In*:

> For two decades unemployment has been a grim fact of British life, bearing particularly hard on men. As well as those included in the official count who want work and who can't find it, there are millions who are marginalised – prematurely retired or living off inadequate savings or sickness benefit. One in four of the country's males of working age is now either officially unemployed or idle, with incalculable consequences for our well-being and social cohesion.[25]

> ... The former workshop of the world is now Europe's fourth economic power after Germany, France and Italy and in some branches of production is being overtaken by Spain. One in three of the nation's children grows up in poverty. In 1991 one twenty-one-year-old in five was innumerate; one in seven was illiterate. The prison population is the highest in Europe.[26]

These statements express the reality of life for many in this country and are backed up by official figures. Such poverty is partly a result of the effects of the global market economy and partly the result of specific market-driven policies pursued in the United Kingdom. This had been a reality in many parts of the country long before it was confirmed by statistical evidence. When he was Archbishop of Canterbury Robert Runcie acknowledged this by setting up the commission which produced *Faith in the City*. Published in 1985, this piece of work was the result of 'hearings' in some of the most deprived parts of the country and its findings were supported by detailed statistical analysis. In the Introduction to the report, the commissioners state:

> We have to report that we have been deeply disturbed by what we have seen and heard ... We have seen physical decay, whether of Victorian terraced housing or of inferior system-built blocks of flats, which has in places created an environment so degrading that some people have set fire to their own homes rather than be condemned to living in them indefinitely. Social disintegration has reached a point in some areas that shop windows are boarded up, cars cannot be left on the street, residents are afraid either to go out themselves or to ask others in, and there is a pervading sense of powerlessness and despair.[27]

Tragically, little has changed in our society in the decade which has passed between the publication of the report and *The State We're In*. If anything, the problems of structural poverty have intensified. More people are sleeping on the streets, decent rented housing is even scarcer than it was in the mid-eighties, and many of those who can be found begging on the streets of our cities and towns are frighteningly young. Poverty-related diseases such as TB are on the increase, as is the abuse of alcohol and other potentially addictive drugs. The poor are very much part of our society, seemingly in ever-increasing numbers.

The response of the Church of England to the *Faith in the City* report was to set up the Church Urban Fund. Despite its best efforts and those of many other charities, British society still faces a major challenge in its response to the endemic cycle of deprivation. Because the problems faced are so large, agencies which have significant but limited resources can only hope to make a marginal impact on the overall situation. Nonetheless, the Church Urban Fund, in its criteria as a grant-making Trust has incorporated the principle of 'walking with' those whom it is trying to assist. Any scheme which receives a CUF grant for instance, must show that it is attempting to meet needs which are not already being met. Furthermore, it must demonstrate that it has real support both from the local community and from ecumenical bodies, and the participation of those who are to be served is actively encouraged. The Church Urban Fund is firmly based within the structures of the Church of England, and is primarily a grant-making body. Another community initiative in which significant numbers of Anglicans have become involved is that known as 'Broad Based Organising' (BBO). This movement, which involves participants undertaking a radical critique of the exercise of power, is based upon the work done by Saul Alinski in the United States. BBO aims to create a new power-base consisting of groups which are already rooted in the local community. It is already well-established in several British cities, and consists of a coalition of local churches, other faith communities, schools and community bodies. By training its members in techniques which involve the building of confidence and the empowerment of local people, and by choosing appropriate and commonly agreed goals which are achievable for 'actions', it can claim to have been moderately successful in its early life. The strength of both these attempts to 'walk with' others in the pursuit of a just society is that both eschew the 'service-delivery' model of social action. Such an approach is still an influential one in British society, and it locates power and influence predominantly in the hands of the 'service deliverer'. By highlighting the desirability of participation and partnership in all their projects the Church Urban Fund and Broad Based Organising can be seen as pioneers of a new way of approaching the alleviation of poverty.

Such an approach assumes that there must be a significant shift in thinking by all who are committed to the search for justice. So, for instance, the Church of England, along with other agencies committed to the poor, has to see itself as not only contributing to the good of society, but also to its existing and perceived evils. The Church can only become the critical spirit of society 'if she develops a more critical conscience with regard to the influences she herself experiences from economic, political and cultural structures.'[28] It also means that the Church in its mission cannot afford to retain any sense of being a patron of work with the poor. Rather, by embracing partnership and participation, it must rediscover the God who is already at work through and in the poor: an idea most powerfully stated in Jesus' parable of the sheep and the goats (Matt. 25.31–46).

The weakness of such initiatives lies not in their fundamental methodology but in the fact that what can be achieved by them will be limited. The resources available to any society are not limitless and are heavily dependent upon macro-economic decisions. While the effects of such decisions are felt and must be addressed at the grass roots, or micro level, any actions targeted at specific local problems can only have a very partial influence upon global policy-making. Thus while local achievements will be attained, success will always be partial. This does not in any way diminish the importance of such local activity, especially for those actively involved. It does, however, point to the need for the Church also to address those who control power at national and international levels. This will involve a continuing 'walking with' those who operate the global economic meta-narrative. John Atherton, writing about the way of interaction between the reality of the economic market and its challenges, gives an example of how this might be done, warning against a simplistic attempt to regard economic principles as God's laws. 'It is the time to recognise the contribution of various traditions, and not to seek to reformulate any one of them.'[29] This approach frees Christian people from the need to search for pre-determined answers, and enables them instead 'to share fully in what is really going on from a perspective of Christian belief'.[30]

The Church, the distinctive Christian community inextricably stained as it is by the world, has to take seriously the contribution of economics to the debate about society, and to contribute its own perspectives. 'It is ... about becoming free in order to engage the market and its challenges, holding the market, at the moment, as the principal partner in that process. It is about being open to whatever might emerge out of that dynamic interaction. It is about taking the contemporary context so seriously that we can engage the future with realism and therefore hope.'[31] Such exercises in dialogue have taken place in places such as St George's, Windsor, for many years. Initiatives such as this need adequate resourcing and an opportunity to develop and influence the ongoing mission of the Church.

The engagement of the Church with those who make decisions affecting our society expresses an important principle, that of inculturation. While Atherton speaks of the pressing need 'for human and Christian concern for a common language' in the field of economics and the market, this holds good also for other areas of human activity and experience and has to include a critical look at how the Church expresses that which is specifically religious. The Church needs to speak differently within each part of a culturally pluralistic society. This will involve not only learning the appropriate language appertaining to a particular culture, but also affects the way in which the Church expresses its own life through its liturgy. Genuine inculturation allows the local church a free discourse and real dialogue with others so that they are not only heard by the Church but also freed to make an effective contribution to the process of nurturing mutual respect. Such a method of evangelisation is much less directed from the centre. It is also much less dependent upon set-piece evangelistic techniques, which can often be a form of spiritual service-delivery. It is not really possible for the Church to imagine that it is unaffected by interpretations of reality which differ from its own. Such a recognition will facilitate a way of 'walking with' those outside the Christian community, and illuminate the relationship of the Church with many of its nominal adherents. As John Reader puts it:

> First, we need to become more aware of the major narratives which are at work inside ourselves. Second, we need to be willing to bracket or to let go of those major narratives enough to be able to listen to others who live with different narratives. Third, one of the most valuable services which the church has to offer is the opportunity to create spaces within which others can share their own stories and listen and learn without entering into direct conflict.[32]

Such critical awareness, coupled with the dynamic which drives Christians to a love and concern for all aspects of human life, means that the local church in its outreach will seek to work co-operatively with a widely differing range of people and groups. When this happens, as can already be seen in many CUF Projects and BBO Actions, the church will be expressing in its life a real mutuality, respect and value for others. Only when the church does this, can it challenge and question its partners in the search for the common good. Evangelisation then becomes not a form of faith-sharing, in which it is assumed that one group has a faith which it generously shares with others, but a rooted involvement with the rest of the local community.

Such a methodology of evangelisation is well articulated by Häring:

> The disciples of the Lord who are dedicated to the Gospel, individually or in community, cannot claim to have a superior culture. They recognise that there would be no greater sacrilege than the one accomplished by making the mission of evangelisation an instrument of culture, whatever that culture may be ... The apostle is all things to all men: Hebrew to the Hebrews, Greek to the Greeks, and not for any vain strategy! The Church cannot be a boastful museum of multiple treasures of the past, especially if this is to the detriment of her evangelising mission, which can develop with a spirit of humility and simplicity only through actual cultures.[33]

The Church as sacrament

> In the last analysis, it is a question of meeting with the more deci-
> sive human experiences, seen however in the light of the Christ, the
> great Sacrament, the 'visible image of the invisible God'. This
> approach is always valid, but it presupposes a very deep experience
> of the sacraments and the sacramentality of the Church in relation
> to the whole of human life, and furthermore, a certain sensitivity
> to the signs and fundamental acts in which the heart of man and the
> qualities of the community are expressed.[34]

In the above passage, Häring assumes both that the Church relates to
human life sacramentally and also that it views the whole of life as
sacramental. This idea developed by several modern Roman Catholic
theologians, and based upon the work of Second Vatican Council,
roots all the sacramental life and systems of the Church firmly in the
authority and authenticity of the person of Christ who is the primordial sacrament. By doing this, they build in a systematic way upon the
insights of Anglican theologians of an earlier generation, such as Gore
and Quick, who saw the sacraments as extensions of the incarnation.
The theological approach can be sketched as follows. God took the
initiative in the redemption of the world in the person of Christ. By
doing so he embraced his own creation, using the stuff of that creation
in the word made flesh; and in his life, death and resurrection Jesus
acted as the expression and agent of what it means to be fully human,
a child of God. Therefore, the Church is called to be a visible sign of
that reality until the Lord comes. It can be seen that one of the key
elements of such an approach is the emphasis it places upon what it
means to be human, because it takes as its benchmark the person of
Jesus, who is true God and true man. Because this is the case, the
Church as a sacrament of Christ is a sign of the image of God in
humanity, after the order of both creation and redemption. In Christ
God is restoring the fullness of his image within us enabling us to
become his children (Gal. 4.4–7). Thus, because it is an extension of
the life of Christ, the sacramental life of the Church will offer new
models and resources for human beings in their ongoing exploration
of what it means to be fully human. One of the implications of such
an approach is that a divorce between 'spiritual' and 'material' is
precluded and is replaced by a creative tension between the two. The
sacramental outworking by the Church of the implications of Christ,
the primordial sacrament, has to be done in and for the created world.
    This model of the Church offers to society a different way of under-
standing what it means to be human. It declares that all human life,

indeed all of creation, has a sacramental potential, and that there is a depth and mystery to all human experience which can be most effectively encountered and articulated in the sacraments. The sacraments are therefore, not arcane and exclusive rites, but the means by which people may continue to discover 'life in all its fullness'. By maintaining such a view of the potential sacramentality of life itself, the Church not only challenges the post-modern view of reality, but is also drawn into dialogue with those who see human beings as simply consumers or highly complex biological mechanisms. Such a sacramental view of all reality is encapsulated pre-eminently in the eucharist, which is why Häring can speak of the Church finding 'its centre of life and mission in the Eucharist' which is in itself 'an expedition in the name of Christ to the very ends of the earth.'[35]

It would be true to say that this sort of sacramental approach to life has never held undisputed sway in the life of the Church of England. Such a view, however, is consistent with the other two models of the church described in this chapter, and has the advantage of containing at its heart a Christocentricity which is unique without being exclusive. It also contains within itself a dynamic which can equip the church to engage in the wider debate about the meaning of life. The fact that the church's contribution to this debate is not exclusively expressed in verbal terms but also by actions which are rooted in its common life means that it can be multi-faceted and therefore accessible to many more people. If in practice the whole of the Church of England were to promote the centrality of the eucharist, and the creative tension between word and sacrament which lies at its heart, then its dialogue with society would be both creative and potentially challenging to many other ways of viewing reality.

Such a development can already be discerned in the ongoing debate about gender, personhood and sexuality. The General Synod's decision to permit the ordination of women to the priesthood has placed these concerns, which are of course not limited to Christians, at the heart of its life. This is so, because once the president at the eucharist is a woman, the issues surrounding gender and personhood become incarnated. Consequently, those who would want to maintain that gender is primarily a biological and an ontological category which in turn rests upon God's revelation of himself, find it impossible to accept a woman as a priest. Those, on the other hand, who would see gender as primarily a social construct, and would speak of the essential complementarity and equality of women and men find that there is no problem at all in receiving the sacrament consecrated by a female celebrant.

Similarly, the church's eucharistic life and practice may hold an important clue as to how it should approach the ongoing debate about human sexuality and its expression in different sorts of relationships. In the recent Synod report, *Something to Celebrate,* the authors accept that life in the nuclear family is no longer normative for many people. This being the case, the church is faced with the problem of having to decide whether there are any kinds of relationships which, if entered into by individuals, would render them unacceptable as communicants. (There was a time, for instance, when divorced people were not welcomed at many Anglican altars.) The decisions which the church makes, both nationally and locally, on the issue of excommunication, will be more significant than its official pronouncements. It will also indicate, as do, for example the rubrics in the Prayer Book concerning the disposal of the unused eucharistic elements, where its priorities and beliefs actually lie. Thus, on gender and sexuality, Elaine Graham raises the sort of issues which the church in its common life will have to go on addressing in the coming century:

> What strategies can we adopt as women and men to explore the possibility of difference without appropriating such traits as subordinate or deterministic; of speaking through distinctive gender experiences without doing so through categories of power and discrimination? Is it possible to talk about distinctive gender experience without using the language of otherness, inferiority and polarisation? Can women and men speak from gendered vantage points without recourse to strategies of power and difference? What new ways of being human can be drawn from culture and theories of gender that offer a more authentic and less distorted account than the inherited models? ... Are there alternative models of human nature other than those of dualism – which informed ancient classical accounts inherited by Christian theology – that give an account of human nature as gendered, that is consistent both with the available cultural evidence and orthodox Christian anthropologies?[36]

The church will be able to consider such questions about what it means, to be human (gender, personhood and sexuality being only some of many) in the light of Christ 'the great sacrament'. Shifting the focus of debate from one which is primarily analytical and word-based to one which is holistic, synthetic and incarnational will mean that the church's insights on the reality of human nature will be of great importance in the ongoing exploration of the 'human project'.

Postscript

When faced with social change, and the problems and opportunities associated with it, the reaction of some can be a desire to produce instant solutions to problems and to respond immediately to opportunities. The models of the Church as the body of Christ, the people of God, and the base sacrament, which have been suggested as starting points for a consideration of the Church of England's mission in society in the twenty-first century, do not lend themselves to so speedy an application. Any exploration of the nature of the Church and its vocation does not permit an easy passage to a clear set of specific policies or strategies. This may not necessarily be a negative factor in promoting effective mission. Such would be Thomas Merton's view, in *Contemplation in a World of Action:*

> He who attempts to act and do things for others or for the world without deepening his own self-understanding, freedom, integrity and capacity to love, will not have anything to give to others. He will communicate to them nothing but the contagion of his own obsessions, his aggressiveness, his ego-centred ambitions, his delusions about ends and means, his doctrinaire prejudices and ideas. There is nothing more tragic in the modern world than the misuse of power and action to which men are driven by their own Faustian misunderstandings and misapprehensions. We have more power at our disposal today than we have ever had, and yet we are more alienated from the inner ground of meaning and love than we have ever been. The result of this is evident. We are living through the greatest crisis in the history of man; and this crisis is centred precisely in the country that has made a fetish out of action, and has lost (or perhaps never had) the sense of contemplation. Far from being irrelevant, prayer, meditation, and contemplation are of the utmost importance in America today.[37]

Such a critique, whilst written from an American perspective, can well be applied to England at the end of this millennium. The twenty years which have passed since Merton made his observations have seen an increased adoption in British society of an American lifestyle both in leisure and at work. As a result, his critique of his own society has a strikingly contemporary application when applied to England. A strong case can be made that the same malaise, which Merton observed in 1973, can also be discerned in the Church of England in 1998. The Church of England is marked by great activism at all levels of its ecclesial life. There is no shortage of organisational activity; indeed, much time is expended in setting goals and establishing and refining management systems. At the same time more clergy are suffering from symptoms of stress, breakdown and 'burnout', than in the past, and many of the laity are overworked. Also, for a variety of reasons, more English parish churches are locked up for most of the week, and it is rare to find the people of God engaged in the daily activity of common prayer within their walls.

While this is happening in the structures and life of the church, more people in society are looking for what Merton in the previous quotation names as 'self-understanding, freedom, integrity and capacity to love', and are doing this in a variety of ways. Counselling and psychotherapy are booming, and thousands of young people head for the ecumenical community at Taizé every year, in order to experience a depth of prayer and contemplation which they often do not find in their local churches. Retreat houses are full of people who are yearning to continue their spiritual pilgrimage, and there is no shortage of interest in what is on offer from the rich spiritual traditions of other faiths. New Age spiritualities are on the increase, as is the re-emergence of many, basically benign, forms of paganism.

Faced with such trends, which could well be symptoms of a growing disillusion with the prevailing orthodoxies of the market economy and its potentially dehumanising side-effects, the Lambeth fathers in 1998 could well do worse than to designate the first years of the new millennium as a 'Decade of Contemplation', during which the people of God would be encouraged to meditate upon what it means to be the Church. Such a proposal might well be dismissed in the present ecclesial climate as naïve quietism, or as a retreat from relevant activity. However, it should be noted than many of the most prominent and influential Christian thinkers of the passing century have made the life of prayer their first priority. A continued rooting of the life of the Church of England in deep and persistent prayer could well give it both the discernment and the resources which it will need to engage with society in a creative and liberating way.

Häring puts the call to contemplation thus:

> And since the faith is not an ideology to be put beside so many others, we shall be in a position to communicate the novelty of the gospel and of its morality only in the measure in which the experience of faith has deepened in us the joy, the gratitude and the knowledge of Christ and of the Father and his design for all men. It follows, evidently, therefore, that the evangelisation of the world demands first of all the spirit of authentic prayer and meditation on the gospel, never however separated from readiness for the existential translation of the word mediated.[38]

And St John of the Cross:

> Let those that are great activists and think to gyrate the world with their outward works take note that they would bring far more profit to the Church and be far more pleasing to God if they spent even half this time abiding with God in prayer ... of a surety they would accomplish more with one piece of work than they now do with a thousand, and that with far less labour.[39]

Notes

1. W. Temple, *Christianity and the Social Order* (Penguin, London, 1956), p. 24.
2. *The Economist* (October, 1930), quoted in P. Kennedy, *Preparing for the Twenty-First Century*, (HarperCollins, London, 1993), p. 329.
3. C. Handy, *The Empty Raincoat* (Arrow Books Ltd, London, 1995), p. 66.
4. *The Independent* (21 July 1996).
5. W. Hutton, *The State We're In* (Jonathan Cape, London, 1995), p. 15.
6. J. Cornwell, *The Tablet* (20 July 1996).
7. T. Merton, *Contemplation in a World of Action* (Image Books, New York, 1973), p. 49.
8. F.G. Belton, *A Manual for Confessors* (Mowbrays, London, 1931), p. 201.
9. D. Hey, *Religious Experience Today. Studying the Facts* (Mowbrays, London, 1990), p. 75.
10. W. Hutton, op. cit., p. 6.
11. P. Kennedy, op. cit., p. 64.
12. D. Bosch, *Transforming Mission. Paradigm Shifts in Theology of Mission* (Orbis, New York, 1991), p. 519.
13. W. Temple, op. cit., pp. 27-9.
14. K.B. Osborne OFM, *Sacramental Theology. A General Introduction* (Paulist Press, New York, 1988), p. 76.
15. C. Davis, *The Temptations of Religion* (Hodder & Stoughton, London, 1973), p. 111.
16. B. Häring, *Evangelisation Today* (St Paul Publications, Slough, 1990), pp. 41-2.
17. R. Frankenburg, *Communities in Britain* (Penguin Books, London, 1969), p. 238.
18. A. Shorter, *Evangelisation and Culture* (Geoffrey Chapman, London, 1994), p. 116.
19. R. Warren, *Being Human, Being Church. Spirituality and Mission in the Local Church* (Marshall Pickering, London, 1996), p. 16.
20. C. Handy, op. cit., pp. 255-7.
21. ibid., p. 76, 99, 118, 119.

22. Häring, op. cit., p. 142.
23. G. Davie, *Religion in Britain since 1945: Believing without Belonging* (Blackwell, Oxford, 1994).
24. Quoted in G. Davie, ibid., p. 77.
25. Hutton, op. cit., p. 1.
26. ibid., p. 2.
27. *Faith in the City. A Call for Action by Church and Nation* (Church House Publishing, London, 1985), p. xiv.
28. Häring, op. cit., p. 130.
29. J. Atherton, *Christianity and the Market* (SPCK, London, 1992), p. 269.
30. ibid., p. 272.
31. ibid., p. 275.
32. J. Reader, *Local Theology. Church and Community in Dialogue* (SPCK, London, 1994), p. 18.
33. Häring, op. cit., p. 34.
34. ibid., p. 61.
35. Quoted in Häring, ibid., p. 29, derived from L. Newbigin, 'La Chiesa missionaria nel mondo di oggi' (Roma, 1968).
36. E. Graham, *Making the Difference. Gender, Personhood and Theology* (Mowbray, London, 1995), p. 56.
37. Merton, op. cit., p. 179.
38. Häring, op. cit., p. 39.
39. St John of the Cross, *Spiritual Canticle* 29.3.

6

New Dimensions in Ministry: Towards 2000

Timothy Bradshaw

Traditional ecclesiological orientation

Anglicans regard themselves as in the tradition of Christianity rooted back in the very earliest era of the faith in these islands. The Church of England is merely the reformed catholicism which traces back to the early Fathers and the Apostles and Prophets. It does not seek to mark out a particular style or distinctiveness all its own, hence the emphasis on the Scriptures, the creeds and the continuing flow of church life through history marked particularly by the practice of ordination through the hands of episcopally-consecrated bishops. This is simple and reformed church life open to all. There is no distinctive Anglican confession of faith beyond the Thirty-Nine Articles of Religion and their Augustinian emphasis on grace.

Perhaps the Anglicans who rejoice most in this heritage today are the evangelicals, to whom the Articles are congenial, although today the occasional polemical note is to be regretted. According to Article Nineteen, 'The visible Church of Christ is a congregation of faithful men, in which the pure Word of God is preached, and the Sacraments be duly ministered'; this is a definition no doubt deficient in terms of what it omits, for example the theology of the body of Christ and the Holy Spirit, but it emphasises the evangelical orientation of the Church as the people of faith who hear the word and receive the sacraments of Jesus Christ.

The ministry of the Church must be of people lawfully called and sent, by those who have public authority given to them in the congregation to call and send ministers into the Lord's vineyard, that is the bishops. Anglicans point to the continuing line of ordination and consecration back through time as well as to the continuance of the people of faith, those who constitute the Church by their faith, worship and witness. The ministry is very much the pastoral ministry of word and the two sacraments of baptism and holy communion. In the ordination service the bishop charges those to be ordained to the priesthood 'to be Messengers, Watchmen and Stewards of the Lord; to teach and to premonish, to feed and provide for the Lord's family; to seek for Christ's sheep that are dispersed abroad, and for his children who are in the midst of this naughty world, that they may be saved through Christ for ever'.[1] There could hardly be a greater emphasis on the pastoral task among the people of God. The ordained are daily to weigh the Scriptures for the resources wherewith to carry out this heavy office.

Presbyters are called priests in the Anglican tradition, but not mediating or sacrificing priests in the Old Testament sense; rather, as the elided form of the word 'presbyter'. The people and the presbyter are in the same relationship to God, and the ministry holds no special dimension of grace on which the laity depend. The Book of Common Prayer and the Ordinal make clear that the ordained are pastoral ministers of the gospel, not a mediating priesthood. 'It emerges above all from the pre-Nicene literature that the ancient church had difficulty in calling the church leaders "priestly". According to the New Testament, Christ and the Christian community alone were priestly; the leaders were at the service of Christ and the priestly people of God, but are themselves never said to be priestly.'[2] This modern Roman Catholic scholar's opinion has long been held by the classical Anglican theology and the evangelicals, who claim to be at the centre of the Anglican tradition.

The Church should never be without apostolic ministry for its upbuilding and maintenance in the faith of Jesus. The ordained ministry is vital and irreplaceable; it is an office of immense importance; its function is to build up and extend the Church through the gospel ministry of word and sacrament. The ministry of pronouncing absolution after the confession of sin, says Bishop Westcott, concerns 'the reality of the power of absolution granted to the Church, and not of a particular organisation through which the power is administered'.[3] The whole Church is the human agency in the world bringing reconciliation and forgiveness to those who will receive the gospel. Within the Church the ordained minister declares the gospel word of forgiveness to the faithful, who are already in the Spirit. The Christian minister is, according to a classical essay by Bishop Lightfoot on the ministry,

God's ambassador to men: he is charged with the ministry of reconciliation; he unfolds the will of heaven; he declares in God's name the terms on which pardon is offered; and he announces in God's name the absolution of the penitent. This last-named function has been thought to invest the ministry with a distinctly sacerdotal character. Yet it is very closely connected with the magisterial and pastoral duties of the office, and is only priestly in the same sense in which they are priestly ... throughout his office is representative and not vicarial. He does not interpose between God and man in such a way that direct communion with God is superseded on the one hand, or that his own mediation becomes indispensable on the other.[4]

The Church transcends history and space, since it exists before the face of God and indeed was chosen in Christ before the foundation of the world, according to the Epistle to the Hebrews. It exists in time and place, as local communities of faith. There is debate as to which is the basic local unit of church life. Is it the local congregation with its pastoral ministry, or is it the regional grouping of congregations under the wider pastoral care of the bishop? The Thirty-Nine Articles speak of a church as a congregation of the faithful where the word is preached and the sacraments ministered, indicating that a local church is the unit ministered to by a presbyter, the bishop therefore providing *episcope* for the cluster of churches and ministers which are present in a region or diocese.

But there is something of a tension in that Anglican documents also refer to the diocese as the basic unit of church life with the bishop as the pastor who delegates his care to presbyters as his curates.[5] To define the diocese as 'the local church', with the bishop therefore as the local minister seems to deprive the presbyter of the proper pastoral role which he exercises under the *episcope* of the bishop but precisely not instead of the bishop. While not being congregationalist, the evangelical Anglican regards the actual congregation as the unit of the local church, over which the bishop exercises *episcope*. The bishop is not the pastor of the local congregation, but has oversight over these, and has the duty to ensure that presbyteral ministry is provided.[6]

The bishop exercises oversight over his diocese of local churches, and also acts in the name of the whole Church of God in ordaining presbyters who have been lawfully called and sent by congregations and tested by those representing the whole Church. The bishop also is charged with being a trustee of the faith and practice of the Church diachronically, through time.[7] In this he is never apart from the whole community of faith, and this emphasises the point that the bishop does not constitute the visible church, but rather is part of it. Apostolic succession means succession in the gospel, and the bishop has a particular responsibility to hand on gospel tradition first articulated by the apostolic circle. The ministry is pastoral, and also a teaching ministry, essentially conservative in orientation. There is a content to the gospel, and this needs to be preserved and articulated. The liberal wing of the Church of England finds this aspect of evangelicalism unpalatable – the notion that truth can be articulated, that doctrine has a cognitive content as well an existential impact.[8] This means that the church is a teaching church under the authority of the apostles and prophets, responsible to that Christological and trinitarian tradition of theology and ethics. The Open Synod Group issued a conference report lamenting Protestant 'confessions of faith', doctrines which divide, in favour of sacramentalism which unites, said to be the Roman Catholic mode of operating.[9] This is a very odd claim for several reasons, the most obvious of which is that each new convert to Rome has to promise to obey a large set of papal propositional teachings; but further the notion that sacraments are devoid of noetic content, including both historical and metaphysical knowledge, is naïve. Existential faith in the risen Christ entails various forms of truth which the mind, as well as other aspects of human capacity, can understand. Anglican priests promise at ordination to 'instruct the people' on the basis of Scripture, not simply to enable individuals to explore their own experience.

Evangelical Anglicanism, especially in the light of the grave weakening of the conservative Anglo-Catholic wing of the church, will have a renewed zeal for guarding that aspect of faith which the mind can understand, the cognitive content of faith about Jesus, the God of Jesus, and that deep tradition which should orientate our subjective narratives of life. Evangelicalism also speaks to the heart, fosters *fiducia* as well as *assensus*, since faith means communion and participation with the Son of God. The life and way of Jesus of Nazareth, the dynamo of renewed commitment by evangelicals towards deeper involvement with the poor in society, cannot be simply intuited existentially but requires the historic narratives about Jesus.

The classical minister or priest is the pastor–teacher, the person in whom the local congregation can put their confidence for leading the local church in the direction of Jesus Christ, someone theologically mature at the heart of the parish who will use the structures of the parish to promote faith and worship, to bring people closer to their Lord. This is the appropriate person to preside at the celebration of the sacraments of baptism and holy communion. It is doubtful in the extreme if this basic model of the minister will change, but new dimensions of this ministry are developing.

Recent developments and influences

Post-Keele Anglican evangelicalism decided to look positively to the whole Anglican structure rather than acting as a victimised group within it.[10] Evangelicals began to involve themselves in ecumenism, the study of liturgy, ethics and hermeneutics. The Congress of 1977 at Nottingham repented of neglect and complacency over poverty and deprivation in the urban areas and made a commitment to help address this social challenge.[11] There was a widening of the focal lens of the evangelicals in the Church of England, who came to terms with a 'comprehensive' kind of church containing a mix of opinion.[12] 'He who chooses Anglicanism finds himself ... in a large, loose, complex church structure with a conservative tone but a seemingly endless willingness to tolerate cultured heretics,' thinks Packer,[13] who believes that this is not a good thing in itself but that the best ecclesial policy is for radical ideas to be tested and debated rather than banned.

> The formalist idea of orthodoxy as a matter merely of keeping yesterday's dogmatic formulae intact seems inadequate to evangelicals, vigorously as they often defend these formulae; the orthodoxy that evangelicals seek is one which, while wholly faithful to the substance of the biblical message, will be fully contemporary in orientation and expression, and they know that to this end experiments in re-statement must be allowed.[14]

Packer commends a subtler theology of the church and doctrinal orthodoxy than may have been expected by liberal critics. It embodies the fact of appreciating Anglican structure and ethos while retaining evangelical gospel imperatives; he also believes that the Church of England has correspondingly been influenced by its evangelicals in a conservative direction.[15]

The charismatic movement continues to influence, and to polarise, opinion in the Church of England, not so much with regard to doctrine but pastoral and liturgical praxis. In terms of the ministry of the church it has led to a greater diversity of ministries perceived to be needed in church life. The conduct of worship, for example, may well be deemed by charismatics to be led by someone with a special 'gift' of leading worship rather than simply by the ordained minister. Healing and prophesying likewise are recognised as apostolic ministries arising in the church congregation. Often, however, an ordained father-figure will retain authority and control in the background of such worship and practice, allowing it take place within the Anglican framework, and bishops rarely intervene. The charismatic movement, within which one includes such phenomena as the 'Toronto Blessing', undoubtedly attracts while it also alienates. The traditional Anglican parishioner is not used to people being 'slain in the Spirit' in Pentecostal fashion, and does not feel at home with such dramatic religion. Here the difficulty of evangelicalism existing within an established church structure is very keenly felt. Should the ordinary parishioner be protected, by the bishop, from Pentecostal excess which is not licensed by Anglican liturgy or doctrine? Is one task of the presbyter to protect the congregation from the powerful personality claiming the Spirit's inspiration to legitimate novelty?

It has to be said that this tension in a way expresses an historic divide throughout church history, and the Church of England would be showing less signs of spiritual life if such phenomena were not appearing. Wesleyan revival exhibited such charismatic incidents,[16] and caused immense friction between the prophetic movement and the established church. In the early centuries of church life the authority of the confessors in time of persecution conflicted with that of the ordained ministry in the Decian persecutions of AD 250 and thereafter. Moreover, as to some of the more bizarre phenomena associated with modern 'enthusiasm', similar instances can be adduced in the late sixth century. Jerome tells us that Paula, a Roman pilgrim, 'shuddered at the sight of so many marvellous happenings. For there she was met by the noise of demons roaring in various torments, and, before the tombs of the saints, she saw men howling like wolves, barking like dogs, roaring like lions, hissing like snakes, bellowing like bulls ...'[17] Such events acted as convincing testimony of the superiority of God and the Christian saints in areas later to become settled dioceses and parishes. 'Enthusiasm' remains a potent and influential strand in evangelical Anglicanism, with the inherent latent tensions of that synthesis. If this does continue, then the presbyteral leadership in the parish will be essential to hold different emphases together.

Evangelicals since the time of Charles Simeon (1759–1836), the great leader of the Evangelical Revival, have developed structures and organisations within the life of the Church of England, some of which play important roles in the whole church: for instance, the Church Pastoral Aid Society with its programmes of training and support for clergy and parishes, and its patronage influence. Missionary Societies also illustrate this evangelical tendency to practical and missionary endeavour leading to parallel ecclesial networks within the Anglican system. The patronage system has become an important element in evangelical survival in the Church of England, and trusts which influence the choice of incumbent have managed to ensure the retention of evangelical clergy in parishes, often despite episcopal preferences in

other directions. There can be little doubt that this structural historical relic has prevented liberal bishops, regarded as the natural party
of government by the senior appointments boards, from excluding
such clergy, as seems to have happened in other parts of the Anglican
communion, notably Canada. The evangelical theological colleges
recognised by the Advisory Board for Ministry are also highly significant in this regard. They are independent colleges, governed by trust
deeds, which train clergy in the evangelical tradition. The alternative
diocesan training courses are widely held to exclude the evangelical
strand of opinion and ethos. Evangelicals have a strong interest in
maintaining the current delicate balance of informal, semi-independent
structures such as the patronage system, theological colleges and the
missionary societies. The latter are not controlled by a central
Anglican board, and any proposal to bring this about would be
resisted as a bureaucratisation of charisma.

For evangelical Anglicanism the great focus is the parish. The
parish means the worshipping congregation set in the area for which
the incumbent is responsible for mission and pastoral care, and the
structures noted above all have their final goal in servicing the parish
ministry. Wider dimensions of church life are little considered.
Education, for example, has long been abandoned as a significant
evangelical cause, in terms of primary, secondary or tertiary education. Diocesan education officers are very rarely evangelicals.
Trustees of what were set up as 'church colleges' seldom regard the
evangelical, or indeed the Christian, faith as relevant to these institutions, even when the trust deeds demand some such effort.
Organisations for social action, justice and peace do not attract mainline evangelical Anglican support or initiative. The few evangelicals
who are made bishops struggle to shift their vision to the wider
regional and national mode of being church; they are really parish
ministers set on 'fishing and shepherding' for Christ. Different
'sector' ministries, for example, dealing with what the liberation
theologians call the structures of society, are difficult to engage and
are therefore solidly occupied by liberals whose theology tends to
identify the gospel with cultural insight arising from the human spirit.

The suspicion must be that a current evangelical Anglican temptation is to lean towards pietism; hence the reason for the great lack of
interest in the engagement of the gospel with wider structures of
humanity than the congregation of the faithful. In other words, the
conversion and sanctification of souls remains so focal as to neglect
the wider challenges of the kingdom of God to contemporary culture.
'Maturer evangelicals', says Packer, 'have always recognised that
though personal conversion is the starting-point Christians must learn

a biblical God-centredness and seek after "holiness to the Lord" in all departments of the church's worship, witness and work and in every activity and relationship of human life.'[18] It is only when evangelicals do more than monitor the drama of divine activity in their own souls that the creation as a whole becomes the theatre for the playing out of the kingdom of God.[19] Bebbington picks out four characteristics of evangelicalism: conversionism, activism, biblicism, and crucicentrism,[20] and it is evangelical activism in support for aid organisations, as an outworking of faith, that represents the effort to implement the kingdom dimension in society. Individuals in society may act as 'salt and light' in this dark world, but how the church as an institution should so act is not a question considered.

One way in which evangelicals have sought to enter the wider aspects of church is in their contribution to Anglican scholarship in the second half of the century, particularly in the field of biblical studies and hermeneutics, but also in areas not formerly known as their field of interest, such as liturgy. In this regard a widening of mind has been evident and there is no doubt that a more subtle approach to the authority and interpretation of Scripture has emerged as a result of this involvement with contemporary theology and hermeneutics,[21] wherein Scripture is generally appreciated for the richness of its texts, and yet also for the normative authority of these.[22] Evangelicals have not, however, produced a doctrinal theologian to articulate the faith in modern categories.

Cultural pressures and patterns of community

The financial pressures now affecting the Church of England are leading to the possibility of increasing reliance on non-stipendiary presbyters and of cutting down on residential theological training for ordination. It may also lead to the increased use of trained lay readers and lay ministries of various kinds being deployed by parishes. Many evangelical parishes now are happy to employ ordained people on their own payroll, outside the official diocesan clergy numbers, indicating that parish finances are stronger than diocesan and national finances, among evangelicals at least. The Church Commissioners' recent loss on investments led to a certain 'congregationalism' among significant wealthy evangelical churches, prompting a 'quota capping' movement. This is exacerbated when diocesan bishops of such parishes are felt to be unorthodox in their ethical and doctrinal teachings and hence prone to misuse the monies donated by evangelical parishioners.

The centrifugal tendencies caused by financial paucity at national level are leading to the appointment of 'lay assistants' to undertake pastoral work, and this is now a familiar position in parishes. Paid administrators are also common, to take care of buildings and non-pastoral administrative affairs. If there can be no curate allowed because of diocesan numbers, other internally-funded posts will be created. Such posts are sometimes accompanied by training. Unpaid ordained ministry tends to be primarily sacramentally oriented and, paradoxically, not necessarily of immediate interest to the evangelical congregation unless the presbyter in question has particular gifts to be used in the parish and the time to give in deploying them. A non-stipendiary minister arising from the congregation will generally be someone recognised as having qualities and gifts of leadership, so that the sacramental functions will always be linked to pastoral oversight of some kind.

The phenomenon of new paid lay posts has led to some losses in evangelical parish life which will not be recovered. If an administrator or youth worker is paid, why not the Sunday School teacher? One can foresee the break-up of the traditional and theologically based voluntary pattern of working for the good of the church by lay people with the introduction of paid lay posts to carry out parish functions. One very notable change already well established over the past decade is the disappearance of the 'vicar's wife' as a role in church life. This person, who staffed the vicarage, ran mother and children groups, and generally provided a caring presence to many in need, is now a rarity; she now almost always holds down some secular job, often to help with the family income. Alternatively, if a wife desires to engage in church work today, she is likely to seek ordination in tandem with her husband or seek a salary from the parish for her services. It might be said that the expansion of paid lay posts has been a move from community responsibility to a more contractual, functional system of church service and ministry.

Training for the various ministries within the church carried out by lay people will become an important factor in the future of evangelical Anglicanism. The present restriction of significant theological training to the presbyterate, in effect not only limits the effectiveness of the lay contribution, but concentrates power in the hands of the clergyman in a way which goes beyond the natural respect and authority of the pastoral leader of the community. The priestly theological education reinforces the gulf between lay and ordained, rendering the former almost a superior 'gnostic' with special knowledge to bestow, in effect a more drastic form of power than the reservation of the task of presiding at the eucharist. Evangelical ecclesiology has long claimed to dislike the width of the gulf between lay and ordained, but may hiddenly have reinforced it by its stress on the trained preacher/teacher figure at the centre of the community. Concentration of power in the presbyter by effectively keeping the laity ignorant means a depotentiation of the lay contribution as agents for Christ in the Church and the world.

A resolution by the 1995 Anglican Evangelical Assembly recommended 'That the House of Bishops consider ways of encouraging colleges and courses to train lay evangelists and lay leaders alongside ordinands, in a mission-oriented programme, so that mission and evangelism is seen as the work of the whole people of God'.[23] This recommendation seeks to foster a greater degree of teamwork in ministry, to enable lay leaders to understand the training clergy undergo, and to provide a similar standard for themselves. Diocesan training courses could possibly meet such an aim, although they are currently not well trusted by evangelicals. It is possible to foresee large evangelical parishes setting up training courses for their lay workers. There is a sense among evangelicals that the gifts and talents of the laity have for too long been frozen, regarded as a threat by the clergy, and needing to be released to work alongside the ordained ministry in witness and mission.

The prospect of increasing numbers of non-stipendiary ordained ministers raises again the sociological question about the nature of the Anglican presbyterate. It is already recognised as representing a narrow band in terms of social class, and an increase in non-stipendiary priests will probably exacerbate that, since it is the professional classes who are most likely to offer for this role. Reliance on non-stipendiary ministers may also affect the availability of ordained ministry in the inner city areas, where confidence is much lower in congregations and their leading lay figures reluctant to offer for ordination. The sociology of the ordination of women is also interesting to note. It is probable that very few women from backgrounds other than the middle class are ordained. It is also likely that married women being ordained are married, in the main, to professional husbands with salaries; this undoubtedly affects the sense of sacrifice generally concomitant with the life of the ordained presbyter.

The *anomie* and alienation of modern life has led to a felt need for community and for spirituality, as well as the missionary imperative instinctive to evangelicals. The new Christian needs a community, a church as a way of being together with others sharing in the life of Christ. The fact of being Anglican as well as evangelical means that close-knit groups which meet for prayer and mutual support are set within the parish structure, and this itself will mitigate against an over-cosy and isolationist mentality. The community of worship cannot close its doors to the outsider and the seeker, cannot become a sect within the church. Community and mission, both rooted in worship, will remain the aims of evangelicals into the next millennium, and these aims are set out now even in quasi-official documents.[24] Community is a vague word with many different meanings, but mission requires a real Christian community in which the newly converted can have a spiritual home. Newbigin argued passionately for this principle in the Indian church context, making it the compelling rationale for the forging of the united Church of South India out of the different denominations; how could a convert from Hinduism survive without a new culture in which to live, a united culture?[25] Mission and community were simply inseparable.

On the other hand 'believing without belonging' is now recognised as a major phenomenon in a wide section of the population.[26] In other words, there are millions of people who consider themselves believers but rarely darken the doors of churches. Such people believe a God broadly defined in Judaeo–Christian terms, a God who hears prayer and cares. Millions of people do worship and serve this God in private, regarding the Church as at best not very relevant and at worst distorting. A version of the Christian faith is therefore lived out in society without ecclesial bonds, or rather with such bonds being provided by the occasional offices of the church, and by Christian material mediated by other agencies such as the BBC. It is not, however, only the 'nominal' Christians who have a belief without feeling the need to belong. Evangelicalism, at its left wing, can exhibit a like tendency in rejecting the church as a structured community; John Drane says of such people: 'The uncomfortable truth is that the church has been all too eager to adopt the secular standards and practices of our prevailing Western culture', that is bureaucracy, hierarchy, power struggles and propaganda.[27]

Notably the younger generation of evangelicals find the culture of traditional church life difficult to live in and find authentic corporate worship in events such as Spring Harvest and March for Jesus,[28] occasional regional and national events of interdenominational character. Paradoxically Anglican identity means less to such young evangelicals than to the nominal believers who do not belong. Retaining the Anglican loyalty of the rising generation of evangelicals will be a massive challenge. The current cultural movement is described as post-modern. This indicates a break-up of the old frameworks of morality and rationality in favour of a range of modes of life chosen on the basis of the emotional drives of individuals rather than on objective truths about the nature of the universe or morality. This means that reality is regarded as constructed by our tastes and needs, rather than that we recognise the shape of reality and then adapt ourselves to it.

Radical pluralism reigns culturally, or at least in the mindset of the younger generation. This is certainly, at the very least, a prophecy being set forth daily by much of the media in its emphasis on different cultural groups having different, and equally valid, values and norms. Absolute truth is discounted in favour of mutually-accepting relativism, many stories displacing an overarching story of humanity and human value. The 'meta-narrative' is not wanted and not available. The coming cultural forces, given that this analysis of the situation is correct as so many think, mean that Christianity will tend to exist in small groups of like-minded people. In terms of Ernst Troeltsch's famous categories, the 'sect type' and 'mystical type', more voluntaristic and experiential, will become increasingly attractive over against the 'church type'.[29]

The future, according to this cultural analysis, holds out a flourishing evangelical and Pentecostal movement alongside a steep decline in what were the 'mainline' denominations. Pannenberg has predicted this decline, leaving Rome with the free evangelical groups as the two movements surviving in the next century. Rome, of course, can offer the 'mystical type' to complement its 'church type' juridicalism, and this will continue to provide a religious appeal to virtually opposing personality types. It may be that the two Anglo-Catholic strands will also be able to capitalise on sacramentalist mysticism, while offering very different ideas of the moral dimension of the gospel. Anglican evangelicalism, however, specifically lacks the mystical and aesthetic appeal of catholic spirituality, although it traditionally shares a similar ethical sinew with classic Anglo-Catholicism.

The shape of the ministry: unity and diversity

Given such predictions, how should evangelical leadership evolve itself into the next century? There is a real danger of the next generation of evangelicals leaving the Anglican structures as being too constraining liturgically and evangelistically, especially in contrast to neo-Pentecostalist modes of the faith. Evangelicalism is committed to the Bible as the authority for faith and practice, and also to the state of convertedness of the heart to Christ. These facets were unpicked and divided at the Enlightenment by Schleiermacher who rejected the former in favour of the latter, doctrines in favour of heartfelt knowledge of God, *assensus* in favour of *fiducia*. In the language of Martin

Buber, this distinction falls between I–it knowledge and I–Thou knowledge. To understand biblical statements about God is not the same thing as to have a living faith in God. Schleiermacher relegated 'I-it' statements to a very subsidiary position behind experience of God in his theology.[30]

Evangelicalism concerns faith in Christ, an I–Thou personalist trust. This entails a definite christological content given in Scripture, a type of I–it cognition, which gives definition and orientation to faith. The faith of the heart is an informed faith. Both aspects remain vital to the evangelical faith. The modern concern for feelings over rationality ought to fit into the evangelical strength. But when the second, biblicist, aspect gains the status of an end rather than a means, evangelicalism can become cerebral and rationalist, dry and lacking in humanity. This mode of evangelical life seems destined to shrivel away the more its christological centre gives way to worship of doctrines and ethical rules.

Dynamic living faith in the risen Christ, bringing forgiveness of sins and true worship, will always remain attractive and ministry must retain this as its central aim, the building up of the Christological centre. But the biblicist dimension remains important, although this challenges, apparently, the cultural movement away from truth claims. Christ, the saviour and recreator, the king and the judge, is the central character in the divine meta-narrative, a truth insisted upon with particular force by Karl Barth, the greatest evangelical theologian of the century and indeed of many centuries. This is a truth, inseparably related to the Bible, which evangelical ministry must affirm despite cultural scepticism about any meta-narratives, any all-encompassing claims to truth. Whatever changes in ministry are allowed to occur, theological training in the key doctrines of the faith will remain a priority, and this against the moves towards purely 'experiential' preparation for ordination, along the lines advocated by some colleges and, particularly, non-residential courses. This is because one crucial aspect of the ministry, whether presbyteral or episcopal, is that of being a trustee of the apostolic tradition, affirming the truth of the divine meta-narrative in the face of the powerful cultural claim against the possibility of any such truth.

Keeping faith with the 'big story', overarching the many stories and readings of human experience, will be perhaps the greatest challenge to orthodox Christianity in the ideologically pluralist West. Anglicanism, of all the denominations, makes a virtue of pluralism within the church and is constantly stretching outwards towards cultural and religious trends beyond the church. Establishment is often interpreted in this way, as an obligation to shadow and echo social mores, never appearing distanced. The popularity of multi-faith worship among the liberal governing class of the Church of England exemplifies the growing difficulty to many Anglican hierarchs in affirming the meta-narrative of Jesus Christ as saviour of the world, that 'scandal of particularity'. The doctrine of salvation, as distinct from revelation, through Christ appears to be increasingly difficult for the predominantly liberal bench of bishops to accept, yet this is precisely the content of the grand narrative of the gospel.

Any new directions in episcopal ministry by the very few evangel-ical bishops will need to take into account the media. This is because the image of the church is created by the media in the minds of millions of people. Even regular churchgoers gain their understanding of what their bishops believe and teach mainly through the radio, TV, and newspapers. The identity of the church nationally and regionally comes through these channels. This all too often produces a sense of estrangement and alienation in the hearts and minds of parishioners, who are treated to a fairly consistent image of episcopal pragmatism, complacency and relativism.

No doubt some of this image is fair, but some is simply media construction. How the Church of England can project an image of itself which includes its conservative traditional dimension and the actuality of parish life, is a problem resting with the bishops collec-tively. Some means of regularly demonstrating the Anglican commitment to the central truths of the gospel need to be developed. This may entail developing internal Anglican networks of communi-cation, as a means of countering media constructs. But in terms of the wider national image, the church is going have to ensure that it has some media-friendly charismatic leaders specialising in conveying the Christian message as Anglican leaders. The privatisation of the BBC and the almost inevitable development of religious channels for churches will require an Anglican policy, and a whole new dimension of Anglican ministry, albeit one which will seek maximum ecumeni-cal participation.

To find ways of affirming the meta-narrative of Christ will prove to be the key role of the presbyter at local level. This will mean a radical criticism of current standards of preaching and teaching which are so often didactic and boring, a virtual repetition of the text of Scripture with little effort to explain or relate it for today. The growth of lay theological education will help the church to relate the gospel to the world in which people live out their lives. The testimony of the Christian about God's relevance to life in the workplace, or the family, for example, will bring the current horizon into play in a way often missing in sermons. New methods of teaching and preaching will need to emerge, perhaps allowing more for questions and answers to flow between preacher and congregation by way of dialogue and application, a more corporate mode of deepening common life in Christ.

The meta-narrative of Christ includes the narratives of his people, for whom he is God with us and for whom his life and death and resurrection was enacted. The story of every Christian disciple relates to the story of Jesus and to the formation of the Church. The message of the 'way, the truth and the life' makes sense within that community context. The common story of Jesus makes claims on the lives of individuals within the community of faith, and liberates them for the kingdom of God in this world. The narrative of Jesus Christ simply is given and experienced as true, and true for all across the ages and spaces; church people are those who have been spoken to by this life story of God to creation, and so must declare its universal truth. Leaders in the church are charged with special responsibility for promoting the telling of this story as universally true, as catholic.

Evangelical leadership will not only be faced with the need to hold to the truth against the fragmenting tendency of culture, but with the task of fostering community in a church which regards itself as a continuum of sinners and saints, wheat and tares, which only God can judge. Maintaining the community of the faithful within an established church which claims to exclude no one who wishes to participate is difficult, and one of the tensions of evangelical Anglicanism. A parish is nominally a community of all those residing in the parish, and yet the active Christians taking part in the life and worship of the parish church form what is the fellowship of the believers within that formal geographically-defined grouping. The local church of the future will need to provide a definite sense of community as the values of society generally continue to fragment and contradict those of Christianity.

In order to promote the way of the kingdom of God over against the dynamic of what some have called the pagan society, churches will need to develop a far better educated and confident laity, possibly by means of lay academies. These could educate lay people in Christian ethics for example, to enable them to make mature assessments and judgements in the modern world. One major new development in evangelical ministry will have to be in the area of spirituality and worship. This is perhaps the greatest weakness of the whole evangelical constituency in the Church of England, that is lack of guidance on personal prayer and public worship. Most evangelicals do set aside time to pray daily, but need more suggestions and help in the way this can be done to add to the simple Bible reading and responsive prayer routine. Ways of approaching Scripture could easily be developed for such a use, for example, as could ways of assessing the life style of the individual believer before God.

Corporate evangelical Anglican worship undoubtedly needs a deeper seriousness and a deeper joy. The widespread phenomenon of family services may have helped attract young families, but has not kept the interest of teenagers as they grow older and away from children's talks, overhead projectors, visual aids and short repetitive choruses. Hymn-singing has traditionally been a major part of evangelical worship, and the hymns have also had a good deal of theological content. It is said that Anglicans imbibe doctrine through liturgy; it is equally true that evangelical hymns have brought home the Pauline gospel to the hearts of the faithful in a most powerful fashion. But such hymns are generally Victorian and set to tunes of earlier cultures. The challenge of bringing evangelical music forward to relate to the cultural rhythms of the new millennium is a huge one. Musical directors and co-ordinators are now commonplace in large churches, and often these are people with knowledge of ancient and modern, an extension of the parish organist and choirmaster certainly, but with a wider brief in terms of width of music.

Radically divergent tastes exist not only in music but also in types of worship services themselves, and this divergence increasingly seems to be a matter of generation. This divide almost certainly extends to questions of ethics and possibly doctrine. The younger generation finds not only Victorian hymns uninspiring but much of the current liturgical diet. Both Pentecostal and mystical approaches prove attractive to the younger generation, and conservative Christian ethics are often felt to be outmoded and even failing to accord with the imperative of love found in the Bible. To return to the model of the meta-narrative of Jesus as catholic and normative, future evangelical ministers are going to have to work with the increasingly pressing truth that the meta-narrative contains sub-narratives, or different ways of reading the overarching narrative. A kind of pluralism already exists in worship patterns, and this is even reflected in the way that General Synod authorises liturgies for different contexts. The church is going to have to reconcile itself to the fact that it contains different cultures, and different age groups coinciding with such cultural differentiation. Some like the Book of Common Prayer, others more free-wheeling styles of praise and worship. Holding different forms of worship in the same building at different times already betokens different communities, at present united by the fact that a single ministry serves them both. Perhaps the youth culture type of congregation will need its own minister, in some form of team ministry, along with other clergy looking after the more traditional flocks.

The fragmentation of society into different segments of cultural type is to be contrasted against the meta-narrative of God, but it may need to be reflected to an extent in the ecclesial outworking of the gospel. Not only the obvious differentiation of age groupings apply here, but socio-economic factors such as employment patterns may cause pressure for other sub-groupings within parishes, for example those who need to worship corporately on a day other than Sunday. 'Except in very simple static societies, modern communities consist of various overlapping groups whose members are related through language, work, culture and common interest. In order to be effective in missionary outreach the Church may have to encourage the formation of distinct forms of ministry and eucharistic fellowship for different groups in the same area.'[31] That is the opinion of the Reformed–Anglican International Agreed Statement, and they say that the unity of all such groups is fostered by their participation in the life of the diocese, presbytery or association. The point is that modern culture produces groups not definable simply in terms of place, and ministry must evolve to cope with and even take missiological advantage of such segmentation. The whole question of what 'the local church' is will become a vital question.

One way in which diversity is formally recognised ministerially is by the provision of 'episcopal visitors' as extended episcopal oversight for presbyters who dissent from the ordination of women to the priesthood, thus forming a kind of movement within the Church of England for a certain type of priest and congregation, a non-geographically defined group choosing the spiritual oversight of a conservative bishop who has a national, peripatetic scope of ministry. If radical ethical opinions continue to gain ground and secret acceptance by bishops, it is increasingly foreseeable that many conservatives in the church would opt for such oversight by bishops committed to traditional ethical principles.

Such pressure to segment the church even within a parish, let alone a diocese, into culturally coherent groups will need the most careful handling. Is such a group ever going to be 'catholic', if for example it fails to include children or the aged as possible members? Should the church not represent all humanity in its makeup? Ministry will need to be able to handle centrifugal and centripetal movements, perhaps even to recognise something akin to the 'orders' which grew up in the monastic movement as special communities of worship, self-selecting and therefore not fully 'catholic', yet linked to the whole Church. Ministry to particular groups of people or special communities has generally been regarded as chaplaincy work, and may diversify to accommodate modern pluralism in society, with ordained ministers, stipendiary and non-stipendiary, keenly aware of the sociological and cultural character of their particular congregation.

The specifically monastic mode of Christian living itself arose in response to social and economic movements which provoked a flight from the corrupt world towards simplicity. Some similar response to modern Western consumer society may be expected at some stage, a revulsion at the hedonism and materialism of the age. Young people rebelling against the whole sexual theatre of modernity might well be moved to set up community houses in which a celibate Christian lifestyle was practised, and service to the local neighbourhood given, in the context of a life of prayer. The ecumenical acceptability of the retreat movement shows that this could well be possible and become part of parish life, offering a new sort of ministry. Historically the monastic movement, putting down small communities in pagan areas, spread the faith in Europe. There is no reason why small worshipping communities, committed to praxis and witness, should not become centres of spiritual life in urban areas. This could, and perhaps should, become a new form of apostolic and evangelical ministry.

Anglican ministerial structures, in the light of this suggestion, do seem very presbyteral and geographical. The ministry is attached to a geographical area, diocese and parish, with offices to minister in these places. This is a type of a pattern rooted back in the patristic era and the apostolic church as it bedded down in major areas of population. But there always was another strand of ministry of a more peripatetic and charismatic type, the ministry of the apostles exemplifying this travelling missionary type. The monastic movement, as it spread centres of faith and worship in Britain, also embodied strong strands of this sort of apostolic ministry, taking the faith into unevangelised areas and attracting converts. The presbyteral ministry, and the episcopal which oversees it, essentially ministers in principle to the converted, although the congregation itself should form a caring and witnessing body of believers with an impact on their neighbours.

The distinction between the presbyteral and the prophetic was an example used by Max Weber for his famous sociological typology of the 'routinisation of charisma'.[32] An established church must be likely to become 'routinised' or bureaucratised in structure and to lose touch with the prophetic, charismatic strand of ministry. In the medieval church the rise of the Franciscan movement in the face of the massive wealth and power of the Roman Church might be regarded as charisma bubbling up and renewing a spiritual life in what had become hidebound. The Methodist movement in England likewise could similarly be interpreted, but tragically was not incorporated into the life of the Church of England; the crossing of parish boundaries was one of the causes of great offence taken by the Anglican leadership: the presbyteral resisting the charismatic. New movements, new initiatives of the Spirit usually seem to the current clerical leadership as hopelessly naïve and disruptive of existing order. The Church of England in particular has a very poor record in this regard.

The diaconate, the shrivelled office in the much-vaunted threefold order, could be reinvigorated as more than a year's pupillage pending priesthood if lessons were learned from the Reformed tradition, and the Church of England, as an institution, began to formulate a policy for meeting social need. At present the Church of England regards its role in this as one of pricking the conscience of government and getting the State to act. The church has pulled out of health care for example, and social service, except for the voluntary efforts of its members as individuals. Given the needs of those who are told that they will receive 'care in the community', for example, should the church not begin to develop institutional means of support, through existing structures such as dioceses, deaneries, parishes and even cathedrals? It may be time for praxis to be taken more seriously, and an obvious ministry to develop for such purposes is that of the diaconate.

Diaconal ministers in parishes, deaneries or dioceses with the task of promoting Christian caring, or indeed peripatetic ministers who travel widely, would bring a whole new dimension to the life of the Church of England. Ministry to those released from prison is another obvious example of a gap in the state system, indeed an example of the personal kind of ministry which is better provided by Church than State. This kind of initiative would be best done in conjunction with other churches and using the network of *Churches Together in England*. The grassroots relations being built up quietly and widely through ecumenical sharing will increasingly effect new initiatives in ministry designed to meet needs. Such initiatives might well also prove inspirational to many young Christians who are seeking avenues of service as disciples of Christ.

Social patterns of leadership and the ministry

The Church constantly faces the task of discrimination of social trends. Society throws up energies which are hostile to faith and the kingdom of God, such as individualism and hedonism. But also God is to be seen at work in some social movements, and society is not simply negative – a long-standing insight of the Anglican tradition developed through the theology of F.D. Maurice in the last century, and recently espoused by Vatican II in the constitution *Gaudium et*

Spes. Current models of leadership in society have been suggested by the philosopher Alasdair MacIntyre as being represented by the figures of the manager, the aesthete and the therapist.[33]

One can perceive the temptation offered by each of these and the combination of the three as models of ministry for the future. The manager is perhaps the most prominent type of leader in our society today. Management techniques are trusted as being in touch with reality. Cost cutting and efficiency improvement are watchwords now for all political parties. Bureaucratic culture will survive general elections, as the history of the Department for Education reveals perhaps most starkly, as it has become an educational establishment with an ideology impervious to criticism from traditionalists. The manager implements measures to achieve change and enlarge the company's balance sheet; this is so for the BBC, the National Health Service, universities, and commercial corporations. Managers wish employees and consumers to be mildly content with things and seek to massage a 'feel-good factor' into the culture. Needless to say, political leaders are very much managers in the late twentieth-century West.

How might this model be affecting notions of ministry among evangelical Anglicans? The manager of the mega-church is indeed an attractive concept, superficially, for the evangelical mind: large numbers of believers gathering together to hear the sermon, to attend meetings, to call upon the Lord for all kinds of good causes and for more souls to be won. Success is assumed in terms of large numbers, of 'throughput' especially on Sundays. Effective evangelistic strategies are planned and implemented, the gospel is spread. This caricature can equally well be applied to the Catholic priest's control of the flock, the demand for giving exclusive loyalty to the denomination. The strongly managerial mode of ministry is a temptation to the evangelical Anglican who is an evangelical in a hierarchical structure providing the means for controlling church life. Indeed, one of the virtues of the episcopal system in comparison with the presbyterian is said to be that the endless committees of the latter prevent decisive action, whereas individual leaders invested with power can act.

Large organisations, including large congregations and dioceses, need strong leadership, and a move toward more managerial awareness may be good in providing a clear vision for churches. The phenomenon of bureaucratic management in secular society as described by MacIntyre, however, is that of technique without concern for the moral ends of the organisation. Church ministry must be Christologically oriented in mode, placing power under the mark of the cross for the sake of the body of believers. Some attempts to impose commercial practice on the Church of England, such as that of five-year contracts for priests, have revealed the mismatch of such practice with an ancient traditional community of faith which values the presbyter in the parish as more than a functionary in the hand of a higher line manager who can hire and fire. Ironically, at the very time that church leaders are implementing business practices, industry is discovering the truth of what the church has long known, that people need to trust each other in teams and groups, need security and mutual respect, if they are to work well and consistently.

The therapist is another modern figure of authority in society. Any public disaster brings out the media message of the availability of counselling, for example, as if this were a vital part of coping with life. Therapy brings the feel-good factor into one's personal life, enabling the individual to surmount the difficulty of lack of confidence and self-esteem, even the difficulty of guilt feelings. Psychotherapy has affected many dimensions of society, including church life and ministerial training. Some ministers regard their role as helping people come through personal problems into a smoother place of happiness and self acceptance. This has been a new direction in ministry since at least the late 1960s and the influence of the Clinical Theology movement associated with Frank Lake. Once again this contained a necessary balance towards recognising the genuine humanity of the congregation, away from a kind of docetism or perfectionism of the perfectly ordered and poised soul. Christians did have problems; it was acceptable to admit this and seek to deal with them humanly and Christianly.

Whether the minister should be a primary counselling figure is questionable. The therapist becomes a figure of dependency; the Roman Catholic confessional prefigures the therapist's treatment and likewise provides a version of absolution, untying oneself from problems of the self. False expectations can be created that a state of complete psychological wholeness is somehow available. Ministers becoming committed to a version of therapy as their primary role will be sidetracked from their main tasks of evangelism and worship.

Therapists and counsellors work in a chain of command, each having a senior supervisory figure to whom they report. Who counsels the counsellor? Who heals the therapeutic vicar? Who is on hand to help the therapist clergyman from developing a control complex and from operating outside his competence in matters of mental health? Structures in the counselling profession are not in place for clergy, and this was painfully demonstrated in the unfortunate case of the Sheffield Nine O'Clock Service experiment, over which there was no proper *episcope* exercised by the diocesan structures. In particular this is the case when such therapy is coupled to a charismatic kind of healing model, claiming the intervention of the Spirit to unravel the psychological tangles of the inner self. The dangers of undue ministerial power over individuals are obvious. This type of ministry can all too easily produce a new version of clericalist control.

The fostering of Christian community life is probably the more biblical way of helping church members feel accepted by others and of worth. The 'sharing group' of committed believers who honestly desire to deepen their discipleship and cope with their problems of all kinds has met many needs. Mutual confession, mutual openness, in the context of prayer and trust in the Spirit's work within the group, diminishes the possibility of one individual exercising too much influence and control. The fellowship of this model of godly counsel links friendship to inner growth, surely a good ecclesial approach, and one which acts against modern individualism and even consumerist approaches to inner well-being, since each member is helping the others: no one is simply a passive recipient of encouragement and help. All are needy in the school of Christ, all have a contribution to bring. The cult of the self-sufficient expert therapeutic minister jars with the pastoral emphases of the gospel of grace.

The aesthetic side of modern life provides pleasure and the sense of meaning and self-transcendence, a necessary complement to the bureaucratically-oriented mode of life commonly lived out in society generally. The minister as the liberal arts lecturer became something of an icon of the sixties and seventies, the figure who provided options of meaning for people who cared to listen. Today however the very legitimate concern for spirituality and the need to develop one's personal prayer life is a more likely equivalent function to that of the secular aesthete. Evangelicals are realising their weakness in teaching spirituality, forms of prayer and devotional patterns of life. Evangelicals can become attracted to more Catholic and Orthodox modes of spirituality, with their greater use of the created human senses in both private and public worship.

Today evangelical ordinands are very likely to have encountered a range of spiritualities in their training, and a greater sense of their role as spiritual advisors. The 'spiritual director' is now a commonplace amongst evangelical clergy. The importance of this ministry will grow. At present it seems to be a borrowing from other traditions, and even spirituality imaginatively using the Bible is often articulated by Roman Catholics rather than evangelicals.[34] The acknowledgement of this great need, and the falling-off of defensiveness about using insights from other traditions, means that this aspect of ministry will grow. Whether it needs to be confined to clergy is quite another matter, but clergy know its importance. At the level of regional *episcope*, it is strange that diocesan advisors exist on many areas, but rarely on prayer.

Conclusions

Evangelical ideas about ministry are surprisingly Anglican and clerical. New directions in ministry will address the new diversification of society and seek to preserve the unity of the story of Jesus Christ against its relativisation, while seeking to encompass various modes of discipleship in the complex society of the West. This concern for truth and its life means a renewed concern for community and indeed communities, for praxis and spirituality being promoted more energetically than at present. All this sounds surprisingly 'catholic'.

What may emerge is a diversification of ministry so that it seems a more shared mode of service in church, with a more corporate and less individualistic focus. Without question evangelical congregations will involve more trained laity in carrying out a wider band of ministry in and outside the local church. It is theologically interesting that the charismatic influence brings with it a greater sense of the ministry of the body, and this in turn ensures a counterweight to individualistic spiritual 'enthusiasm'. Ideally the Spirit and church order are complementary, not antagonistic, and a strong corporate dimension fosters this integration.

Evangelicals must become more evangelical, more prepared to look to Jesus and to the mode of Kingdom life he portrays, in order to enrich spirituality and to promote the good works of caring for the needy, for example, which are currently perceived to be preserves of the 'catholic' and 'liberal' constituencies. Why should this be so? A defensive mindset, reacting against other strands of Anglicanism, has arrested the development of such key elements of church ministry. True evangelicalism is not wooden dogmatism, nor simply warm-hearted pietism, but genuinely Christological and apostolic. If this agenda controls future developments in ministry, then they can be gladly anticipated by all sections of the Church of England and beyond.

Notes

1. The Book of Common Prayer, The Ordering of Priests.
2. Eduard Schillebeeckx, *Ministry: a case for change* (SCM, London, 1981), p. 48.

3. This is Westcott's commentary on the text in John's Gospel in which Jesus says to the disciples, 'If you forgive the sins of any they are forgiven; if you retain the sins of any, they are retained', John. 20.23. Westcott, *St John* (James Clarke, London, 1880 [1958]), p. 295.
4. J.B. Lightfoot, 'The Christian Ministry', in *Dissertations on the Apostolic Age* (Macmillan, London, 1892), p. 236.
5. See for example the report of General Synod entitled *Episcopal Ministry: The Report of the Archbishops' Group on the Episcopate* (Church House Publishing, London, 1990), p. 21: 'That community might, in time, come to consist of several worshipping congregations in a "diocese". But in the episcopal Churches it has remained spiritually and structurally the "local church"...'
6. This ministry of *episcope* is structured in synodal form by the German Lutherans, who regard their regional synods as ensuring that ministry is being carried out, the word preached, sacraments ministered and praxis enacted. Evangelical Anglicans are likely to accept that this is a legitimate mode of *episcope*, forced on the German church by the contingencies of history.
7. W. Telfer, *The Office of a Bishop* (Darton, Longman and Todd, London, 1962).
8. An attempt to state this can be found in my *The Olive Branch* (Paternoster Press, Carlisle, 1992), pp. 285ff.
9. *By What Authority? The Open Synod Group report on authority in the Church of England*, ed., R. Jeffrey, (Mowbray, London and Oxford, 1987), p. 75.
10. Colin Buchanan, 'Anglican Evangelicalism: The State of the "Party"', in *Anvil* vol. 1. 1 1984, pp. 7ff, gives a good account of this development.
11. *The Nottingham Statement: the official statement of the second National Evangelical Anglican Congress held in April 1977* (Church Pastoral Aid Society, London, 1977).
12. J.I. Packer, *A Kind of Noah's Ark: the Anglican Commitment to Comprehensiveness* (Latimer House, Oxford, 1981) demonstrates this intra-Anglican ecumenism by a conservative evangelical.
13. ibid., p. 34.
14. ibid., pp. 35–6.
15. Packer notes the following points as being broadly accepted: the supremacy of Scripture, the majesty of the redeemer Jesus Christ, the sanctifying presence of the Holy Spirit, the need for conversion as convertedness, the priority of evangelism and the fellowship of believers as the essence of the church's life. ibid., p. 6.
16. 'Enthusiasm', says Rack, 'was the bugbear of decent and ordinary Anglicans, and was a charge which in many ways included all others, for it implied not only religious excess but also social subversion.' Henry Rack, *Reasonable Enthusiast: John Wesley and the Rise of Methodism* (Epworth, London, 1992), p. 275.
17. Peter Brown, *The Cult of the Saints* (SCM, London, 1981), p. 106.

18. op. cit., p. 6.
19. 'The sort of pietism which withdraws from all constructive links with the church and the world save those with other evangelicals should not ... be seen as an evangelical Anglican norm.' Packer, op. cit., p. 7.
20. D. Bebbington, *Evangelicalism in Modern Britain* (Unwin Hyman, London, 1989), p. 19.
21. Anthony Thiselton's *The Two Horizons: New Testament Hermeneutics and Philosophical Description with special reference to Heidegger, Bultmann, Gadamer and Wittgenstein* (Paternoster Press, Exeter, 1980) constitutes one of the major contributions from scholars in the evangelical tradition.
22. An interesting indicator of the spectrum of opinion within evangelical Anglicanism on this can be found in the debate between Cray and Benn recorded in the account of the Anglican Evangelical Assembly 1995 entitled *Rough Places Plain* (Latimer House, Oxford, 1996), pp. 96–106.
23. *Rough Places Plain*, op. cit., p. 41.
24. For example, Robert Warren, *Building Missionary Congregations* (Church House Publishing, London 1995), Board of Mission Occasional Paper no. 4.
25. L. Newbigin, *The Reunion of the Church* (SCM, London, 1948).
26. Grace Davie's telling phrase which appears in the title of her sociological analysis, *Religion in Britain since 1945: Believing without Belonging* (Blackwell, Oxford, 1994).
27. John Drane, *What is the New Age Saying to the Church?* (Marshall Pickering, London, 1991), p. 236.
28. Dave Tomlinson in *The Post Evangelical* (Triangle, London, 1995), p. 20, describes the growth of these interdenominational events involving hundreds of thousands of young people.
29. Ernst Troeltsch, *The Social Teaching of the Christian Churches* (George Allen and Unwin, London, 1931).
30. The same fissure is being opened up as some evangelicals are being weaned from the apostolic ethic on homosexual practice, on the ground that the personal narrative of homosexuals affirms such practice. Liberal evangelicalism is a regular feature of Anglican history as shown in *Some Tendencies in British Theology*, J.K. Mozley, (SPCK, London, 1952) as well as Bebbington, supra note 20.
31. *God's Reign and Our Unity: The Report of the Anglican–Reformed International Commission*, (SPCK/St Andrew Press, London/Edinburgh, 1984), p. 70.
32. H.H. Gerth and C.W. Mills (eds.), *From Max Weber: Lectures in Sociology* (London, Routledge, 1984).
33. Alasdair MacIntyre, *After Virtue* (Duckworth, London, 1992), p. 72.
34. Gerard Hughes, *The God of Surprises* (Darton, Longman and Todd, London, 1985) being a good example.

7

Education and Schooling

Leslie J. Francis

Introduction

It is a matter of empirical fact that, as the twentieth century draws to a close, the Church of England remains significantly involved in the fields of education and schooling. The most visible presence is within the state maintained sector of schooling through voluntary aided, voluntary controlled, voluntary special agreement and church-related grant maintained schools. According to figures provided by the Department for Education and Employment, at January 1995, 4,615 primary schools (including middle schools deemed primary) and 204 secondary schools (including middle schools deemed secondary) belonged to the Church of England. Within Wales a further 180 primary and five secondary schools also belong to the Anglican church. Additionally, a significant proportion of schools outside the state maintained sector claim some relationship with the Church of England either in their constitution, their board of governors, or their promotional literature. At the post-secondary level, the Church of England's presence is seen in eight free-standing colleges of higher education and in partnership with other institutions in three institutes of higher education and one university. One further Anglican college of higher education remains in Wales.

This significant institutional presence is said to allow the Church of England's voice to be heard at the highest level of educational policy and practice in England.

Even a memory for recent history, however, will recall that this not insignificant presence in education is a paler reflection of a more substantial presence. The 4,795 Anglican primary schools in England and Wales (including middle deemed primary) recorded in 1995 have survived from the 8,251 primary schools (including all age schools) recorded in 1953. The colleges of higher education recorded in 1995 have survived from the twenty-five colleges recorded in 1969.

In order to shape the educational agenda for the Church of England of the twenty-first century, it is necessary to assess the roots from which the Church of England's strength in education emerged, to evaluate the trends which have shaped the present situation, and to identify the major issues which have to be faced. These proper tasks, however, need to be set against the backcloth of the more general failure of the Church of England in the recent past to take seriously its historical investment in and commitment to education.

Voices from outside

The clarity with which the Church of England perceived its role in education and schooling during the latter part of the twentieth century is best assessed not by reviewing the public statements of the Board of Education but by listening to the perceptions of the wider church. Such perceptions emerge most clearly from those bodies and reports which attempt to take an overview of the Church of England.

In theory, at least, the Partners in Mission Consultation held in 1981 enabled internal and external partners to construct and to assess a picture of the Church of England as a whole. For ten days the external partners visited seventeen dioceses, attending services, meetings, parties and house groups. They spoke with bishops, clergy, teachers, churchwardens and church members at every level. They visited Church House, the Church Commissioners and Lambeth Palace. The internal partners included the General Secretary of the General Synod Board of Education.

Having observed what was happening in practice and having listened to the theory, the Partners in Mission Consultation was far from convinced that the Church of England was deploying its resources committed to education in the most efficient and effective manner. In particular the partners recommended a radical withdrawal from institutional involvement in schools and colleges.

> The Church itself should consider making more of its resources available to help 16–19 year olds ... The proceeds of the sale of many church schools and colleges of education should be used for this, even if it requires a change in the law to enable this to happen.
>
> The churches ecumenically should undertake a major review of church schools, retaining only those which can be seen to have a particular mission in the community as a whole.[1]

A more recent insight into the way in which the Church of England's involvement in education is perceived is provided by the Report of the Archbishops' Commission on the Organisation of the Church of England, *Working as One Body*.[2] This time the clues are provided by both what is not said and by what is said.

Working as One Body begins by locating the task of the commission within the context of what is defined as the three fold mission of the local church. The components of this three fold mission are characterised as worship, service and witness. Each component is discussed briefly and illustrated. No mention is made of education, schools and colleges. An analysis is offered of the local resources available to promote the three fold mission in terms of people, buildings and money. Each area of resource is itemised. The people include priests and bishops alongside the dedicated laity 'who sustain the church by their giving and voluntary service'. The buildings include churches, cathedrals, parsonages and houses for bishops, as well as diocesan and national offices. The money includes historical and contemporary sources. No mention is made of church schools and church colleges, their historic endowments and contemporary value, or the professionally-trained men and women who run and resource them. A case is made for the number of partnerships to which the Church of England has obligations and from which it derives benefits. These partnerships include relationships with other denominations, the Anglican communion, voluntary missionary agencies, and the state as embodied in establishment. No mention is made of the partnership in education, in spite of the continued emphasis on this notion promoted by Board of Education publications as underpinned by the green paper *A Future in Partnership*.[3] These are the clues provided by what is not said.

Working as One Body proposes a new central structure comprising four main areas of work. The four areas of work are defined as resources for ministry, mission resources, heritage and legal services, and finance. Under this new structure the Board of Education would become part of mission resources, alongside the Board of Mission, the Board for Christian Unity and the Board for Social Responsibility. These are the clues provided by what is said. The first clue is provided by the notional downgrading of the chair of the Board of Education and the General Secretary of the Board. Such downgrading is not designed to enhance the parity with which the Board of Education is able to meet with the Minister of State for Education to forward the historic partnership in which Church and State have promoted the education of the nation's children. The second clue is provided by subsuming the work of education within the overall description of mission. Such nomenclature is not designed to allay suspicions entertained either by the secular community or by the other faith communities regarding the Church of England's motivation for involvement within the state maintained sector of education.

Historical roots

To the observer from outside, uninformed about the history of education in England, the Church of England's involvement in schooling presents three puzzles. The first puzzle concerns the sheer number of church schools, both in terms of those that remain active and open and in terms of the closed schools where the buildings have been converted to other uses. The second puzzle concerns the distribution of church schools, with emphases placed in the primary sector, in rural areas and in maintaining small schools. The third puzzle concerns the principles on which the schools are operated. While Jewish schools within the state maintained sector appear to have been established to serve the Jewish community and Roman Catholic schools within the state maintained sector appear to have been established to serve the Catholic community, the Church of England state maintained schools appear to have been established to serve the local neighbourhood. The clue to all three puzzles lies in the fact that the original initiative to provide education for England's children was taken not by the state but by voluntary societies.[4]

The crucial initiative was taken in 1808 when a group of Free Churchmen founded the Royal Lancasterian Society from which the British and Foreign School Society emerged in 1814, supported primarily by nonconformists and some liberal Anglicans. British schools were established to promote 'the education of the labouring and manufacturing classes of society of every religious persuasion'. Religious instruction in British schools was confined to scripture and 'general Christian principles'. It was one of the society's original rules that 'The lessons for reading shall consist of extracts from the holy scriptures; no catechism or peculiar religious tenets shall be taught in the schools, but every child shall be enjoined to attend regularly the place of worship to which its parents belong.'

The National Society was founded in 1811 as a direct response to the Royal Lancasterian Society and had the backing of the great body of Anglicans. National schools were established to promote 'the education of the poor in the principles of the established church'. Religious instruction in National schools was to include the doctrines, catechism and liturgy of the established church. In its early days the

National Society was willing to be liberal in its outlook and made allowances for children whose parents objected to the religious instruction given in the schools. The Royal Commission of 1818 made it clear that at this stage 'The church catechism is only taught and attendance at the established place of worship only required of those whose parents belong to the establishment.' Later, however, National schools generally took a harder line and insisted on attendance for religious instruction and attendance at an Anglican church on Sunday as conditions of entry to the school.

Very soon the greater resources of the National Society, in association with the parochial clergy, enabled it to draw ahead of the British and Foreign School Society. By 1830 the National Society had established 3,678 schools, educating approximately 346,000 children.

The state did not enter the field of public education until 1833, and then it did so not by establishing state schools, but by distributing public funds to the National Society and the British and Foreign School Society. A government grant of £20,000 was distributed between the two societies to assist with school building. The government grant was essentially in 'aid of private subscription', being available only to those voluntary bodies which could raise the first half of building costs and guarantee to meet all future running costs. Because of the greater voluntary resources available to the Church of England, by 1839 about 80 per cent of the state grant went to Anglican schools.

In 1839 a committee of the Privy Council was set up 'to superintend the allocation of any sums voted by Parliament for the purpose of promoting education'. Between 1833 and 1870 the state continued to contribute to public education solely through the administrative system provided by voluntary societies. In 1847 the state was spending £100,000 on education; a decade later it was spending £500,000. In 1847 it was spending public money only on school buildings; a decade later it was contributing towards teachers' salaries, the provision of apparatus and, by means of capitation grants, towards the annual income of the schools.

With the provision of state grants, the number of schools established under the sponsorship of the two societies continued to grow. By 1851 there were 17,015 Church of England schools with nearly 956,000 pupils, and 1,500 nonconformist schools with 225,000 pupils.

By the 1850s the Methodist Conference and the Catholic hierarchy had also established machinery to receive grants from the state to build schools. The overall consequence of leaving school building to voluntary initiative was threefold. In areas where denominational rivalry was strong and well-financed, denominational schools were built to compete one with another. In areas where the Church of England retained a monopoly on resources the Anglican school became the only option. In areas of rapid industrial expansion, where schools were most needed but where neither church nor chapel were well resourced, educational provision remained erratic. When the 1870 Elementary Education Act established the machinery of school boards for building schools in areas where voluntary provision was inadequate, the intention was to supplement the work of the denominational societies, not to supplant them. By the end of the nineteenth century voluntary provision still accounted for 71 per cent of the nation's schools.

Legacy of the 1944 Education Act

Although church schools came under increasing financial pressure during the first four decades of the twentieth century, by the time of the 1944 Education Act the churches still owned a sufficiently high proportion of the nation's schools to place them in a very strong position to influence the details of that act. The partnership between church and state in state maintained education as we know it today is a direct result of the way in which the power of the churches was used.[5]

The 1944 Education Act set out to reconstitute the educational system after the Second World War. At the heart of its thinking was provision of secondary education for all. To make this possible a large number of schools required extension, modernisation and re-equipment; new senior schools were needed. On the one hand, the churches could not afford to maintain their voluntary schools and to bring them up to the new standards required. On the other hand, the state could not afford to buy up the church schools and was reluctant to annex them. In short, the denominational schools presented a major political problem.

The compromise achieved by the 1944 Education Act enabled the churches to give up some of their control over church schools in return for greater control over certain aspects of the rest of the state maintained sector of schools. There were three components to this compromise. The first component established school worship as obligatory in all state maintained schools. Although collective acts of worship had been a major feature of the English educational scene, they had never previously been made a statutory obligation. The second component made religious instruction obligatory in all county schools and specified that such instruction shall be in accordance with a locally agreed syllabus. Moreover the churches, and the Church of England in particular, were guaranteed a key role in determining the content of the locally agreed syllabus. The third component extended to voluntary schools the choice between 'aided' or 'controlled' status. This choice enabled schools which could afford to retain a high level of independence to do so, while those that either could not afford or did not desire to retain such a high level of independence could nevertheless retain something of their church-related character.

The voluntary aided school approximated the status of the non-provided school, and involved the churches in continued financial liability. The managers or governors of a voluntary aided school were responsible for the capital expenditure on alterations required by the local education authority to keep the premises up to standard, for external repairs, improvements and extensions to school buildings. Government grant aid was made available to meet 50 per cent of these costs. In return for their continued financial involvement, the churches retained the right to appoint a majority of the school managers or governors and to provide denominational religious instruction and denominational worship. If the managers or governors of a voluntary aided school decide that they no longer wish or can afford to maintain voluntary aided status, the school may become voluntary controlled.

The voluntary controlled school gave the churches reduced rights, but involved no ongoing financial liability. In this case, the churches retained the right to appoint a minority of the school managers or governors. Religious instruction is given according to the agreed syllabus, but parents may ask for denominational teaching 'during not more than two periods each week'. Provided the teaching staff of the voluntary controlled school exceeds two, up to one-fifth of the staff can be 'selected for their fitness and competence to give such religious instruction'. These are called 'reserved teachers'. The daily act of worship is in accordance with the trust deed and may, therefore, be denominational in character. Once a voluntary school had accepted controlled status, the act made no provision whereby the school could become aided.

The denominations responded differently to the compromise offered by the 1944 Education Act. Free Church opinion generally considered that the provisions for worship and religious education in county schools obviated the need for continued investment in church schools. The Roman Catholic Church rejected the greater state influence over voluntary controlled schools and opted for voluntary aided status. The Church of England remained divided on the issue. Some Anglicans, like Bishop Brook of St Edmundsbury and Ipswich, adopted the view that the Christian presence in education could best be preserved through non-denominational religious education in county schools. He argued that 'It is my conviction that so far as religious education is concerned it is neither buildings, syllabuses, nor timetables that matter most. What matters is that the teachers in all the schools whether voluntary or county shall be Christian men and women.' Others, like Bishop Kirk of Oxford, took a completely different line: 'Undenominationalism is the first step on the road to complete irreligion, and ... true religion is only possible by virtue of active and loyal membership in a worshipping community. Our church schools are essential means towards making our witness effective; we must not let them go.'

In the absence of an agreed central policy on the comparable merits of voluntary aided and voluntary controlled status, each diocese formulated its own recommendations, which the school governors within its area could choose to follow or to ignore, at least as far as their independent sources of finance would permit. Some dioceses, like London, Southwark and Blackburn, opted heavily for voluntary aided status; other dioceses, like Bristol, York, Coventry and Lichfield, opted mainly for voluntary controlled status.

Legislative context

Following the 1944 Education Act, government initiatives and educational legislation left the church school issue relatively unaffected until the early 1980s, apart from three significant developments. The first of these developments had positive implications for church schools, while the other two developments had negative implications.

The first issue concerned the cost to the church of maintaining voluntary aided schools. According to the settlement of the 1944 Education Act government grant aid was made available to meet 50 per cent of the capital costs borne by the governors. Right from the outset the Catholic authorities argued the injustice of the financial burden carried by the church, in comparison with the much more favourable arrangement secured in Scotland under the 1918 Education Act.[6] During the years after the 1944 Education Act, the churches' inability to meet their financial commitment to church schools became increasingly clear. In subsequent legislation the government grant was raised in three stages: to 75 per cent in 1959, 80 per cent in 1967 and 85 per cent in 1974. While these increases were generous in comparison with the expectations set in 1944, they may not have been sufficiently generous to compensate for the disparity between rising costs and dwindling church resources. The nature of the problem was well reflected in the title of a working party report prepared in 1972 by the Schools Committee of the General Synod Board of Education, *Crisis in Church Schools: a report on finance*.[7]

The second issue concerned the structuring of secondary education proposed by the government circular 10/65. The reorganisation of secondary education had one important implication for primary schools. In requesting local education authorities to submit plans for comprehensive reorganisation, circular 10/65 listed a system of middle and upper schools, either of nine–thirteen and thirteen–eighteen or eight–twelve and twelve–eighteen, as one legitimate way of implementing change.[8] Local education authorities which opted for middle schools immediately placed two pressures on the Church of England dioceses to which they related. The first pressure concerned the decapitation of church primary schools. Given the fact that a high proportion of church schools are small rural schools, the removal of the upper classes of primary pupils reduced the total number of pupils below the level of viability. The second pressure concerned the financing of new middle schools deemed large enough to satisfy government criteria for secondary reorganisation.

In a detailed analysis of the response of one rural diocese, St Edmundsbury and Ipswich, to the challenge of circular 10/65, Francis documented the rapid closure of church schools in the villages and the inability of the church to develop a viable network of middle schools.[9] One particular minute of the diocesan education committee summed up the situation: 'The position of the Church of England was most uncertain, there being no money to implement proposals.'

The third issue concerned the question of small schools. This debate was re-established by the Plowden Report in 1967. Here the case against small schools was advanced in educational terms, suggesting that small schools can restrict their pupils' social, emotional and intellectual development, limit their social opportunities to mix with their peers, deprive them of the benefit of working within the range of teachers needed to offer different skills, and curtail their acquaintance with educational resources, curriculum materials and extracurricular activities.[10] The case against small schools was bad news for the Church of England's large investment in small rural primary schools. This pressure on small schools was exacerbated during the 1980s by increasing financial concerns. For example, in 1981 the government circular *Falling Rolls and Surplus Places* advised a minimum primary school size of 100 pupils, while the White Paper, *Better Schools*, in 1985 recommended that schools catering for five–eleven year olds should have at least one form of entry.[11] The continued importance of this issue for the Church of England is reflected in two booklets published by National Society in 1991 and 1995 respectively, *The Future of Small Schools*[12] and *Small Schools*.[13]

From 1980 onwards the impact of legislation on church schools accelerated considerably. In a paper presented to the first international symposium on church school studies, convened in Durham during July 1996, David Lankshear examined the impact of the following legislation on church schools: the 1980 Education Act, the 1981 Education Act, the 1986 Education (No. 2) Act, the 1988 Education Reform Act, the 1992 Education (Schools) Act, the 1993 Education Act, the 1994 Education Act and the 1996 Nursery Education and Grant Maintained Schools Act.[14]

The 1980 Education Act changed the constitution of governing bodies and strengthened the role and responsibilities of governors. The implications for church schools were enormous. First, in view of the autonomy of each school trust, the provision of new instruments and articles of government for Anglican schools took many years following this act, not least because of the complexity created by the need to ensure that the tradition of parochial involvement in the governing bodies was continued to the satisfaction of every parish. The response to this legislation was costly to the church. Second, the introduction of parents and teachers to the governing body began to shift the balance of power and range of opinion. While in voluntary aided schools the foundation governors continued to outnumber other governors their majority was reduced from the two-thirds guaranteed by the 1944 Education Act. Third, governors were obliged to provide a range of information for parents, including a clear statement regarding admissions policy. From this stage onwards admissions policies needed to be explicitly stated, fairly operated, and subject to appeal procedures. This proved to be no simple task for church schools.

The 1986 Education (No. 2) Act carried three implications for church schools. First, a further revision was required for the instruments of government of voluntary controlled schools, despite the fact that in some areas the instruments created under the 1980 act had not yet been implemented. This involved further administrative effort. Second, the governors of all schools were required to meet once a year with the parents and to make a report to them. The third consequence of the act might have been beneficial to the church. Since 1944 it had been possible for voluntary aided schools to become voluntary controlled, but no mechanism existed for voluntary controlled schools to become voluntary aided. The 1986 act at last provided a route for voluntary controlled schools to gain or regain voluntary aided status.

In view of the difficulty and costliness of this route, few schools have benefitted from the change in law.

The most significant issue to face church schools as a consequence of the 1988 Education Reform Act concerned the option of grant maintained status.[15] On the surface there appeared to be many advantages to the church in opting for grant maintained status. As far as the religious provision of the school is concerned, the same principles apply as to the status prior to opting out. In other words, grant maintained schools which were formerly voluntary controlled can continue to provide denominational worship, while grant maintained schools which were formerly voluntary aided can continue to provide denominational religious education as well as denominational worship. The advantage of opting out for the voluntary aided school is that governors cease to be responsible for 15 per cent of capital expenditure. The advantage of opting out for the voluntary controlled school is that, having opted out, the foundation is responsible for appointing a majority of governors, rather than a minority as applied to voluntary controlled status.

The National Society and General Synod Board of Education greeted the opportunity for grant maintained status with caution. A booklet published in 1988 included the following two warnings.[16]

> Governors of Church schools will need carefully to balance a proper self-interest with a Christian concern for the effects of their actions on the rest of the maintained system in their area. Going grant-maintained may be a means of escaping threats of closure or grudging ministrations from an unsympathetic local authority. It may also be a means of an already privileged, strong school gaining more privileges and becoming stronger at the expense of other schools (including church schools) in the area.
>
> The absence of any continuing financial input from the church could strengthen the arm of any future government wishing to abolish church schools.

The second challenge faced by church schools as a consequence of the 1988 Education Reform Act concerns the claims that the act has given to other schools much of the autonomy previously only enjoyed by church schools. As a consequence the church has needed to become clearer about the distinctive role of church schools within the state maintained system in order to justify its continued involvement.

Thirdly, the 1988 Education Reform Act made the provision of Standing Advisory Councils for Religious Education a statutory requirement on all local education authorities. The distinctive role of the Church of England within the structure of the Standing Advisory

Councils for Religious Education has raised the wider expectations placed on diocesan education teams.

The 1992 Education (Schools) Act developed a whole new system of school inspection. According to this system all schools became subject to a regular inspection conducted by the Office for Standards in Education, at four-yearly intervals. Within the act this became known as section 9 inspection. Church schools also became subject to a separate denominational inspection, known as section 13 inspection. In voluntary controlled schools section 13 inspection concerned the school worship, while in voluntary aided schools section 13 inspection concerned the religious education as well as the worship. In addition the governors could invite the section 13 inspectors to report on the wider school ethos. The National Society responded to the challenge of section 13 inspection by establishing a training programme for inspectors and by developing appropriate guidelines and literature.[17] Under the 1996 School Inspections Act, section 13 inspection became known as section 23 inspection and section 9 inspection became known as section 10 inspection.

The 1993 Education Act strengthened the government's commitment to promoting grant maintained status. As a result of this act, governing bodies of all county and voluntary schools were required to review annually the status of their school and decide whether or not to become grant maintained. Revising its guidelines on grant maintained status, the General Synod Board of Education continued to remain cautious, although recognising that the progressive weakening of local education authorities in some areas vitiated the old model of partnership.[18]

> Church school governors, in deciding whether or not to apply for grant-maintained status, will consider the gains and losses for their own school, but the decision will not rest there. *Every church school is a part of the church's total participation in the education system of the nation* and governing bodies need to reflect on the impact of their decision on other schools in the locality and on the churches' total contribution to the national system of education.

The 1994 Education Act promoted the development of school-based initial teacher training. This development carried two implications for the Church of England's involvement in education. The first implication concerns the proper participation of Church of England voluntary aided and voluntary controlled schools within the overall provision of initial teacher training. Church schools may be disadvantaged in the sense that they tend to be both small and rural. In this case fewer teachers may be exposed to the church school experience during their initial training. The second implication concerns the role of the church colleges of higher education which have traditionally relied heavily on the intake of students for initial teacher training courses.

The 1996 Nursery and Grant Maintained Education Act promoted the development of nursery vouchers. This development has left church schools with an opportunity, but raises a crucial question regarding the adequacy of resources with which to respond to this opportunity.

Challenges to church schools

The Church of England's continued involvement within the state maintained sector of education is not without significant and formidable challenge. In particular three main sources of challenge need to be recognised.

The first challenge to church schools is rooted in educational philosophy. The best known proponent of this challenge is Professor Paul Hirst, whose position is summarised in two key papers.[19] In the first paper, published in *Learning for Living* in 1972, Hirst argues that the concept of 'Christian education' is a contradiction in terms. On this account, the theologian is precluded from making a distinctive contribution to *educational* theory. In the second paper, published in the *British Journal of Religious Education* in 1981, Hirst extends the argument to church schools. On this account, the church school is precluded from making a distinctive contribution to *educational* practice. The main strand in Hirst's argument rests on his understanding of what is to count as education; another strand rests on his analysis of the educational implications of secularisation.

Hirst's first point is that 'there has already emerged in our society' a concept of education, according to which education constitutes an area of discourse autonomous in its own right. Hirst (1976) illustrates what he means by this autonomy by developing the parallel between education and science. He argues that:

> Just as intelligent Christians have come to recognise that justifiable scientific claims are autonomous and do not, and logically cannot, rest on religious beliefs, so also, it seems to me, justifiable educational principles are autonomous. That is to say that any attempt to justify educational principles by an appeal to religious claims is invalid. I am anxious that the terrible story of the long battle which Christianity waged and lost over science and religion be no longer repeated in the area of education and religion.

For Hirst, to speak of Christian education is a misleading anachronism.

Hirst's second point draws a distinction between a *primitive* and a *sophisticated* concept of education. The primitive concept is 'concerned with passing on to children what we believe, so that they in turn come to believe it to be true'. The sophisticated concept is not 'determined by what any group simply believes but by what on publicly acknowledged rational grounds we can claim to know and understand'. The goal of the sophisticated concept of education is to develop 'a rationally autonomous person whose life is self directed in the light of what reason determines'.

Hirst argues that, because of their religious beliefs, Christians are involved in the primitive concept of education. It is, however, the sophisticated concept of education which has a place in schools and which excludes the possibility of a distinctively Christian contribution to the curriculum. Hirst argues that according to the sophisticated view of education:

> The character of education is not settled by any appeal to Christian, Humanist or Buddhist beliefs. Such an appeal is illegitimate, for the basis is logically more fundamental, being found in the canons of objectivity and reason, canons against which Christian, Humanist and Buddhist beliefs must, in their turn and in the appropriate way, be assessed. When the domain of religious beliefs is so manifestly one in which there are at present no clearly recognisable objective grounds for judging claims, to base education on any such claims would be to forsake the pursuit of objectivity.

Hirst's third point is to develop a distinction between *education* and *catechesis*: 'In catechesis ... the aim is from the stance of faith, the development of faith.' Hirst argues that when the churches are in business to educate, they need to play by the same rules as secular schools; when the churches are involved in catechesis, they cannot be said to be engaging in education. While theologians may contribute to the theory and practice of catechesis, they are firmly excluded from being allowed a contribution to the theory and practice of education.

Hirst's fourth point is that church schools need to take seriously the distinction between education and catechesis. According to this argument, the two activities obey different rules and are in fact logically incompatible. A school undertaking both activities would find itself 'at one and the same time committed to trying to develop commitment to reason and commitment to a particular faith'. The consequence of attempting to combine these incompatible activities would be confusion for both pupils and teachers.

While Hirst does not pursue his case to its logical conclusion of arguing that church schools, like Christian education, are necessarily a contradiction in terms, he does wish to impose stringent limitations on the church school. According to Hirst, the important condition that can legitimate church schools being involved both in education and catechesis is that these two activities are 'sharply separated within the school, being self-consciously and deliberately presented to the pupils as clearly different in character and objectives'. In practice, this means separating the two activities both in time and place and by the use of quite different personnel to make out the differences between those involved in 'teaching' and 'preaching'.

Thus, Hirst is not simply arguing that there are difficulties either in formulating a coherent theological understanding of education or in putting this understanding to work through church schools. He is arguing that the very *logic of education* outlaws the possibility of the churches having a distinctive contribution to make to educational theory and practice. Hirst's argument did much to undermine the church's self-confidence in church schools before considered responses began to challenge this position.[20]

The second challenge to church schools is rooted in an analysis of the implications of denominational schooling for social integration within a multi-cultural society. The sharpest presentation of this position was advanced by the committee of inquiry into the education of children from ethnic minority groups in the report, *Education for All*.[21] After reviewing the arguments for and against voluntary schools for other ethnic and religious groups, the majority voice of the committee stresses 'misgivings about the implications and consequences of "separate" provision of any kind'. Having come to this view, the majority voice of the committee faces the consequence that 'our conclusions about the desirability of denominational voluntary aided schools for Muslims or other groups, by extension seriously call into question the long established dual system of educational provision in this country and particularly the role of the churches in the provision of education'. Six members of the committee dissented from this conclusion and formulated a different minority recommendation, supporting the provisions of the 1944 Education Act concerning voluntary schools and wishing to enable other ethnic and religious groups to benefit from these provisions. 'We believe that it is unjust at the present time not to recommend that positive assistance should be given to ethnic minority communities who wish to establish voluntary aided schools in accordance with the 1944 Education Act.'

In an oral statement to the House of Commons on the afternoon of 14 March 1985, following the publication of the Swann Report, Sir

Keith Joseph, Secretary of State for Education, gave an immediate assurance that the government does not 'wish in any way to call in question the present dual system of county and voluntary schools'. The clear division of opinion within the committee of inquiry, together with the Education Secretary's immediate response, added a new sharpness and immediacy to the debate about the future of church schools within a multi-cultural society.

The year before the publication of *Education for All*, reports from both the Roman Catholic Church[22] and the Church of England[23] had given consideration to this issue. The Anglican report, *Schools and Multi-Cultural Education*, specifically emphasised the view that church schools can function as important centres of reconciliation among people of different races and creeds.

The third challenge to church schools is rooted in an analysis of the implications of denominational schooling for equality of educational opportunity. The sharpest presentation of this position has been advanced in a series of papers from the Socialist Education Association. In their 1981 discussion document, *The Dual System of Voluntary and County Schools*, a key appendix focuses on two primary objections to church schools.[24] The first objection concerns the problem of religious privilege in a pluralist society. This objection acknowledges that, if certain churches are permitted to operate voluntary schools, every sect and faith should be allowed the same privilege. It is argued that this would lead to 'divisive sectarianism and some of the difficulties already evident in a place like Northern Ireland'. The second objection concerns the political problem of privilege itself within a socialist educational system. This objection argues that 'the continuing existence of the segregated voluntary school sector will frustrate the achievement of the truly comprehensive system'.

The Socialist Education Association's 1986 document, *All Faiths in All Schools*, reports that the majority of those who sent comments on the original document supported the view expressed in this appendix.[25] The new report proposes:

> The eventual establishment of a new unified system of maintained schools, in which voluntary schools – without sacrificing their ethos and individual approach – could gradually develop the capacity to educate a greater diversity of intake from their own local communities, and where county schools – without sacrificing their unifying secular approach – could gradually develop the capacity to meet more widely the religious and cultural needs of their intakes.

In 1990 the Socialist Education Association again confirmed the policy on voluntary aided and voluntary controlled schools, demanding that no new such schools should be opened and requested that the Labour front-bench teams conduct talks with the churches regarding transferring voluntary schools to the county sector.[26]

With such weight of criticism, there is clear need for the Church of England to maintain a coherent agenda for church schools into the twenty-first century.

Empirical context

During the past fifty years the study of education has clearly developed in Britain as a discipline grounded in empirical methods.[27] Given both the politically sensitive nature of the issues raised by church schools and the size of the contribution which Anglican schools make to the state maintained sector of education in England, it is surprising that so little educational research has focused on the character, distinctiveness and effectiveness of Anglican schools. Existing research in this area can best be summarised under six main headings.

The first strand of research has focused on the pupils who attend Church of England schools. Four separate studies have employed attitude scaling techniques and multiple regression to assess the comparative influence of Church of England schools on their pupils' religiosity. In a paper in *British Educational Research Journal* Francis reported on three studies conducted in East Anglia in 1974, 1978 and 1982 to assess the comparative influence of Church of England, Roman Catholic and county schools on the religious attitudes of their year five and year six pupils.[28] All three studies point to the positive influence of Catholic schools and the negative influence of Anglican schools on pupil attitudes, after using path analysis to control for other influences, like sex, age, church and home. In *Religion in the Primary School* Francis examined the religious attitudes of year six pupils in Roman Catholic, Church of England and county school in Gloucestershire.[29] This study, too, pointed to the positive influence of Roman Catholic primary schools on pupils' attitudes toward Christianity. In this study Church of England voluntary aided primary schools exerted neither a positive nor a negative influence, while Church of England voluntary controlled schools were found to exert a negative influence. At the secondary level, Francis and Carter examined the religious attitudes of pupils in year eleven attending Church of England voluntary aided, Roman Catholic voluntary aided and county schools.[30] These findings provided no support for the notion that church voluntary aided secondary schools exert a positive influence on their pupils' attitudes toward religion. A second study by Francis and Jewell among year ten pupils attending the four county and the one Church of England voluntary secondary schools serving the area around the same town also found that the Church of England school exerted neither a positive nor a negative influence on its pupils' religious practice, belief or attitude.[31]

A fifth study by Levitt undertook a longitudinal case study among 38 families in Cornwall from Penvollard county junior school, the Church of England voluntary aided school and a neighbouring voluntary aided village school.[32] The author concludes that this study 'points to the possibility that Anglican schools are popular because they are seen as "good" schools which do not affect children's religiosity unduly'.

The second strand of research has focused on the parishes which support church schools. Francis and Lankshear reported two studies conducted in rural[33] and urban[34] areas to assess the impact of Church of England primary schools on quantitative indicators of local church life. Both studies point to the positive impact of church schools on church life, after using path analysis to control for other influences, like the size of the parish, the church electoral roll and the age of the priest. For example, in rural areas the presence of a church school is shown to augment slightly the village church's usual Sunday contact with 6–9 year olds and with adults. The presence of a church school is also shown to have a small positive influence on the number of infant baptisms, the number of 6–13 year olds in the village church choir and the number of young confirmands under the age of 14 years.

The third strand of research has focused on whether in practice Church of England voluntary aided and voluntary controlled primary schools display a different religious ethos and character from county schools. In a detailed study of the primary schools in Gloucestershire Francis found that, although the church schools were serving specific local neighbourhoods in the same way as county schools, they continued to express more signs of church-relatedness than county schools.[35] Church of England schools in Gloucestershire encouraged more contact with the clergy and with the church. They held more explicitly Christian assemblies and gave more emphasis to the church-related aspects of religious education.

O'Keeffe conducted research in 102 county secondary and Church of England secondary and primary schools in London, the North West and the West Midlands with a special concern to explore the role of church schools in multi-racial and multi-faith Britain.[36] She concludes that: 'For the most part church schools do not admit "other faith" expressions within the area of school activity and in addition tend towards a policy of selectivity in their admission of other than Christian pupils and staff. Culture often seen as Christian, for many schools, means belonging to the historic British or European tradition.'

The fourth strand of research has focused on the governors of church schools. Gay, Kay, Newdick and Perry compared the views provided by 99 heads of Church of England primary schools and 100 chairs of governors in the Diocese of London.[37] This study revealed that 82 per cent of the chairs of governors thought that the head teachers should be practising Christians; 61 per cent thought that senior members of the teaching staff should be practising Christians; 34 per cent thought that the teachers should be practising members of a Christian church. This study is not, however, able to explore the extent to which the views of the chairs of governors reflect the views of the governing body as a whole. Kay, Piper and Gay analysed the views of 843 governors from the 81 Church of England voluntary aided primary schools in the Diocese of Oxford.[38] This study found that the foundation governors were markedly more committed to preserving the religious ethos of the school than the other members of the governing bodies. The authors conclude that 'in contrast parents of children in the school tend to value the Christian ethos of the school less. Since this is a group that we can expect to see increasing in numbers and influence, this is potentially a worrying situation for those who value the distinctiveness of the church school.' These findings are confirmed in a study among 486 governors from the 55 Church of England voluntary aided schools in the Diocese of Chichester conducted by Francis and Stone.[39] The findings from this study indicate that governors' attitudes toward the religious ethos of Church of England voluntary aided primary schools are closely related to their age, personal religious commitment and role on the governing body. More positive attitudes are held by older, churchgoing and foundation governors.

The fifth strand of research has focused on the teachers who work in Church of England schools. This strand of research may be of particular importance in understanding the dynamics which determine the distinctiveness and effectiveness of church schools on the grounds that it is the teachers themselves who implement the policy of the school and communicate that policy to the pupils. Francis analysed the views of 338 teachers employed in the 20 Church of England voluntary aided and 91 voluntary controlled first, primary and middle schools within the Diocese of St Edmundsbury and Ipswich.[40] This study demonstrated considerably more goodwill towards the church school system than antipathy against it and more support for the distinctiveness of church schools than rejection of this potential for distinctiveness. At the same time, this study also noted that there is considerable variation in the attitudes of teachers in both voluntary aided and voluntary controlled church schools.

In order to understand this variation in attitudes from one teacher to another, Francis (1986a) identified three main attitudinal clusters and constructed an attitude scale to measure each of these areas. Then he employed path analysis to model the major influences on the scores recorded on each of these scales. This analysis found that age and personal religious commitment were key predictors of attitudes toward church schools. Older teachers and churchgoing teachers held a more positive attitude toward the church school system and tended to give more emphasis to the distinctiveness of church schools. These findings suggest that, as younger teachers replace the more senior members of staff in church schools, so the desire to assert the distinctiveness of church schools will decline.

Francis' findings in St Edmundsbury and Ipswich were later tested by Wilcox and Francis in a second study in the Diocese of Newcastle.[41] This second study conducted a decade later and in a different part of England confirmed the finding that older teachers and teachers who attend church hold a more positive attitude toward church schools and are more likely to wish to emphasise the distinctiveness of church schools.

The sixth strand of research has focused on an analysis of the section 13 inspection reports which voluntary schools were required to undergo under the 1992 Education (Schools) Act. In theory these inspection reports should provide the Church of England with a regular and reliable barometer regarding the denominational aspects of church schools. In an analysis of the reports produced during the first year of mandatory inspection, 1994–5, Jane Lankshear demonstrated both the potential value of these reports and the need for the inspectors to follow tighter guidelines if the information were to be really useful to the church.[42]

With the developing body of empirically grounded information about the church school system, there is clear need for future policy to take proper account of what is known about the present situation.

Educational policy

The Church of England's original rationale for involvement in schools was clearly set out in 1811, within the terms of reference for the National Society, to promote 'the education of the poor in the principles of the established church'. Such terms of reference have needed re-evaluation and reformulation in response to social, political, cultural and religious changes. It is the Durham Report, published in 1970, which provides the coherent starting point for understanding the Church of England's policy regarding church schools during the latter part of the twentieth century.[43]

While the Durham commission was established as 'an independent commission to inquire into religious education', the report devoted a whole chapter to the discussion of church schools. This chapter made two crucial points which have shaped the Church of England's self-understanding in education throughout the rest of the twentieth century.

First, the Durham Report developed and sharpened the distinction between the Church of England's two historic motives for involvement in education. The report styled these two motives as the Church of England's *domestic* and *general* functions in education. The domestic function characterises the inward-looking concern to 'equip the children of the church to take their place in the Christian community'. The general function characterises the outward-looking concern 'to serve the nation through its children'. The Durham Report recognises that historically the two roles were 'indistinguishable, for nation and church were, theoretically, one, and the domestic task was seen as including the general'.

Second, the Durham Report evaluated the contemporary relevance of these two distinct functions and came to the conclusion that emphasis should now be placed on the general function rather than on the domestic function. Recognising that 'nowadays no one would pretend to claim that nation and church are coextensive', the Durham Report argues that the domestic task can no longer be seen as including the general task. Consequently 'the church should for the present see its continued involvement in the dual system principally as a way of expressing its concern for the general education of all children and young people rather than as a means for giving "denominational instruction".' The report underlines this point again by recommending that 'religious education, even in a church aided school, should not be seen in domestic terms'. Elsewhere the report argues that many of the difficulties associated with church schools 'would disappear if the aided school were looked on as a service provided by the church, rather than something provided for the church'.

Following the Durham Report in 1970, the Church of England's next major statement on church schools appeared in the green paper *A Future in Partnership*.[44] While the Durham Report was the result of a commission of inquiry, *A Future in Partnership* was a somewhat more personal document drafted by Robert Waddington, General Secretary to the National Society. Two main pointers emerge from this green paper. Set starkly side by side these two pointers may appear to be looking in somewhat different directions.

The first pointer builds on the Durham Report's commitment to the church's general function in education. The green paper argues that the idea of *partnership* should be stressed in preference to the *dual system* and that the *voluntary* aspects of church schools should be stressed in preference to *denominationalism*. The emphasis of this aspect of the green paper argues for a balance of power in state maintained education over an increasing trend towards educational dominance by central government. The church is seen as one component, alongside other political, community, parental and professional bodies, in an educational partnership which offsets the claims of central government in determining educational policy and practice. It is argued that the maintenance of church schools gives the church an institutional credibility in this context. On this account, the Church of England sees its rationale for involvement in education to be in terms of balance, partnership and voluntarism, rather than in terms of denominationalism, religious distinctiveness or the dual system.

The second pointer draws on the resources of theology to construct a model of church schools in the light of the doctrine of the Trinity. According to this model, church schools may be distinguished by ten key characteristics. Waddington's ten characteristics of the church school have been repeated in several subsequent National Society publications.[45] When pressed, these characteristics indicate a renewed commitment to the religious distinctiveness of church schools which goes beyond the aims of service to engage with the aim of nurture and formation.

For example, Waddington's first characteristic affirms that 'Christian inferences are built into the ethos and teaching as signals for children to detect'. The fifth characteristic defines church schools as a 'house of the gospel in which, starting at governor and staff level, there is a deliberate attempt to link the concerns of Christ's gospel with the life of the school'. The sixth characteristic sees church schools as 'a place of revelation and disclosure in which the rigour of learning and the art of acquiring skill are seen as parables of the revelation of God and his continuous involvement in his creation'. The eighth characteristic speaks of church schools as 'a beacon signalling the transcendent by the development of awe, mystery and wonder through the curriculum, exemplified in acts of corporate worship including contact with the Christian calendar and sacraments'. Such a view of distinctiveness is reinforced by the final paragraph of the green paper which begins: 'Within that web of partnership, the Christian churches must provide a distinctive contribution, one that grows out of theological reflection on the nature and practice of education. The contribution must be educationally excellent, Christian in style and content, adventurous in its willingness to face change and to create new patterns of ministry in the education service.'

The sequel to the green paper, the General Synod paper, *Positive Partnership*, returned to the analysis of the twin aims of the church's involvement in education.[46] *Positive Partnership* paraphrases the green paper's strategy for church schools and makes the claim that the green paper argued 'that in every church school even today both these aims should be consciously present – contributing to the provision of general education in the neighbourhood, and yet providing a specifically Christian form of education'.

Following the General Synod debate on *Positive Partnership* in 1985, the mind of the National Society on the nature and future of church schools is perhaps glimpsed most clearly through the writings of the Deputy Secretary and Schools Officer. Since 1985 two individuals have occupied this position, Geoffrey Duncan followed by David Lankshear. Both have written with a distinctive voice.

Geoffrey Duncan's voice emerged clearly in his chapter in the collection of essays *Faith in the Future*, published in 1986 to mark 175 years of the National Society.[47] After reviewing a number of trends in church schools Duncan concludes in this chapter that 'For Church of England schools many of the tensions will cluster around the twin aims of fulfilling a general/community role and a domestic/nurture role, discussed in some depth by the Durham Report.' He recognises that in an increasingly secular and multi-cultural society there are growing tendencies both to set up independent Christian schools and to emphasise the domestic or nurture role for voluntary aided schools. Against such trends Duncan clearly wishes to re-emphasise the service role of church schools. In a second paper, two years later, Duncan writes explicitly to the theme 'Church schools in service to the community', arguing that[48] 'Difficult as it may be to hold the tension between a school's Christian foundation and the need to serve a population that is largely non-Christian, such a model still has much mileage in it.'

While Geoffrey Duncan chose the theme of service as the central notion underpinning his writings on church schools, his successor, David Lankshear, shifted the emphasis more to distinctiveness. This transition was facilitated by the new political climate initiated by the 1988 Education Reform Act and confirmed by subsequent educational legislation. In *A Shared Vision: education in church schools*, the first question which Lankshear addresses to his readers is this. 'What differences are observable in your local community between Anglican and county schools?'[49] Beginning from a perspective grounded in empirical observation of what is actually happening in church schools, rather than in doctrinaire prescription of what should be happening in church schools, Lankshear draws out and affirms the practical evidence of distinctiveness already there.

In a second publication in 1992, *Looking for Quality in a Church School*, Lankshear once again starts from the empirical reality of the different emphases in church schools.[50] 'Some schools serve a geographically defined community and offer education to all children within the area. Other church schools offer a Church of England education mainly to the children of parents who can claim membership of the Church of England. Most church schools fall somewhere in between these two different positions.' Accepting this diversity, Lankshear argues that 'The school itself should witness to the gospel both in its daily life and in the way in which it makes contact with the communities beyond its gate. It is part of the Body of Christ and as such will recognise a special relationship with the parish, the diocese and the wider church.'

Lankshear recognises that such a view has implications for the weight given to Christian commitment in making staff appointments, participation in worship, prayers before and after meetings, and a pastoral and spiritual concern for all members of the school community.

In a third publication in 1992, *Governing Church Schools*, Lankshear makes the point that the lives of the two communities, local church and church school, should be 'so interwoven that there is never an opportunity for people at the school to feel neglected, nor for members of the church to feel ignorant about the school'.[51] In a fourth publication in 1996, *Churches Serving Schools*, Lankshear argues that church schools have a responsibility to ensure that[52] 'no one can be in any doubt that they are church schools. Such schools will demonstrate that they have a clear understanding of what it means to be the church school in the location in which it is set.'

Theology and education

A church which takes seriously its involvement in education needs to underpin such involvement in mature theological reflection. While the theology of education never appears to have been particularly high on the Anglican agenda, there are some significant indicators pointing to the value of this enterprise when properly undertaken.

With characteristic thoroughness the Durham Report devoted its second chapter to 'theology and education'.[53] The way in which this chapter conceives the theology of education is both illuminating and limiting. The chapter has four major strengths. First, the chapter provides a masterly overview of the developments in theological thinking from the early nineteenth century. Second, the chapter identifies seven key points at which the contemporary theologian needs to interact with modern thought: urbanisation, the philosophical revolution, psychology, sociology, the debate between science and religion, globalisation, and secularisation. Third, the chapter cites the field of Christian ethics as a prime example of the complexity of the interface between theology and the issues of modern living. Finally, the chapter assesses the significance of these developments for religious education at school. It considers the educational significance of the subject, the relationship between religious education and worship, the study of other religions, the moral strand in religious education, and the status of religious knowledge. In this sense the theory of religious education advanced in the report is grounded in theological reflection.

Less satisfactory, however, is the report's consideration of the application of theological reflection to wider educational issues. Nevertheless, the report raises the key question 'What are the implications [of Christian theology] for a theory and practice of education?' and speaks in terms of identifying 'the "theology of education" which lies behind our report'. The report responds to these questions by emphasising the contribution of Christian theology to key questions like critiquing the perspectives on humanity in contemporary educational thought and responding to the issue 'What kind of being is this whom we seek to educate?' The report stops short, however, of developing from these basic questions the foundations of a theology for church schools.

The green paper, *A Future in Partnership*, also includes a chapter on theology, boldly entitled, 'No apology for theology' and subtitled 'relating the Christian tradition to the life of the school'.[54] The green paper argues robustly that the education officers of the church 'have a duty to make it plain that their contributions are illuminated by faith and mature theological reflection'. At the same time the green paper recognises that these very education officers of the church have been significantly handicapped by the lack of concern which theologians have generally displayed for educational matters.

It seems strange that education, a process which helps to shape the vision humans can have of a particular cultural world and which indicates how personal and communal fulfilment within a particular society might be achieved, has aroused relatively little interest among theologians. In spite of the vigorous contributions that have been made since the 1870s to validate the contribution of the Church of England to the education service of the nation through its schools, there has been little written within the vision of faith as articulated in theology.[55]

However, the vision of faith articulated by the green paper itself remains somewhat opaque and draws on two different starting points. The author's first starting point is rooted in ecclesiology, a theological discussion of the nature of the church. Two main arguments emerge from this starting point.

The first argument sees the church as the community of the baptised. Attention is then turned to the theology of baptism and to the relative merits of open and rigorist baptism policies. Relevance for church schools is achieved by drawing parallels between baptism policies and school admission policies. Theologically such parallels can only function at a very superficial level, since the sacramental nature of baptism as the point of entry into the body of Christ necessarily involves an understanding of the activity of God which is not transferable to discussion about church schools. While church schools may be a sign of God's activity in the world, they are not sacramental in the same sense as the traditional Christian understanding of baptism and eucharist.

The second argument sees the church as the sign of the Kingdom and contrasts two opposing theologies of the relationship between the church and the world. One view sees the church attempting to direct all the energies of its members to itself and ceasing to be an effective instrument of the Kingdom in the world. The other view sees the church attempting to direct all the energies of its members to the world and ceasing to retain distinctive commitment to the Kingdom. Once again parallels are drawn between the nature of the church and the nature of church schools, emphasising the distinction between inward-looking and outward-looking admission policies. Theologically, however, such parallels only work successfully if church schools are seen as an extension of the church itself, whereas in the present system of state maintained education church schools constitute a proper hybrid, being extensions both of the church and of the secular educational system.

The author's second starting point is rooted in a theological discussion of the nature of God, revealed as Father, Son and Holy Spirit. Implications are then drawn for the church school from an understanding of each person of the Trinity. God as Father points toward the mystery of transcendence, the order within creation and the respect for justice and truth. God as Son points toward the powerful images of discloser, Jesus as teacher and Christ as suffering servant. God as Spirit points toward creativity and inspiration. Each of these suggestions, however, deserve much more extended development.

Following the green paper, Professor Stewart Sutherland began to emerge as the Anglican voice on the theology of education in two short essays entitled 'Education and theology'[56] and 'Theological reflections.'[57] In the first essay Sutherland identifies areas of educational debate to which theologians have a contribution to make, including critiquing the implicit anthropology. He concludes by arguing that 'educationalists must insist that theologians accept their intellectual responsibilities' in this area. In the second essay Sutherland articulates the fundamental educational question with which theology must engage in the following way. 'Behind this, of course, lies the question of what the point of education is and the answer to that question will include a declaration of what one considers to be of fundamental value for human (individual and social) flourishing, and of the role which education can play in helping individuals and societies achieve this.'[58]

Three more recent voices to have contributed to the debate are those of Leslie Francis,[59] Adrian Thatcher[60] and John Hull.[61] Francis argues for the theology of education to be resourced by the prophetic tradition within Christianity. Thatcher argues for an informal approach to theology of education which takes its cue from the difficulties and problems which Christian people encounter in their day-to-day work in education and then introduces the resources of theology (scripture, tradition, reason, and so on) to these issues. Hull argues for a theological view of education which is anchored not in maintaining Christianity but in promoting Christian-ness, as a true reflection of the nature of God as Trinity. The growing vitality of the interface between theology and education is also demonstrated by two recent readers, *Christian Perspectives for Education: a reader in the theology of education*[62] and *Christian Perspectives on Church Schools: a reader.*[63]

Higher education

Consideration of the Church of England's involvement in education is incomplete without an account of the church colleges. The story here goes back to 1839 and the 1840s when colleges were founded in such places as Cheltenham, Chester, Chichester, London, Winchester and York. Then new developments during the 1960s established further colleges in Canterbury and Lancaster. In the early 1970s there were twenty-five separate Anglican colleges in England at Abingdon, Birmingham, Bishops Stortford, Bristol, Canterbury, Cheltenham (St Mary's and St Paul's), Chester, Chichester, Derby, Durham (St Hild's and St Bede), Exeter, Lancaster, Lincoln, Liverpool, London (All Saints', St Gabriel's and Whitelands), Norwich, Plymouth, Ripon, Salisbury, Winchester and York. A further two colleges were in Wales at Bangor and Carmarthen. Each of these colleges has its own clear story of individual development.[64] At the same time institutional autonomy has inhibited any overall coherent strategy for the sector.

Restructuring of higher education in England and Wales during the 1970s saw a radical reduction in the number of Anglican colleges. The situation in 1994 when the report *An Excellent Enterprise: the Church of England and its Colleges of Higher Education*[65] was presented to the General Synod looked like this. Seven completely autonomous colleges remained: Canterbury Christ Church, Cheltenham and Gloucester (from a merger between St Paul's, St Mary's and the higher education element of the Gloucester College of Art and Technology), Chester, King Alfred's Winchester, Ripon and York St John, St Mark and St John Plymouth and St Martin's Lancaster. In addition Bishop Grosseteste had become a School of the University of Hull with all students spending the second year of their course away from the college in Hull. St Katharine's College Liverpool had federated with the Roman Catholic institution of Christ's and Notre Dame to form the Liverpool Institute of Higher Education. Whitelands College London had joined the Froebel Institute, Southlands College (Methodist) and Digby Stuart College (Roman Catholic) to form the Roehampton Institute of Higher Education. Bishop Otter College Chichester had become part of the West Sussex Institute of Higher Education. Bishop Lonsdale College had become part of the University of Derby. One further church college remained in Wales: Trinity College Carmarthen.

The role of the church colleges has also changed considerably since they were first established in the nineteenth century to train teachers. By 1994 only Bishop Grosseteste had remained monotechnic. Within all twelve colleges in England in 1994 there were 22,414 undergraduates on courses leading to a qualification other than teaching, compared with 10,619 undergraduates on courses leading to a teaching qualification. At the same time there were 2,037 students on a postgraduate teacher training course, compared with 346 students on other postgraduate courses. A further 4,527 students were registered on professional and other courses.

During the 1990s the church colleges began to face two further problems. First, the 1992 Further and Higher Education Act purported to abolish the 'binary line', which had distinguished between the financial and administrative arrangements relating to universities on the one hand and to polytechnics and colleges of higher education on the other hand. However, once polytechnics had seized the opportunity to become universities, the reality was not the abolition of the binary line, but the redrawing of the line to distinguish between the enlarged university sector and the reduced college sector. The church colleges remain significantly disadvantaged. Second, government moves to reform initial teacher training by placing more emphasis in schools and less emphasis in colleges has impacted particularly heavily on those smaller institutions in which teacher training continues to represent a comparatively high proportion of student intake.

At the same time, the church colleges have been challenged to reflect on their identity and to assess their distinctiveness. Recognising the importance of distinctiveness, the General Synod Report, *An Excellent Enterprise*, analysed the mission statements of the colleges and distilled the following six key qualities:

–   a commitment to good educational quality and to maintaining a caring and collegiate environment for students and staff, which includes for all who seek it worship, fellowship and service;

–   the serious study of Christianity;

–   a commitment to support the caring professions and the Christian contribution to human welfare including teaching, social work, youth work, nursing and ancillary health care;

–   a commitment to provide appropriate services to the community and to the church;

–   a commitment to foster equality of opportunity;

–   a commitment to develop a research capacity and to include within this a focus upon church affairs and church development.

Reviewing the implementation of the mission statements, *An Excellent Enterprise* concludes that in a 'rich variety of ways the church colleges serve the needs both of the community of the church and the community which the church itself serves'.

Looking to the future, *An Excellent Enterprise* identifies four main priorities for the colleges to consider. First, while acknowledging the autonomy of each institution, the report emphasises the added strengths of closer relationships between the colleges and with the

central institutions of the church, not simply as a defence against
perceived external threats but as a positive support for 'Christianity
and the ministry and mission of the Church of England'. Second, the
report recommends closer engagement between the colleges and the
church at local and regional levels. Third, the report rehearses the
potential contribution of the church college to ministerial education
and training. Finally, attention is drawn to an initiative known as
Engaging the Curriculum sponsored by the colleges jointly in order to
examine the ways in which the curriculum might be different in
church-related institutions of higher education.[66]

One of the consequences of the closure of some of the Anglican
colleges was the development of ten Church College Trusts: All Saints
Educational Trust, Culham Educational Foundation, Hockerill
Educational Foundation, Keswick Hall Charity, St Gabriel's Trust, St
Hild and St Bede Trust, St Luke's College Foundation, The
Foundation of St Matthias, the Sarum St Michael Educational Charity
and the St Peter's Saltley Trust. One further trust was established in
Wales: St Mary's College Trust, Bangor.[67] The autonomy of each
trust remained to further the intentions of the trust deed as the trustees
saw fit. In some cases new institutions grew from the former colleges.
For example, the Culham Educational Foundation sponsored the
Culham College Institute and the St Hild and St Bede Trust sponsored
the North of England Institute for Christian Education. In some cases
the trusts invested heavily in the institutions which had purchased the
old college buildings. For example, the St Gabriel's Trust supported
the chapel and a staff salary in the religious education department
after merger with Goldsmith's College; and the St Luke's College
Foundation decided to support the St Luke's chaplain and the St
Luke's Foundation Chair in Theological Studies within the University
of Exeter. In some cases the trusts decided to sponsor individual
students or individual projects. For example, the All Saints
Educational Trust annual report for 1987/88 indicated that 180 individuals had shared personal awards totalling £123,000, while
twenty-two groups had shared corporate awards totalling £145,000.
Very little of the resources from the closed college trusts, however,
have gone to support the work of the other Anglican colleges which
continue to struggle for survival in an increasingly competitive educational climate.

Although the church colleges have undergone enormous transformation within the past two decades, the issue of the Church of
England's involvement in higher education has undergone surprisingly
little intellectual scrutiny during this period. Three main initiatives are
worthy of note.

First, the Bradwell Consultation emerged during the mid 1970s as an informal group of people concerned about the apparent lack of policy concerning the church's strategy in the field of higher education. Debate was stimulated by essays from Charles F. Carter, Anthony Dyson, Elizabeth Maclaren and George Tolley and the findings were published in 1977 under the title *The Language of the Church in Higher and Further Education*.[68] The working party discussion paper which built on the Bradwell Consultation emphasised the importance of identifying the possible characteristics for a Christian curriculum.[69]

The second initiative was stimulated by John D. Gay. Gay's first study, *The Christian Campus?* was published in 1979.[70] Making good use of empirical research findings from North America, Gay formulated a model of a high impact college environment in which clear institutional objectives and a carefully selected Christian staff are combined with a small residential unit. He argues that such a value-laden college ('sub-college, which clustered like-minded students and faculty in a supportive environment') should be part of a much larger secular organisation so as to combine the strength of both the small Christian college and the large-scale secular university and at the same time retain the valuable characteristics of each. Then as Director of the Culham College Institute, Gay co-ordinated a significant empirical enquiry into *The Future of the Anglican Colleges* published in 1986.[71] This study concludes that 'there is widespread support for the view that the colleges can make a distinctive contribution, based on their Anglican foundation, to the future educational system of this country'.

The third and most prophetic initiative is that of Gordon McGregor, who between 1989 and 1994 contributed three essays under the title 'Church colleges for the twenty-first century' and a fourth essay entitled 'Church universities in the making'.[72] Throughout these essays McGregor is motivated by the view that 'There will be continuing pressures against the survival of relatively small institutions of higher education. Unless we make strenuous and successful efforts there may be no church colleges in the new century.'

In the first two of his essays McGregor identifies ten characteristics of a church college which he describes as 'an advisory Decalogue'. These are stated in no particular order of priority as: Christian insights and experience; open, participatory style; a sense of collegiate community; political awareness and determination; wide range of degree courses and professional training; a major role and open context in teacher education; encouraging international higher education; a context in which the practice and study of the Christian faith are taken seriously; obligations and opportunities for governors; and high quality education. In the third of his essays McGregor offers some prioritisation among these characteristics and argues that 'the curriculum is the biggest task that confronts us in the argument for a distinctive Christian ethos'. In his fourth essay McGregor challenges both the church and the secular world to recognise the immense transformation already experienced by the church colleges. While the old teacher training college image dies hard, the reality is that of diversified institutions offering a range of professional degree programmes, BA and BSc courses in humanities, arts and sciences, taught masters' programmes and research degrees. Already, he argues, these are church universities in the making.

Looking to the future

Having reviewed the nature of the Church of England's involvement in education and schooling during the post-war years, it is hard to avoid the conclusion that education has rarely been a matter at the top of the church's agenda during this period. As a consequence key questions now need to be raised, in recognition of the fact that the alternative to decisive action may be continuing drift and erosion of influence within an area in which the Church of England was once very strong. The following is an attempt to order twelve questions which may need answering within the next decade.

The first question concerns the Church of England's perceptions of its relationship with wider society and of the state maintained system of schools operated by that society. If the Church of England is placed within a society which is fundamentally based on Christian principles and if these principles permeate the value structure of state maintained schools, then its attitude toward involvement with schools will be quite different from what would be the case if it were located within a society which is fundamentally post-Christian and where the value structure of state maintained schools is not founded on Christian principles. In one case the Church of England might want to serve the nation by maintaining a network of neighbourhood schools. In the other case the Church of England might want to offer a radically distinctive alternative network of schools for parents who explicitly wish their children to be educated in a Christian environment.

The second question concerns the Church of England's perception of its relationships with other Christian denominations. If the Church of England is placed in a society in which the fundamental distinctions are between the different denominations, it may wish to emphasise a distinctive network of Anglican schools in contrast to, say, Catholic schools. If the Church of England is placed in a society in which the fundamental distinctions are between the Christian churches and a secular culture, the Church of England may wish to explore ways in which greater ecumenical co-operation can be expressed through the development of church schools.

The third question concerns the Church of England's perceptions of its relationships with other faith groups. If the Church of England perceives itself to be in a society in which cultural assimilation should be promoted as the greatest social good, it may wish to help individuals from other faith traditions to feel properly accommodated by county and Church of England schools. If the Church of England perceives itself to be in a society in which cultural and religious identities should be promoted as the greatest social good, it may wish to help other faith groups achieve distinctive religious schools within the state maintained system.

The fourth question concerns the balance of responsibility and power in education between the various levels of the local school and parish, the dioceses and the central church structures. The Church of England needs to be able to assess the relative strengths and weaknesses between protecting the autonomy of the local and being able to speak authoritatively from the centre. Just as was the case in 1944, central government continues to look to the churches for a policy voice on education. The Church of England may need to reassess the clarity and authority with which it is able to respond to such invitations.

The fifth question concerns the extent to which the local churches are properly informed regarding the changes which are taking place in education and the Church of England's involvement in and responses to these changes. If local churches are to be asked to continue to finance the Church of England's education arm, local congregations (and clergy) need to be properly informed. Perhaps much more use could be made of the opportunities provided by Education Sunday each year.

The sixth question concerns the administrative resources which the Church of England needs at central and diocesan level to service adequately the churches' involvement in education. This involves the proper evaluation of the training, career structure, and resourcing of diocesan education officers and the staffing of the Board of Education and the National Society.

The seventh question concerns the intellectual resources which the Church of England needs in order to resource its involvement in education. Such resources may be needed at three levels. At the level of theology, Christian theologians may need to be challenged to take the area of the theology of education seriously and to contribute more vigorously to this field. At the level of educational research, much more may need to be known about the potential distinctiveness and effectiveness of church schools. At the level of curriculum development, new initiatives may be required to stimulate the distinctive development of the church school curriculum. All three areas may require the identification and resourcing of particular scholars.

The eighth question concerns the professional development of teaching staff for church schools, both within the context of initial teacher training and in-service training. The Church of England may wish to assess the emphasis which should be placed on the opportunities currently available through the church colleges' certificate programmes (in religious studies and church school studies) and the taught masters' programmes offered by the church colleges in church school studies.

The ninth question concerns maximising the opportunities provided by the current system of school inspection, especially in relationship to the provision of the section 23 denominational inspection. These opportunities may involve giving further attention to training inspectors, developing more formal guidelines for inspection reports and enabling schools to respond effectively to the inspection process and reports.

The tenth question concerns the interrelationships between school education and the programmes of Christian nurture offered to young people within the context of parish education. The Church of England needs to continue to assess the extent of the gap between the curriculum of the secular school and the educational assumptions of the worshipping community.

The eleventh question concerns the future of the church's involvement in higher education. The Church of England needs to ask how well the fiercely-guarded autonomy of the individual church colleges has served either the interest of the individual colleges themselves or the church's overall presence in higher education. Within the changing context of higher education in England, the Church of England also needs to ask whether there is a continuing place for a church-related presence and, if so, what form that should take. The case for the survival of individual colleges validated by neighbouring universities needs to be assessed alongside the case for a federal Anglican university in England.

The twelfth question concerns the appropriate use to be made of the many educational trust funds administered in the name of the Church of England, especially perhaps those resulting from the closure of former Anglican teacher training colleges. While the autonomy of individual groups of trustees needs to be respected, the Church of England also needs to ask whether, within a changing educational climate, the church as a whole needs to offer some advice regarding the priority allocation of scarce resources. Are Anglican funds best deployed, for example, by supporting individual students, desperately seeking sponsorship as an alternative to accepting educational loans, or by strengthening church-related educational initiatives? Are Anglican funds best deployed by sponsoring posts and projects within secular universities or by resourcing the remaining church-related institutions of higher education?

While none of these questions necessarily has an obvious or easy answer, it would be irresponsible of the Church of England to leave them unanswered and for the consequent policy to emerge by default rather than through decision.

Notes

1. *To a Rebellious House? Report of the Church of England's Partners in Mission Consultation 1981* (CIO Publishing, London, 1981), p. 38.
2. *Working as One Body: the report of the Archbishops' Commission on the organisation of the Church of England* (Church House Publishing, London, 1995).
3. *A Future in Partnership* (National Society, London, 1984).
4. See M. Cruickshank, *Church and State in English Education* (Macmillan, London, 1963) and J. Murphy, *Church, State and Schools in Britain 1800–1970* (Routledge and Kegan Paul, London, 1971).
5. See, for example, R.A. Butler, *The Art of the Possible* (Hamish Hamilton, London, 1971).
6. See J. Scotland, *The History of Scottish Education* (University of London Press, London, 1969).
7. *Crisis in Church Schools: a report on finance* (General Synod, London, 1972).
8. See, for example, A. Hargreaves and L. Tickle (eds.), *Middle Schools: origins, ideology and practice* (Harper & Row, London, 1980).
9. L.J. Francis, *Partnership in Rural Education* (Collins Liturgical Publications, London, 1986).
10. Plowden Report, *Children and their Primary Schools* (HMSO, London, 1967).
11. For further detail, see L.J. Francis, 'Primary School Size and Pupil Attitudes: small is happy?' *Educational Management and Administration* 20 (1992), pp. 100–4.
12. Small Schools Working Party, *The Future of Small Schools* (National Society, London, 1991).
13. D.W. Lankshear, *Small Schools* (National Society, London, 1995).

14. D.W. Lankshear, 'From research to policy 1980–96: the case of the Church of England school' (unpublished paper presented to the first international symposium on church school studies, University of Durham, July 1996).
15. See, for example, M. Flude and M. Hammer (eds.), *Education Reform Act 1988* (Falmer Press, Basingstoke, 1990).
16. *Grant-Maintained Status and the Church School* (National Society, London, 1988).
17. See D.W. Lankshear, *Preparing for Inspection in a Church School* (National Society, London, 1993) and A. Brown and D.W. Lankshear, *Inspection Handbook* (National Society, London, 1995).
18. *Grant-Maintained Status and the Church School: after the 1993 Education Act* (National Society, London, 1994).
19. P. Hirst, 'Christian Education: a Contradiction in Terms', *Learning for Living* 11, 4 (1972), pp. 6–11 and P. Hirst, 'Education, Catechesis and the Church School', *British Journal of Religious Education* 3 (1981), pp. 85-93.
20. See, for example, L.J. Francis, 'The Logic of Education, Theology and the Church School', *Oxford Review of Education* 9 (1983), pp. 147–62; and E.J. Thiessen, 'A Defence of a Distinctively Christian Curriculum', *Religious Education* 80 (1985), pp. 37–50.
21. The Swann Report, *Education for All* (HMSO, London, 1985).
22. Catholic Commission for Racial Justice, *Learning from Diversity* (Catholic Media Office, London, 1984).
23. General Synod of the Church of England Board of Education, *Schools and Multi-Cultural Education* (Church House Publishing, London, 1984).
24. Socialist Education Association, *The Dual System of Voluntary and County Schools* (Socialist Education Association, London, 1981).
25. Socialist Education Association, *All Faiths in All Schools* (Socialist Education Association, London, 1986).
26. See report in *Education*, 2 November 1990, p. 370.
27. See, for example, R.H. Thouless, *Map of Educational Research* (National Foundation for Educational Research, Slough, 1969) and P. Gordon (ed.), *A Guide to Educational Research* (The Woburn Press, London, 1996).
28. L.J. Francis, 'Denominational Schools and Pupil Attitudes Towards Christianity', *British Educational Research Journal* 12 (1986), pp. 145-52.
29. L.J. Francis, *Religion in the Primary School* (Collins Liturgical Publications, London, 1987).
30. L.J. Francis and M. Carter, 'Church Aided Secondary Schools, Religious Education as an Examination Subject and Pupil Attitudes towards Religion', *British Journal of Educational Psychology* 50 (1980), pp. 297–300.
31. L.J. Francis and A. Jewell, 'Shaping Adolescent Attitude towards the Church: Comparison Between Church of England and County Secondary Schools', *Evaluation and Research in Education* 6 (1992), pp. 13–21.

32. M. Levitt, 'The Influence of a Church Primary School on Children's Religious Beliefs and Practices: a Cornish Study' (unpublished PhD dissertation, University of Exeter, 1993).
33. L.J. Francis and D.W. Lankshear, 'The Impact of Church Schools on Village Church Life' *Educational Studies* 16 (1990), pp. 117–29.
34. L.J. Francis and D.W. Lankshear, 'The Impact of Church Schools on Urban Church Life', *School Effectiveness and School Improvement* 2 (1991), pp. 324–35.
35. L.J. Francis, *Religion in the Primary School* (Collins Liturgical Publications, London, 1987).
36. B. O'Keeffe, *Faith, Culture and the Dual System: a comparative study of church and county schools* (Falmer Press, Barcombe, 1986).
37. J. Gay, B. Kay, H. Newdick and G. Perry, *A Role for the Future: Anglican primary schools in the London diocese* (Culham College Institute, Abingdon, 1991).
38. B.W. Kay, H.S. Piper and J.D. Gay, *Managing the Church Schools: a study of the governing bodies of Church of England aided primary schools in the Oxford diocese* (Culham College Institute Occasional Paper 10, Abingdon, 1988).
39. L.J. Francis and E.A. Stone, 'The Attitudes of School Governors Towards the Religious Ethos of Church of England Voluntary Aided Primary Schools', *Educational Management and Administration* 23 (1995), pp. 176–87.
40. L.J. Francis, *Partnership in Rural Education* (Collins Liturgical Publications, London, 1986a).
41. C. Wilcox and L.J. Francis, 'Church of England Schools and Teacher Attitudes: Personal Commitment or Professional Judgement?', in L.J. Francis, W.K. Kay and W.S. Campbell (eds.), *Research in Religious Education* (Gracewing, Leominster, 1996), pp. 311–33.
42. J.F. Lankshear, *Denominational Inspection in Primary Schools* (National Society, London, 1997).
43. *The Fourth R: the Durham Report on Religious Education* (National Society and SPCK, London, 1970).
44. *A Future in Partnership* (National Society, London, 1984).
45. See, for example, G. Duncan, *The Church School* (National Society and SPCK, London, 1990).
46. *Positive Partnership* (National Society, London, 1985).
47. G. Duncan, 'Church Schools: Present and Future' in G. Leonard (ed.), *Faith for the Future* (National Society and Church House Publishing, London, 1986), pp. 67–8.
48. G. Duncan, 'Church Schools in Service to the Community' in B. O'Keeffe (ed.), *Schools for Tomorrow: building walls or building bridges* (Falmer Press, Barcombe, 1988), pp. 145–61.
49. D.W. Lankshear, *A Shared Vision: education in church schools* (National Society, London, 1992).
50. D.W. Lankshear, *Looking for Quality in a Church School* (National Society and Church House Publishing, London, 1992).

51. D.W. Lankshear, *Governing Church Schools* (National Society, London, 1992).
52. D.W. Lankshear, *Churches Serving Schools* (National Society, London, 1996).
53. *The Fourth R: the Durham Report on Religious Education* (National Society and SPCK, London, 1970), pp. 29–73.
54. *A Future in Partnership* (National Society, London, 1984), pp. 60–72.
55. ibid., p. 60.
56. Stewart Sutherland, 'Education and Theology', in G. Leonard (ed.), *Faith in the Future* (National Society and Church House Publishing, London, 1986), pp. 35–41.
57. Stewart Sutherland, 'Theological Reflections', in B. O'Keeffe (ed.), *Schools for Tomorrow: building walls or building bridges* (Falmer Press, Barcombe, 1988), pp. 182–90.
58. ibid., p. 182.
59. L.J. Francis, 'Theology of Education', *British Journal of Educational Studies* 38 (1990), pp. 349–64.
60. A. Thatcher, 'Making the Difference: Theology of Education and Church Schools' (unpublished paper presented to the first international symposium on church school studies, University of Durham, July 1996).
61. J.M. Hull, 'The Holy Trinity and the Missions of the Church School' (unpublished paper presented to the first international symposium on church school studies, University of Durham, July 1996).
62. L.J. Francis and A. Thatcher (eds.), *Christian Perspectives for Education: a reader in the theology of education* (Gracewing, Leominster, 1990).
63. L.J. Francis and D.W. Lankshear (eds.), *Christian Perspectives on Church Schools: a reader* (Gracewing, Leominster, 1993).
64. See, for example, G.P. McGregor, *Bishop Otter College: a policy for teacher education 1839-1980* (Pembridge Press, London, 1981); M. Rose, *A History of King Alfred's College Winchester 1840-1980* (Phillimore, London, 1981); L. Naylor and G. Howat, *Culham College History* (Culham Educational Foundation, Abingdon, 1982); G.P. McGregor, *A Church College for the 21st Century? 150 years of Ripon and York St John* (University College of Ripon and York St John, York, 1991); P.S. Gedge and L.M.R. Louden, *S. Martin's College Lancaster 1964-89* (Centre for North-West Regional Studies University of Lancaster, Lancaster, 1993).
65. *An Excellent Enterprise: the Church of England and its Colleges of Higher Education* (General Synod of the Church of England, London, 1994).
66. See further J. Habgood, 'Engaging the Curriculum', in G.P. McGregor (ed.), *Toward True Education* (University College of Ripon and York St John, York, 1994), pp. 92-100.
67. See J.D. Gay, 'The Church College Trusts', in T. Brighton (ed.), *150 Years: the Church Colleges in Higher Education* (West Sussex Institute of Higher Education, Chichester, 1989), pp. 99-117.

68. M. Pye (ed.), *The Language of the Church in Higher and Further Education* (The Bradwell Consultation, London, 1977).
69. *Christian Involvement in Higher Education* (National Society, London, 1978).
70. J.D. Gay, *The Christian Campus? The Role of the English Churches in Higher Education* (Culham College Institute, Abingdon, 1979).
71. J. Gay, B. Kay, G. Perry and D. Lazenby, *The Future of the Anglican Colleges* (Culham College Institute, Abingdon, 1986).
72. G.P. McGregor, 'Church Colleges for the Twenty-first Century', in T. Brighton (ed.), *150 Years: the Church Colleges in Higher Education* (West Sussex Institute of Higher Education, Chichester), pp. 172–89; G.P. McGregor, 'Epilogue: a Church College for the Twenty-first Century', in *A Church College for the 21st Century* (University College of Ripon and York St John, York, 1991), pp. 260–5; G.P. McGregor, 'Church Colleges for the Twenty-first Century', in G.P. McGregor (ed.), *Toward True Education* (University College of Ripon and York St John, York, 1994), pp. 79–91; G.P. McGregor, 'Postscript: Church Universities in the Making', in G.P. McGregor (ed.), *Toward True Education* (University College of Ripon and York St John, York, 1994), pp. 114–16.

Part Three:
Faith and Praxis

8

Liturgy and Worship

Gordon P. Jeanes

We exist in order to glorify God. That may not be the whole truth, but it is a very great part of the truth. The importance of worship is about our very being. Worship is also about the Church's mission: it is often described as its shop window; it is where much of the teaching, pastoral and social life is focused. But worship matters above all because it is the response of the Church to God the Father. We are called to live as the body of Christ in the communion of the Holy Spirit, and that is embodied in the regular gathering of the church for worship.

Liturgy, the language of worship, frames the way in which we behave as Christians. It can make us sensitive to some issues and immune to others. In part our thoughts are directed by the liturgy; in part our unconscious assumptions are fed by it. But also our lives reflect back on the public language and reshape it, and the liturgy is constantly changing, perhaps not in the text of worship, but in its performance and context. There is no time when it is static and unchanging. Perhaps the most important changes, because they are so much part of us, are hidden from us.

Worship is in a state of great turmoil. The years of revision from the 1960s found a conclusion in the publication in 1980 of the *Alternative Service Book* (henceforth ASB). There was a hope at the time that this would mark the end of a chapter, but revision and additional texts have continued unabated. Seasonal material has come in *Lent, Holy Week, Easter*, and *The Promise of His Glory* which covers the Christmas period. *Patterns for Worship* adopts the form of a directory or resource book for liturgy, offering many more options than those provided in the ASB. In the 1980s there seems to have been a broad consensus in many parishes about how the ASB was to be used. But now with the revisions leading to the replacement of the ASB in 2000, and with greater variety already being used, the future looks

243

entirely open. It also remains to be seen what difference will be made by the wide range of new ministries, clerical and lay. At the moment, the most radical initiative, the local non-stipendiary ministry ordained as part of a ministry team, is too novel for us to see what effect it will have on our worship.

Many people, if asked what is the prime issue in liturgy today, would probably say that it is the question of language. For some that would be a gender issue; others would recognise the far wider problems of creating a modern rhetorical style for public worship in a culture which has little or no place for the formal spoken language. While these are serious issues, there is very little that one can, at the end of the day, say about them. One learns the proper use of language by using it. When the Church of England set out to create a new liturgical style in the 1960s (as did other denominations at about the same time) it was very much starting from scratch. The early attempts, seen in Series 2, were sparse and functional. The ASB is fuller in language, sometimes to the point of verbosity, but abstract and conceptual. Recent work has tried to introduce concrete imagery and symbolism, to appeal more to the imagination than the intellect. With the hindsight of a generation, we can smile at the childish endeavours of our predecessors, but complacency must be tempered by the realisation that we are by no means beyond our adolescence in such things. Hopefully further experience will allow better results in the future. Certainly to stop our activities would only freeze us in our present inadequacy, and stifle the incentive to learn from our mistakes. As for particular issues in language, the decisive battles will be fought elsewhere. Gender inclusiveness became an issue in the Church of England in 1989 with the publication of *Making Women Visible*, though no one had noticed that all new Liturgical Commission writing since 1980 had been gender inclusive. But it is society as a whole which will decide what forms of language are permissible or not, and how one negotiates the tricky alternative for the third person singular pronoun 'he' meaning he or she. As for gender language about God, the language of the Trinity obviously has a liturgical context, but overlaps with historical and systematic theology. Any solution involves both a reflection on current experience of the Trinity and a re-examination of the history of Trinitarian thought, so an adequate discussion would go beyond the bounds of this chapter. More exciting than 'issues' is a new awareness of the power and sensitivity of language, and the study of liturgy from the standpoint of the hermeneutics of language is opening entire vistas.[1]

But perhaps the greatest issue facing worship in the Church of England today is the bewildering variety of services in its churches every Sunday morning. A newcomer would expect to learn the ways of a congregation in just the same way as when joining any new group or indeed entering someone's home. Every guest knows how to keep an eye open and try to fit in with the host. Different styles of music, different sizes of congregations, different approaches to intimacy, affection, intellect, charismatic worship, use of symbols, enthusiasm, all have their effect. But even the landmarks are seen to be shifting. The service itself may be matins, or a family service, or a eucharist, to say nothing of rave services and the like. Even in a eucharist celebrated using the ASB two services could have virtually no common material at all. The Lord's Prayer is commonly to be found in three versions (ignoring the question of the doxology).

At present the problem is not too bad. The variety (goods competing in the market place?) sets out to meet the various needs and wants of people. However the worship of God is not simply one more commodity like washing powder or breakfast cereal, to be shaped and changed according to whim. And it would be ironic if the process of renewal of our worship over the last century, commonly known as the Liturgical Movement, having begun with a very strong emphasis on the community, were to end up as a service industry for the individual consumer. It has been mooted that, 'one possible scenario for the future of liturgical reform ... is a sudden centrifugal outburst, resulting in a kaleidoscope of patterns and forms both between and within Churches', or, as a reaction to this, that we may see 'a recrudescence of a conservatism that could well impede further liturgical experimentation and even blur the impact of what has been achieved'.[2] At present the former seems the greater threat. And the centrifugal outburst could bring about the disintegration of liturgy as a public language.

Already worship has all but retreated from the world. To a large extent the reason is the decline of corporate activities, from youth groups to local political parties to football supporters' clubs. And there is an impatience with formality and tradition: where they are 'preserved' they are being recast, and it may well be that we are living in an age when we are re-inventing our traditions as radically as did the Victorians. But while worship slips inside the safety of the walls of the church, not only is the world left behind but also other congregations may be as well. Increased mobility and minority church attendance have stretched the relationship between a church and the community around it. If worship continues to diversify, what is to prevent more and more congregations developing their private language? Already the secular world finds itself bemused by the services in the average parish church. How much further can diversity go before one's fellow Anglicans from the next parish are equally bemused? Or can congregations develop the necessary allowance for one another, and respect for common forms of worship, to enable the Church of England to develop as one body? Alarm at this extreme could easily result in the backlash of the 'recrudescence of conservatism', but it is impossible to put the genie back in the bottle, and churches which have tasted liturgical development are unlikely to go back very far. A clumsy attempt to put on the brakes could result in the loss of control altogether.

Liturgy and uniformity

The history of liturgy in the Church of England in this century has largely been one of the struggle to find a pattern of uniformity broad enough to embrace legitimate diversity. That may sound like a contradiction in terms, but historically it is not altogether unfair. Research into the evolution of Cranmer's own Prayer Books of 1549 and 1552 still leaves open the question whether he always intended the latter book (or even a third edition, one hundred times more perfect!) or whether he might have been content with the first if consensus had been established around it. But what is becoming more clear is the huge effort expended by the government at the time in seeking to forge agreement around the 1549 liturgy. Questionnaires and discussions abounded, partly in order to cajole the traditionalists into line but also in an attempt to identify and meet their objections. When that failed, Cranmer moved on to 1552 without his opponents' company. But even that volume bears witness to the pressures of consensus, with the issue of kneeling communion very much to the fore in the Black Rubric, and many other controversial issues unresolved.[3]

The 1662 liturgy was no different. The Puritan suggestions for reform were for the most part ignored, though extremists at the other end of the spectrum, such as Cosin, also achieved far less than they had hoped for. Like its predecessors, 1662 did not win free consent. Unlike its predecessors, it could not successfully be imposed on an unwilling constituency. Nonconformity became a fact of British religious life.

The years between 1662 and the beginning of this century were not uneventful, especially the nineteenth century when there were various attempts to enforce liturgical conformity. The tale is a sorry one of a failure of legal and spiritual authority and also of the destructive aspects of ritual controversy which still leaves the study of liturgy with the aura of nit-picking pedantry. But at the same time there was the serious issue as to whether the worshipping patterns of a church could be allowed to grow and change and, if so, how these may be directed and controlled. The Prayer Book as proposed in 1927 and 1928 represents the last gasp of an attempt to impose conformity and uniformity at least in the sense of a very narrow range of options, since in the book there are generally two alternatives allowed, the 1662 form and its 1928 equivalent.

Ronald Jasper summed up his account of the failed 1928 Prayer Book with this comment: 'An exercise which began as an attempt to solve problems of discipline became confused with an attempt to meet pastoral and devotional needs no longer entirely satisfactorily met by 1662'.[4] However it is possible that Jasper is unfair to the endeavour. We may look back to the Royal Commission of 1906 which began the long odyssey of the proposed Prayer Book, and see the Commission's report as saying, in effect: that discipline had broken down; that one of the reasons for that breakdown was the narrowness of liturgical provision offered to clergy and congregations; that the liturgy should therefore be revised so that discipline could be maintained. Thus the Commission's message to the bishops was that they should come up with something which could be enforced, and then enforce it. According to this view, there is no logical inconsistency or confusion in the 1928 revision. Whether it was successful for what was intended is another matter.[5]

Such a view takes full account of the Commission's Conclusion: first, its famous description of diversity which is quoted by virtually every study of the period:

> The law of public worship in the Church of England is too narrow for the religious life of the present generation. It needlessly condemns much which a great section of Church people, including many of her most devoted members, value; and modern thought and feeling are characterised by a care for ceremonial, a sense of dignity in worship, and an appreciation of the continuity of the Church, which were not similarly felt at the time when the law took its present shape. In an age which has witnessed an extraordinary revival of spiritual life and activity, the Church has had to work under regulations fitted for a different condition of things, without that power of self-adjustment which is inherent in the conception of a living Church ...

But then (in a less often quoted passage) the Commission goes on to bewail the breakdown of the machinery for discipline, and then to state:

It is important that the law should be reformed, that it should admit of reasonable elasticity, and that the means of enforcing it should be improved; but, above all, it is necessary that it should be obeyed ... With regard to the future we desire to state with distinctness our conviction that, if it should be thought well to adopt the recommendations we make in this report, one essential condition of their successful operation will be, that obedience to the law so altered shall be required and, if necessary, enforced, by those who bear rule in the Church of England.[6]

In the event the revision that arose out of the Commission's findings was rejected, twice, by Parliament and never became the authorised liturgy of the Church of England. The archbishops stated that its use would, in the light of the impasse, be regarded as not disobedient to the laws of the church, and many of its provisions passed into common use. In particular much of the funeral liturgy (perhaps most distinctive among the reforms in the book in that it owed much to the pastoral experience of the chaplains in the trenches of the First World War) is used to this day. But the eucharistic prayer, over which infinite pains were taken by the church, was generally ignored by clergy who continued to use 1662, either as it stood, or by adding the Prayer of Oblation to the end of the Prayer of Consecration: the so-called Interim Rite. In any event, what passed into common use in the Church of England was due, not to its legality or illegality, but to how it was valued pastorally and theologically by priest and people. And it was the Interim Rite that was to prove the pattern for subsequent revision of the eucharistic prayer in the Church of England up to the ASB.

In effect the failure of either the bishops or Parliament to fashion and enforce a standard form of worship was a victory for the parishes, at least in the short term, in allowing them to carry on with their worshipping practices (with or without the connivance of the bishop) instead of reining them in, to accord with the new benchmark. The success of 1928 would have been an admission that worship had moved over the centuries, but that control by the central authorities was possible and desirable. The failure of 1928 left the locus of control at a lower level, with the diocesan bishop, or even at parish level.

Parliament and Synod

Legally, Parliament is still the supreme authority in liturgical provision as in other aspects of the government of the Church of England.

However, over the years this has been devolved in various ways to the episcopate and General Synod. At the Reformation, papal authority in England was not so much abolished as assumed by the Crown, and this authority came to be exercised by Parliament. It was by Act of Parliament that the successive Prayer Books were authorised in 1549, 1552 and 1662, and it was in the House of Commons in 1927 and then 1928 that the proposed revision of 1662 came to grief. Throughout this period the Church of England was governed by Parliament and regarded by many as in effect the religious aspect of the State. The ritualist controversies of the nineteenth century brought to a new pitch the old High Church concern about Erastianism, but one important blow was struck by Archbishop Benson's ruling in favour of Edward King, Bishop of Lincoln, over matters of ritual. Benson took into account the history and tradition of the church over against previous Privy Council judgements. And, to their credit, the Privy Council acquiesced in the archbishop's findings. This episode stands as a landmark in the struggle of the church to determine the authority for its worship and life.[7] However, it was in the aftermath of the 1928 fiasco that the archbishops made an explicit declaration of the claims of the church to some independent status:

> It is a fundamental principle that the Church – that is, the Bishops together with the Clergy and Laity – must in the last resort, when its mind has been fully ascertained, retain its inalienable right, in loyalty to our Lord and Saviour Jesus Christ, to formulate its Faith in Him and to arrange the expression of that Holy Faith in its forms of worship.[8]

And in accordance with this principle they proceeded to declare that use of the 1928 Prayer Book would not be regarded as 'inconsistent with loyalty to the principles of the Church of England'.[9]

In the 1950s the Church of England once again set itself the serious task of redefining its position with regard to the State. The revised canons of the Church of England set out to determine the lawful authority of the church in allowing deviations from the 1662 Prayer Book.[10] In 1964 the *Prayer Book (Alternative and Other Services) Measure*, invoking the new canons, was approved by the Church Assembly, and this allowed for the Church of England to adopt optional and experimental alternatives to the Prayer Book of 1662. The first collection to be approved for use was the *Alternative Services First Series*, much of which was an adoption, and therefore legalisation, of 1928 material which had become widely used over the years. On the other hand the *Alternative Services Second Series* was of new material compiled by members of the Liturgical Commission. The so-called Series Two was the first attempt to compose liturgical material in a more contemporary vein, abandoning the 'Prayer Book English' which had been followed for the most part by 1928 and Series One. While it was only with Series Three that 'thou' gave way to 'you', the exploration of a new liturgical language began with Series Two.

The Measure passed in 1964 by the Church Assembly had still left revisions by the church subject to Parliament. In 1974 the *Church of England (Worship and Doctrine) Measure* was passed through Parliament, allowing the church itself to authorise liturgical change. The Prayer Book was excepted from this provision and remains as the definitive liturgy of the church, but the shift of authority from Parliament to Synod is a real one nevertheless.

Centralised authority and the parish

The question of authority in worship has often been presented in terms of the legally competent body for regulating and revising the liturgy. As such it was debated acutely in the nineteenth century, and forcibly in the twentieth, in terms of the legal establishment and the relations between Parliament and Convocation or Synod. However, there is another issue distinct from this first one, namely the relation of the church to society as a whole. Parliament had often portrayed itself, when debating ecclesiastical affairs, as representing society in this respect, and Paul Welsby sees the Parliamentary debates in 1974 as encapsulating the problem:

> What emerged most significantly from the debate was the fact that there appeared to be two 'Churches of England'. One was composed of committed members, who were regular worshippers, who were dedicated to mission and who played their part in synodical structures. The other was the 'vague mass', who attended worship spasmodically, who took no part in the Church's mission, and who held aloof from the synodical structures, but who nevertheless regarded themselves, rather than the first group, as 'the Church of England'. The Worship and Doctrine Measure polarised the two and posed the question: Which of these two is the real Church of England?[11]

It is a mistake to see Parliament or Synod as embodying either side in this debate. They represent the two sides and defend them, but they do not embody them. For the actual debate is to be found at its fiercest at the local level. From the point of view of the village or urban church, Synod and Parliament are both somewhat distant, centralising powers that legislate from on high. They can make rules about what text is used, and expend great effort in its felicity of phrasing or equilibrium of theology, but they cannot determine, except in the very broadest manner, the way in which a service is celebrated. It is a truism among liturgists that the ritual actions can convey more meaning than the words on the page, and it has been suggested, rather wickedly, that a proper regulation of worship should prescribe the acceptable theology of the denomination through the actions of the ministers, but could safely ignore the text. For example, if a Roman Catholic church were to celebrate the eucharist in the usual manner, with elevation and veneration of the sacrament, but using the text of the United Reformed Church, most people in the congregation would perceive the rite to convey the usual theology of their church. And likewise a minister of the United Reformed Church could use a Roman Catholic prayer, but not the ceremonial. But who prescribes the ritual act? Outside the Roman Catholic Church, directions are minimalist and can be interpreted only within the living tradition of the denomination and of each congregation. The way in which people worship is determined not by centralised authority but by the tradition of the community.

In recent history the congregation has become steadily more important as the place for determining the style of worship. The Liturgical Movement has placed a renewed worship at the centre of the church's life in all denominations of the Western world, and it has also led to a new awareness of the needs of the congregation in worship. John Fenwick and Bryan Spinks see the rationale for this going back to the Enlightenment emphasis on a human-centred approach to life: the needs of people are more important than previously.[12] The wider aspects, those of the state or of tradition, are bound to suffer. The most obvious features of the Movement have been the drive to make the liturgy comprehensible and accessible to members of the congregation (hence the need for vernacular, or contemporary, language), the teaching of the faith (the restoration of preaching and lectionary reform in many traditions) and the active participation of the laity (hymnody, active lay participation in prayers and ceremonial, reordering of churches to integrate clergy and laity within one body). If the members of a congregation are able to participate so fully, then it is natural that they will want to have a say in how the worship is ordered. Village churches have always had the more difficult task of seeking to please as many people as possible, but urban and suburban churches have often traded on differences between one another, and those laity who cared sufficiently about such things found themselves in the position of liturgical consumers. When liturgical revision was

begun in the Church of England, congregational choice was demonstrated in the adoption (or rejection) of new alternatives, which has
added to the competitive nature of the marketplace. It could be said,
however, that this marketplace approach has at least maintained a
generally high standard of worship in the various traditions. Some
other denominations, with a less varied and competitive market, have
not maintained such a high standard.

Church and society beyond Parliament and Synod

The movement of authority in worship away from Parliament can be
seen as evidence of disestablishment by degrees on the one hand and
of secularisation on the other. However, neither should be exagger-
ated. In terms of the former, there is nothing of itself incongruous in
an established church taking charge of its worship life (though that
may imply a particular form of establishment). With regard to the
latter case, even full disestablishment would not imply that the institutional church would be free to order its worship without reference
to society, or that society as a whole has no interest in what the church
does, even if Parliament takes no account. Legal establishment is only
one aspect of the role of a church in society. Writing as one who is
at present in the Church in Wales, it would seem to me that the disestablishment of 1920 has resulted in virtually no difference at all in her
position in society compared with that of her sister across Offa's
Dyke. That thing called secularisation is of more importance than
establishment: how far does the church identify itself with society, or
society with the church; or are the two radically distinct? Recent work
by sociologists has suggested a very complicated picture of secularisation in Britain, epitomised by the slogan *Believing without
Belonging* which is the subtitle of Grace Davie's summary of the
issue, *Religion in Britain since 1945*.[13] At the popular level, services,
especially rites of passage, belong to the whole community, and the
church may be seen more as the trustee than as the owner of the
liturgy. The individual may not identify with the institution of the
church, but may still feel an entitlement to the occasional offices and
a concern for how they are administered.

The worship of the church is easily spoken of, but more difficult to
define. The question, 'What is the church?' is like, 'Who is my neigh-
bour?' Only the most simplistic and artificial answer can avoid the
uncomfortable implication that there is no one competent authority for
the regulation of worship either in a congregation or in the church as
a whole. Authority takes various forms: the memory of particular

communities; the life and growth of an individual congregation; the minister as worship leader; the church as represented in its provincial synod and its structures.

It is perhaps at this point that the complicated role of worship is seen at its most acute. I have had conversations in which traditionalists have blamed liturgists for some great liberal agenda which cannot leave things alone. I have also had conversations in which more progressive worship leaders have clearly resented the liturgist's appeals to the Anglican tradition and theological consensus. In both extremes there is an intolerance of the 'expert' perspective which only serves to complicate matters. But more worrying than this healthy distrust of the specialist is an impatience with the complicated nature of the church today. In former, more hierarchical, ages it was relatively straightforward to legislate for the church, for the predominant virtue was conformity. In the middle ages, one conformed to the traditions of the community and diocese; in the Reformation period centralised government had been developed and exercised its new-found muscles, being able for the first time, thanks to printing, to specify a new text for the worship of every congregation in the realm, and having the will and power to enforce it. The modern age is less respectful of either: hierarchy is a dirty word and community is as substantial as the Cheshire Cat's smile. The advent of the word processor and the photocopier is quickly annulling the centralising effect of the printing press, and forms of worship are increasingly produced locally, and so can only be controlled locally. The locus of authority in the worshipping life of the church often devolves onto the clergy and active laity of the congregation, and they function as a sub-group within society rather than as a microcosm of it. But there is no point in bemoaning the issue or looking elsewhere for 'the community' as a group with a view or a voice. There is no silent majority; rather, there is a number of silent minorities. And here the church – the whole people of God in every congregation and at every level of the hierarchy – must be able to give a lead, for in the 'first past the post' democracy that we live in, minorities often get a raw deal, and consensus and compromise get pushed to the side. The church must do better, and that begins with the way in which it worships God.

The situation created is extremely complex – and challenging. As far as the rarely attending, 'believing but not belonging' group are concerned, one might easily meet two items in the agenda. For the liturgy to be recognisable and useful as worship or as effecting the particular rite of passage, it needs to be familiar as a worship form. In other words, it needs to be traditional, sometimes radically so. (Here we are simply thinking of the reaction of the worshipper to the familiar. Below we will also discuss the advantage of tradition in effecting rites of passage.) But at the same time, for the rite to be meaningful it has to speak to the present age and its agenda. That the traditional liturgy often cannot do. For example, the 'traditional' funeral service is often requested, but a simple use of 1662, eschewing any sermon and never even mentioning the name of the deceased, completely fails to meet the most common basic requirements of the contemporary funeral.

The regular worshipping congregation, on the other hand, is in an altogether different situation. While the basic needs of familiarity and relevance are there, frequent attendance and a strong identification with the other worshippers enables the individual to cope with, and indeed want, far greater variety and novelty. The practical result is that when one has a mixture of regular and occasional worshippers, leading the service can be somewhat like holding a meeting when half the group is on *terra firma* and the other half on a travelator.

But more than the practicalities, we need to consider the theological self-understanding of the regular worshipping congregation. Ironically it is perhaps here that we may find the best evidence of 'secularisation', where the church and the world occupy totally separate compartments. John Gladwin has pointed out for us how, while the Book of Common Prayer has a specific and concrete conception of church and society, the *Alternative Service Book* 'has no conscious idea of what understanding of the place and mission of the Church it is trying to sustain'.[14] While society is lost in the cloud of unknowing, the consciousness of the church has turned in on itself in a way which is all too specific and indeed confident. The loss of transcendence within the modern liturgy is almost total. To take one particular but very significant example, in the eucharist we are no longer to be brought to eternal life but are kept within it, both in the absolution and also in the words of communion. In effect, the congregation claims to be already in full possession of the Kingdom of God, which is a claim both to God and to the world outside. The message spoken by 'keep you in eternal life' is, stay where you are, and all will be well. Now this is a criticism of the liturgical work of the 1970s, and nothing is more galling than wisdom which comes twenty years after the event. More recent proposed revisions are all too aware of the problem overall and in various ways attempt to reintegrate a sense of the transcendent, but it is still very much a current issue in the worshipping congregations, where the language of twenty years ago is reinforcing its effect each week.

One of the most important steps forward is the report *On The Way*, sponsored jointly by the Board of Mission, the Board of Education and the Liturgical Commission, looking together at the whole area of mission and the integration of new members into the life of the church. The motif of the church as the pilgrim people of God, adopted by that report, is in part designed to overcome the static picture we have seen of the church already in total possession of the Kingdom. But also we have the proposal to introduce into the church the 'inquirer', that is, the person who is on the path of conversion and integration into the church and preparing for sacramental initiation. The inspiration for this is to be found in the Roman Catholic cate-chumenate. In Europe catechumens are still a rare species, the reason being that, for the most part, those coming into active Christian disci-pleship are already familiar with the basic values of Christianity. But as 'Christendom' recedes within our society, the number increases of those for whom the church is a totally novel and foreign world. Such people need time to adjust as they are integrated into the life of the church. The catechumenate movement, as it is known, seeks to inte-grate conversion as a process along with learning the facts about the Christian gospel, growing in prayer and the Christian life, and inte-gration into the community of the church. All these things are necessary in any instance of bringing someone to discipleship. But to adopt the new 'category' of an inquirer alongside that of the commu-nicant members of the church and the non-communicants, mainly children, is both a statement of the commitment of the church to mission, and an acknowledgement of the growing distance between the church and society which can be bridged only by such a radical innovation.

It is hard to avoid the conclusion that one of the prime symptoms of the division between the habitual and the occasional churchgoer is the dominance of the eucharist in modern Anglican worship. The pattern of cause and effect is complex, and certainly it is inadequate simply to say that the eucharist is off-putting to occasional worship-pers and therefore should be celebrated less often. What is perhaps more distinctive than the dominance of the eucharist is the collapse of Morning Prayer as the main Sunday service and the eclipse of Evening Prayer. But while the latter has been lost largely through the demise of evening services in general (most people now only go to church once on a Sunday, and evening attendance, once general, has become the mark of particular evangelical churches), the former has lost out to the eucharist but also to the family service. It is as though the habit of worship has changed: the thoughtful, word-based service has given way either to the symbol-based eucharist or the musical and affective family service, one demanding and the other eschewing a high personal commitment on the part of the individual. There is no middle ground. The shift in habit is something which has happened almost entirely at the grass-roots level. The Parish Communion movement provided the theological apparatus for the eucharist, but the shift is far wider in that the family service has no such undergirding. There is no doubt that the latter attracts the larger congregations, and in that respect at least is the more popular and successful. However, clergy often dislike it for being shallow and trite; in part this is snobbery, but also it is hard to avoid the problem that growth in the Christian life includes growth in worship, both for the individual and for the community. And whatever one's tradition, the sacraments of the gospel frame one's Christian self-understanding and worship. It is not just academic theory but experience that confirms the capacity of sacramental worship to engage us at a radically deep level and give us a unique language to worship God. And while this form of worship may seem opaque, impenetrable even to the newcomer, it sustains many a congregation in the Christian life.

How does one provide a bridge to the eucharist from the family service? It is largely in this context that one may see the work of the Liturgical Commission in its *Patterns for Worship* and related material. In part it seeks to give substance to the otherwise insubstantial family service; in part it is also trying to train congregations and worship leaders in a style of worship which involves use of the symbol and the action and has less reliance on the written word cn the page. The immediate context was the response of the church to the needs of the inner city, but that is only the thin end of the wedge. Many middle-class people are put off by books just as are the working-class people described in *Faith in the City*. And, as I have just mentioned, action and symbol enable much fuller engagement in worship than does the spoken and heard word. People need to be trained in this mode, the sacramental, spoken of warmly by St Augustine and the sixteenth century reformers as 'visible words'. But also the 'Service of the Word' in *Patterns for Worship* is the kind of service aimed at as the proper successor to Morning Prayer: something besides the dominical sacraments, which stands in its own right as fitting worship of God and feeding the congregation.

One problem in all this is the question of novelty and tradition. As I have already mentioned, the regular congregation tends to demand more variety than the occasional worshipper may be happy with. But at the official level of liturgical writing, there is seemingly a limitless appetite for the production of new versions, shapes and texts. Back in 1974 John Halliburton imagines, beside pictures of the Bachs all playing and the Breughels all painting, 'all the liturgists busy writing canons'.[15] Since then, besides the considered works of the Liturgical

Commission and the occasional offerings of diocesan committees, there is a veritable industry of liturgists whose status may be described as charismatic rather than institutional, and are perhaps more popular (at any rate less derided) than the institutions. For all these, *amour-propre* is naturally on the side of new writing rather than the conservation of the old.

To some extent we are faced by an unusual problem, namely the artificial 'freezing' of the Anglican liturgy from 1662 until the beginning of the nineteenth century. Much water had gone under the bridge in the meantime, and while liturgical needs had changed, the liturgy remained static. To say that a liturgy is timeless is a condemnation rather than a compliment. So there was much making up to do. The head of water was such that, when the dam burst, the torrent swept all before it. Babies were washed away with the bath water. The Lord's Prayer is a classic example of how radical change came in because it seemed to the liturgical drafters that gradual change still lagged dangerously behind. With Series 2 'which art' and 'in earth' became 'who art' and 'on earth'. Virtually no one blinked and, if the path of gradualism had been given time, another generation could easily have coped, say, with the demise of 'trespasses'. And so on. But gradualism was not given that space. A new translation, ecumenically and internationally sponsored, entered the lists and we find ourselves with competing texts for the prayer which many Christians would consider their birthright. At a time when the collapse of a common Christian education leaves a huge proportion of the population ignorant of any Lord's Prayer, the church cannot decide which alternative to encourage. It is ironic that the old justification of a fixed liturgy, that a traveller will find the familiar in any church in the world, has just become relevant at a time when common forms are being abandoned.

The Lord's Prayer is only one example of the problem we find ourselves in, with congregations becoming increasingly distanced both from the world and from one another. The church is in danger of subdividing into a number of groups, each with its own approach to worship. Movement from one to another is liable to become increasingly difficult.

Common prayer

The issue of 'common prayer' has been one of the major topics over the last decade. The Liturgical Commission raised the question in print in its directory of services, *Patterns for Worship*. (Report stage

1989). The approach of the Commission merits quotation at some length.

> 'Common prayer' does not in fact exist, in the sense of being able to walk into any church in the land and find exactly the same words to follow. Nor should we pretend that it would be either good or right to return to a position – well over a century ago – when that might have been the case. Rather, 'common prayer' exists in the Church of England in the sense of recognizing, as one does when visiting other members of the same family, some common features, some shared experiences, language, patterns or traditions. To accept a variety of forms, dictated by local culture, is part of our Anglican heritage, spelt out by Archbishop Thomas Cranmer in his 1549 *Preface:* 'it often chanceth diversely in diverse countries'.
>
> What are the marks of Anglican worship that we might expect to find (or have a right to find?) in any service? We believe that some of the marks which should be safeguarded for those who wish to stand in any recognizable continuity with historic Anglican tradition are:
>
> –   a clear structure for worship
> –   an emphasis on reading the word of God and on using psalms
> –   liturgical words repeated by the congregation, some of which, like the creed, would be known by heart
> –   using a collect, the Lord's Prayer, and some responsive forms in prayer
> –   a recognition of the centrality of the eucharist
> –   a concern for form, dignity and economy of words ...
>
> Another mark of Anglican worship is a willingess to use forms and prayers which can be used across a broad spectrum of Christian belief. This may sometimes mean that, for the sake of the unity of the Church, we refrain from using some words which reflect one of the traditional 'party' positions.[16]

Is the Commission attempting to describe or is it seeking to propose a form of Anglican liturgy? If the former, then it makes a poor job of it. Historic Anglicanism from the mid sixteenth to the mid twentieth century is unrecognisable when no mention is made of the Prayer Book. And while it is wrong to overemphasise the uniformity at the parish level, variety dictated by local culture cannot be projected onto Archbishop Cranmer. The Commission's quotation (actually of the last words of *Of Ceremonies*) refers to the variety not of forms of worship but of its abuses and the steps necessary to erase them. Certainly Cranmer proposed the right, if not the duty, of a state to legislate for its own liturgical provision, but there is no room for variety within the State. In the Preface of the Prayer Book, diversity is clearly regarded as a regrettable state of affairs resulting from an inability to understand the government's directions properly, and is something to be resolved by seeking a ruling from the bishop.

The issue was taken up by the Prayer Book Society, which of course had a rather different idea of common prayer than that described by the Liturgical Commission. At an eirenic meeting in November 1992, members of the Society and the Commission could happily agree that once flexibility is pursued beyond a certain point unity is destroyed, but there was no consensus where the point lies.[17] The Commission took the discussion further in its collection of essays, *The Renewal of Common Prayer*, in which it discusses the notion of Common Prayer using the notion of a 'core' rather than the old contrast of freedom and variety. In a sustained treatment, Michael Vasey speaks about 'identifying the core' under the headings of 'patterns and structures', 'presentation', 'familiar words', 'agreed norms and boundaries', and 'hymnody'.[18]

A liturgical core?

Rather than discuss Michael Vasey's piece in detail, I would like to draw out some ideas about the core by suggesting my own headings, and examining very briefly how liturgy might matter in different ways to different people. For the 'core' can mean several quite different things. In practice these often overlap, but it is important here to keep them distinct in our minds.

1. *Textual Core.* When a centralised authority writes texts for use, then there has to be a standard text from which copies or versions are made. The core text itself may never actually be used. For example the Roman Catholic *editio typica* of a new rite is written in Latin and then translated into the various vernaculars for use, but there is no necessity for the *editio typica* itself to be used in worship.

2. *Theological Core.* A text or action may be the core since it is held to embody certain theological doctrines or agreed conventions. As such we may be speaking either about a whole service book, like the Book of Common Prayer, or a set phrase which has become theologically conventional. The Dixian four-fold shape might come under this heading since it is something which belongs in many ways to academic reflection rather than congregational consciousness.

Instances of the Theological Core can be divided between two groups which I shall describe as *standard* and *compromise*.

– Standard. The Standard forms are close to the idea of the Textual Core. These are where we begin, and in the Church of England the Book of Common Prayer of 1662 is the doctrinal standard of worship, from which the alternative forms are held not to deviate in any essential manner.[19] In this respect, like the Textual Core, it would remain the Standard even if it were not actually used.

– Compromise. Many expressions in the liturgy are the result of theological compromise and 'fruitful ambiguity'. It has been ever thus. The 1662 version of the Book of Common Prayer has its full share. Unlike the Standard Core, which has a claim to permanence, the Compromise Core is, in principle, ephemeral. However, it often has its own status in that people tend to look for historical precedent for compromise. For example the 1549 Prayer Book has provided instances of compromise more broadly ambiguous and acceptable than can be offered by 1662. In the eucharist, the 1662 'Prayer of Consecration' is, when read literally, a prayer for those receiving communion. (The 1662 version inserted references to consecration of the bread and the wine into the 1552 prayer by giving it the title mentioned above, by adding the manual acts and by inserting an *Amen* before the administration of the sacrament.) Revisions of the eucharist from Series 2 to the ASB have borrowed the 1549 Prayer Book's very ambiguous formula, that the bread and wine 'may be to us' the body and blood of Christ. And in the funeral service, the composers of modern funeral services, wishing to do more than commit the body to the ground, as is the case in 1662, look to 1549 for precedent in commending the departed to God. And these particular phrases have become almost 'Standard' in their own right.

The problem with the 'Compromise' Core is keeping it in proper relation with other issues. If we ignore it then we tread carelessly on the delicate balance of the traditions within Anglicanism. There is a very healthy principle in liturgical composition, namely that what one person is allowed to use, all must feel able to use. The 'Compromise' Core preserves this. But at the same time over-concern for areas of theological controversy can blind the eye to other issues. And it is all too easy to end up defining points of controversy as the points worthy of special note. For example, in *Patterns for Worship*, this logic is seen in the comment, 'One way of securing doctrinal orthodoxy and avoiding the divisions caused by "party" texts would be to have some parts of the service with a limited number of options: for example, the creed, confession and absolution, specific prayer about the departed, and the Eucharistic prayer.'[20]

3. *Legal Core*. Closely related to the question of Core is that of legality, above all in the marriage service but not irrelevant elsewhere. The Law has its own criteria but these need only be mentioned but not discussed here.

4. *Archetypal Core*. Some liturgies are composed from the point of view of archetypal situations, and varieties may then be provided for other cases. For example in the ASB, adult baptism, confirmation and eucharist is provided as the archetypal initiatory rite, and from it are derived other rites. The eucharistic service is composed with a parish Sunday eucharist in mind, but there are only insignificant variations for weekday use or celebrations with large numbers of non-communicants.

5. *Efficient Core*. Some parts of a service are necessary because otherwise the service would not do what it set out to do. This core may be set as a theological core, but not necessarily so. The core of the marriage service would include the section required by law. Also the congregation will have its own idea about what constitutes the efficient core. For some, a funeral service is not complete without a particular hymn, or a description of the deceased. And it is likely that to hear the words, 'earth to earth, ashes to ashes, dust to dust' is more important than the language of commending or committing, and to hear about the character of the deceased matters more than the precise terminology of how the dead are remembered or prayed for.

6. *Evangelistic Core*. The liturgy is about groups and communities, but above all it is about the love of God in Christ. Worship must be faithful to the gospel and seek to communicate it both in teaching the faith and in seeking to appropriate it in this instance, by word, prayer and sacrament. Sometimes there can be a real conflict, for example, when a minister is serving a mourning family who do not wish to use very much if anything of the Christian funeral service. They want a sermon about the deceased and the hymn, 'The old rugged cross'. The minister's pastoral response in trying to meet the mourners' wishes and yet remain faithful to the Christian gospel of dying and rising with Christ as taught and celebrated in the liturgy is a different approach from the two cores already considered, though obviously it overlaps.

7. *Structural Core*. What I call the structural core enables a service to be used and followed by the worshippers, and this is a regular feature of all styles of worship in all traditions. A Free Church minister used to 'unstructured worship' will still joke about how the

congregation will react if they sing one more or one fewer hymn than usual in a service. An established pattern lets people feel at home. But it is not simply a matter of the order of prayers or the number of hymns. Content is equally important. Set phrases, for example beginning the eucharistic prayer with the *sursum corda*, enable people to know where they are in the rite. Congregational participation moves everyone along together at these points. In congregations with a more fluid structure of worship, or where there are any number of strangers, the contribution of the worship leader is necessary in telling people what is going to happen next.

8. *Responsive Core.* This is my term for the texts that stick in the memory and affection of individuals, and includes not only the Lord's Prayer and the Grace but also such things as the Collect for Purity, the General Thanksgiving and the Prayer of St Richard of Chichester. This criterion would seem to be the basis for the list of the 'core texts' in Michael Vasey's article[21] and for much of the discussion in the whole book.

9. *Pastoral Core.* This was championed by Alan Wilkinson in an article in the *Church Times* on 1 May 1992. Wilkinson bemoaned the lack of well-learned prayers, psalms and Bible texts which people could know and rely on in times of crisis. In earlier generations there had been good manuals produced giving the essence of the Christian faith, some popular and useful prayers and providing relevant texts for ministry to the sick and so on. Wilkinson's Knapsack (as this proposal is generally known, from an analogy he draws from his army days) is directed to the needs of the individual but there is an obvious and important link with public worship. And Wilkinson blames modern fashions for the decline in familiarity with these key texts: 'By the 1980s ... this common stock had largely been destroyed by liturgical change, by ecumenism which resulted in a loss of Anglican identity, by individualism clerical and lay, by the growth of non-liturgical worship, by secularisation and by the rejection of the habitual and ritualised in favour of the spontaneous and personal.' The liturgy needs to build up the individual member, and that is done not just by teaching or by sharing in uplifting worship, but also by providing texts to lean on in times of need. These must be familiar, and ideally known by heart so that they can be spoken from the heart. But for this to be aided by public worship, then there must be a greater reliance on the simple, the memorised, the well-worn. Wilkinson appeals for a period of 'concentration and convergence' after the recent years of variety and experimentation, but admits, 'that would require a degree

of discipline and self-abnegation unfamiliar to many Anglicans'. He asks for convergence, not for conservatism. This is no attempt to turn the clock back.

Fixity and importance

Within the context of core texts, we must consider the question of the fixity of forms of words. Again this is a matter of historical description rather than prescription. There is no *a priori* reason why there should be unchanging prayers and formulae. The first centuries of Christian worship were marked by considerable variety, and since the Reformation some traditions have reclaimed that ancient style. But, as a general principle, words become fixed when they are deemed to be important, and fixity gives an impression of importance. A classic example is that of the words of institution in the various eucharistic prayers in the Church of England and the Roman Catholic Church. They have a special importance in Western eucharistic thought, with a heritage of their being words of consecration. One of the more curious liturgical discussions which I have attended was at a conference for Diocesan Liturgical Committees in York in September 1990, when a straw vote was solicited backing the Liturgical Commission's call for variable words of institution in new eucharistic prayers. (If I remember rightly, the bishops had wanted the same formula in all the prayers.) And it was said at the conference discussion: they are not words of consecration; they do not need to be marked out by being fixed. This is true enough; but what we can see from the discussion is the natural tendency to show that something is important by making it to be fixed in form, and contrariwise that fixity of itself seems to mark out something as being theologically important (and words of institution are deemed to be words of consecration).

Let us now apply the same principle of fixity to other services. The marriage rite is remarkable in the ASB for being a very conservative revision, especially in the marriage vows. And they remained virtually unchanged in Cranmer's revision, losing only the wife's promise to be bonny and buxom in bed and at board, and substituting the more prosaic 'to love, cherish and obey' (the husband too had the novelty of undertaking to love and cherish his bride). In effect the most important words that most people say in their lives have remained virtually unchanged since perhaps the mid fourteenth century.

To explore this point verges on the sentimental. But the principle comes to the heart of many ceremonies as rites of passage, where our identity is conferred on us not by how we stand apart from other individuals but by how we are united with them. This raises in many contemporary people in our society bemusement or even horror, and the urge is strong to privatise rites of passage, opting out of the marriage service and stealing away with the cremated remains. It is a rare experience, limited now to country areas, for the bride to walk to church past the grave of her grandparents or great-grandparents, or only a little less rare for a child to be baptised in the same font as had been his or her father or mother. When it happens it is often taken for granted, but the occasional response convinces me of the hidden strength of these occasions. But localised fixity is becoming a rarity even in village life, and would be almost unknown for the urban majority of our population. Hospices and crematoria are taking on something of the role, but they are involved only with death. Marriages are possible not only at the local church or register office, representing the community where the couple live, but also at places of their choice: football grounds or historic buildings. The church is ceasing to be the 'shrine' for its community. Indeed people are learning to do without such community shrines altogether, but that is a reflection on the community rather than on the shrine.

Fixity is seen also in the liturgical formulae of the rites of passage. I am baptized, married, and buried with the same words as those who came before me and will come after me. The words of committal of the departed form part of the general consciousness, and 'dust to dust, ashes to ashes' is a well-known phrase, just as 'till death us do part' was well enough known to have formed the title of a BBC comedy show.

These formulae are texts couched in performative language. It is one of the features of performative language that it is governed and given its force by conventions within society.[22] At one level the required convention for the due enactment of a liturgical performative text is that it be authorised by General Synod. Whether this is sufficient convention I doubt. Unless the congregation recognises and 'owns' the text and its conventions it is difficult to see how it could function. Presumably there must have been considerable problems in the mid sixteenth century over the loss of publicly-owned conventions and texts, not that Cranmer would have held that to be at all important. His liturgy was imposed on the public for their good, not offered for their choice. The liturgical texts would have gained strength as performative texts only with time. But it is within this context that we can understand the particular advantage of the slow evolution of the vows in the marriage service. Changes have definitely happened, and many a couple must be glad that the bride's behaviour at bed and board were no longer specified from the sixteenth century, and that she no longer has to obey in the late twentieth. But at the same time the formula is recognisably the same, and the institution of marriage is maintained by the continuity as well as (most would affirm) served by the emendations.

Moving forward

At the time of writing, the liturgical world in the Church of England is coming to terms with the General Synod's rejection of the six new eucharistic prayers which were part of the new eucharistic rites to succeed those in the ASB. Clearly there are many causes for their failure; here I wish to suggest a weakness in them which would at least make them open to those negative influences. As Colin Buchanan suggests, the lack of continuity with standard Church of England texts would have had a debilitating effect: 'the Church of England at large was not quite ready to rally to the innovatory, and so the consensus did not appear'.[23] Why such a lack of continuity? In effect the prayers adopted both a new content, being much less conceptual and more based in concrete imagery, and also new structures, with a large number of different congregational responses. There was very little for the Synod members to identify with, which left the opponents with a free hand. The failure of the prayers leaves open the question of what prayers are to go in the new rite. But what is far more troubling is the overall lack of direction given by Synod. As Bryan Spinks complained in a letter to the *Church Times* (15 March 1996),

> [The prayers] were compiled in response to the cacophony of conflicting and contradictory criteria which emanated from Synod and the wider Church: user-friendly language, but poetic, evocative and resonant; suitable for UPAs, but also for rural areas, and, at the same time, for the whole Church; for family worship and 'normal' Sunday worship; responsive, but unitary; language for children, but not language which adults would find childish; concerned with creation and justice, but 'classical' in content; different in style from the ASB, but not too innovative; different forms of institution narrative, but at the same time making the narrative a common formula.

This is indeed a serious complaint, and compounded by the frustration when a bishop can make an objection to the prayers in Synod which he has not made on 'up to seven previous occasions open to him'.[24] But if these prayers should have failed, how might some of them have fared if they had gone to Synod in the versions first published, in the report edition of *Patterns for Worship*? There we have the Sanctus at the end of two prayers, an even greater variety of congregational responses, and a totally unparallelled (in Church of England rites) form of petition for consecration, that God may 'show' the bread and wine to be the body and blood of Christ.[25] These were removed by the due process of committee, a classic example of the tendency of liturgical revision to begin with radical new ideas and move back, stage by stage, to the familiar. In the revised versions which came to Synod, the Sanctus is to be found in the position familiar to users of the ASB,[26] and 'show' is abandoned in favour of 'may be for us': a phrase closer to the old Anglican precedent of the 1549 rite.[27]

But it is ironic that, at virtually the same time as this débâcle in General Synod was unfolding, Paul Bradshaw should have been asking for greater diversity in liturgy, in his address to the Congress of *Societas Liturgica* in Dublin in August 1995.[28] He does not by any means ask for an 'anything goes' variety, rather that the divergence should reflect the ecclesiological diversity of the different Christian traditions rather than the mid twentieth century ecumenical sameness. He claims that there is a diversity and richness in the worship of all Christian traditions, but historically it is hard to see how this can be claimed without important qualifications. He asks for 'a greater attentiveness to tradition – to the whole of tradition and not just to a selective sampling of it'.[29] But it is hard to imagine which denominational tradition is really adequate to the task of resourcing the modern British situation. At the most basic level, is hymnody to be resisted by Roman Catholics, or lectionaries by Free Church ministers, for they belong more to ecumenical borrowing than to the particular traditions?

At one level these instances may seem like trivia, but they affect the entire culture of a worshipping tradition. A service of Morning or Evening Prayer or of the Holy Communion from the Book of Common Prayer with choral music but without hymnody is today virtually unknown and would seem even to most traditionalist Anglicans as verging on the bizarre. In one respect 1662 remains the touchstone of the liturgy of the Church of England, in another it is unrecognisable and unusable. How do we fulfil Bradshaw's challenge, to discover richness and yet enter into our own tradition?

By way of conclusion, I wish to make a number of observations and suggestions which sum up much of what has been discussed throughout the chapter.

First, the two scenarios feared by John Fenwick and Bryan Spinks, of a centrifugal outburst of diversity, or a recrudescence of conservatism, must both be avoided. We must not lose our identity. At the same time it is impossible simply to stop, still less to go backwards. Any attempt to force this to happen would run the risk of shattering what little consensus there is. How do we plot a safe course between Scylla and Charybdis? Alan Wilkinson's watchword of convergence offers us a model of going forward while avoiding yet more needless variety. New liturgy and radical initiatives still need to be made (and the catechumenate is an outstanding example), but modest change, conserving where possible the traditional, must be a higher priority than it has been in the recent past.

The task of liturgical revision is always led by the desire to improve. Now, this is worthy in itself, but there is no end to possible improvements. The ability to write a better form of service is in itself not sufficient reason why a Liturgical Commission should propose one, or why a parish priest should replace what is provided with a home-made version. Regardless of its quality, a prayer has a certain status as the property of the whole church and its heritage and should be respected as such. Gradual improvement is generally better than wholesale demolition. And unless the new is mingled with the old, then it proves indigestible. Public worship seems to be one exception to our Lord's dictum about wine and wineskins, but in commanding his disciples to continue the established customs of shared meals and ritual lustrations – with a new meaning – perhaps he himself allowed the exception.

In particular, major changes of structure should not happen at the same time as major changes of content. That was attempted, in a comparatively modest form, in the new eucharistic prayers, and failed. Other forms of service which are soon to be revised by the Liturgical Commission, such as the marriage and funeral rites, would benefit from improvement, but not from someone seeking to reinvent the wheel.

Creativity needs to be properly channelled rather than stifled. One challenging feature of some of the new eucharistic prayers was that the celebrant was invited to compose a proper preface. There are countless options in the ASB for new compositions – the intercessions, prayers when the bread and wine are brought to the table, prayers after communion – which could be exploited but are not. The possibilities with music are limited only by the vision and ability of the musicians. Much could happen without any need to change core texts. But respect for core texts and basic structures requires that virtue which Alan Wilkinson describes as 'a degree of discipline and self-abnegation unfamiliar to many Anglicans'. I am not saying that everything must be squeezed into a straitjacket of 1662 or the ASB.

But both texts can be used far more creatively than they are, and are often quite unnecessarily abandoned in favour of an alternative which is beautiful only in the eyes of its maker.

Services belong to the worshipping congregation rather than to the Central Board of Finance of the Church of England. Discussion of the various types of core liturgy bring out the many different aspects to be considered, and in particular how important is the response of the worshippers. The academic theology, the legal authorisation, are only one side of the equation. The context of the community and the response of the individual also are important, but so easily forgotten or undervalued. There is a curious form of blinkering in the clerical mind which can propose that the only words of the funeral service known to all: 'earth to earth, ashes to ashes, dust to dust', should be made optional.[30] Care needs to be taken to identify what is important to people and if possible to preserve and enhance it. And 'people' includes the outsider, the irregular attender and the member of another tradition within Anglicanism as well as one's own fellow travellers.

The closure of churches (during the week and permanently), less frequent Sunday attendance, the privatisation of public ceremonial, have all led to a diminution in the role of churches as the 'shrines' for their communities. If the Church of England wishes to hold on to its role as the 'established' church of this country, then this is a greater problem than its relations with Parliament. And if we are convinced of the virtue of the community as the proper forum for the great events in individuals' lives, then we need to fight back against the growing privatisation.

What happens in individual congregations cannot be controlled by legislation; it must be directed by education. Ordinands are given an introduction to academic and pastoral liturgy as part of their training. But experienced clergy also need to reflect on their liturgical ministry more closely than happens at present. And, above all, the laity, both leaders and participants in worship, also need to reflect on and learn from what they are doing Sunday by Sunday and day by day. This raises the question of resources. The world of liturgy is populated by enthusiastic amateurs. But if the worship of God is what the Church exists for, then we need a more sustained approach to the whole issue. Finance needs to be forthcoming; the study of liturgy needs to be supported by scholars from the whole range of disciplines (theological, historical, sociological, linguistic ...) which reflect the role and importance of worship in the life of the Church. And programmes of clergy and lay training need to be sponsored and funded so that the whole people of God can participate more fully and contribute with greater ability, confidence and genuine creativity to the worship of God.

Notes

1. Bridget Nichols, *Liturgical Hermeneutics: Interpreting Liturgical Rites in Performance* (Peter Lang, Frankfurt am Main, 1996), though a book for the specialist, offers many new ideas and is far more manageable than some other writers in the discipline.
2. J.R.K. Fenwick and B.D. Spinks, *Worship in Transition* (T&T Clark, Edinburgh, 1995), p. 196.
3. The immense amount of research into Cranmer's Prayer Books is ably summarised by Diarmaid McCulloch in *Thomas Cranmer* (Yale University Press, New Haven and London, 1996).
4. R.C.D. Jasper, *The Development of the Anglican Liturgy 1662-1980* (SPCK, London, 1989), p. 128.
5. I owe this approach to Gareth Lloyd, whose study of the period awaits publication.
6. *Report of the Royal Commission on Ecclesiastical Discipline* (His Majesty's Stationery Office, London, 1906), paras 399-401, pp. 75-6.
7. See J. Bentley, *Ritualism and Politics in Victorian Britain* (Oxford University Press, Oxford, 1978).
8. *Church Assembly Proceedings*, 1928, pp.114-19, quoted by R.C.D. Jasper, op.cit., p. 147.
9. R.C.D. Jasper, ibid., p.147-8.
10. For the Canon Law background, see Donald Gray, 'The Revision of Canon Law and its Application to Liturgical Revision in the Recent History of the Church of England', *The Jurist*, 48 (1988), pp. 638-52.
11. P. Welsby, *A History of the Church of England* (Oxford University Press, Oxford, 1984), pp. 222-3.
12. J.R.K. Fenwick and B.D. Spinks, op. cit., p. 16.
13. G. Davie, *Religion in Britain since 1945: Believing without Belonging* (Blackwell, Oxford, 1994).
14. 'Liturgy in its Social Context', in Michael Perham (ed.), *The Renewal of Common Prayer* (SPCK, London, 1993; = GS Misc 412), p. 40.
15. 'The Canon of Series 3' in R.C.D. Jasper (ed.), *The Eucharist Today* (SPCK, London, 1974), p. 95.
16. *Patterns for Worship* (Liturgical Commission Report: GS 898, Church House Publishing, London, 1989), pp. 5-6.
17. The papers at this meeting are published in Michael Perham (ed.), *Model and Inspiration* (SPCK, London, 1992).
18. 'Promoting a Common Core', in Michael Perham (ed.), *The Renewal of Common Prayer*, op. cit., pp. 81-101.
19. Cf. e.g. Canons A5, B4.
20. *Patterns for Worship*, Commended edition (Church House Publishing, London, 1995), p. 6.
21. 'Promoting a Common Core', in M. Perham (ed.) *The Renewal of Common Prayer*, op. cit., pp. 93-4.
22. See J.L. Austin, *How to Do Things with Words* (Oxford University Press, Oxford, 1975), e.g. p. 14.

23. *News of Liturgy* (255, March 1996), p. 5.

24. Michael Vasey, letter, *Church Times*, 15 March 1996.

25. *Patterns for Worship,* Liturgical Commission Report, pp. 239–51. Prayers B and C use 'show' (pp. 244, 248) and invoke the precedent of a Patristic Greek formula. (For the background of these prayers, see *Patterns for Worship: Essays on Eucharistic Prayers*: GS Misc. 333 n.d.)

26. The ASB structure of the eucharistic prayer is of course radically different from that in the 1662 Communion Service where we have the order: Preface, Sanctus, Prayer of Humble Access, Prayer of Consecration, Communion, Lord's Prayer, Prayer of Oblation or Prayer of Thanksgiving. The joining together of the Preface, Sanctus, Prayer of Consecration, Prayer of Oblation into a single eucharistic prayer was the aim of the so-called Interim Rite. But this was not so much a novelty as a conscious rejection of the 1552/1662 shape in favour of 1549 and Patristic and medieval models. For the long history of such rejections of 1552/1662 from the Laudians onward, see e.g. G.J. Cuming, *A History of Anglican Liturgy*, 2nd edn (Macmillan, London, 1982), pp. 106ff., and K.W. Stevenson, *Eucharist and Offering* (Pueblo, New York, 1986), pp. 149ff.

27. 1549 has 'may be unto us'. But even the small difference of 'for' may have influenced some suspicious Synod members towards rejection. For similar examples of 'reversion to type', one may think of the rejection of the 1928 eucharistic prayer in favour of the Interim Rite, or the troubled origins of the eucharistic prayer of Series 2, both described by R.C.D. Jasper in *The Development of Anglican Liturgy*. This is also good evidence for the usefulness of having many committee hoops for any proposed rite to jump through before it comes to Synod. Those who propose the disbanding of the Liturgical Commission should realise that it would only mean the end of this sieving process, and that Synod would find itself dealing with much less mature proposals for liturgical revision.

28. 'The Homogenization of Christian Liturgy,' *Studia Liturgica* 26 (1996), pp. 1–15.

29. ibid., p. 15.

30. The ASB note 5, p. 306 says the words are to be omitted in the case of burial at sea, but many clergy also feel that the words are not suitable in a crematorium. I would have thought them to be eminently appropriate.

9

The Ecumenical Agenda

Mary Tanner

This essay is a reflection on ecumenism taken as the movement of Christian churches seeking for unity, a unity in truth expressed in doing the will of God in every area of life and work, and participating in the mission of God to the world.[1] Christians share many concerns and make common cause with people of other faiths and ideologies. Inter-faith dialogue will inevitably gain in importance in the next millennium. Nevertheless, there is an appropriate concern for Christian unity which lies at the heart of the ecumenical movement.

An ecumenical agenda for the Church of England for the next century needs to be charted, recognising both what the Church of England is and its place in an already well-established and changing ecumenical movement. Continuity and renewal, preservation and transformation are basic principles for ecumenism and they will provide a focus for the present enquiry.

At the Reformation the Church of England understood itself as living in continuity with the ancient Church, though now independent from foreign papal jurisdiction. It reckoned its faith, sacraments and ministry as those of the catholic Church, reformed by the insights of the sixteenth century. This sense of continuity, catholicity and reformation is essential for understanding the Church of England's ecumenical relations today and its ecumenical future. The sense of belonging to the One, Holy, Catholic and Apostolic Church has been, and remains, fundamental for ecumenical engagement. It explains why relations with other Christian churches have always formed part of the Church of England's life. There were close links with the Reformed in France in the sixteenth and seventeenth centuries, the Orthodox and Moravian churches in the late nineteenth and early twentieth centuries, the Scandinavian and Baltic Lutheran churches in the early years of the twentieth century, the Old Catholics in the 1930s, the German Evangelical churches in the period between the wars and even through the last war, and with Roman Catholics in the Malines Conversations of the 1890s which intensified through the Anglican–Roman Catholic International dialogue in the 1970s and 1980s. These relations with other Christian traditions point to an Anglican sense of belonging to a wider Christian family, the fellowship of all the baptised, around the world and through the ages.

A recognition of the Church of England's understanding of itself as the continuing catholic church in this country, and a reminder of close relationships with those of other traditions from the Reformation onwards, is important for mapping out an ecumenical agenda for the future.

Also important for the ecumenical future is an understanding of the Church of England's place today within the worldwide Anglican Communion, an expanding fellowship of 37 provinces.[2] This Communion is open to a wider fellowship of those gathered by the Archbishop of Canterbury to the Lambeth Conference: the United Churches of South India, North India, Pakistan and Bangladesh, the Philippine Independent Church, the Mar Thoma Syrian Church of India, the Old Catholic Church and, most recently invited, those Nordic and Baltic Lutheran churches which have signed the Porvoo Agreement. The presence of these other churches, together with ecumenical observers, is a witness to the Anglican intention to search for a greater unity, a unity 'beyond Anglicanism'.

At its best the Anglican Communion provides the Church of England with a sense of belonging to a worldwide communion. It is a window into an even greater unity with an even richer diversity which is the promise held out by the ecumenical movement. It provides an experience of interdependence and mutual responsibility shared by those who live out their common faith in very different cultural contexts.

It was the Lambeth Conference that provided Anglicans with a skeletal statement of the bonds of their unity in the Chicago–Lambeth Quadrilateral. The Quadrilateral (adopted by the House of Bishops of ECUSA in Chicago in 1886 and by the Lambeth Conference of 1887) designates not only the essential marks of Anglican unity but also describes the marks of the unity which Anglicans seek to bind them together with all Christians in visible communion.

a.   The Holy Scriptures of the Old and New Testament, as 'containing all things necessary to salvation' and as being the rule and ultimate standard of faith.

b.   The Apostles' Creed, as the Baptismal Symbol; and the Nicene Creed, as the sufficient statement of the Christian faith.

c.   The two Sacraments ordained by Christ himself – Baptism and the Supper of the Lord – ministered with unfailing use of Christ's words of Institution, and of the elements ordained by Him.

d.   The Historic Episcopate, locally adapted in the methods of its administration to the varying needs of the nations and peoples called of God into the Unity of his Church.[3]

The Quadrilateral describes both that unity which God has given and that to which he calls. The Quadrilateral, in its basic form, has provided and continues to provide, an agenda for Anglican involvement in the ecumenical movement. There are some Anglicans who would want to add to these four essentials a statement on the collegial and conciliar life of the church, with a ministry of primacy exercised within that life for the sake of the maintenance of communion. Since the formation of the Quadrilateral Anglicans have developed structures of communion at a world level – the Lambeth Conference, the Anglican Consultative Council and the Primates' Meeting. The Archbishop of Canterbury exercises a personal ministry of unity for Anglicans which is valued by the provinces of the Communion.

Setting an ecumenical agenda for the Church of England for the next decade must take into account both the Church of England's understanding of itself as the continuing catholic church in England, and also its place today within the worldwide Anglican Communion. In deepening its ecumenical relations there is a delicate balance to be held by the Church of England (as for any other province of the Anglican Communion) between the unity enjoyed within the Anglican Communion and the growth to unity with other Christians in any particular region of the world. The unity of the Church has its local, regional, worldwide and universal dimensions.

The charting of an ecumenical agenda for the Church of England into the next millennium needs also to emerge from a realistic assessment of the ecumenical situation in England today. At the end of a century that has been called 'the ecumenical century', the ecumenical scene is complex and untidy, not easy to describe or to assess. After intense activity and high expectation, particularly after the entry of the Roman Catholic Church into the ecumenical scene following on Vatican II, it has become fashionable to talk of 'a winter of ecumenism', of an ecumenical movement that has ground to a halt. However, this judgement hardly does justice to the facts. It fails to acknowledge the dramatic change in attitudes of Christians of different traditions to one another, or to recognise the ecumenical dimension which is a normal part of the life of all the churches in

England today. Nor does it acknowledge the substantial formal agreements entered into in the last ten years.

As far as the Church of England is concerned it is clear that there has never been a period of so much ecumenical activity touching so many of its members. The primary place of ecumenical involvement is at the local level. Almost every church is part of some form of churches together in the locality. Some of these groupings share only a minimum of activities and in some places are losing some of their former enthusiasm, even for the annual celebration of the Week of Prayer for Christian Unity. In other places, however, churches share in many activities of worship, common life and witness. The Church of England is a member of more than 700 formal Local Ecumenical Partnerships. In different configurations, with Methodists, Baptists, Reformed, Roman Catholics, Moravians, Black Majority churches, a shared life may include a shared building, common baptisms, joint confirmations, shared worship – including the giving and receiving of eucharistic hospitality – shared ministry (though not interchangeable ministry), service to the wider community and evangelism. This shared living is governed by formal ecumenical canons.[4] New Christians find it hard in these situations to think of themselves as Anglicans or Methodists or Reformed, identifying themselves with the Christian community in that particular locality. More recently, ecumenical developments have seen the growth in ecumenical activity at an intermediate or county level with the sharing together of those who exercise oversight in the different churches, the sharing of specialist agendas and resources. In two places there has been the development of a regional, ecumenical council as well as the appointment of an ecumenical moderator in Milton Keynes. At national level the Church of England has seven ecumenical observers at the General Synod who may speak (though not vote) in debates. In return it sends representatives to the national governing bodies of the other major denominations. At national level, new ecumenical instruments, Churches Together in England (CTE) and the Council of Churches in Britain and Ireland (CCBI) help all the churches to act together in those things which it is possible to do together. The Roman Catholic Church and the Black Majority churches are now full members of these new structures. Using new patterns of collaborative work, with one church working on behalf of all the churches, or appointing one shared member of staff, the churches are working more closely together in the social, political and educational spheres. Annual gatherings of church representatives provide experience of shared worship and the exchange of common concerns. The Conference of European Churches and the World Council of Churches provide opportunities for wider ecumenical commitments and engagements.

None of this ecumenical activity at local, intermediate or national level is easy. In theory it makes sense to share resources and not to duplicate efforts and to do all that can be done together now. In practice ecumenical work is often cumbersome and slow to respond to areas of need. There is frustration about the untidiness and confusion of the ecumenical scene and the overload of structures servicing ecumenism. Some see resources as being diverted from what they believe is the primary task of the Church, namely its mission. There is sometimes uncertainty about the theological basis for such co-operation, particularly for Local Ecumenical Partnerships, and unclarity about where all of this sharing is supposed to be leading. On the other hand, the joint testimony of Archbishop Derek Worlock and Bishop David Sheppard of Liverpool remains: it is 'better together', and the prayer of Jesus, 'may they be one so that the world may believe' continues to be the guiding principle for many Christians.[5]

It is not always recognised that the advances in ecumenical living at the local and intermediate levels in England, paradoxically, owe much to the rejection by the Church of England of two major schemes for unity. The failure of the Anglican–Methodist scheme in the 1970s led to the promulging by the Church Assembly of Canon B15A which allows for the offering of eucharistic hospitality to those of other Christian traditions. Later it was the failure of the Covenanting proposals (with the Methodist, United Reformed and Moravian churches), that led to the promulging of Canons B43 and B44, the ecumenical canons, making possible the closer shared life, both generally and in designated Areas of Local Experiment, a name which perhaps more accurately points to the dynamic on the way to greater unity than the more recently adopted Local Ecumenical Partnerships.

The theological justification for the degree of ecumenical living in England today is there in the work of the earlier Anglican–Methodist conversations and in the work of the Covenanting Council. Both of these conversations registered a high degree of agreement in faith, sacraments and ministry, including a threefold, episcopally ordered ministry, as well as in the area of mission. The issue which remained the stumbling block was the lack of agreement on how to reconcile an episcopally-ordered ministry in the historic succession with the ministry of churches which, while they have a ministry of oversight, do not see the need for an episcopal ministry within the historic succession.

The theological justification for the growth in relations at local, intermediate and national level lies also in the impressive degree of ecumenical convergence and consensus arrived at in the international, multilateral, theological documents of the Faith and Order Commission of the World Council of Churches, and in the international bilateral dialogues of which the Church of England has been a part through its membership of the Anglican Communion. From 1972 onwards many impressive documents have been published. *Baptism, Eucharist and Ministry*, the report of the Faith and Order Commission of the World Council of Churches, provides evidence for converging agreement in areas of sacraments and ministry and offers a sure base for the ecumenical sharing which is developing in England.[6] The report of the Anglican–Reformed dialogue, *God's Reign and Our Unity*, perhaps the most visionary of all the dialogue reports, unfolds the picture of the unity of the Church and offers insights on the reconciliation of sacraments and ministries within the context of unity for mission and the vision of the Kingdom of God.[7] It again provides a theological rationale for Anglicans and Reformed in England to share more of their life and mission. Many would reckon the reports of the first and second Anglican–Roman Catholic Commission (ARCIC) the most remarkable and hopeful of all achievements.[8] The view of the Church of England, as indeed of the Anglican Communion as a whole, was that in the *Final Report of ARCIC I* it could recognise 'the faith of the Church of England' (the faith of Anglicans). This, together with subsequent work on ecclesiology, justification by faith, and the moral life provide a challenge to deepen Anglican–Roman Catholic relations in this country today. To these reports can be added those of the international conversations with the Orthodox, Lutheran and Methodist Churches

The theological basis for the degree of shared life developing in England is to be found in these bilateral and multilateral theological texts. However, the churches in England have generally been slow to draw the consequences for their life from these theological advances and to see how they might support an even closer commitment. Nevertheless, the most recent agreements between the Church of England and the Evangelical Church in Germany, between the Anglican churches of Britain and Ireland and some of the Nordic and Baltic Lutheran churches, and between the Church of England and the Moravian Church are hopeful and promising signs of what can be achieved when the theological conversations inspire a convergence in life.

These three agreements, and the relationships established by them, are very different but they each work with the same dynamic pattern. First, agreement is set out on the shared goal of visible unity and a commitment to go on seeking together that deeper communion in faith, sacraments, ministry and conciliar life in order to strengthen the

Church's service and mission. Next comes the setting out of explicit agreements in faith that exist between the partners.

Both *The Meissen Common Statement* with the Evangelical Church in Germany and *The Fetter Lane Common Statement* with the Moravian Church are honest about the remaining areas of difference that need to be tackled before visible unity is possible.[9] With the German churches the ministry of bishops and historic episcopal succession remain outstanding areas where more agreement is needed. With the Moravians the reconciliation of ministries, and how two churches of such very different size can live together in visible unity in the same territory without the one losing its distinctive ethos, remain issues to be faced. With a realistic acknowledgement of remaining differences both these agreements have enabled the churches to make a formal declaration of mutual acknowledgements and commitments, establishing a new and closer communion. The first five years of the Meissen Agreement have seen an active implementation of the commitments, an increase in sharing in many areas of life and a serious engagement with the outstanding theological difference which prevents visible unity.

In the case of the *Porvoo Common Statement*, the agreements in faith contain a breakthrough in reaching a common agreement on episcopacy in the service of the apostolicity of the Church, including agreement on the historic episcopal succession as sign.[10] This has made possible the ratification of a formal declaration containing mutual acknowledgements and commitments to share a common life in mission and service, to regard baptised members of all churches as members of our own, to establish a single interchangeable ministry (in accordance with any regulations in force at any particular time), to participate in episcopal consecrations, and to establish appropriate forms of collegial and conciliar life.

The story of these new and closer relationships gives the lie to talk of an ecumenical winter. Not only are Anglican, Lutheran, Reformed, United and Moravian churches being brought closer together, but the Anglican churches of Britain and Ireland are also experiencing something of their Anglican communion. In each of these agreements the concerns to manifest unity for the sake of a more credible witness to the gospel message of reconciliation and for a more effectively resourced mission have been dominating concerns. In a Europe seeking for its own unity and diversity, the calling of the Church to be a sign and instrument of unity has been a motivating force.

The agreements have been entered into in the light of already existing relations, on the basis of common statements of faith and with the expressed intention to live together in closer unity. Each sets out a vision of visible unity which is common to all and agreements in the essentials of the faith based on common bilateral and multilateral sources. In this way consistency and coherence is maintained, not only between these European agreements, but with agreements made in other parts of the Anglican Communion which seek to 'receive' the fruit of the same ecumenical reports. The theological convergences of the dialogues achieved with much patience and over many years are beginning to support new and committed relations in life. These agreements seem to prove both the degree of agreement in faith that churches already share, as well as the degree of communion that already exists between them.

What then in the light of where we are in the complex, all-round, all-level and multi-activity ecumenical movement with its mixture of failures and achievements, with the despondency of some and the continuing enthusiasm of others, ought to be the agenda of the ecumenical movement for the Church of England?

High on the Church of England's ecumenical agenda must be the task of clarifying, both with other provinces of the Anglican Communion and with ecumenical partners, a common understanding of the kind of Christian unity we seek to live together in this world. Bishop Lesslie Newbigin once wrote that a sincere intention to seek unity is incompatible with an intention to remain permanently uncommitted to any particular form of unity. The ecumenical movement in this country, as well as worldwide, needs a compelling, common portrait of the kind of unity God is calling us to live out in this world – the kind of unity that would be a foretaste and sign of the unity of God's Kingdom. In his Encyclical *Ut Unum Sint*, the Pope writes: 'What is needed is a calm, clear-sighted and truthful vision of things, a vision enlivened by divine mercy, and capable of freeing people's minds and of inspiring in everyone a renewed willingness, precisely with a view to proclaiming the Gospel to men and women of every people and nation'.[11]

Without a compelling portrait of the kind of united life Christians seek to live together, the ecumenical movement may be in danger of disintegrating into diverse, unconnected, episodic, even competing tasks with no continuity or overall direction. The old divisions between the tasks of faith and order, life and work and missionary endeavour have not yet been brought together within an overall understanding of unity. Unnecessary rivalries and jealousies between those who work in these several areas occur at all levels of the ecumenical movement.

A common portrait of visible unity needs to show that unity is required above all for the fitting praise and worship of the one God,

Father, Son and Holy Spirit. It is as Christians worship together that they experience at the deepest level, through the power of the Holy Spirit, what being in Christ is. In worship they are formed with a common identity as they encounter together the gospel message and make memorial together of the saving events of Christ's death and resurrection. From worship they are sent out together to witness and serve in the places where they are set.

A common portrait of unity must show how Christians united in the local church and at all levels of the church's life will in fact be more effective and credible in carrying out the church's missionary task. The unity and reconciliation of the churches ought to offer a convincing model of the possibility of reconciliation and unity in the human community. The question what sort of church for what sort of mission is crucial for those who seek a motivating portrait of unity. The unity of the Church is inseparable from the mission of the Church. Both belong to the very nature of the Church.

The unity and mission of the Church are inseparable from the diaconal work of the Church. What this might mean for a united Church has most recently been explored in the work on ecclesiology and ethics done by the World Council of Churches.[12] Christians are called to live together in God's world embodying and promoting just relations, engaging in concrete actions for justice and peace and showing that the Church exists for the entire creation.

A common portrait of unity must also convince that to talk of Christian unity is not to talk of clever ecclesiastical joinery which somehow manages by deceptive compromise to bind together those who have been divided. The unity Christians seek to live is one which will make evident the promise of a life lived together within the orbit of God's own trinitarian life. A common understanding of the Church as *koinonia* (communion) has become a central concern in almost every recent ecumenical document.[13] *Koinonia* is not one more image which, along with others, illustrates the kind of Church we seek to be. It is the concept which, when biblically explored, most aptly illuminates the character of the Church's fundamental unity.[14] A deeper ecumenical exploration of this concept would lead to a greater emphasis on the quality of life the Church of England seeks to live with other Christians. Unity entails qualities which reflect the personal and relational life of the God who binds Christians together in his own life and love. Personal and relational attitudes are the 'living tissue' of unity and a sign that unity is grounded in God's own life: patience, forbearance, generosity, the sharing of joys and the sorrows, constant repentance, forgiveness and, above all, love.

The portrait of unity needs to convince that the unity Christians seek to live involves the breaking-down of human divisions: the divisions of black and white, men and women, rich and poor, and of those with different abilities. These divisions insidiously affect the language, symbols and imagery in which the faith is proclaimed, the way the sacraments are administered, the way ministry is exercised, the way the Church's structures work and who is present in the places of power and authority. The ecumenical movement is about each church being renewed into unity. Unity and renewal are inseparable.

It is often asserted that visible unity is not to be confused with uniformity. 'Unity in Christ does not exist despite of and in opposition to diversity, but is given with and in diversity'.[15] The ecumenical movement has found it difficult so far to render a convincing view of the sort of diversity that will be held in unity. Diversity is not weakness or a concession to a negative human tendency to disagree. Authentic diversity reflects the many gifts of the Holy Spirit to the Church, as well as God's gifts in creation. Only a united Church which is richly diverse will match the love of God for variety which is so positively evident in the universe and in history. Nevertheless, there are 'limits to diversity' if communion is to be maintained in the face of never-ending challenges to the faith, order and moral teaching of the Church. The Canberra Assembly of the WCC in 1991 was challenged to give some preliminary description of what those limits are as it sought to draw a portrait of the visible unity of the Church. It was reticent but clear: 'diversity is illegitimate when, for example, it makes impossible the common confession of Jesus Christ as God and Saviour, the same yesterday, today and forever, or when it makes impossible the confession of salvation and the final destiny of humanity as proclaimed in the Holy Scriptures and preached by the apostolic community'.[16] There are tolerable limits to diversity but these are likely to be fewer than is usually asserted.

The more emphasis that is placed on the promise of diversity, the more there is need to develop a common understanding of those thin, steel-like bonds which bind Christians together in a united life, baptism and the one faith, the eucharist and the ordained ministry, synodality or conciliarity, and a ministry of primacy. The agenda set by the Lambeth Quadrilateral must remain an important skeletal framework for Anglicans in the ecumenical future. But much more exploration needs to be done in ecumenical exchange on how these steel-like bonds will help Christians in local churches around the world to live rich and textured lives of 'thickness' in the specificity of different cultures and the particularity of historical contexts: how they can encourage and support diversity. The Church is most effective when it is embodied within a local place, challenging wrongs, healing relationships, standing with the vulnerable and marginalised, and opening up new possibilities for mutual service, respect and love.

The portrait of unity will need to offer a greater clarity than has so far been reached in the ecumenical movement about structures of conciliar communion. What kind of structural co-operation would provide for local churches the awareness of belonging to a wider Christian fellowship and make for more effective ministry and mission? What kind of structures would serve a church that will always be confronted with new questions, will always be in dialogue, always searching to discern truth afresh under the Spirit's guidance? What kind of structures, collegial, communal and primatial, at each level of the Church's life (local, regional and worldwide) would provide for an interconnected life? What kind of structures, working with respect for subsidiarity, would enable the Church to live in fidelity to the apostolic faith, keeping Christians mutually accountable?

There must be a renewed emphasis on the possibilities offered by a united Christian life in the local church. 'It is in "each place" (however defined) where Christians rub shoulders daily and, more importantly, are observed by their non-Christian neighbours, that the reality of Christian fellowship is put to the test.'[17] But that has to be held together with a sense of belonging to the worldwide fellowship of Christians around the world today and the company of the faithful Christians through the centuries. When the local church glimpses this company of the faithful then it knows something of the true catholicity of the Church. The process *Called To Be One,* set up by Churches Together in England, is showing that it is precisely on how the local church is related to the universal Church that the churches in England lack a common understanding.[18] Some emphasise the local church at the expense of other dimensions, others emphasise the world level and neglect the richness of the local. The promise of ecumenism is that Christians will help one another to reach a more balanced ecclesiology and a common understanding of the relation of the local church to the other dimensions of the Church's life and how that is to be structured in practice.

The most important thing on the agenda for the Church of England, the Anglican Communion and for the ecumenical movement is to clarify a compelling portrait of the sort of united Church, devoted to its Lord and active in mission, Christians seek to become by God's grace; a portrait that would help to move them beyond the limits of the landscape that any of them at present knows.[19] It only confuses the matter to ask whether this is a model of 'organic union', 'full communion', 'reconciled diversity', or 'united not absorbed'.

A second item on the ecumenical agenda of the Church of England for the next decade ought to be to give encouragement to Christians to experience in their own lives, here and now, the degree of unity that already exists. Regular acts of joint worship, ecumenical cells of prayer and bible study should complement the celebration of the annual Week of Prayer for Christian Unity which suffers too often from being an isolated and forced time together. 'When brothers and sisters who are not in perfect communion with one another come together to pray, the Second Vatican Council defines their prayer as the soul of the whole ecumenical movement.'[20] The work of the liturgical movement has brought much more commonality to the liturgical life of the mainstream churches. Nevertheless, rich and distinctive liturgical traditions exist in each and are a potential rich common inheritance. Ecumenical worship needs to be more about sharing the riches of different traditions than sinking to the lowest common denominator of the pick-and-mix variety.

The encouragement of shared worship inevitably means facing the continuing divisions around the eucharistic table. There are not only two views: those who share the eucharist and those who do not. There are those who believe the eucharist is a means to unity and welcome all to an open table. There are others who believe that a degree of eucharistic hospitality, offered and received, does signify the degree of unity that already exists. Anglicans (and Roman Catholics in a much more restricted sense) represent this position. There are those who hold that eucharistic unity is an expression of the fullest unity possible in this life and can only be enjoyed in a united Church. Each of the different positions has its own integrity and makes an important witness within the current state of the ecumenical movement. But the growing impatience of many laity and young people with the existing rules ought to be a reminder to all who exercise leadership in the churches that the theological dialogue and ecumenical practice must progress.

Experiencing the unity that already exists through sharing in worship needs to go hand in hand with experiencing unity in acts of joint mission and service. Archbishop Desmond Tutu described the force of Christians from separated churches joining together in struggles for justice and peace and for the preserving of the world around them in South Africa. Unity in service cannot be optional; 'apartheid is too strong for a divided church': 'We ought to get on with the business of redeeming the world, making it more hospitable for human beings, making it a more humane environment with room for love, compassion, joy, laughter, peace and prosperity, sharing and caring'.[21] Archbishop Desmond Tutu explained that from his experience in Southern Africa in fighting apartheid, there could be no question at all that a united Church is a far more effective agent for justice and peace.

It was in their common struggle that Christians in South Africa learned to acknowledge a unity that already existed. This experience is open to Christians in England if they have the will to engage together in issues that confront them: unemployment, third world debt, questions of the environment and a range of issues raised by scientific and technological development. Finding unity in this country in a common response to contemporary challenges should be more about shared debate and exploration than about arriving at premature, ill-formed and uniform answers.

Some leading ecumenists have stressed that the real ecumenical action in the next decade will be less and less in church to church dialogue than in new forms of Christian solidarity emerging through local struggles for justice.[22] To experience unity in common struggles for justice and peace is a powerful incentive towards Christian unity. But it can also be deceptive. Archbishop Desmond Tutu asked sharply where is unity to be found when the struggle against apartheid ends? The churches in South Africa have been sent back to rediscover a unity in faith, sacraments, ministry and conciliar life, a necessary foundation and inspiration for their continuing common witness for justice and peace.

Christians experience the unity that already exists in worship and in common service most immediately in the places where they live, in the local church. The potential for the growth in the number of Local Ecumenical Partnerships presents a very particular challenge to Christians in England. There are many more places in England which lend themselves to formal and committed partnerships. But there is also an urgent need for a review of these developments and a more explicit theological rationale to be provided for their existence. LEPs must be recognized as living within the complex reality of the ecumenical scene, as well as pointing towards a greater visible unity. An ecumenical statement on the goal of visible unity might help LEPs to locate their local life together within an explicit intention of the churches to move onwards towards unity. The danger that LEPs become isolated congregations with little 'connectedness' with any one of the participating churches at national level, let alone world level, will only lead to a weakening of unity, rather than a deepening of unity.

More progress needs to be made in places where Local Ecumenical Partnerships are not the appropriate way of experiencing a greater unity, for example rural areas where the parish church is the only physical church presence. How the Church of England lives out its ecumenical vocation by helping to keep alive the traditions of the Christians who worship in the parish church regularly is a challenge for the future.

Sharing resources and developing ecumenical living at intermediate level is perhaps where most practical effort is needed now. The symbolic value of those who exercise oversight in the different churches being seen to work closely together is a powerful incentive to the whole Christian community to live together. The exhortation of the Pope to his brothers in the episcopate is one which is appropriate for all in ministries of oversight.

> I therefore exhort my Brothers in the episcopate to be especially mindful of this commitment. The two Codes of Canon Law include among the responsibilities of the Bishop that of promoting the unity of all Christians by supporting all activities or initiatives undertaken for the purpose, in the awareness that the Church has this obligation from the will of Christ himself. This is part of the episcopal mission and it is a duty which derives directly from fidelity to Christ, the Shepherd of the Church.[23]

Bishops in their dioceses, and the college of bishops in the Church of England, need to take a greater responsibility for guiding the ecumenical movement in this country. Lambeth Conferences since 1867 have acknowledged the key role of the bishops in formulating the ecumenical agenda of the Anglican Communion. There is much theological talk about the bishop as a focus of unity. This makes little sense without an obvious and expressed commitment in the way a bishop exercises the ministry of oversight entrusted to him.

Developing a common portrait of the kind of unity we seek, and deepening the experience of the unity we already share, will inevitably throw into sharp relief the remaining areas of difference which need further work. Already it is easy to predict what some of those areas are likely to be. Many of them, though not all, continue to relate to the ordained ministry: the authorisation of lay people to preside at the eucharist; the nature of the threefold ministry; the role of the diaconate; the exercise of a personal ministry of oversight; the way continuity and apostolicity are carried in the life of the Church; the relation of the apostolicity of the whole Church to the apostolicity of the ministry; the personal, collegial and conciliar exercise of oversight; the ministry of primacy; the ordination of women; the way towards the reconciliation of ministries; the way the local church is connected to the worldwide Church; how the authority of Christ in the Church is exercised; the processes of discernment and reception and the ethical witness of the Church, not least of all in those issues relating to an understanding of sexual orientation and its expression.

Recent ecumenical convergence on some of these issues ought to give hope that these 'neuralgic' areas can be seen in new ways when they are set within an understanding of the Church as *koinonia* and find their proper place within an overall vision of the unity of the Church, and as the experience of Christians living together is brought to bear on these issues. The recent work on apostolicity and succession shows how a renewed and a much broader understanding of the apostolicity of the Church helps us to understand historic episcopal succession in a new light.[24] There has been no giving up on the Anglican position as set down in the Chicago–Lambeth Quadrilateral but, by locating episcopal succession within the apostolicity of the whole Church and the Church's fidelity to the apostolic teaching and mission, a more intelligible and convincing understanding has emerged. At the same time there has been no weakening of agreements made with Roman Catholic and Orthodox partners on the place of the historic episcopal succession as an 'effective sign'.

The search for agreement in faith, that which is sufficient and required for unity, must continue to be high on the Church of England's ecumenical agenda. The work of the international bilateral and multilateral dialogues is vital for each world communion as well as for local and regional developments. The reception of the insights of the dialogues into the life of the churches at all levels is the way to coherence and consistency. This search inevitably brings with it old as well as new questions of ecumenical method. How in ecumenical dialogue do we use Scripture? How do we understand the Tradition of the Church? What is the relation between Scripture and Tradition? What place do we give to experience in ecumenical dialogue? What weight do we place on the multiple expressions of faith, life and witness that are emerging in different parts of the world? How should churches respond to the restatement of faith when it is in language which is not identical with their own traditions? In other words, how are ecumenical texts to be formulated and how read and received? The work on Scripture, Tradition and traditions of the Montreal World Conference on Faith and Order in 1963 was formative for the last period of faith and order work.[25] However, new questions have arisen with developments in biblical scholarship and intercultural hermeneutics. The current work of the Faith and Order Commission on ecumenical hermeneutics is much needed if progress is to be made in the development of the ecumenical agenda.

Defining a vision, experiencing the degree of unity that already exists, seeking for further theological convergence and consensus are indispensable items on the ecumenical agenda. The Church of England must at the same time nurture the formal committed relationships that already exist with the Moravian Church in this country, with the Evangelical Church in Germany and the Nordic and Baltic Lutheran churches. But a more puzzling question is whether to engage now in England at national level in multilateral moves to unity, or bilateral moves. The question is a complex one. The work of the Anglican–Roman Catholic International Commission and responses to it demonstrate that Anglicans and Roman Catholics share a high degree of agreement in faith. Their agreements extend beyond those reached in any other international bilateral conversation in which Anglicans have been engaged. These agreements stretch into areas of what collegial and conciliar structures will enable the Church to live in unity, as well as agreement on the need for a primatial ministry. Moreover, Roman Catholics and Anglicans agree that they are committed to steps and stages on the way to visible unity. But while Anglicans in different regions of the world have been able to take committed steps towards unity with other churches on the basis of a degree of expressed agreement in faith, this has not yet been possible with the Roman Catholic Church. The Roman Catholic Church's understanding of the fundamental and integral relationship between the elements necessary for unity – the faith, sacraments, ministry, conciliar and primatial structures – makes it more difficult to take gradual steps or to move in one region of the world, especially if these entail a degree of offering and receiving of eucharistic hospitality.

There is urgent need in the immediate future for a high level international meeting of Anglican–Roman Catholic Church leaders to assess the enormous gains of the work of ARCIC and to ask with some rigour the question that was set before the two churches as long ago as 1984 – 'whether the *Final Report* (and to that ought now to be added the work of ARCIC II) offers a sufficient basis for taking the next concrete step towards the reconciliation of our churches grounded in agreement in faith'. The Church of England in response to that question in 1985 did make clear suggestions which have never been followed up.[26] Unless Anglicans and Roman Catholics can begin to make some more official recognition of each other and move to a more committed relationship, then these spectacular theological agreements, won with such patient and devoted work, will become outdated pages on a library shelf. But much more seriously, an opportunity for the whole ecumenical movement will be lost. An opportunity will have been missed for the reconciliation of divisions within the western Catholic Church. A move between Anglicans and Roman Catholics could be a move which would set in motion new hope and dynamism in the whole ecumenical movement and help set the terms for visible unity for the next ecumenical decade. The Pope has expressed his hopes for unity at the dawn of the millennium – what could be a more important part of that agenda?

The bilateral relationship with the Methodist Church is currently on the Church of England's agenda. A decision will be made by both churches by the middle of 1998 about whether to proceed to formal conversations. *Commitment to Mission and Unity* sets out an agenda of issues that would need to be faced.[27] Among them the question of how to unite two churches, one of which has women in the ministry of oversight while the other excludes that possibility. Can both churches risk moving together with all the messiness and complexity of life that this would inevitably create, agreeing together that discernment on the matter belongs within the universal Church? The report sets out the reality of the situation and leaves the churches themselves to decide whether they dare risk moving. The difficulties are enormous, but reconciliation is always costly. If Anglicans and Methodists were able to find a way to fuller unity – a way which lived realistically with, and through, these complexities – this might prove a catalyst for other reconciliations.

However, the present degree of living together in many Local Ecumenical Partnerships involves Anglicans and Methodists living closely with the United Reformed Church, the Baptists and other partners. This might argue for a rather broader initiative than a bilateral move. This will need to be weighed up carefully by those who set the detailed agenda. What is clear is that any gain in one bilateral move does give encouragement to others, and makes theological breakthroughs which can then be seen to have wider implications and applications. The ecumenical map needs to be kept open in front of us all the time so that the consequences of developments in one partnership flow into others, and what is achieved in one region of the world stimulates other regions. Only in this way will there be coherence in the 'all-round' and 'all-level' ecumenical movement.

The pursuit of bilateral partnerships in England ought not to be set over against a multilateral partnership. By its very nature the ecumenical movement must be an open and inclusive movement, inclusive of all who claim to confess Jesus Christ as Lord and Saviour. The challenge to recognise the common faith Christians hold, and the urgency to proclaim it together in words that turn into life, is a very special one for entry into the third millennium. The Faith and Order Commission of the World Council of Churches has spent almost twenty years in providing an ecumenical explication of the faith of the Scriptures, a faith borne witness to in the Niceno-Constantinopolitan

Creed.[28] It has begun to explore, in the broadest ecumenical forum that exists, the challenges to that faith that come from the contemporary secular, scientific world as well as the challenges of the faith to life today. If Christians in England from many traditions could get hold at a deeper level of the faith which they have in common, and explore ways of living that faith, then the barriers of ecclesial division would be seen for what they are – a denial of the message that the churches proclaim. The suggestion that leaders of the Christian churches should gather together and celebrate the Millennium by proclaiming a common faith – perhaps in the words of the ancient creed – deserves to be followed up. Symbolic gestures have a place in the ecumenical movement.

It is inevitable that the ecumenical agenda for the Church of England for the next decade will be complex. So much has already been achieved with so many partners, locally, nationally and internationally. The 'all-round', 'all-level' and 'multi-activity' ecumenical commitment of which Archbishop Runcie spoke at the opening of the 1988 Lambeth Conference needs to be continued with determination and patience. There must be more clarity about the sort of unity Anglicans are seeking to live with their ecumenical partners, a greater attention given to seeing that the different advances are consistent and coherent with one another, and a more careful consideration of how advances with different partners each fit within the one ecumenical jigsaw.

Working for visible unity with other Christians needs to go hand in hand with maintaining the unity, with diversity, of the Church of England itself. The unity of the Church of England and the Anglican Communion is currently being tried over the matter of the ordination of women to the priesthood and the episcopate. It may be that there is a lesson to be learnt from this uncomfortable, painful experience, about living with difference, accepting the position of others in a genuine and open process of discernment and reception of Christian truth. This may prove to be a crucial insight for the kind of visible unity we seek.

Establishing close relations with other ecclesial traditions in this country and in continental Europe must not be at the expense of unity enjoyed within the Anglican Communion. This means that the unity of the Anglican Communion itself must be strengthened. The Anglican Communion needs more effective structures of unity, if it is to hold the provinces together in a life of interdependence. There are issues in the ecumenical agenda of the Church of England, and of other provinces, that need an Anglican-Communion consensus before action is taken to enter visible unity with another ecclesial body.

Unless urgent attention is given to this by the bishops at the 1998 Lambeth Conference moves to unity in some provinces might prove to be at the expense of Anglican unity. It has been argued by some that the new relationship established in the Porvoo Agreement, with its implications for a united ministry, ought first to have been agreed by the bishops at the Lambeth Conference.

Discovering and making visible unity and communion with another church must not be at the expense of surrendering the signs of continuity with the Church through the ages which have been received as gifts by Anglicans. Historic episcopal succession has been maintained in the Anglican way since the Reformation, not as a guarantee of fidelity to the apostolic faith and witness but rather as a powerful sign of the Church's intention to remain faithful, and as a sign of God's promise to be ever with the Church. Anglicans need to find a more convincing way to offer this gift to others so that judgement is not passed on the fruitfulness of their ministries. Through mutual acts of giving and receiving all can move into a more complete and faithful life, in continuity with the faith and mission of the Church through the ages.

Bishops focus the unity and continuity of the Church – its apostolicity and catholicity. A clearer lead, and a more effective promotion of the ecumenical agenda, from those who exercise oversight, both individually and collegially, at the level of the Church of England and the Anglican Communion would greatly strengthen the ecumenical movement in the next decade. There is evidence from the responses to the Called To Be One process that the laity are looking for a stronger lead from the bishops. It is no accident that unity matters have played a major part in the agendas of Lambeth Conferences.

There must be no turning back. The message to the churches from the Fifth World Conference on Faith and Order in Santiago de Compostela in 1993 was: 'there is no turning back, either from the goal of visible unity or from the single ecumenical movement that unites concern for the unity of the Church and concern for engagement in struggles of the world.'[29] 'The balance between continuity and renewal, preservation and transformation, the ecumenical movement needs at all times and particularly now.'[30] The Church of England has not found this balance easy to strike in the past. In the end unity is not simply the Church's calling; it is God's gift. However carefully the ecumenical agenda is set and however patiently it is taken up, without an openness to receive God's gift, and a willingness to be transformed in receiving that gift, there will be no progress on the way to visible unity.

Notes

1. Nicholas Lossky, José Miguez Bonino, John S. Pobee, Tom F. Stransky, Geoffrey Wainwright, Pauline Webb, *Dictionary of the Ecumenical Movement* (WCC, Geneva, 1991), p. xii.

2. The term Anglican Communion appeared for the first time in 1851, cf. A.M.G. Stephenson, *Anglicanism and the Lambeth Conference* (SPCK, London, 1978), pp. 7f., cited in P. Avis, What is 'Anglicanism?' in S. Sykes and J. Booty (eds.), *The Study of Anglicanism* (SPCK/Fortress Press, Minneapolis, 1988), pp. 405ff.

3. J. Robert Wright, ed., *A Communion of Communions: One Eucharistic Fellowship* (Seabury Press, New York, 1979), pp. 231–2.

4. Ecumenical Relations, Canons B43 & B44: Code of Practice (Church House Publishing, London, 1987).

5. David Sheppard and Derek Worlock, *Better Together* (Hodder & Stoughton, London, 1988).

6. *Baptism, Eucharist and Ministry,* Faith & Order Paper 111, (WCC, Geneva, 1982).

7. *God's Reign and Our Unity, The Report of the Anglican – Reformed International Commission, 1981 – 1984* (SPCK, London and St Andrews Press, Edinburgh, 1984).

8. *The Final Report of the Anglican – Roman Catholic International Commission* ARCIC (Catholic Truth Society/Church House Publishing, London, 1982). *Salvation and the Church*, ARCIC II (Catholic Truth Society/Church House Publishing, London, 1987). *The Church as Communion*, ARCIC II (Catholic Truth Society/Church House Publishing, London, 1992). *Morals, Communion and the Church*, ARCIC II (Catholic Truth Society/Church House Publishing, London, 1984).

9. *The Meissen Common Statement, On the Way to Visible Unity* in *The Meissen Agreement: Texts,* CCU Occasional Paper No. 2 (Church House Publishing, London, 1992): *Anglican Moravian Conversations, The Fetter Lane Common Statement with Essays in Moravian and Anglican History*, CCU Occasional Paper No. 5 (Cromwell Press, Wiltshire, 1996).

10. *Together in Mission and Ministry, The Porvoo Common Statement with Essays on Church and Ministry in Northern Europe* (Church House Publishing, London, 1993).

11. Papal Encyclical, *Ut Unum Sint*, Encyclical Letter of the Holy Father John Paul II on Commitment to Ecumenism (Catholic Truth Society, London, 1995).

12. *Costly Unity*, 1993; *Costly Commitment*, 1995; *Costly Obedience: Towards an Ecumenical Community of Moral Witness* (WCC, Geneva, 1997).

13. Thomas F. Best and Gunther Gassmann (eds.), *On the Way to Fuller Koinonia*, Official Report of the Fifth World Conference on Faith and

Order, Faith & Order Paper No. 166 (WCC, Geneva, 1994).

14. John Reumann, 'Koinonia in Scripture: Survey of Biblical Texts' in *On the Way to Fuller Koinonia*, op. cit., pp. 37–69.

15. *Ways to Communion,* Roman Catholic–Lutheran Joint Commission (LWF, Geneva, 1981), para. 9 quoted in *The Porvoo Common Statement*, para. 23.

16. The Canberra Statement, in *Signs of the Spirit*, M. Kinnaman (ed.), (WCC, Geneva, 1991), pp. 172ff.

17. Oliver Tomkins, 'The Chicago – Lambeth Quadrilateral and the Ecumenical Movement', Jonathan Draper, (ed.), *Communion and Episcopacy* (Ripon College, Cuddesdon, 1988).

18. *Called To Be One* (CTE Publications, London, 1996).

19. Ian Crichton Smith, *Collected Poems* (Carcanet Press, Manchester, 1992), p. 9.

20. *Ut Unum Sint,* op. cit., para. 21.

21. Desmond Tutu, 'Towards Koinonia in faith, life and witness', in *On the Way to Fuller Koinonia*, op. cit., p. 96.

22. Konrad Raiser, 'The Future of the World Council of Churches and the Role of Faith & Order within the Ecumenical Movement' in *On the Way to Fuller Koinonia*, cf. op. cit., pp. 168ff.

23. *Ut Unum Sint*, op. cit., para. 101.

24. *Apostolicity and Succession*, House of Bishops' Occasional Paper No. 1 (Church House Publishing, London, 1994).

25. *The Fourth World Conference on Faith & Order*, Patrick C. Rodger and Lukas Vischer (eds.), Faith & Order Paper No. 42 (SCM Press, London, 1994).

26. *Towards a Church of England Response to BEM & ARCIC*, GS 661 (Church Information Office Publishing, London, 1985).

27. *Commitment to Mission and Unity, Report of the informal conversations between the Methodist Church and the Church of England*, GS Misc 477 (Church House Publishing and Methodist Publishing House, London, 1996).

28. *Confessing the One Faith*, Faith & Order Paper No. 153 (WCC, Geneva, 1991).

29. *On the Way to Fuller Koinonia*, op.cit., p. 223.

30. *Crisis and Challenge of the Ecumenical Movement: Integrity and Indivisibility* (WCC, Study of the Institute for Ecumenical Research, Strasbourg, 1994), p. 41.

10

Anglicanism and the Theology of Culture

Robert Hannaford

Anyone attempting to survey the current state of theology within the Church of England is confronted with a complex task. Since many Anglicans insist that their church has no distinctive theology of its own, the commentator is confronted immediately with the problem of identification. Closely related to this is the problem of establishing the *locus standi* for Anglican theology: who speaks authoritatively for Anglicanism? Moreover, there are practical problems as well as theoretical ones. While the last twenty years has witnessed a burgeoning of boards and committees of the General Synod, each producing an increasing number of reports and working papers on theological and other matters, the number of theologians publishing work that is self-consciously Anglican has declined considerably. Church of England theologians such as Bishop Stephen Sykes and Paul Avis have contributed greatly to our understanding of the history and identity of Anglican theology, especially the theology of the Church, but, as Sykes pointed out in his book *The Integrity of Anglicanism*, published in 1978 when he was still Van Mildert Professor of Divinity at the University of Durham, Anglicans have by and large neglected the task of systematic or doctrinal theology. Systematic theology, as Sykes defines it, is that discipline which 'presents the substance of the Christian faith with a claim on the minds of men'.[1] Unlike historical theology or the study of the history of Christian doctrine, a discipline in which Anglicans have generally excelled, systematic theology concerns itself with the continuing question of the credibility and coherence of the Christian tradition. Sadly there is little evidence that this neglect has been redressed in the intervening years.

This, briefly, is the backdrop to our enquiry. In order to establish a coherent framework for what follows I shall begin by looking again at the question of Anglican theological identity. Clearly, this is no simple task, since many claim that what is distinctive about Anglicanism is precisely that it has no distinctive theology of its own. Fortunately, however, most commentators agree that the appeal to reason and a sense of historical perspective are particularly characteristic of the Anglican approach to theology.[2] As this is at its clearest in the question of the theology of culture we shall take this as the main axis of our whole enquiry. Following a critical survey of the treatment of this question in recent Church of England reports and in the work of various influential Anglican theologians, I shall conclude with some reflections on the challenge confronting the church as it pursues its dialogue with contemporary western culture.

I

The question of Anglican theological identity

Unlike the confessional Churches of the Reformation or the Roman Catholic Church with its established dogmatic tradition, the Church of England does not possess agreed and canonically binding dogmatic interpretations of the Scriptures and Christian tradition. It is perfectly true that this has not prevented the Church of England from publicly endorsing the dogmatic implications of ecumenical documents such as the Agreed Statements of the Anglican–Roman Catholic International Commission, but it is not an easy matter to substantiate these agreements from Anglican historic formularies. Anglican formularies, such as the Book of Common Prayer and the Ordinal, are couched in the language of liturgy and inevitably permit a number of interpretations, a possibility which is deliberately foreclosed by the language of dogmatics. This has led to difficulties over the acceptance of the reports by the Vatican. Anglicans are being asked to support their ecumenical gestures by clearer reference to confessional documents, but it is the absence of these which plays an important part in defining their ecclesial identity.[3] To those possessed of a doctrinal *magisterium* the Church of England, and indeed the Anglican Communion of churches as a whole, appears theologically pragmatic and doctrinally plural.

It is true that Anglican doctrine is not easily identifiable but it is a mere caricature to suggest that the Church of England has none. The fact that a great deal of freedom is granted to Anglican theologians does not mean that the same degree of latitude occurs at every point in the church's life. Anglicans, for example, have been hesitant about joining in certain ecumenical schemes because of their commitment to episcopacy. Although it is not defined dogmatically, Anglican practice presupposes a particular ecclesiology, which is reflected in the dignity and importance accorded to the episcopal office. Then again, Anglican liturgical practice, although more varied in both form and content than the Roman Catholic Church, is nonetheless premised on the centrality of the eucharist. Generally speaking the lesser or pastoral offices are seen as either a preparation for or a response to the eucharistic rite, and this is even clearer in the newer Anglican liturgies. Anglicans may not be publicly committed to a single doctrinal interpretation of the eucharist but their collective life makes the rite central. The compilers of the 1981 report of the Church of England Doctrine Commission, *Believing in the Church* comment that it is 'more typical of Anglicanism to rely upon custom, ceremonial and, above all, its forms of public prayer, to reveal its doctrine by implication'.[4] The public face of Anglican doctrine resides principally in its liturgy and canons.

It is at this point that the question of Anglican identity becomes especially complex. Doctrinal identity cannot easily be established if it has to be inferred from the language of the liturgy. At least it will be difficult if one is seeking to identify a single cohesive set of beliefs. Unlike the language of dogmatics, which is exclusive in character, the language of liturgy is expansive and inclusive. Whatever can be inferred from it is likely to be patent of a number of different inter-pretations. This is why the Church of England, and the Anglican Communion as a whole, include a number of schools of thought, each claiming to offer an authentic interpretation of Anglican doctrine, and each appealing to the same documentary evidence. Perhaps, then, we should speak of Anglican doctrine as existing at two levels: first, at the level of its public liturgies and formularies, and, secondly, and more informally, at the level of its different traditions of interpreta-tion. Both levels are features of the public face of Anglicanism, and it is not always easy to disentangle one from the other. For example, debates about the form of new liturgies often involve careful negotia-tions between the different traditions within Anglicanism, and the wording of the resultant, 'official', liturgies reflect this internal doctrinal dialogue. As I have suggested elsewhere, the search for an implicit Anglican theological identity ignores the dialectical nature of the doctrinal debate within Anglicanism.[5] Official liturgies may well imply doctrines, but they also reflect and reinforce the theological diversity within Anglicanism. Any account of Anglican identity must include the fact of doctrinal diversity and plurality.

Many apologists for Anglicanism insist that its distinctiveness lies not so much in its doctrines as in its approach to method in theology. A.M. Ramsey made such a claim when he addressed the question 'What is Anglican Theology?' in a paper published in 1945:

> There is such a thing as Anglican theology and it is sorely needed at the present day. But because it is neither a system nor a confession (the idea of an Anglican 'confessionalism' suggests something that never has been and never can be) but a method, a use and a direction, it cannot be defined or even perceived as a 'thing in itself', and it may elude the eyes of those who ask 'What is it?' and 'Where is it?' It has been proved, and will be proved again, by its fruits and works.[6]

H.R. McAdoo, like Ramsey, finds this method exemplified in the work of the great Anglican divines of the seventeenth century. In his book *The Spirit of Anglicanism*, published in 1965, Bishop McAdoo sees the absence of an official theology within Anglicanism as 'something deliberate which belongs to its essential nature', for, he continues, 'it has always regarded the teaching and practice of the undivided Church of the first five centuries as a criterion'.[7] Like Ramsey before him, McAdoo regards the Anglican way of theology as nothing less than the attempt to recover and reappropriate the undifferentiated Catholicism of the early Church. It never seems to occur to Anglican apologists that this can seem like a monstrous conceit, especially when it is supported by appealing to the theological controversies of seventeenth-century England. Notwithstanding this, McAdoo is not alone in identifying the balanced appeal to Scripture, Tradition and Reason as the distinctive contribution of the seventeenth century to the formation of Anglican theological method.

> Seventeenth-century Anglicanism ... saw no solution to the problem of authority which did not admit of the mutually illuminating relationship of Scripture, antiquity and reason, and refused any solution which insulated authority against the testing of history and the free action of reason. It must be such an authority as can stand investigation and command freely-given adherence.[8]

Time does not allow us to trace the origins of this particular appreciation of Anglican self-understanding, but it has undoubtedly established a firm place in Anglican apologetics. Once again, one cannot avoid commenting that most Christian theologians, of whatever tradition, would presumably want to own these three sources. Certainly, very few systematic theologians would quarrel with the claim that reason plays a central role in the theological enterprise, although in an increasingly plural culture there is obviously room for a healthy debate about the nature and limits of reason. When the conditions for a consensual view of the nature of reason no longer exist this item in the Anglican theological agenda becomes problematic. Recognition of the historically and culturally conditioned nature of reason makes it difficult to treat it as a neutral arbiter in the debate about truth. The answer for many philosophers and commentators on modern culture lies in a frank acknowledgement that reason is linked to the changing patterns of human language and belief. We shall consider the implications of this for a contemporary account of the theology of culture in the final section of the essay, but we turn now to a brief survey of the current theological climate within the Church of England.

The theological climate[9]

Twenty years ago the Doctrine Commission of the Church of England produced a report entitled *Christian Believing* which, in the words of the subtitle, explored 'The Nature of the Christian Faith and its Expression in Holy Scripture and Creeds'.[10] The report caused enormous embarrassment, signalling as it did the failure of a group of leading Anglican theologians to reach agreement about the nature of belief. Of the report's one hundred and fourteen pages the agreed statement runs to only forty-two pages, and many of these are descriptions of divergent positions. The main bulk of the report consists of appendices and position papers by Commission members. The impression created is of a divided and confused church whose theologians cannot even agree about the Christian attitude towards faith and belief let alone the content of doctrine itself. The Commission's chairman, Professor Maurice Wiles, admitted that the report had not been easy to write.[11] In the concluding section of the agreed statement the compilers analyse various approaches to the place of creeds in Christian life, and comment:

> The issues here – on the one hand loyalty to the formulas of the Church and obedience to received truth, on the other adventurous exploration and the Church's engagement with the contemporary world – appear to point in very different directions and to reflect different conceptions of the nature of religious truth. It is, to say the least, very difficult to explain divergences of this fundamental kind merely as complementary aspects of the many-sided wisdom of God. Plainly, when differences go as deep as this, they cannot

help generating conflict and giving rise to profoundly felt unhappiness and pain.[12]

Conventional Anglican notions about theological complementarity are abandoned in the face of mutually exclusive views about the nature of religious truth. As the report acknowledges, conflict was inevitable since the differences have to do with the foundations of Christian theology itself. Resolution is impossible when there is disagreement about the framework for disputation. The report continues, rather optimistically given the nature of the disagreements, 'The tension must be endured. What is important is that everything should be done (and suffered) to make it a creative tension – that is, not a state of non-communication between mutually embattled groups but one of constant dialogue with consequent cross-fertilisation of ideas and insights.'[13]

The contrast between *Christian Believing* and *The Mystery of Salvation: The Story of God's Gift*, the latest report of the Doctrine Commission, could not be greater.[14] Where the former signalled fundamental theological divisions, the latter was published as a unanimous statement by all the members of the commission. While many of the contributors to *Christian Believing* were at best agnostic about the historical foundations of credal faith, the later report gladly affirms the 'particular historical experiences of the saving power of God' that underpin the Christian account of salvation.[15] Furthermore, where the earlier report emphasised the exploratory nature of Christian faith, the later report boldly endorses its essential givenness. As Bishop Alec Graham, the Commission's chairman, states in the Foreword to the report: 'Our aim has been to express the Church's faith as received by us from Scripture and from the Church's subsequent understanding of its inheritance, in such a way that we are true to the tradition received and give fresh expression to it'.[16]

Unlike *Christian Believing* and the famous 1938 report *Doctrine in the Church of England*, both of which handled the absence of unanimity on the Commission by presenting the divergent views then held by members of the Church of England, the authors of the current report have not hesitated to arrive at agreed positions on the substantive issues. A careful reading shows it to be a balanced and considered work, faithful to classical Christian doctrine but also attuned to the contemporary context for Christian mission. Sadly, however, the report was largely dismissed in the press as an example of theological reductionism. Journalists fastened onto the brief discussion of hell, and the implied rejection of the idea of eternal punishment, and failed to understand the accompanying argument about human freedom and divine omnipotence.[17] Many in the Church took their lead from the press and dismissed *The Mystery of Salvation* as a further sign of the Church of England's doctrinal confusion.

Although the negative reaction to *The Mystery of Salvation* is entirely misplaced it is illustrative of the doctrinal and theological task facing the Church of England. Even though the Doctrine Commission regained recognition as an advisory board just before the publication of its 1981 report *Believing in the Church*[18] and confirmed this with the publication of two further reports, *We Believe in God*[19] in 1987 and *We Believe in the Holy Spirit*[20] in 1991, the fact is that many of the faithful no longer trust the church's theologians to reflect the faith that they celebrate in worship. Public perception remains fixed on the theological liberalism of the 1960s and 1970s.

The liberal theological legacy within English Anglicanism

As we have noted, the compilers of *Christian Believing* freely acknowledged the radical nature of the views espoused by some of them. The kind of liberalism in theology adopted by many of the contributors is clearly incompatible with traditional Christian doctrine. Take, for example, the essay by D.E. Nineham on the historical foundations of Christian doctrine. Few would disagree with Nineham's definition of the doctrinal theologian's task: 'to understand and formulate the faith in a way acceptable with integrity today'.[21] However, many would disagree profoundly with his conclusion about what this implies: 'It means removing all *unnecessary* obstacles to acceptance of the faith, which have arisen simply as a result of cultural change, and relieving us of any necessity to "believe what we know cannot possibly be true"'.[22] Amongst the 'unnecessary' obstacles that 'cannot possibly be true' Nineham includes belief that Jesus is God's agent in ushering in his eschatological kingdom, and belief in the atoning nature of his death. Moreover, according to Nineham, it is not the case that the time for these beliefs has simply passed; they never have been credible, for they involve an unwarranted and 'presumptuous' attempt to explain the story of God's work.[23] A 'reverent agnosticism', unavailable to first-century Christians is more in keeping with the hidden or secret nature of God's work in the world.[24] We should reject all attempts to explain this, and distance ourselves from the language and thought forms of the Bible.[25] It is clear from this that Nineham rejects traditional Christian doctrine on theological grounds as well as historical ones. His approach is as much determined by an understanding of the nature of religious language and truth as it is by a commitment to critical history. His disagreement with the traditional believer is not simply about the available evidence but about the type of evidence acceptable to the critically aware believer. Such a person simply cannot entertain any longer the idea of a God whose actions can be traced directly in history.

The scepticism of English academic theology in the 1970s was even more evident in a symposium entitled *The Myth of God Incarnate*, edited by John Hick and published in 1977.[26] The contributors included many of the leading Anglican theologians of the day: Maurice Wiles, Leslie Houlden, Don Cupitt and Dennis Nineham. The standpoint adopted in the book can be gauged from a question posed by Dennis Nineham in his epilogue: 'Is it any longer worthwhile to attempt to trace the Christian's ever-changing understanding of his relationship with God directly back to some identifiable element in the life, character and activity of Jesus of Nazareth?'[27] It is clear that the authors expect a negative answer to this question. They are convinced that modern historical scholarship makes it impossible to regard the traditional doctrine of the incarnation as anything more than a mythological or poetic way of expressing Christ's significance for us.[28] Furthermore they regard this as a question of truth and not merely of interpretation.[29] The doctrine of the incarnation is rejected not because of the evidence, or rather the lack of it, but because no such event could ever have taken place. The authors dismiss the idea that any single event or set of circumstances can provide a basis for universal or absolute truth-claims. This in effect constitutes an objection to any and all accounts of the incarnation, for any doctrine of revelation presupposes the uniqueness of certain events.

Looking back it is hard to explain why these works received the attention that they did. *The Myth of God Incarnate* could hardly be described as a major book when compared with other work in Christology then being produced in Germany and elsewhere. Recent studies in Christology barely give it a mention. John Macquarrie dismisses it in a single sentence in his recent major survey of modern Christology.[30] Moreover, Alister McGrath is surely correct when he accuses the contributors of parochialism. Having set out to discuss the central Christological question of the incarnation they barely mention, let alone assess, the significance of two of the most influential works on Christology available at the time: Wolfhart Pannenberg's *Jesus – God and Man* (1968) and Jürgen Moltmann's *The Crucified God* (1974).[31] Notwithstanding this the liberal scepticism epitomised in these works continues to colour the public perception of the theological life of the Church of England. This calls for some explanation and analysis.

A first and fairly obvious point is that many clergy and church leaders received their theological education during the 1970s when this particular brand of theological liberalism was at its height. Secondly, there is usually a time lag between developments in academic theology and their dissemination at the popular level. Even though the sensational nature of some of the proposals ensured wide interest and discussion at the time the debate lasted well into the 1980s. Furthermore, the sheer audacity of the liberal programme should not be discounted. This more than anything guaranteed it a degree of public attention not usually accorded to works of theology. Non-believers were confirmed in their doubts, and the faithful were perplexed by figures who appeared to speak on behalf of the Church of England. As Adrian Hastings comments in his major survey of modern English Christianity,

> Pleasing or displeasing, the consequence of their conclusions could hardly be other than the necessity of winding up historic Christianity, with a minimum of pain to all concerned, as unacceptable to the modern mind. If *The Myth* produced excitement, it was principally the smirking excitement of an agnostic world amused to witness the white flag hoisted so enthusiastically above the long-beleaguered citadel of Christian belief, the stunned excitement of the rank and file of weary defenders on learning that their staff officers had so light-heartedly ratted on them.[32]

The impression that this movement represented a fundamental threat to traditional Christianity was confirmed in 1980 when Don Cupitt, a leading member of the group, published *Taking Leave of God*, his anti-realist account of the language of theism.[33]

Hastings points out that the Church of England was particularly vulnerable to attack from this quarter. Because of its stress on the role of reason in theology, the Church of England has traditionally looked to theologians at the ancient English Universities to provide a lead. This school of thinking, centred as it was on Oxford and Cambridge, was strategically placed to exert an influence that was not necessarily commensurate with its scholarly significance or its bearing upon the life of the church. In the end Hastings' judgement is surely correct:

> No Church can continue for long without a theology possessing a fair measure of internal coherence, one related organically both to the actual religious practice of believers and to certain basic requirements of credibility or utility posited by contemporary society ... By the 1970s the central tradition of English academic theology, particularly Anglican theology as taught at Oxford and Cambridge, was hardly any longer fulfilling these needs.[34]

Liberalism in its 1970s guise ultimately failed the Church of England. First of all it exacerbated the existing gap between University-based academic theology and the beliefs and experiences of the ordinary believer. Theology is critical in the sense that it has to be a rigorous and intellectually disciplined activity but its roots lie in the faith and practice of the Christian community. Theologians who simply reflect the piety of the faithful are failing in their task but those who reject it out of hand have abandoned their charter and their calling. The technical nature of academic theology often leads to problems of communication but in the case of modern liberalism the problem was one of credibility. The average believer could no longer recognise his or her faith in its proposed reformulations. It is not simply that these were unorthodox, although they certainly were, but that they amounted to a rejection of the framework upon which faith is based, namely belief in a God who acts in human history. A theology which leads some of its exponents not only to reject the idea of revelation, but also – as in the case of Cupitt – the reality of God himself, has long since abandoned the Christian frame of reference. In this respect Stephen Sykes was right when he insisted that this brand of liberalism is a cuckoo in the nest, surviving as a parasite upon that which it ultimately subverts.[35] Classically liberalism takes the form of a reaction against received tradition and authority. At its best it comes as a corrective: in this form it marks a rejection of much that is perceived as fundamental to Christian theological identity. Including it within the mainstream of Anglicanism tests the idea of comprehensiveness to destruction.

The second reason why this movement must be judged a failure has to do with its perception of the credibility gap between Christian teaching and modern western culture. Christian theology has always been conducted in dialogue with the prevailing culture. The question here is whether liberalism truly gauged the temper of the modern age. Liberalism was marked not only by its anti-supernaturalism but also by a profound scepticism about God's immanence in the world. This appears to have been based upon two judgements about modern western culture: first, that it is essentially secular in nature and secondly, that as a consequence, it is no longer credible to attribute universal significance to particular historical events.

The secularisation model of culture was undoubtedly very popular in the 1960s and 1970s. Even if it did not offer an explanation for the decline in the formal observance of religious belief and practice in the West, it offered a persuasive interpretation of this phenomenon. Generally the argument focused on claims about the disappearance of the transcendent in modern western culture rather than simply on the statistical facts of declining church attendance. Modern men and women, it was argued, are increasingly materialistic in their view of life, rejecting the idea of the transcendent as a component of reality. Liberalism accepted this interpretation of modern culture in its entirety and either radically modified or abandoned altogether the idea of a transcendent world interacting with this world. What it failed to notice was the persistence of religion in western culture. Men and women might have abandoned the mainstream churches, but, as the sociologist Peter Berger pointed out, there are continuing signs of transcendence permeating modern western culture.[36] Moreover recent sociological studies have highlighted the importance of folk religion, a 'popular' faith existing in tandem with 'official' Christianity. Although it might not seem so to members of the western intelligentsia, religion remains a potent force in world affairs, the West included. It is not entirely fanciful to suggest that abandonment of the transcendent in liberal Anglican and Protestant Christianity helped to create the conditions for the remarkable emergence of New Age religion. Men and women who looked in vain to the western churches for insights into the transcendental dimension of human experience turned instead to paganism or eastern religion.[37] Liberalism abandoned transcendentalism precisely when the young were treading the pilgrims' path to the East in the search for truth. As Alister McGrath comments sardonically: 'Liberalism, which set out to make Christianity more relevant to the modern age, seems to have ended up achieving something like the reverse of its stated intention'.[38]

Liberal denial that historical events or sets of circumstances can ever be used as a basis for universal beliefs touches upon the heart of Christian belief about the person of Christ. However, as a proposal about the theological response to modern culture this too is open to question. How can such a claim be made at all? On what basis might one argue that no belief can ever be regarded as universal? The claim itself is universal in scope and in that sense begs the question. This conundrum nicely illustrates a contradiction at the heart of liberalism, namely, that it sets out to relativize all truth but does so on the back of a universal judgement about the nature and limits of reason.

Quite apart from the logical oddity of this position there are also serious doubts about whether liberalism has drawn the right conclusion here about the intellectual shape of modern culture. The claim that universal beliefs of the kind that Christians hold about Jesus are no longer credible provokes the question: precisely for whom are they no longer credible? On the face of it liberalism appears to catch the relativistic spirit of the age. The difficulty in obtaining anything like a consensus on questions of value and belief does seem to be a prominent feature of contemporary pluralistic culture and some thinkers, such as the American philosopher Richard Rorty, have adopted this as a distinctive philosophical perspective. However, it is one thing to claim that our culture is pluralistic; it is quite another to argue that thoroughgoing relativism is the necessary consequence of this. One of the characteristics of modern culture, leading some to label it 'post-modern', is the growing sense that truth and meaning are tied to historical contexts. What you believe and the language you use to articulate this depends upon your community or culture. This certainly means that archimedean judgements about what must be true in any culture (what post-modern thinkers label meta-narratives) are no longer tenable. We do not have the degree of intellectual consensus about beliefs and values to sustain this kind of universalism. In other words, pluralism spells the end of judgements that compare and arbitrate between the beliefs of disparate traditions.[39] Relativism, however, does precisely this, arguing that no one is ever entitled to believe in the universality of their own tradition-specific beliefs and judgements. Once again one is forced to ask, from what privileged and necessarily archimedean perspective thinkers such as Rorty are entitled to claim that relativism is true as an account of beliefs? This view appears to be self-subverting. Relativist philosophies can only claim to be one view amongst many but in reality they set out to end all discussion. In the guise of liberal pluralism they close all exits except the one marked 'liberal'.

Modern culture is not so much characterised by the absence of the transcendent or the impossibility of universal beliefs as by a plurality of such beliefs. Men and women still hold beliefs that they regard as universal in nature. What is lacking in our culture is a common or widely-shared interpretation of them that transcends all interest groups. It is not so much that God or the divine is absent from contemporary western culture but that there are many different conceptions of this.

In its one-sided commitment to a particular reading of modern culture, liberalism appears to have overlooked the real consequences of pluralism. A generation of liberal theologians assumed that the world is a reflection of the fashionable scepticism of Oxbridge senior common rooms. It is clear that this is no longer the case, even if it ever was. The confident assumption of generations of western intellectuals that all thought and belief is based on certain commonly-agreed norms of rationality and intelligibility is breaking down. The modern age, marked by the emergence of the Enlightenment in the eighteenth century and its confident rationalism, is giving way to post-modernity. Where once philosophers and theologians could assume agreement on the basic criteria of truth and meaning, increasingly this is no longer the case. Western culture agonises over the difficulty of sustaining a community of shared values. In so doing it confronts its own intellectual inheritance. Paradoxically, liberal theology stands indicted for its failure to be modern enough. Its assumption that the many could be convinced by a single brand of accommodation is precisely a manifestation of the modernism that is no longer tenable. Peter Berger comments pungently on the irony of this state of affairs:

> The various efforts by Christians to accommodate to the 'wisdom of the world' in this situation becomes a difficult, frantic and more than a little ridiculous affair. Each time that one has, after an enormous effort, managed to adjust the faith to the prevailing culture, that culture turns around and changes ... Our pluralistic culture forces those who would 'update' Christianity into a state of permanent nervousness. The 'wisdom of the world', which is the standard by which they would modify the religious tradition varies from one social location to another; what is worse, even in the same locale it keeps on changing, often rapidly.[40]

II

Theology and culture

Anyone facing the confusing complexity of contemporary western culture could be forgiven for reaching in desperation for the confident certainties of fundamentalism or narrow traditionalism. However, both represent a retreat from one of the major theological tasks facing the church today. Although we have been sharply critical of liberal accommodation to culture we do not fault the desire to develop a theology of culture. If anything our criticism has been that liberalism misrepresents the pluralism of modern culture. How then should the church respond theologically to a culture undergoing profound change? Given the stress on the rational dialogue with culture in Anglicanism, this is obviously a matter of strategic importance within Anglican theology. The rest of the paper will be concerned with this question.

Twentieth-century theology is marked by significant differences over the relationship between theology and culture. Early in this century the great Protestant theologian Karl Barth thundered his 'No!'

to culture in defence of the unique foundation of the gospel in the revelation of God. Barth published his first great statement of dialectical theology, a commentary on the Epistle to the Romans, in the aftermath of the First World War.[41] Those who had witnessed this carnage could no longer share the optimism of late nineteenth-century liberal theology nor its assimilation of the gospel to human culture. Barth and his followers stressed the unbridgeable gulf between time and eternity and the gospel and human culture. Later on the church struggle in Nazi Germany was to confirm Barth in his absolute rejection of any theology of culture.[42] The opposite point of view – exploring Christian theology in a conscious dialogue with human culture – is represented classically by the work of Paul Tillich. In his method of correlation Tillich set out to establish an agenda for theology by reflecting on the questions of meaning and truth thrown up by human culture.[43] His whole theological project was based on the belief that theology must identify and respond to the existential questions that animate culture. The Roman Catholic theologian Karl Rahner took this a stage further, arguing that, as a feature of human self-transcendence, culture is already a manifestation of divine grace at work. The theologian does not address a world from which God is absent but one which is already graced in advance and in anticipation of the definitive revelation of God in Christ.

The debate about the place of culture in theology has often been highly polemical. The positions adopted tend to be sharply drawn: either one is faithful to the gospel and disregards the insights of human knowledge and reason or one embraces the humanly-constructed insights and uncertainties of culture, exposing theology to the corrosive power of reason. Such are the terms in which the discussion is conducted: in reality the situation is more complex. Even those, like Barth, who explicitly reject the idea of securing a rational foundation for theology cannot help adopting a position on culture, albeit a negative one. In effect Barth's 'No!' constitutes a kind of negative theology of culture. Moreover, there is more than a little truth in the claim that Barth was doing precisely what he accused the liberals of doing, namely, echoing the cultural mood of the time, in this case disillusionment with nineteenth-century optimism. On the other hand, those who explicitly turn to culture as part of their theological programme do not thereby automatically renege on the Christian tradition. Tillich, for example, recognised that the traffic between theology and culture runs both ways, with theology serving culture as it strives to formulate its own existential questions. Theology has its own insights to bring to the study of culture and comes to the dialogue to give and not only to receive.

One of the most exciting and significant developments in recent English-speaking theology is the Gospel and Culture project initiated by Bishop Lesslie Newbigin.[44] Avoiding self-defeating reductionism on the one hand or the revelatory positivism of neo-orthodoxy on the other, Newbigin and his colleagues have argued that fidelity to the missionary imperative of the gospel demands that we develop a theology of culture. At a fairly obvious level the church needs to be aware of its receptor culture. The communication of the gospel needs to be in language that is intelligible, and that means using patterns of thought that resonate with the prevailing culture. Traditionalists are often sceptical about this, seeing it as a cloak for reductionism. It is of course true that some theologians have been uncritical in their adoption of a theology of culture but this does not invalidate the process itself. Indeed we do not have a choice in this matter. It is not the case that there is a 'primitive' culture-free gospel that is passed from generation to generation untainted by historical contingency and the changing patterns of human thought. As Newbigin reminds us:

> Neither at the beginning, nor at any subsequent time, is there or can there be a gospel that is not embodied in a culturally conditioned form of words. The idea that one can or could at any time separate out by some process of distillation a pure gospel unadulterated by any cultural accretions is an illusion. It is, in fact, an abandonment of the gospel, for the gospel is about the word made flesh. Every statement of the gospel in words is conditioned by the culture of which those words are a part, and every style of life that claims to embody the truth of the gospel is a culturally conditioned style of life. There can never be a culture-free gospel.[45]

The Bible is no exception to this general rule. Like any historical text it too is affected by culture. On every page it is clear that the authors were men and women of their times and this presents particular problems of interpretation for the modern reader. Nonetheless, as Newbigin continues, 'the gospel, which is from the beginning to the end embodied in culturally conditioned forms, calls into question all cultures, including the one in which it was originally embodied'.[46] The Word embodied in the historical circumstances of Jesus' life and that of the early Church is also the definitive revelation of God. The gospel, proclaimed as it is in the language and forms of human culture, is also a manifestation of the kingdom which is not of this world. God's self-emptying in the human event of proclamation is not an abrogation of his sovereign freedom but an exemplification of it.

Attention to the theology of culture is not only a factor in the communication of the gospel to non-believers, it also has a direct bearing upon the identity of the Christian faith itself. The Christian perception of reality – what an earlier generation of scholars termed the Christian mind – is itself deeply affected by the prevailing culture. Christians are as much a product of their own culture as their non-believing neighbours. It is by now widely recognised that, whether knowingly or not, western missionaries acted as agents of western culture when they introduced the Christian faith to Africa in the late nineteenth and early twentieth centuries. The struggle by the former missionary churches to re-contextualise the faith, placing it more explicitly in the setting of their own cultures, is both inevitable and understandable.

Although the Church cannot avoid the influence of culture it must also avoid the danger of wholesale assimilation. As the servant of the word made flesh the Church has a duty to engage positively with culture. However, as the Kingdom that it serves is not of this world, its engagement with culture is necessarily prophetic. One of the crucial tasks of the theologian is to negotiate this delicate line between engagement and prophetic distance. Paradoxically, western culture, which played such an important role in the expansion of the Church in the last century, poses a serious challenge to the Church. It is clear that there has been a sharp decline in the formal observance of the Christian faith when measured in terms of church attendance. However, more significant even than this is the belief that western culture is increasingly inhospitable to crucial aspects of the Christian view of life, particularly Christian belief in the autonomy of the created order. The doctrine of creation *ex nihilo* asserts the world's utter dependence upon the will of God, but it also underscores the proper and distinctive reality of the world. The world exists by the gracious will of God but it exists as a reality that is other than God. Caution needs to be practised when attempting to translate this into universal judgements, but this element of Christian belief brings it into conflict with secularism and its denial of the distinctive reality of God, and relativism, which calls into question the autonomous reality of the world. Where pantheism sees the world as simply an extension of God, relativism in effect sees the world as an extension of human consciousness or language. (As we shall see in due course, acceptance of pluralism does not thereby commit one to a relativistic view of reality.)

None of this means that theology should retreat from the engagement with culture. On the contrary it makes that engagement ever more urgent. At the same time it also underlines the importance of maintaining the critical balance already mentioned. As John Milbank reminds us in his seminal work *Theology and Social Theory: Beyond*

Secular Theory, it would be foolish to assume that secular reasoning offers a benign or neutral environment for the interpretation of faith.[47] Faith must observe its own critical distance from culture even during the process of engagement. In the modern environment failure in this respect would simply confirm the secular in its Godforsakeness. Moreover, as we have seen, faith also has its own insights to bring to the analysis and critique of culture. Liberal accommodation or assimilation not only misrepresents the integrity of the gospel, it also inhibits the unique contribution that Christian theology can make to the debate about culture. Milbank's book is an excellent example of a genuinely critical dialogue between faith and culture. On the whole the liberal approach to the theology of culture accepts the secular account of social reality and then works to identify a place for religion within these terms of reference. The end result is the reduction of religion to an epiphenomenon, a secondary effect of secular social forces regarded as more fundamental and foundational. Milbank sets out to reverse this by insisting that there is nothing more basic in human experience than the reality and power of religion. Social theory must be explained in terms of theology and not vice versa. Milbank summarises his own complex position in the following terms:

> If the analysis given ... is correct, the sociology of religion ought to come to an end. Secular reason claims that there is a 'social' vantage point from which it can locate and survey various 'religious' phenomena. But it has turned out that assumptions about the nature of religion themselves help to define the perspective of this social vantage. From a deconstructive angle, therefore, the priority of society over religion can always be inverted, and every secular positivism is revealed to be also a positivist theology. Given this insight, sociology could still continue, but it would have to redefine itself as a 'faith'.[48]

Milbank exposes the metaphysical foundations of modern social theory. Paradoxically, his case is that social theory – the term and idea are essentially modern – is itself completely indebted to the very forms of thought that it rejects. So far from an accommodation of theology to secular social theory, Milbank envisages a reconfiguration of social theory in terms of its own 'theological' origins. We will consider some criticisms of Milbank's approach to the theology of culture in due course; for the moment we should note some positive outcomes. First, his work illustrates the benefits to be gained from a genuinely critical approach to the theological dialogue with culture. In this case fresh light is cast not only on theology but also on social theory itself. Secondly, this particular exercise reminds us of the importance of adopting an historical perspective in the approach to culture. It is in the nature of a culture that it embraces us in a definitive and global view of life. This makes it very difficult to recognise that cultures are contingent and that what seems obvious and plausible in one age does not in another. It would be foolish to suppose that we can ever completely transcend our own particular culture in order to survey it objectively, but we must beware of the danger of becoming transfixed by the overwhelming power of what seems so obvious to the many. At the very least the theology of culture offers the academic community an alternative – some would say, in the present climate, counter-cultural – perspective on our collective engagement with truth and meaning. In our desire to engage with culture we should not underestimate the potency of theology as an interpretative and analytical tool in its own right. Milbank demonstrates very effectively the light that theological analysis can cast on the historical evolution of culture and its hidden roots. As we turn more specifically to the question of a contemporary theology of culture we must begin by considering the historical context.

III

The emergence of post-modernity

The modern age in Europe is normally dated from the beginnings of the Enlightenment in the late seventeenth and early eighteenth centuries. It is at this time that western culture witnessed the emergence of a new approach to reason typified in the work of the rationalist philosopher Descartes. Impressed by the achievements of mathematics and natural science, Descartes wanted to establish a similarly secure foundation for all knowledge. His employment of the famous method of doubt – calling into question all that he had been taught to believe – and his subsequent identification of the thinking self (the *cogito*) as the ultimate basis of all knowledge are well known. Man discovers within his own consciousness the basis of indubitable knowledge. I can doubt the existence of material things, including my own body; I can even doubt that God exists, but what I cannot doubt is that I am thinking (*cogito ergo sum*). Two points are clear here: first, that Descartes re-interpreted reason in terms of self-evidence, or what Ernest Gellner more accurately describes as 'inner compulsion';[49] secondly, that the autonomous thinking self has become both the substance and the guarantor of its own certainty. Gellner characterises the Enlightenment, and Descartes' philosophy in particular, as marking a self-conscious rejection of custom and tradition in favour of a new pattern of autonomous reasoning. Enlightenment man was searching for epistemological freedom and autonomy as well as political liberation. Reason itself is drawn into the struggle with the *ancien régime*. Gellner summarises the rationalist programme very effectively:

> It is opposed to the acceptance of the reality of the world on trust. It knows no loyalty to a culture and its custom. On the contrary, it views culture with the utmost suspicion ... The rationalist, hence anti-dogmatic or anti-authoritarian stance, sees the mind as facing the problem of knowledge of the world, without a prior commitment to (or faith in) *any* world and, *a fortiori*, to any particular culture. It is the expression of a mind determined to accept only rationally defensible cognitive claims, judged by laws of reason which transcend any one culture and any one world.[50]

Reason, formerly situated within the historical and contingent realm of culture and tradition, was redefined and relocated to the transcendental conditions of human consciousness. This double movement of interiorisation and universalisation reached its culmination in the critical philosophy of Immanuel Kant. In Kant's philosophy it is the categories of the human mind that are conceived as the transcendental ground of the unity of experience. The unity and uniformity of the world is not a feature of the world as it is in itself but of the world as it is perceived by the human self.

Robert Solomon coined the term 'transcendental pretence' to characterise the leading theme of the Enlightenment story.[51] The search was on for a universal account of reason, one moreover with its ground and basis in the human self. Of course the self in question was the transcendental self: timeless, universal and common to each and every human being.[52] It is this transcendental self that was identified as the ground and basis of all things, the measure by which the existence of all other things is judged. It is no mere coincidence that the beginnings of the Enlightenment coincided with the Age of Revolution in Western Europe and North America and the emergence of the bourgeoisie. The self that is raised to the level of transcendentality is a mirror image of this newly confident Enlightenment man: autonomous, free and sure of its status as a universal icon of humanity. Solomon's characterisation of this captures its strangeness for those more accustomed to cultural pluralism:

> The transcendental pretence is the unwarranted assumption that

there is universality and necessity in the fundamental modes of human experience. It is not mere provincialism, that is, the ignorance or lack of appreciation of alternative cultures and states of mind. It is an aggressive and sometimes arrogant effort to prove that there are no such (valid) possible alternatives. In its application the transcendental pretence becomes the *a priori* assertion that the structures of one's own mind, culture, and personality are in some sense necessary and universal for all humankind, perhaps even 'for all rational creatures'.[53]

The expression 'post-modernity' is in grave danger of being overworked but it does serve to signify the profound changes overtaking contemporary western culture. From the perspective of the late twentieth century the confident certainties of the Enlightenment seem increasingly unreal: it is clear that the common culture that made such universalism in thought possible is now virtually non-existent. Although it seemed otherwise to generations of western thinkers, the human self is too fragile, too fallible, to bear the weight of such awesome responsibilities. The transcendental self of modernity is being transformed slowly into the fractured self of post-modernity.

The pretence of universal identity could not survive for long the arrival of mass communication and the evident proximity of other, very different, ways of being human. This also impacted on belief in the possibility of identifying a universal pattern of rationality, the other leg of the Enlightenment pretence. Increasing contact with others, who are passionately committed to very different views of human life, compels us to question our own cherished assumptions and the rational processes that underpin them.[54] Enlightenment thinkers confidently believed that the autonomous human self, set free from culture and custom, could identify the self-evident ground of all reason. Ultimately the transcendentality of reason proved to be an illusion. Rationalism was self-subverting, unable to survive the consequences of its own basic convictions. Descartes believed that the mind is the ground of indubitable truth, but it is a short step from this to the belief that the mind alone has reality and that the world around us is a mental construct. Rationalist thinking cannot escape from the circularity of its own basic premise: when the reality of the world is made dependent upon the priority of the knowing self, then the independent vindication of the former is rendered impossible. It is but a short step from Descartes' rationalism to the constructivist epistemology of Kant, where the categories of the human mind become the sole guarantors of an ordered world. It is an even shorter step from that to the constructivism of modern social anthropology where the compulsiveness of our basic ideas and beliefs is located in their social and communal origins.

So the wheel has come full circle: the rationalist programme of the Enlightenment begins with the Cartesian flight from culture and convention but ends with the frank acknowledgement that our inner compulsions are socially contrived and induced. As Ernest Gellner puts it: 'Descartes, when he wished to elude social prejudice, used as his guide and saviour in the flight from the social *precisely that which is in reality the voice of society within us*! He sought escape from the daemon who would mislead us: and he found the salvation precisely in that which the daemon instils in us'.[55] Shorn of its transcendentalism, the autonomous self faces only the stark reality of choice with no guarantee that others will choose the same truth. Post-modern pluralism is, as it were, the obverse of rationalistic transcendentalism. Unable to validate independently its own self-evident world the transcendental self of the Enlightenment loses its main access of identity and collapses in upon itself.

Post-modernity and theology

At first sight it might seem that the most appropriate form for a contemporary theology of culture lies in a bold re-assertion of the universality of reason and the self. However, our analysis so far suggests that, given the absence of a publicly acknowledged framework for the resolution of such questions, such an enterprise would be doomed to failure. Furthermore, as we suggest in more detail below, the assertion of a universal shape to human experience already presupposes a particular way of conceiving the world. In the absence of a common language about the transcendent, the dialogue between culture and theology needs to be radically reconceived. The traditional model of dialogue, which was classically exemplified in natural theology, presupposed the acceptance of a shared metaphysical vision. It is precisely this that is now in question. An alternative approach, which is beginning to suggest itself to many theologians, lies in the recovery of a sense of the distinctiveness of the Christian tradition and a significantly greater stress on the prophetic distance mentioned earlier.

One of the most striking features of recent Christian theology, especially in Western Europe and North America, is the renewed interest in the doctrine of the Trinity. Anglican, Catholic and Protestant theologians appear to be recovering aspects of the Niceno-Constantinopolitan Creed that have long lain dormant. From the Protestant side Karl Barth saw the triune nature of God as the controlling factor in revelation and hence as the fundamental basis of all theology.[56] The Roman Catholic theologian Karl Rahner presents the Trinity as the definitive mystery of Christian faith, the theme in all the variations of theology.[57] In his *Mystical Theology of the Eastern Church* Vladimir Lossky, an Eastern Orthodox theologian, presents a profound theological meditation on the doctrine of the Trinity, seeing it as the high point of revelation and the goal of all authentic theology.[58] Many others have contributed to this renaissance but, as the report of the British Council of Churches Study Commission on Trinitarian Doctrine Today notes, these three are generally regarded as representing the fountainhead of recent discussion of the Trinity.[59] A number of theologians have also turned to the wider question of the trinitarian shape of all Christian theology. In his book *Trinity and Society* Leonardo Boff sees the communion of the Trinity as the basis for social and political liberation.[60] John Zizioulas, a Greek Orthodox theologian, appeals to the dynamic trinitarian theology of the Cappadocians as the basis of his claim that personhood constitutes being. Zizioulas insists that communion rather than substance is the basis of being, and this trinitarian insight allows him to develop an account of the Church as a way of being.[61] In his 1992 Bampton lectures, delivered in the University of Oxford, Professor Colin Gunton continued his significant engagement with the doctrine of the Trinity by essaying a trinitarian theology of culture and creation.[62] A number of theologians have argued that the long neglect of the trinitarian doctrine of God has led not only to an accommodation to monolithic theism but also to a general impoverishment in the Christian account of reality. In his major new study of the Christian doctrine of God Thomas F. Torrance reminds us that the formulation of the doctrine of the Trinity signalled a decisive moment in the historical development of the Church:

> There took shape within the ecumenical thinking of the Church a specifically apostolic frame of understanding the truth of the Gospel which soon came to be revered as the distinctive *mind* or *phronēma* of the Catholic Church. It was to this *mind* that the great fathers and theologians of the Church intuitively appealed in forming theological judgements and making conciliar decisions.[63]

As Torrance points out, the doctrine of the Trinity established a 'theological paradigm of understanding' that came to exert a definitive influence on the whole life of the Church.[64]

What is significant about this renaissance in trinitarian thinking is that it represents the recovery of a specifically Christian theological language. The doctrine of the Trinity constitutes the grammar of

Christian theology; as well as encapsulating the Christian understanding of God, it also provides the conceptual substance of Christian theological discourse. Paradoxically, this evidence of the recovery of a specifically Christian tradition of thought, focused on the Trinity, is in itself indicative and illustrative of the condition of post-modernity.

Although post-modern culture is said to be characterised by a rejection of authority and tradition, pluralism means that people are inevitably thrown back onto various 'narratives' in order to secure a sense of identity. The fractured self of post-modernity can no longer rest secure in the grand narratives of modernity and looks elsewhere for coherence. It is not so much that modern western culture is lacking in creeds or values but rather that few if any retain a general hold on the population. The world of publicly-accepted truth is shrinking and being replaced by a plurality of private commitments. This does not mean that post-modern culture rejects absolutely the idea of a transcendent reality – that would be alien to its pluralism – but it does imply a rejection of what one might term foundational metaphysics. Traditional metaphysics involved the search for a universal reading of ultimate reality. It was foundational in the sense that it sought a single coherent basis for all knowledge and truth. Pluralism sounds the death knell to any form of absolute foundationalism. Post-modernism is mistrustful of any view of reality that claims a privileged status in the arena of public debate. The Modernist or Enlightenment presumption of a single overarching pattern of rationality is giving way to pluralism and the co-existence of many different structures of meaning.

Karl Barth more than any other twentieth-century theologian represents the rejection of metaphysics and rational foundationalism, and the self-conscious recovery of a specifically Christian pattern of theological reflection. Traditional metaphysics, with its search for a single account of reality, inevitably involved a negotiation between competing theologies and philosophies, and it was precisely this that Barth rejected. He argued that there can be no compromise in the formulation of Christian theological truth. Barth's insistence on the priority of the Word of God and his rejection of any correlation between theology and culture are paradoxically very much in tune with aspects of post-modernism. Barth rejects the universal in favour of the unique particularity of the gospel, insisting that there is no universal truth that is greater than the unique events of the life, death and resurrection of Jesus Christ. Theology has no ground other than the gospel itself: it must grow and develop by constantly returning to its own internal roots in the trinitarian revelation of God. Barth, of course, rejected natural theology, and the dialogue with culture, on theological rather than pragmatic grounds. His 'No!' is not based explicitly on a reading of modern culture. However, with the benefit of hindsight it is now possible to see the Barthian recovery of tradition or orthodoxy as culturally as well as theologically significant. Barthian neo-orthodoxy may with some justification be regarded as post-modern theology ahead of itself.

Although Barth may be described as the first major post-modern theologian, the term can only be applied to him retrospectively. More recently a number of theologians have begun to respond explicitly to aspects of the post-modern condition in their articulation of the Christian tradition. In the process they have raised far reaching questions about the nature of theology and its relation to culture. We shall examine briefly the work of two theologians. The first reinforces the particularity of Christian theological language, while the second interprets religious traditions as languages or forms of life that constitute the experience of believers.

We have already mentioned John Milbank's major contribution. Like Barth he is quite clear that 'it is theology itself that will have to provide its own account of the final causes at work in human history, on the basis of its own particular, and historically specific faith'.[65] He is quite clear that there can be no appeal by the theologian to a neutral and universal mode of rational justification, for there is no such court of appeal in a post-modern culture, only a series of different rational discourses. Milbank is equally insistent that theology cannot be isolated from Christian practice. Theology is first and foremost an ecclesiology, an account of the specific form of Christian history.[66] 'Abandoning all scholastic attempts to graft faith onto a universal base of reason,' post-modern theology 'instead turns to the Church Fathers, and indeed goes beyond them, in seeking to elaborate a Christian *logos*, or a reason that bears the marks of the incarnation and Pentecost. At the same time, it seeks to define a Christian *Sittlichkeit*, a moral practice embedded in the historical emergence of a new and unique community.'[67] The extent to which such a post-modern theology represents the recovery of a specifically Christian frame of reference is clear from what Milbank has to say about reason in theology. The belief that theology must accommodate itself to an all-embracing account of reason is rejected in favour of a pattern of understanding and cognition focused on the saving events of the gospel. Reason is nothing more nor less than the conceptual and logical framework for thought. In Milbank's view theology has to uncover the *logos* or framework implicit in the Christian story. Events such as the incarnation and Pentecost cannot be interpreted in the light of a neutral or external pattern of reason for they themselves constitute the basis of the Christian apprehension of reality.

Milbank's argument is addressed to theologians and social theorists alike. It involves both a systematic theology and a critique of secular modernity. As he himself admits, his study can also be read as an exercise in sceptical relativism.[68] In this connection it is important to underline the fact that Milbank's work illustrates and reinforces aspects of the post-modern analysis of culture. Although he is clear that the recovery of a distinctive Christian *logos* is beneficial to theology in its own right, it is equally clear that he sees no alternative. The liberal approach of testing theology against the criteria of secular reason, as well as the scholastic attempt to 'prove' the truths of revelation, are rejected for their dependence on a universalising and a-historical view of reason. In a post-modern culture one is inevitably thrown back upon the specifically historical contexts of human believing.

The recovery of the idea of theology as the articulation of ecclesial tradition is clearly evident in the so-called Yale school. An important example of this is to be found in George Lindbeck's influential book *The Nature of Doctrine. Religion and Theology in a Postliberal Age.*[69] Since at least the advent of the Enlightenment, generations of western theologians have assumed that the various world religions are simply different ways of expressing the universal experience of religion. Two assumptions were made: first, that religious belief expresses pre-linguistic experience, and, secondly, that these experiences have a universal character. At first sight, this recognition of pluralism at the level of belief and practice seems consistent with the post-modern analysis, but this is misleading. At one level difference is acknowledged but at another it is treated as superficial and unimportant. The significance of specific expressions of belief is in effect relativised by the insistence on the uniform nature of the underlying 'experience' of religion. A particular religion is but one expression of a universal phenomenon that could just as easily be expressed by another. Lindbeck rejects this approach to religion. He not only denies that there is a universal 'experience' of religion but also the implication that religious beliefs depend upon a pre-lingustic experience. Quite reasonably, he asks how one might identify or specify such a pre-linguistic experience; every specification of experience after all presupposes the use of language. As Lindbeck puts it, 'There are numberless thoughts we cannot think, sentiments we cannot have, and realities we cannot perceive unless we learn to use the appropriate symbol system'.[70] To claim the contrary is to say that we have access to a language that bypasses the various cultural forms within which experience is specified. As Lindbeck identifies it, the mistake lies in thinking that religious belief involves a two-stage process: first, the pre-linguistic experience, and then the expression of this in formal terms. Lindbeck insists that the two stages are indistinguishable: the experience cannot be had apart from its linguistic formulation. In fact one might more accurately say that the religious experience is constituted by belief and practice and not vice versa. Experiencing the world as a Christian means seeing it from the perspective of the Christian story and encoding this in religious language. 'A religion', Lindbeck states, 'is above all an external word, a *verbum externum*, that moulds and shapes the self and its world, rather than an expression or thematization of a pre-existing self or a pre-conceptual experience.'[71] Becoming a Christian is not a matter of choosing a language to describe pre-formed experience but rather of 'learning the story of Israel and of Jesus well enough to interpret and experience oneself and one's world in its terms'.[72]

Lindbeck describes his as a 'cultural–linguistic' approach to religion. The focus here is on the communal, tradition-orientated, nature of belief and its regulative role in human experience. A particular religion is not to be regarded as a single manifestation of a universal phenomenon that could just as easily be expressed in other ways. On the contrary a religion, like any culture or language, constitutes the life and experience of its participants. Hence what is stressed here is the embodiment of religion in specific forms of life:

> It is a communal phenomenon that shapes the subjectivities of individuals, rather than being primarily a manifestation of those subjectivities. It comprises a vocabulary of discursive and nondiscursive symbols together with a distinctive logic or grammar in terms of which this vocabulary can be meaningfully deployed. Lastly, just as a language (or 'language-game' to use Wittgenstein's phrase) is correlated with a form of life, and just as a culture has both cognitive and behavioural dimensions, so it is also in the case of a religious tradition. Its doctrines, cosmic stories or myths, and ethical directives are integrally related to the rituals it practices, the sentiments or experiences it evokes, the actions it recommends, and the institutional forms it develops.[73]

The recovery of tradition: retreat or advance?

Advocating the recovery of tradition as an appropriate post-modern theology of culture might seem a contradiction in terms to some. How can one engage in dialogue from this base? We must take such reservations seriously. For the moment I want to spell out two positive advantages. First, and most obviously, constructive dialogue is only possible when one is clear about one's own position. The difficulty with modern liberalism is that it appears to have come naked to the discussion of the theology of culture, allowing secular scepticism to establish the terms of the debate. As a result Christian theological identity is put at risk, if not lost altogether. Secondly, pluralism should not necessarily be regarded as an entirely negative phenomenon, either theologically or socially. In theological terms it forces Christians to reconsider the sense in which they can claim universality for their beliefs.

Various post-modern thinkers have argued that universal claims are totalizing, demonstrating a desire to control rather than enlighten or liberate. As we shall see in a moment, belief in the universality of Christian doctrine has often been misconceived. Clearly Christians do not believe that God the Holy Trinity is simply their God, nor do they see their story as exclusive. However, their dialogue with culture and their striving after universality has sometimes been premised on the acceptance of a frame of reference regarded as external to their own tradition. Nineteenth-century liberal analysis of Christian doctrine in the light of a general theory of religion is a case in point. Here the universality of Christian beliefs is secured by treating them as an example of a larger and more all-embracing account of human experience. In effect this means that it is religious experience that is treated as universal rather than the tradition-specific claims of Christianity. Universality is secured at the price of granting priority to certain very general concepts or ideas. Karl Rahner and others have argued that a similar pattern of thinking lay behind the submergence of the doctrine of the Trinity.[74] Christian thinkers occluded the doctrine of God within an all-embracing monotheism and in the process sacrificed the distinctiveness of the Christian account of God. The end result of this kind of universalism is that the Christian tradition becomes simply one instance of a general interpretation of experience that can equally well be expressed in other traditions. In contrast to this, what we have termed the recovery of tradition compels us to recognise the historical particularity of the Christian story grounded in the life, death and resurrection of Jesus and Pentecost. This is universally available to all but only by entering into the faith and practice that emerged from this story. As we pursue this discussion, I want to turn to two particular objections, one from a recent review of Milbank's book and the other from a report of the Mission Theological Advisory Group of the Church of England.

In a penetrating analysis of Milbank's *Theology and Social Theory: Beyond Secular Theory* Aidan Nichols accuses the author of 'hermeticism'.[75] He claims that Milbank encloses 'Christian discourse and practice within a wholly separate universe of thought and action, a universe constituted by the prior '*mythos*' of Christianity'.[76] As a contrast to this Nichols points to the Catholic scholastic tradition and its dependence upon belief in the universality of human nature and experience. Theology, he argues, cannot rest upon an absolute appeal to revelation but must also include reference to the insights of 'natural' human wisdom. Nichols reminds us just how much of the ancient Greek conceptual vocabulary entered the tradition of Christian thought. Terms such as substance, person, presence, soul, etc., all played a key role in the evolution of Christian theology.[77] However, these terms were never adopted uncritically or without some significant reformulation. For example, the ancient Greek term 'person' underwent a radical transformation of meaning once it came to be adopted in formulating the doctrine of the Trinity, and this has had a decisive impact on the wider use of the term in Western culture.[78] Then again, not a few theologians have questioned the efficacy of the early Church's adoption of the Greek concept of substance. The Orthodox theologian, John Zizioulas, whose work is steeped in the ancient Greek Fathers rather than contemporary post-modern thought, reminds us that the identification of being with an impersonal 'substance' made it difficult for the Church to come to terms with the trinitarian and hence personal nature of God's being.[79] In the process of confronting this problem the Church both adopted and radically transformed the results of 'natural wisdom'.

As we suggested earlier, Nichols is right to remind us that the Church has always been open to influences from the prevailing culture. However, the very fact of change and development in the Church's self-understanding of faith as it engages with the world underscores the post-modern analysis of the historically contingent nature of reason. The development of a specifically Christian understanding of reality, worked out in dialogue with Jewish and Hellenistic culture, reinforces the case about the malleability of our basic ideas and concepts. In one sense reason or wisdom is far from 'natural'. What we believe about reality has as much, if not more, to do with culture than nature. What one age or culture counts as 'natural' or inevitable will not always seem so to others. What is taken for granted at one time in a culture will seem to have the solidity of nature itself, but ideas and beliefs have their time, and are subject to change, even those that constitute our view of what is rational. One is compelled to ask, then, just which historically contingent conception of reason Nichols wants the Church to engage with? Contemporary secular reasoning is profoundly inhospitable to the Christian conception of reality, predicated as it is upon the denial of the reality of the divine. Furthermore, Nichols' appeal to 'natural wisdom', as the common rational inheritance of Christians and non-Christians alike, is only available to those who, against the grain of contemporary culture, conceive the world as a created given. In other words, the appeal to universal truth or reason in defence of Christian faith already presupposes important elements in the Christian tradition. To point to nature as a solid and reasonable basis for truth is, in our contemporary cultural context, an act of faith, and therein lies the grit in the post-modern case.

The Mission Theological Advisory Group of the Church of England has recently published a report on the Church's witness to contemporary culture.[80] In this they take issue with the theology of culture advocated above, characterising it as a 'back-to-the-wall' approach to culture in which 'the residue of the global character of the Christian message' is called into question.[81] There are two related points at issue here: one to do with the Church's relation to culture; the other touching upon the substance of the gospel message itself. We shall consider them in turn.

As to the first, the suggestion is that grounding the gospel in itself is over-defensive and incompatible with the need for dialogue with culture. At its simplest level, dialogue means 'conversation', and few, if any, would dispute the claim that people from different traditions can and do talk to one another about their respective beliefs. But what form does such a conversation take? The authors of the report clearly take the view that it must include more than the exchange of personal testimony and confession.[82] They take the understanding of dialogue a stage further, moving beyond simple conversation to the mutual search for truth, with agreement in judgement as the ultimate goal. In other words, dialogue is now seen as a factor in theological development as well as mission. It is true, of course, that conversation with those who do not share the faith can form part of the process of theological formation and development. However, there are difficulties with this more ambitious view of the goal of dialogue.

What is at issue here is not simply mission strategy but the question of the foundations of Christian theology. The report implies that discussion of the foundations of the gospel must be open to believers and non-believers alike. This presupposes that the criteria of judgement concerning those foundations must also be shared, at least in part, between the believer and the non-believer. If the search for a common identification of truth is the ultimate goal, then this is only possible when there are shared criteria for resolving questions of truth and falsehood. Not only that, there must also be agreement about what would constitute a definitive conclusion to such a dialogue. A number of philosophers of religion, influenced by the work of Ludwig Wittgenstein, have raised doubts about the logical possibility of such an agreement. In his famous essay 'Is it a Religious Belief that God exists?' the American philosopher Norman Malcolm insisted that the believer and the non-believer cannot mean the same thing when they talk about God.[83] Malcolm's case is complex but, drawing upon Wittgenstein's discussion of meaning in terms of 'language-games' and 'forms of life', he argues that religious concepts only make sense against the background of a whole way of life. It is important to stress here that he conceived this as a logical rather than a psychological observation. It is not the significance or intensity of belief in God that is at issue here, but its meaning. Malcolm points out that the meaning of the concept of God is misrepresented unless it is seen as entering into a believer's whole way of life. When a believer claims that God exists he does much more than simply reiterate one of the many things he happens to believe in. On the contrary, in such statements the believer rehearses the very foundation of his life. This is what Malcolm appears to mean when he argues that belief 'in' God is much more significant from a religious point of view than belief 'that' God exists. Belief 'in' God, which involves affective as well as cognitive commitment, forms a crucial part of the foundational framework of the religious way of life. From this point of view, talk of testing belief in God against criteria regarded as external to religious belief amounts to a conceptual confusion. As the central constitutive component in the Christian form of life, belief in God also determines its criteria of judgement. Hence, appealing to criteria that do not presuppose such a belief means judging one form of life by the criteria of another. As we have already noted, post-modern thinking takes this analysis a stage further, arguing that the cultural conditions for the kind of dialogue envisaged are absent. It is not simply that the nature of religious believing is misrepresented by such an approach, but, rather, that the appeal to shared criteria of judgement is misplaced in a post-Enlightenment culture. Pluralism exposes the futility of the Enlightenment search for a universal pattern of reason and compels us to recognise the tradition-specific nature of believing. Believing, in the end, rests not upon a set of confessionally neutral rational principles but upon the various forms of life that constitute our plural culture. Perversely, then, a frank endorsement of the confessional nature of Christian reasoning might just provide the kind of theology that is best suited to join the general conversation in a post-modern culture.

The second reservation expressed by the Mission Theological

Advisory Group has to do with what they term the 'global' character of the Christian gospel. The Christian community has always understood its message to be universal in character. The gospel is a message for the many and not simply the few. The question is whether grounding the gospel in itself, and refusing to have recourse to external criteria of judgement, is inconsistent with its universality. The resolution hangs upon what is meant by the term 'universal'.

It is important to draw a clear distinction between universality of application on the one hand and universal validation on the other. Clearly, Christians regard the gospel as universal in scope and application but does this mean that they are thereby committed to the search for universal validation? The report does not draw such a distinction, but it is clear from the references to dialogue that the latter is desired as well as the former: Christian beliefs are not only universal in scope, they must also be judged according to the widest possible criteria of validation. The question is, does the one presuppose the other? Is it only possible to believe in the universal application of the Christian message, if one also holds to the *possibility* of its universal validation? We put the requirement at this minimal level because it is clear that to date no such validation has yet been secured. Universal validation presupposes that there are generally recognised criteria of judgement, and this is precisely what is problematic in a post-modern culture. People still hold religious beliefs, many of which they regard as universal in scope, but they cannot verify them without drawing directly upon their own tradition of believing. Indeed, we have already hinted that in a post-modern age, belief in the universality of truth involves an act of faith. To say that there are certain universal truths about the world presupposes that one is already committed to belief in the givenness and objectivity of the world. Paradoxically, belief in the universal or public nature of truth shows that one is part of a community committed to belief in the created autonomy of the world. Establishing that this is true, however, is inseparable from faith in the Christian story of Creation and Redemption. This story, encompassing as it does the creation of the world *ex nihilo* and the victory of Christ over death and nothingness, enshrines a deep belief in the reality of the world. Although the world exists by the will of the creator, it exists as that which is other than him. In this sense Christians are committed to belief in the proper autonomy and reality of the created order. The world, although dependent upon the will of God, exists in its own right; it is neither a projection of the divine mind nor a figment of human imagining. Reality might be infinitely complex but it is not illusory. Although the Christian theology of creation does not necessitate particular universal judgements about the structure of the world, it does presuppose that there is a world about which truth can be told. In a post-modern culture belief in the possibility of universal truth is then an act of resistance, and marks one as a member of a counter-culture. Hence, commitment to public truth-criteria, which has all the appearance of a desire for universal validation, serves rather to identify one as a member of a particular believing tradition.

The urge to universality is a direct outcome of belief in the universal scope of the saving work of God in Christ. The question is whether or not it is possible to frame a theology for addressing this without becoming embroiled in the search for universal validation. Traditionally the validation of faith has been sought in metaphysics or natural theology, most famously in the so-called arguments for the existence of God. Conclusions about the nature and existence of God are drawn from certain general features of reality that are said to be observable by any rational human being. The Enlightenment critique of the classical arguments for the existence of God by philosophers such as David Hume and Immanuel Kant led to the development of a 'critical' natural theology in which attention was transferred from the world in general to human consciousness in particular. This in turn has been criticised as involving a fatal concession to transcendental rationalism. A theology that grounds itself in the human consciousness subverts its own project, displacing God and paving the way for secularisation. In such a 'theology' the universal and autonomous human self takes the place formerly occupied by God. Traditional natural theology has also been criticised for enshrining a generalised and undifferentiated theism. Rational discussion of the existence of God has never entirely succeeded in shaking off the influence of ancient Greek philosophy and its belief that unity rather than multiplicity is the basis of all being, God's included.[84] The end result is that the God of natural theology is seldom, if ever, the differentiated God of Christian trinitarian theism. In his recent Bampton lectures Colin Gunton reverses this process, appealing to the specifically Christian account of God as the basis for a new account of the universal structure of creation. Gunton believes that trinitarian faith generates 'ways of looking at universal features of the world of which we are part and in which we live'.[85] His expectation is that 'if the triune God is the source of all being, meaning and truth we must suppose that all being will in some way reflect the being of the one who made it and holds it in being'.[86]

Disillusionment with metaphysics is usually regarded as a characteristic feature of post-modernism. Certainly, judgements about the ultimate nature of reality are problematic in a culture which has lost both the taste and the wherewithal for making universal truth-claims. Although he rejects the term 'post-modern', Gunton's approach to metaphysics, or the doctrine of creation as he prefers to describe it, is entirely consistent with this distaste for universal validation. Eschewing the transcendental universalism of traditional metaphysics, Gunton embraces instead the idea of 'open transcendentals'. He sees these as universal in character but 'open to many distinct and particular forms of embodiment in different lives'.[87] Gunton compares this idea favourably with Sabina Lovibond's recommendation of a form of 'transcendental parochialism'.[88] In talking about what is ultimate we should renounce false universalism and resist the impulse to escape from the conceptual scheme that culture and the environment has framed for us. Gunton's own version of this parochialism takes the form of an appeal to the transcendental implications of trinitarian faith. Taking the trinitarian being of God as his basis, he extrapolates from this to the universal nature of reality. Hence, although Gunton conceives his work as universal in scope, it is validated by an appeal to the tradition of the Christian community. In other words, what we have here is a metaphysics of faith, a reflection on the ultimate nature of reality in the light of a very particular vision of God. Gunton's pattern of thought is determined by what we might term the logic or symmetry of faith. Recognising the universal scope of the Christian doctrine of God he, nonetheless, refuses to ground the Christian message in anything other than itself. Indeed, a good deal of his book is devoted to uncovering the displacement of God that occurs when Christians seek validation elsewhere.

We began this essay lamenting the baleful influence of modern liberalism on the theological life of the contemporary Church of England. While the liberal analysis of culture and the implications of this for Christian theology were seriously at fault, its perception of the importance of the theology of culture cannot be doubted. No church can afford to neglect this essential theological work. Gunton's work is an example of what can be achieved theologically from a genuinely critical dialogue with culture. In the process of reflecting on the foundations of Christian faith questions are raised that have a very wide bearing upon the general quest for truth and understanding. Although Christian theology has its own proper *logos* or reason, founded upon the saving events that form the substance of the Christian story, it also has a direct bearing upon the human struggle for meaning and truth. It is the prime theological task of the Church to be the setting for this liberative dialogue.

Notes

1. Stephen Sykes, *The Integrity of Anglicanism* (Mowbray, London and Oxford, 1978), p. ix.
2. See, for example, Anthony and Richard Hanson, *Reasonable Belief: A Survey of the Christian Faith* (Oxford University Press, Oxford, 1980), p. ix.
3. See, for example, Joseph Ratzinger, 'Anglican–Catholic Dialogue – Its Problems and Hopes', *Insight* (Hitchin, Hertfordshire) 1 (March, 1983): 2–11; and *Observations on the Final Report of ARCIC* (Vatican City, Sacred Congregation for the Doctrine of the Faith, 1981).
4. *Believing in the Church: The Corporate Nature of Faith.* A Report by The Doctrine Commission of the Church of England (SPCK, London, 1981), pp. 141–2.
5. See my article 'Anglican Identity and Ecumenism' in the *Journal of Ecumenical Studies* (32:2, Spring 1995), pp. 195–206.
6. A.M. Ramsey, 'What is Anglican Theology? (*Theology*, XLVIII, 1945), p. 2.
7. H.R. McAdoo, *The Spirit of Anglicanism: A Survey of Anglican Theological Method in the Seventeenth Century* (Adam and Charles Black, London, 1965), p. v.
8. ibid., p. 410.
9. The following two sections are based on an article forthcoming in the journal *Theology*.
10. *Christian Believing: The Nature of the Christian Faith and its Expression in Holy Scripture and Creeds.* A Report by The Doctrine Commission of the Church of England (SPCK, London, 1976).
11. ibid., Preface, p. xi.
12. ibid., p. 38.
13. ibid.
14. *The Mystery of Salvation: The Story of God's Gift.* A Report by The Doctrine Commission of the General Synod of the Church of England (Church House Publishing, London, 1995).
15. ibid., p. 86.
16. ibid., p. ix.
17. See my review article of the *Mystery of Salvation* in *New Directions* (vol. 1 no. 10, March 1966), p. 4.
18. *Believing in the Church: The Corporate Nature of Faith.* A Report by The Doctrine Commission of the Church of England (SPCK, London, 1981).
19. *We Believe in God.* A Report by The Doctrine Commission of the General Synod of the Church of England (Church House Publishing, London, 1987).
20. *We Believe in the Holy Spirit.* A Report by The Doctrine Commission of the General Synod of the Church of England (Church House Publishing, London, 1991).
21. *Christian Believing*, op. cit., p. 87.
22. ibid., author's italics.

23. ibid., p. 85.
24. ibid.
25. ibid., p. 87.
26. John Hick, ed., *The Myth of God Incarnate* (SCM Press, London, 1977).
27. ibid., p. 202.
28. ibid., Preface, p. ix.
29. ibid.
30. John Macquarrie, *Jesus Christ in Modern Thought* (SCM Press, London and Trinity Press International, Philadelphia, 1990), p. 334.
31. Alister McGrath, *The Renewal of Anglicanism* (SPCK, London, 1993), p. 41.
32. Adrian Hastings, *A History of English Christianity 1920–1990* (SCM Press, London and Trinity Press International, Philadelphia, 1991 (3rd edn), p. 650.
33. Don Cupitt, *Taking Leave of God* (SCM Press, London, 1980).
34. Hastings, op. cit., p. 662.
35. Stephen Sykes, *The Integrity of Anglicanism* (Mowbrays, London and Oxford, 1978), p. 32.
36. See Peter Berger, *A Rumour of Angels* (Penguin, Harmondsworth, 1969).
37. See, for example, Ted Peters, *The Cosmic Self: A Penetrating Look at Today's New Age Movement* (HarperCollins, San Francisco, 1991).
38. McGrath, op. cit., p. 41.
39. As I shall argue at a later point in this essay, such an apparent concession to post-modern anti-foundationalism is not necessarily incompatible with a thoroughly Catholic conception of Christian doctrine. What is in question is not the universal scope of Christian belief in God but the question of whether or not this can be rationally secured. When the 'universal' nature of reason is in question, theologians have to look again at the question of the Catholicity of faith.
40. Peter L. Berger, *A Far Glory: The Quest for Faith in an Age of Credulity* (Free Press, New York, 1992), pp. 10–11.
41. Karl Barth, *The Epistle to the Romans*, English translation of the 2nd edn, translated by Edwyn C. Hoskyns (Oxford University Press, London, 1965).
42. See, for example, Barth's famous dialogue with Emil Brunner on Natural Theology reproduced in *Natural Theology: 'Nature and Grace' by Emil Brunner and the Reply 'No!' by Karl Barth* (1934) translated by Peter Fraenkel (Geoffrey Bles, London, 1946).
43. See Paul Tillich, *Systematic Theology*, 3 volumes (Nisbet, London, 1953, 1957, 1964).
44. See, for example, Lesslie Newbigin, *Foolishness to the Greeks: The Gospel and Western Culture* (WCC Publications, Geneva, 1986), *The Gospel in a Pluralist Society* (Eerdmans, Grand Rapids, Michigan/WCC Publications, Geneva, 1989), *Truth to Tell: The Gospel as Public Truth* (SPCK, London, 1991).
45. Lesslie Newbigin, *Foolishness to the Greeks: The Gospel and Western Culture*, p. 4.

46. ibid.
47. John Milbank, *Theology and Social Theory: Beyond Secular Reason* (Blackwell, Oxford, 1990).
48. ibid., p. 139.
49. Ernest Gellner, *Reason and Culture: The Historic Role of Rationality and Rationalism* (Blackwell, Oxford, 1992), p. 9.
50. ibid., pp. 23f.
51. Robert C. Solomon, *Continental Philosophy since 1750: The Rise and Fall of the Self* (Oxford University Press, Oxford, 1988).
52. This self was also male. cf. Genevieve Lloyd, *The Man of Reason: 'Male' and 'Female' in Western Philosophy* (Methuen, London, 1984).
53. ibid., p. 7.
54. For a more detailed analysis of the post-modern condition see: D. Lyon, *Postmodernity* (Open University Press, Buckingham, 1995); S. Connor, *Postmodern Culture* (Blackwell, Oxford, 1989); J.F. Lyotard, *The Postmodern Condition* (Manchester University Press, Manchester, 1984).
55. Gellner, op. cit., p. 38. Author's italics.
56. Karl Barth, *Church Dogmatics* I.1 (T & T Clark, Edinburgh, 2nd edn., 1975).
57. Karl Rahner, *The Trinity* (Burns and Oates, Tunbridge Wells, 1970).
58. Vladimir Lossky, *The Mystical Theology of the Eastern Church* (James Clarke, Cambridge and London, 1957).
59. *The Forgotten Trinity*. 1. The Report of the BCC Study Commission on Trinitarian Doctrine Today (The British Council of Churches, London, 1989), p. 45. See the bibliography in this report for a more extensive list of relevant modern texts.
60. Leonardo Boff, *Trinity and Society* (Burns and Oates, Tunbridge Wells, 1988).
61. John D. Zizioulas, *Being As Communion. Studies in Personhood and the Church* (St Vladimir's Seminary Press, Crestwood, New York, 1985).
62. Colin E. Gunton, *The One, The Three and The Many. God, Creation and the Culture of Modernity*. The Bampton Lectures 1992 (Cambridge University Press, Cambridge, 1993).
63. Thomas F. Torrance, *The Christian Doctrine of God, One Being Three Persons* (T & T Clark, Edinburgh, 1996), p. ix.
64. ibid.
65. Milbank, op. cit., p. 380.
66. ibid., p. 381.
67. ibid.
68. ibid., p. 1.
69. George Lindbeck, *The Nature of Doctrine. Religion and Theology in a Postliberal Age* (SPCK, London, 1984).
70. ibid., p. 34.
71. ibid.
72. ibid.
73. ibid., p. 33.

74. Rahner, op. cit., pp. 9–20.
75. Aidan Nichols OP, "Non tali auxilio": John Milbank's Suasion to Orthodoxy', *New Blackfriars*, vol. 73 no. 861, 1992, pp. 326–32.
76. ibid., p. 327.
77. ibid., p. 329.
78. See, for example, Torrance, op. cit., pp. 102f.
79. Zizioulas, op. cit., pp. 40ff.
80. *The Search for Truth and the Witness of the Church. An Exploration by the Mission Theological Advisory Group.* GS 1218 (Church House Publishing, London, 1996).
81. ibid., p. 177.
82. ibid.
83. Norman Malcolm, 'Is it a Religious Belief that God exists?' in J. Hick, ed., *Faith and the Philosophers* (St Martin's Press, New York, 1964). See also N. Malcolm 'The Groundlessness of Belief' in Stuart C. Brown ed., *Reason and Religion* (Cornell University Press, Ithaca and London, 1977), pp. 143–57.
84. cf., Zizioulas, op. cit., pp. 29f. In this respect it is tempting to speculate that the recent renaissance in trinitarian thinking amongst Christian theologians is in part a result of the final demise of Greek monism and its replacement with a more dynamic view of being.
85. Gunton, op. cit., p. 145.
86. ibid.
87. ibid., p. 227.
88. ibid., p. 142.

11
Sexual Ethics

Robin Gill

If there is a single issue which is likely to prove the most troublesome and intractable for the Anglican Church over the next few decades it is surely that of sexual ethics. Unlike some of the highly complex areas of biotechnology which affect the few, or the daunting issues of macro-economics affecting us all but which seem beyond individual control, sexual ethics impinges upon the personal lives of almost everyone. Decisions about personal sexual behaviour and strong moral attitudes about the sexual behaviour of others seem to be part of the human condition. Attempts to regulate this behaviour and shape these attitudes can be found in many religious traditions and especially within the Christian tradition. Yet because of the evident changes both within the Church and within society at large in the second half of the twentieth century, the twenty-first century seems likely to bring considerable tensions and debates.

There is a real need to analyse the present situation carefully before offering any prescriptions for the future. In this paper I will try to do this. But a warning is necessary at the outset. Although it has long been a practice in Anglican ethics to present an empirical analysis of an issue first before turning to theology and Christian ethics, this practice has come under increasing attack. Indeed it presents an obvious danger. The empirical 'is' can easily dictate the theological 'ought'; secular practice can determine theological vision; and, in the process, the distinctiveness of Christian ethics can simply be lost. Christian ethics becomes, in effect, a means of legitimating secular moral (or immoral) practices.

To avoid this, it is essential to emphasise that this is not my intention here. Instead, the first part of this paper will seek to understand why Anglicans are both changing and increasingly confused about sexual ethics. There is no assumption here that all of these changes are desirable, or even that all are undesirable, in terms of Christian ethics. The final part of the paper will move from this analytic mode to a more theological and prescriptive mode, searching for theological principles that might unite most Anglicans despite our evident differences. This theological reconstruction, as so often elsewhere in Christian ethics, is considerably more difficult than the analytic task. Yet I remain suspicious of those who believe that it can adequately be achieved without the latter.

I

That Anglicans are both changing and increasingly confused about sexual ethics is evident from two British reports produced in the 1990s. The first of these was the 1991 House of Bishops' *Issues in Human Sexuality*.[1] In his preface the then new Archbishop of Canterbury admitted that there was 'a wide variety of opinions' even amongst the Bishops on the issue of homosexuality. He modestly encouraged congregations 'to find time for prayerful study and reflection on the issues we have discussed' and made no claim that this would be 'the last word on the subject'. The second report appeared four years later and was surrounded by considerable media attention, namely *Something to Celebrate*[2] produced by a working party of the Board for Social Responsibility. This second report was commended in a foreword by the Bishops of Liverpool and Bath and Wells, both of whom had been present at the discussions which produced the first report. They wrote hoping that 'it will prove to be a rich resource for debate across the country', but also warning that 'not every member of the Board would want to support every specific approach that appears here, but all agree that this is a positive contribution to the debate which will encourage widespread reflection and action. *Something to Celebrate* is a resource for Church and society.'

However, the eirenic tone of both of these opening recommendations has done little to resolve the divisions that prompted the reports in the first place. Both well illustrate just how intractable sexual ethics currently seems to be, especially for a broad church such as the Church of England. *Issues in Human Sexuality* was prompted in the first place by the obvious fact that gay priests and lay people, who have long been present especially within the Anglo-Catholic wing of the Church of England, have recently become less covert about their sexual behaviour. And *Something to Celebrate* was prompted by the fact that the children of many practising Anglicans (clergy and laity), some younger practising Anglicans themselves, and even some of the younger clergy, were already cohabiting outside marriage. Herein lay the central existential problem for both reports; actual practice did not accord with current theory even within the church. (Once again it is important to emphasise that this is an analytical point and says nothing at this stage about whether such practice should be condemned, condoned or simply tolerated.)

Faced with these existential problems the two reports responded rather differently, although ironically both were criticised for the way they reacted. *Issues in Human Sexuality* argued that although faithful but active homosexual relationships between lay Christians might be condoned, those between clergy could not be. The bishops argued:

> We have, therefore, to say that in our considered judgement the clergy cannot claim the liberty to enter into sexually active homophile relationships. Because of the distinctive nature of their calling, status and consecration, to allow such a claim on their part would be seen as placing that way of life in all respects on a par with heterosexual marriage as a reflection of God's purposes in creation. The Church cannot accept such a parity and remain faithful to the insights which God has given it through Scripture, tradition and reasoned reflection on experience.[3]

Clearly an underlying belief here is that clergy should be subject to higher professional standards than lay people, and indeed many clergy may well accept such a belief. The secrecy of the confessional and the imperative to maintain non-sexual relationships with those under their care are ethical requirements for several professional groups. Doctors, for example, are just as adamant about the need for patient confidentiality and non-exploitative doctor-patient relationships (curiously, university academics remain ambivalent about both). But why, several theologians asked, should any of this refer to homosexual behaviour, especially if it is faithful and does not exploit parishioners? The answer in the paragraph just quoted seems to be that sanctioning active homosexuality amongst the clergy 'would be seen as placing that way of life in all respects on a par with heterosexual marriage as a reflection of God's purposes in creation'. But why, the same theologians asked, does this consideration apply especially to the clergy? Does it not apply equally to lay people?

Having put this argument, the bishops at once insisted that it would be wrong for them as bishops to be 'rigorous in searching out and exposing clergy who may be in sexually active homophile relationships'.[4] They argued that it is wrong to assume that all those who cohabit have an active sexual relationship and that it would be wrong to carry out intrusive interrogations amongst the clergy. They concluded: 'Although we must take steps to avoid public scandal and to protect the Church's teaching, we shall continue, as we have done hitherto, to treat all clergy who give no occasion for scandal with trust and respect, and we expect all our fellow Christians to do the same.'[5]

Critics soon identified this as the crucial chink in the bishops' argument. They had admitted their internal differences, but had united in their concern about 'public scandal'. Logically their argument allowed for private homosexual behaviour amongst the clergy as long as this behaviour never became a matter of public scandal. Cynics soon interpreted this as an injunction not to be found out. It mirrored Max Weber's concept of 'perceived honesty' when he argued[6] that at the heart of the spirit of western capitalism lay a novel combination of hard work, thrift and perceived honesty. Hard-working and thrifty capitalists would not be trusted with the capital of others unless they were *perceived* by the latter to be honest. If they were privately honest but publicly suspected of being dishonest, they would be as badly placed in business terms as capitalists who were both privately and publicly dishonest. In contrast, successful capitalists might be either privately and publicly honest or privately dishonest but perceived in public to be honest. In the rise of western capitalism, so Weber argued, public perception became the dominant variable. Thus, bizarrely, honesty became a functional commodity and its normal moral meaning became inverted – somewhat like versions of 'ostentatious humility' which are important for promotion in many hierarchical but non-democratic organisations (including some churches).

In a similar way homosexual ordinands in faithful but sexually active relationships soon realised that, if they were to be ordained, they would be unwise to tell their ordaining bishop. The latter appeared most concerned about the avoidance of 'public scandal'. But, critics continued, does this not encourage just the sort of hypocrisy that is most detested by secular society (and which, of course, Jesus in the synoptic gospels persistently criticised)? Just this has been one of the most damaging areas for the Roman Catholic Church on the issue of clerical celibacy. An ideal is upheld despite widespread evidence that in some parts of the world many, perhaps even a majority, of priests do not uphold it and despite a series of very damning instances of western priests and bishops leading double lives. Only when such cases become public scandals do they characteristically receive public reprimand. Ecclesiastical hierarchies would usually rather deal with what they deem to be clerical and, sometimes, episcopal sexual misbehaviour – even illegal forms of misbehaviour such as paedophilia – with private reprimands and, if necessary, discreet career moves. Only when this behaviour becomes public – usually because of reports in the media – is further action typically taken. In other words, the dominant concern is to avoid public revelations, especially in the media, and, thus, public scandal – and it is just this which is often identified in society at large today as public hypocrisy.

Further, the critics continued, which public is it that might be scandalised? This question raises the important issue of possible changes in public opinion, to which I shall turn in a moment. *Issues in Human Sexuality* did little to resolve these critical questions.

Something to Celebrate raised rather different critical questions. Ostensibly the working party that wrote this report supported the bishops' report. For example, having briefly set out their views on homosexuality, they concluded: 'We therefore support the House of Bishops' hope that there will be a continuing growth in understanding and support of gay and lesbian people and a fuller integration of all that they may be able to teach and give through their own particular perspective'.[7] However, they avoided the vexed issue of clerical homosexuality and with it the argument of the bishops that condoning it 'would be seen as placing that way of life in all respects on a par with heterosexual marriage'. Indeed, they annoyed their critics precisely by appearing to put cohabitation – heterosexual and perhaps even homosexual – almost on a par with marriage. For example, they argued that 'the wisest and most practical way forward ... may be for Christians both to hold fast to the centrality of marriage and at the same time to accept that cohabitation is, for many people, a step along the way towards that fuller and more complete commitment'.[8] A little later they claimed that 'some forms of cohabitation are marriages already in all but name ... in terms of the theology of marriage, cohabitation which involves a mutual, life-long, exclusive commitment may be a legitimate form of marriage, what might be called "pre-ceremonial" or "without ceremonial" marriage'.[9] And a few pages later they argued that many gay and lesbian partnerships also involve 'commitment and interdependence' and 'are able to create relationships of high quality, capable of expressing love, joy, peace, faithfulness, endurance, self-sacrifice and service to the outside world beyond their relationship'.[10] Encouragement and support, rather than condemnation, they believed to be the appropriate Christian responses to these 'families'.

Some of the critics of the report caricatured it as little more than a legitimation of secular sexual practices. In reality, the authors of the report argued in several places that the 'Christian practice of lifelong, monogamous marriage lies at the heart of the Church's understanding of how the love of God is made manifest in the sexual companionship of a man and a woman'.[11] At the same time, they did not wish to condemn those who differed from this position:

> The widespread practice of cohabitation needs to be attended to
> with sympathy and discernment, especially in the light of the enor-
> mous changes in western society that have taken place recently and
> the effect these have had on the understanding and practice of
> personal relationships. Anxiety amongst churchgoers about cohabi-
> tation is best allayed, not by judgemental attitudes about
> 'fornication' and 'living in sin', but by the confident celebration of
> marriage and the affirmation and support of what in cohabiting rela-
> tionships corresponds most with the Christian ideal. Being
> disapproving and hostile towards people who cohabit only leads to
> alienation and a breakdown in communications. Instead, congrega-
> tions should welcome cohabitees, listen to them, learn from them
> and co-operate with them so that all may discover God's presence
> in their lives and in our own, at the same time as bearing witness
> to that sharing in God's love which is also available within
> marriage.[12]

The authors of *Something to Celebrate* argued with some passion that
'too often the Church has been censorious and judgemental in matters
of personal ethics' and considered that 'the beginning of a meeting of
minds and hearts is only likely to occur if the Church is honest about
its failure to embody the love of God in its teaching and practice of
marriage and family life'.[13] In contrast to the bishops, the working
party was less concerned about public scandal affecting the church and
more about what they considered to be anachronistic attitudes within
the church. They wrote, perhaps, more as the Christian parents of
young adults in a changing society, than as bishops concerned with
the public reputation of the church. The differing social contexts of
the House of Bishops and the Board of Social Responsibility may well
have contributed to this crucial difference.

Not surprisingly they attracted rather different critics. Nevertheless,
and this is important for my analysis, both of these predominantly
eirenic and non-confrontational reports did attract vehement critics,
within and outside the church. If the first was considered to be too
arbitrary in setting different standards on homosexual behaviour for
laity and clergy (despite the known presence of a substantial number
of actively gay clergy in parts of the church), the second was considered to be too devoid of Christian standards (despite the evident
differences amongst Anglicans on most sexual issues). The two
reports certainly did not represent the full spectrum of sexual attitudes
in the Church of England – for some the bishops were still far too
liberal and for others the working party was too conservative. Yet

together they illustrate some of the deep divisions to be found in many countries amongst Anglicans at the end of the twentieth century – divisions which will surely continue to trouble us in the twenty-first century. To understand these adequately it is important to understand their broader context. It is to this that I must turn next.

II

The most obvious feature of this broader context is that, for better or worse, social attitudes about sexual ethics have radically changed in the second half of the twentieth century. It will be obvious to every-one that this has happened, but it may be less obvious that the attitudes of churchgoers, although somewhat more conservative than those of the general population, do seem to be changing fast as well. Clergy attitudes, too change, but more slowly than other groups. Frequently, it is claimed that 'liberal' clergy have been responsible for these changes amongst churchgoers. From this perspective such clergy, fashioned by the relativism of 'liberal' theology and critical biblical studies, have become agents of secularisation within the church. This claim is frequently made, but it has seldom been made after a careful study of opinion poll data. (Since my own research has been on British opinion polls – analysing in the process some 60 polls conducted over more than half a century – I will confine my analysis to them, yet it is clear that similar trends can be found elsewhere.) Such study suggests that the reverse may in reality be the case – on sexual issues most clergy are more conservative than their congregations and change their opinions on these issues some decades later. Of course opinion polls cannot decide everything, especially in areas as complex as attitudes to sexual ethics. Nonetheless, they do show a remarkable consistency especially when set out longitudinally with a sufficient time gap.

For example, the issue of whether or not divorcees should be allowed to marry in church has been measured for half a century in Britain. In 1947 a Gallup Poll[14] suggested that a third of the general public (34 per cent) thought that they should not and well over half (58 per cent) that they should. By 1955 the negative group had declined somewhat (to 28 per cent) whilst the positive group had changed little (59 per cent) and by 1984 the negative group had declined again to less than a quarter (24 per cent) where it remained in 1996 (by now the positive group is 55 per cent). In other words throughout this period of time a clear majority of the general population thought that divorce should not be a barrier to a church wedding. In contrast, communicant churchgoers in 1955 were distinctly more opposed. A majority of this group (55 per cent) opposed the marriage of divorcees in church and little more than a third (37 per cent) supported it. An opinion poll conducted by the BBC[15] in December 1954 also showed a very similar, sharp difference of attitude on divorce between churchgoers and the general public: a majority (53 per cent) of those who reported that they went to church 'most Sundays' thought that the divorce laws then should be made more difficult, whereas less than a third (30 per cent) of the total sample held this view. Yet by 1984 this difference had largely disappeared. Now a majority of Anglican churchgoers (55 per cent) supported the marriage of divorcees in church and less than a third (29 per cent) were opposed. Exactly half of Roman Catholic churchgoers in 1984 remained opposed and so did a sizeable group of Anglican clergy (44 per cent), with less than a quarter of the latter (21 per cent) positively supporting the marriage of divorcees in church. Yet by the 1990s opposition by the clergy was clearly waning. Ted Harrison's poll[16] in 1994 showed less than a third (32 per cent) opposing it and a Gallup Poll in 1996 showed even less than this (28 per cent).

What had happened in this time? It is not too difficult to guess. Divorce has considerably increased during these five decades throughout the western world and has begun to affect congregations directly. Not only does every parish priest have requests from non-churchgoing divorcees for church marriages, but increasingly they are likely to have such requests from regular churchgoers as well. Despite the fact that the issue has been debated in the General Synod in England several times, there has as yet been no agreement to change at an official level. Yet unofficially change has already taken place in an increasing number of parishes and pressure to change can be found in most parishes. Faced with a strong claim from parishioners, many clergy, despite their generally more conservative views, find themselves following this unofficial path. Far from being the agents of secularisation, a persistent pastoral demand has persuaded them to change.

Another area which shows a similar pattern in opinion poll data is on attitudes towards sex before marriage and cohabitation. Asked in a Gallup Poll in 1964 whether they approved of sex before marriage almost two-thirds (64 per cent) of the sample of the general public replied 'no', a tenth 'yes', and just over a quarter (26 per cent) were 'not worried'. Anglican churchgoers were even more opposed (79 per cent). By 1978 attitudes in the general population appeared to have changed radically: just over a quarter (26 per cent) now replied 'no', 17 per cent 'yes', and a majority reported that they were 'not worried' (55 per cent). *British Social Attitudes*[17] surveys also suggest a shift in public perceptions: in 1983 over two-fifths (42 per cent) responded that sex before marriage was simply 'not wrong' and less than a third (28 per cent) that it was 'always or mostly wrong', whereas in 1993 a majority (54 per cent) held the first position and less than a fifth (18 per cent) the second. In Leslie Francis's extensive research[18] on those aged 13–15 he found that in 1995 amongst churchgoing Anglicans less than a quarter (22 per cent) thought that it was 'always or mostly wrong', and even amongst churchgoing Roman Catholic youngsters it was less than a third (30 per cent). Asking a similar question, but this time whether it is right for a couple to live together without intending to get married, a *British Social Attitudes* survey in 1993 found that almost two-thirds of the general population (64 per cent) thought that it was. A Gallup Poll in 1996 found a very similar proportion (68 per cent), and it also found that a majority (56 per cent) of adult church-going Anglicans also believed this. Once again it was the clergy who were distinctly more conservative: little more than a third of them (36 per cent) agreed: most (52 per cent) disagreed.

This evidence suggests that the general population changes – liber-alises, secularises, enlightens or degenerates (the choice of labels here, of course, signifies one's value perspective) – first, then churchgoers change and finally the clergy change. Such change is seen in bottom-up terms. Yet supposing this perspective is reversed and change is seen as something that is allowed or disallowed by the clergy. According to this perspective it is a duty of clerical leadership to maintain right beliefs and practices amongst the faithful – ortho-doxy and orthopraxis – whatever changes take place in secular society and however much these changes might at times mislead their congre-gations. A strong clerical leadership on sexual issues is considered vital to maintain the distinctiveness of Christian ethics amongst churchgoers.

There is one area which provides evidence about the effectiveness or non-effectiveness of clerical leadership on sexual issues, albeit in the Roman Catholic, not the Anglican, Church. Gallup Poll data suggests that in 1964 a considerable majority of both the general population and non-Roman Catholic churchgoers approved of contraception within marriage. One survey in that year set general approval at 79 per cent and another at 81 per cent: only about one in ten people disapproved. Amongst Anglican churchgoers this approval rose to 85 per cent and amongst Free Church churchgoers it was 75 per cent. Perhaps not surprisingly, it was only amongst Roman Catholic churchgoers that a majority (59 per cent) disapproved of contraception within marriage, although even within this group almost a third (32 per cent) approved. In 1965, before the publication of *Humanae Vitae*, a sample of the general population was asked if it would approve if the Roman Catholic Church were to change its teaching on contraception. Over two-thirds (69 per cent) responded 'yes' and only 4 per cent 'no'. Conversely, in 1968 after publication, most people (59 per cent) did not approve of the Pope's recent teaching on contraception. Apparently it was only Roman Catholic churchgoers who approved of the firm teaching of their church leaders on contraception in any significant numbers.

Yet it soon became apparent that, despite the firm teaching of both Pope Paul VI and Pope John Paul II, sexually active Roman Catholics in many parts of the western world did resort to contraception (and abortion) in proportionate numbers to their non-Roman Catholic counterparts. Perhaps they felt more guilty than others about using proscribed forms of contraception, but the obvious burden of not using barrier and hormonal forms of contraceptive soon persuaded them to act otherwise. Leslie Francis's research amongst those aged 13–15 in 1995 suggests that this generation may not even feel guilty. The attitudes of Anglican and Roman Catholic churchgoing youngsters appear indistinguishable: almost three-quarters of both groups (72 per cent) disagreed with the proposition that contraception is wrong: only one in twenty now believed it to be wrong.

This evidence is highly significant. In the second half of the twentieth century the hierarchy of the Roman Catholic Church has taken a determined, and for some courageous, stand against public opinion on a matter of sexual ethics which affects most sexually active people. Almost alone in any major Christian denomination, this hierarchy has decided to take a stand against prevailing mores and uphold a traditional sexual standard. It may even have done this despite a loss or alienation of many of its own sexually active members. Yet the evidence suggests that this stand has not substantially altered the practice of its members or even the attitudes of its youngest members. Despite one of the most systematic attempts at ecclesiastical teaching and control during this period, Roman Catholic churchgoers now appear little different from the general population in attitude towards, or practice of, proscribed forms of contraception.

The final area that provides an abundance of opinion poll data is that of attitudes towards homosexuality. Here the evidence suggests considerable ambiguity both amongst the general population and amongst churchgoers. Once again clergy appear to be more conservative than other groups. In a Gallup Poll in 1957 little more than a third of the population (38 per cent) thought that homosexuality should be decriminalised for adults. As with the slightly later abolition of capital punishment, British government reform on this issue probably did not have popular support at the time of its introduction. In 1964 again little more than a third of both the general population (36 per cent) and churchgoers thought that society should be tolerant of homosexuals. The *British Social Attitudes* in 1983 and 1993 suggest continuing antagonism towards homosexuality: in both exactly half of the general population thought that homosexual relations between adults were 'always wrong' and a further fifth that they were 'mostly or sometimes wrong'.

Perhaps this evidence is not altogether surprising. In a predominantly heterosexual population, homosexuality is by definition a minority issue. Unlike contraception or sex before or outside marriage, it is an existential issue for the few, not for the many. Nonetheless, there is some evidence here of increasing 'tolerance'. In 1977 a Gallup Poll suggested that two-thirds of the population believed that a homosexual could be 'a good Christian/Jew etc.': by 1981 this had increased to 77 per cent. And some two-fifths of the population in both surveys thought that homosexuals could 'be hired as clergy'. Asked in a different form, in 1984 just less than half of the population (45 per cent) thought that the 'Church can never approve homosexual acts'. Anglican churchgoers were slightly more conservative (52 per cent) and Anglican clergy even more so (61 per cent). The divide between Anglican laity and clergy was again suggested by a *Guardian* survey of newly elected General Synod members in 1996 which suggested that 45 per cent of laity and 70 per cent of clergy agreed that the church could not approve homosexual acts. A Gallup Poll in 1996 suggested a rather narrower gap of 53 per cent of Anglican churchgoers and 59 per cent of the clergy.

However, the most striking evidence of changing attitudes on homosexuality is amongst the youngest age group. Leslie Francis's 1995 sample of 13–15 year old Anglican churchgoers suggested that less than a third (30 per cent) thought that homosexuality was wrong. Most striking of all, Ronald Inglehart's analysis[19] of data from the 1981–2 *World Values Survey* shows significant differences in fourteen out of sixteen countries between the youngest and oldest age groups on the issue of homosexuality. It provides persuasive evidence of what he terms 'cultural shift'. Analysing the responses of those who answered that homosexuality can 'never' be justified, he found that across nations less than two-fifths (39 per cent) of those aged 18–24 responded in this way, whereas almost three-quarters (73 per cent) of those aged 65 or over did. The British figures (31 per cent and 72 per cent respectively) were very close to this international mean. Significantly this is a progressive mean: in every age band the international mean rises, reaching 50 per cent in those aged 35–44.

In statistical terms herein lies the problem for Anglican bishops in many countries, especially where congregations are disproportionately elderly. It appears that it is the elderly who are disproportionately inclined to believe that homosexuality can never be justified. So for this group *Issues in Human Sexuality* was likely to be viewed as dangerously liberal, since it did not condemn faithful homosexual relationships amongst lay-people. Yet for most of the youngest group of churchgoers homosexuality is simply not seen as wrong at all. So any attempt by bishops to proscribe homosexual relationships amongst the clergy is always likely to be viewed by this young group as homophobia or hypocrisy. The middle-aged are likely to sit somewhere between these two perspectives – sharing the ambiguities and confusions of the late twentieth century.

Faced simply with their followers, and disregarding for the moment all theological considerations, the English bishops evidently faced a thankless task when they met to produce *Issues in Human Sexuality*. On a divisive issue such as homosexual relationships they could not expect to please all age groups even within the Church. What appears to be simply wrong to the oldest age group is likely to appear homophobic to the youngest. And on issues where society at large and even a majority of churchgoers have changed their views – for example on the issue of divorcees marrying in church – they are still likely to encounter strong opposition from many of the clergy. If they take a firm line against popular opinion – as the Roman Catholic hierarchy did on barrier and hormonal forms of contraception – they are likely to alienate the faithful or simply be ignored by them. Yet if they take a more liberal line – as the authors of *Something to Celebrate* did – they are likely to be accused by some within the Church of being agents of secularisation. In the circumstances it may hardly be surprising that *Issues in Human Sexuality* is now widely seen as a deeply contradictory document.

Perhaps theology can rescue this situation.

III

Unfortunately biblical and historical scholars are not always very helpful at this point. Just when it is thought that the unified voice of the Bible or church history on sexual ethics might resolve these contradictions and ambiguities, scholars seem increasingly to stress that distinctively Christian resources are themselves surprisingly pluralistic. The problem seems to be two fold: much modern scholarship appears to present a plurality of both contents and methods. At the contents level, many scholars detect crucial differences of perspective on sexual ethics between the Old and New Testaments and between both of these and subsequent church history. At the methodological level, a wide variety of hermeneutical perspectives makes it seem ever less likely that Christian theologians can reach a consensus, especially on those issues such as sexuality which have crucial gender and cultural implications.

Three very recent collections, each with a predominance of Anglican contributors confirm this situation at the contents level. The first of these collections is *New Occasions Teach New Duties? Christian Ethics for Today* edited by Cyril S. Rodd.[20] It consists of articles originally written for *Expository Times* intended to introduce general readers to the current state of scholarship in Christian ethics. This collection opens with two critical articles on biblical ethics. The first, by Cyril Rodd, looks at the use of the Old Testament in Christian ethics, and the second, by Howard Marshall, looks at that of the New Testament. Both offer many more problems than they resolve (even Marshall has surprisingly little positive to say) and present a very effective challenge which is taken up by several of the authors that follow. If the Bible is indeed the central and most distinctively Christian resource for Christian ethics, then how do we resolve its internal pluralism, its anachronisms, its gaps, and the varying synchronic and diachronic interpretations that are made of it? Alister McGrath boldly compounds these problems by noting key differences amongst the Reformers and David Brown by setting Christian ethics in its present-day context of competing philosophies. Richard Jones instructively looks at the differing ways that individual Christians make decisions (for example, about whether they should or should not be ordained). Alan Suggate, John Atherton and David Cook all offer useful but characteristic accounts of their specialist areas in Christian ethics – namely church and state, economics and medical ethics. Stephen Barton, fresh from *Something to Celebrate*, offers a gentle piece on sexuality – although I suspect that it will not satisfy his conservative critics. William Storrar looks at the 'option for the poor', Graham Gould at the Church Fathers, and Peter Bishop at issues of war and peace.

The second collection is *The Family in Theological Perspective*, this time edited by Stephen Barton[21] and the third *Christian Perspectives on Sexuality and Gender*, edited by Adrian Thatcher and Elizabeth Stuart.[22] Both of these collections compound the plurality of distinctively Christian resources on ethical issues evident in the first collection. Not one of the collections offers any clear path through these differences.

Stephen Barton, featuring prominently in all of the collections, is very much at the centre of the recent debate in the Church of England.

In a series of measured articles he seeks to show some of the difficulties facing those wishing to claim that Christians can speak with a united voice on the family or on sexuality. For him it is not the plurality of present-day society which causes these difficulties, but the Bible itself and our relationship to the Bible. He seeks to move readers away from interminable debates about particular biblical texts (for example, the cluster of much-cited verses on homosexuality), and towards a more hermeneutical perspective, seeing us as contextualised late twentieth-century people coming to the Bible for enlightenment rather than for proof texts. But, of course, therein lies the problem: we already come to the Bible with our gender, ethnic and social class differences.

The Family in Theological Perspective consists of eighteen thoughtful papers originally given to seminars at the Durham Centre for Theological Research. Most of the contributors are academics at Durham or Newcastle University. An exception is John Rogerson who gives a very helpful paper on the family in the Old Testament, set alongside similar papers on the New Testament by James Dunn and James Francis. Carol Harrison, Anthony Fletcher and Sheridan Gilley offer papers on the family in historical perspectives. The second half of this collection is a little more disparate with contributions amongst others from Peter Selby, Michael Vasey, Jeff Astley, Jon Davies, Alan Suggate and Gerard Loughlin, all of whom have something interesting to add to the debate. However Susan Parsons presents one of the most cogent papers, outlining the thesis that she sets out so well in her recent *Feminism and Christian Ethics*,[23] on differences between feminists often resulting from the crucial issue of whether they consider gender distinctions to be socially or biologically constructed.

Christian Perspectives on Sexuality and Gender is in effect a reader, since all but one of its 36 articles have been previously published elsewhere. Whereas half of the second collection is concerned with biblical and historical tradition, in this third collection it is covered by just three articles, by Stephen Barton, Richard Price and Daniel Doriani. Of the other sections, that on power and relation (with characteristic and contrasting contributions from Daphne Hampson and Mary Grey), on sexuality and spirituality (James Nelson), sexuality and violence, and families (Rosemary Radford Ruether, Stephen Barton and Susan Parsons again) are all interesting. The tone and standard of the contributions in this collection are not as even and scholarly as those in the other two. Nevertheless, the three books work well together and abundantly illustrate the plurality facing the very heart of Christian ethics.

Of course, despite this evident plurality, there might still be a single and distinctively Christian narrative beneath it. If it were possible to discern such an underlying narrative in the Bible on sexual ethics, would this settle the theological debate? The Roman Catholic Anne E. Patrick's recent *Liberating Conscience: Feminist Explorations in Catholic Moral Theology*[24] argues that it would not, since such a patriarchal biblical narrative would still need correction.

Anne Patrick SNJM, is Professor of Religion at Carleton College, Minnesota, and a past president of the influential Catholic Theological Society of America. Writing very much as a Catholic for other Catholics, she introduces her first chapter with this quotation: 'When I was young ... there never was any question of right and wrong. We knew our catechism, and that was enough. We learned our creed and our duty. Every respectable church person had the same opinions.'[25] This expresses very well the dilemma of many Roman Catholics today. Once church authority and morality were firmly anchored, but today, and despite a strong pope, they are not. In the wake of Bishop Roderick Wright's resignation, even that staunch defender of Catholicism, Clifford Longley, admitted in the *Daily Telegraph* that a Roman Catholic congregation is likely to start collecting for a 'going-away present' for a priest who decides to get married. Anne Patrick herself provides numerous examples of changing Catholic perceptions and values. Yet she teases her readers, since her quotation is from the last century by George Eliot and refers to Anglicans not to Roman Catholics. Her message is clear; just as Anglicans experienced radical changes a century ago, so Roman Catholics are experiencing similar painful changes today. She might have added that Roman Catholics are experiencing these changes at the very moment when some Anglicans are moving to Rome to avoid change. For these Anglicans, Rome represents an unchanging authority – in doctrine, in morality and in the ordination of males alone. Yet for her even this authority is essentially contested and contestable.

Over the last two decades some of the most powerful theological books have been written by Roman Catholic theologians breaking away from traditional antagonisms to biblical criticism and incontestable papal teaching. In liberation theology, feminist theology and hermeneutics generally, it is often Roman Catholic theologians who lead the debate. Anne Patrick's *Liberating Conscience* follows in this radical line.

In this book she argues that Roman Catholic theology has become increasingly polarised. One section, which she terms 'fundamentalist', stresses unchanging authority and doctrine and seeks to enforce them by removing a theologian such as Professor Charles Curran from his job in a Catholic University. The other section, which she calls 'revisionist', still regards itself as orthodox and loyal to Rome, but sees change as a continuing experience of a faithful church. Such change once involved coming to terms with a non-Jewish world; later it involved recognising the evil of slavery; today, so she argues, it involves recognising same-sex relationships, contraception and diverse sexual mores. At the heart of these two positions are radically different paradigms of virtue, the one 'patriarchal' and the other 'egalitarian–feminist'. The first of these paradigms, which she sees as most typical of the Bible, she depicts as follows:

> A patriarchal paradigm for virtue has long dominated Catholic thinking. Its shape has been affected by the otherworldly spirituality, the theological and social patterns of domination and subordination, the misogyny, and the body-rejecting dualism characteristic of Western culture. This paradigm understands virtue to involve the control of passion by reason and the subordination of earthly values to heavenly ones. It articulates many ideals for character but tends to assume that these are appropriately assigned greater emphasis according to one's gender and social status. All Christians should be kind, chaste, just, and humble, but women are expected to excel in charity and chastity, men are trained to think in terms of justice and rights, and subordinates of both sexes are exhorted to docility and meekness.[26]

The second paradigm, which of course she espouses herself, is critical of much biblical and traditional patriarchy. She continues:

> In contrast to the anthropological dualism of the patriarchal paradigm, the egalitarian–feminist paradigm understands reason itself to be embodied, and women and men to be fully equal partners in the human community. Instead of *control*, the notion of *respect* for all created reality is fundamental to this paradigm, which values the body in general and the humanity of women in particular, and promotes gender-integrated ideals for character. Rather than understanding power as control over others, this paradigm operates with a sense of power as the energy of proper relatedness. Discipline is still valued, but it is less rigidly understood. Ideals of love and justice are not segregated into separate spheres of personal and social ethics, with responsibility for realizing them assigned according to gender; instead love and justice are seen to be mutually reinforcing norms that should govern both sexes equally.[27]

My point in quoting this distinction at length is not to suggest that it cannot be criticised. On the contrary, there are many important critical questions that should be raised about how Anne Patrick establishes this second paradigm and even about the degree to which she may exaggerate the prevalence of the first. However, that is not my point here. Rather it is to illustrate that different hermeneutical perspectives can have a radical effect upon one's use and selection of distinctively Christian resources. Once this point is accepted, then the realisation that modern theology offers a range of competing hermeneutical perspectives – of which Anne Patrick's egalitarian-feminism is just one – simply adds further confusion to current confusions about sexual ethics. A generation ago bewildering choices between differing forms of historical criticism made it difficult for the theologian who took them seriously to find a reliable path through them. It was always tempting to bypass them by going back to the 'real' message of the Bible. Today hermeneutics in the form of biblical interpretation has made even this bypass problematic. None of us approaches the Bible without cultural and gender baggage. We are women or men reading Scripture, we are inhabitants of the affluent North or the poor South, we are products of particular histories, tribes and families. Biblical interpretation has shown us just how varied are our interpretations of the Bible both across cultures and across time. How then can we make reliable choices as we do theology?

Vernon Robbins, Professor of Religion at Emory University, argues in his recent but complex book, *The Tapestry of Early Christian Discourse: Rhetoric. Society and Ideology*,[28] that socio-rhetorical criticism can help to give us an overview of these various historical and hermeneutical approaches to the Bible. However, in the process, he also shows just how daunting the task is. Those who study rhetoric start from oral speeches and see a constant interaction between the speaker, the speech and the audience. Speeches typically contain a mixture of repetitions, key words, narratives and differing forms of logic and emphasis, designed by the speaker to persuade the audience. Transferring these observations to written biblical texts, a socio-rhetorical approach sees them as the products of known and unknown authors addressing audiences which are often just implied in the texts and which in any case are very different from the audiences that receive them today. Like speeches these texts also contain forms and styles which can be analysed and assessed using various literary, theological and social scientific methods. Robbins describes in detail four levels of analysis – that of the inner texture, that of intertexture (texts relating to other texts and linguistic forms), that of social and cultural context, and finally that of ideology (texts often imply power relations within communities). For Robbins 'there is not simply a text; texts were produced by authors and they are meaningless without readers. There are not simply readers; readers are meaningless without texts to read and authors who write texts. All three presuppose historical, social, cultural and ideological relations among people and the texts they write and read.'[29]

How is a Church for the twenty-first century ever to find a convincing way through these different hermeneutical levels?

IV

It would be foolish of me to pretend that I can wholly answer this question. Instead I can only point in directions that I have attempted to sketch in *Moral Leadership in a Postmodern Age*.[30] There I started my own theological reconstruction with the 1995 report *The Church and Human Sexuality* produced for the Anglican Church of the Province of South Africa.[31]

This South African report begins with an extended biblical study of sexuality by the retired Rhodes University Professor of Theology, John Suggit, which seeks to identify two key biblical virtues that are held in tension on the issue of sexuality. In the process it allows us to see that there may be abiding Christian virtues which are balanced differently in ever-changing contexts by a rich variety of Christian communities. Two sets of abiding virtues are seen as especially present in both Old and New Testaments – loving-kindness/faithfulness on the one hand and righteousness/justice on the other. God's *hesed* or loving-kindness in the Old Testament is seen as continued in the New Testament in the form of *agapē* and *charis*. Suggit, schooled in the tradition of biblical theology, believes that these abiding virtues can be detected despite differing emphases between the Old Testament/Jewish Bible and the New Testament – for example, the endorsement of celibacy in the latter. A common theme between these abiding virtues is a stress upon the initiative of God's dealings with humans. The South African report sees a creative tension between this set of themes and that in both Testaments of *zedek* – that is, God's righteousness. The balance between these two sets of virtues is expressed in terms of three themes:

1. A Christian sexual ethic of love arises from faith's perception of God's ways with humankind in divine creativity and reconciliation, and in his action by which he sustains and liberates human beings so that they may live with justice (*zedek*) and integrity.

2. A sexual ethic centred in love needs to express mutual commitment between the partners, and to be liberating, enriching, honest, faithful, personally and socially responsible, life-giving and joyous.

3. Love involves an attitude towards the other partner in which the

happiness and welfare of the other is of prime importance, and which is expressed in appropriate acts. In view of the frequent distortion of sexuality by abusive power both within and outside marriage, a Christian sexual ethic is committed to the liberation of sexual expression as mutual enrichment rather than as dominance and submission.[32]

The South African report sees these as abiding theological virtues in tension and then seeks to identify a number of more contingent themes. As a distinctively African report it encourages an understanding attitude towards brideprice, customary unions and polygamy and sees them in quite a different moral light from, for example, sexual promiscuity. For the report promiscuity 'should be seen as a misunderstanding of the meaning of sexuality and a hindrance to the development of full human personality ... as being opposed to God's will for human beings'.[33]

In terms of my theological analysis, the chief merit of this South African report is that it distinguishes carefully between, on the one hand, abiding Christian/Jewish virtues that are held in tension in the Bible and in subsequent Christian history, and, on the other, contingent contexts and recipients that are for ever changing. By identifying at the outset a set of relevant theological virtues, it is able then to bring them to the various moral issues surrounding sexuality and changing patterns of family life. An abiding pattern is faithful and loving monogamy, which is seen as the Christian ideal for both sexuality in general and for the responsible bringing up of children. Nevertheless, customary marriage and polygamy, in the context of African society, are seen as less than ideal but not as inherently opposed to this ideal.

Vernon Robbins' socio-rhetorical criticism acts as an important reminder that, in Christian ethics, author, text and audience constantly interact with each other, changing over time and across time within Christian communities. We change, our context changes and our perception of the Bible changes. If this had not been the case then Christianity would soon have become moribund and anachronistic. Nevertheless we are spared from pure relativism, becoming in the process little more than echoes of our surrounding societies, by our constant interactions with Christian texts especially in a context of Christian worship. It is thus important to distinguish carefully between the abiding and the contingent – a task that might be achieved at three levels:

Level 1 Faithful and righteous family life, based upon love and mutuality, remains an *abiding Christian ideal for all societies*. It is not, of course, the only ideal, since in the New Testament, as well as in much of subsequent Christian history, dedicated celibacy is also an ideal – although, by definition, not a sexual ideal. There has also been a long-standing recognition in Christian ethics that family life can be distorted, either by unfaithfulness or by unrighteousness.

Level 2 Some forms of sexuality, which are sadly present in many societies, are *inherently opposed to this ideal and are thus sinful* – for example, promiscuity (both heterosexual and homosexual), adultery, prostitution, child pornography, active paedophilia, and sado-masochism. From a Christian perspective they remain deeply sinful however much some elements of secular society seek to justify them. Likewise families which are deeply distorted by unfaithfulness and/or unrighteousness can become inherently opposed to the Christian ideal. Monogamy as such is not a guarantee against such distortion.

Level 3 Yet there are other forms of behaviour which, in terms of Christian virtues, are not inherently sinful but which are still less than ideal. That is to say, they *share some of the Christian virtues without exemplifying them all* – this group contains both patterns which are present 'in nature', such as childlessness through spontaneous steril-ity, and others, such as faithful cohabitation, which are products more of changing cultures. Faithful homosexual relationships may belong either to nature or to culture (morally that may not be too important since for both a homosexual orientation is not something an individ-ual chooses).

The third level allows for considerable differences amongst those of us who try to be and hope that we are faithful Christians. Yet if the model that Vernon Robbins offers is accepted, then perhaps the church in the twenty-first century will learn to see these differences as a sign of a vivacious and dynamic church. Christian virtues in tension abide but our application and interpretation of these virtues constantly change. That, I believe, has always been the reality of a living church.

Notes

1. *Issues in Human Sexuality: A Statement by the House of Bishops of the General Synod of the Church of England* (Church House Publishing, London, 1991).
2. *Something to Celebrate: Valuing Families in Church and Society* (Church House Publishing, London, 1995).
3. *Issues in Sexuality*, 5.17.

4. ibid., 5.18.
5. ibid.
6. Max Weber, *The Protestant Ethic and the Spirit of Capitalism* (Unwin, London, 1930).
7. *Something to Celebrate*, p.121.
8. ibid., p.115.
9. ibid., p.116.
10. ibid., p.120.
11. ibid., p.118.
12. ibid.
13. ibid., p.115.
14. Gallup Opinion Poll data can be found in George H. Gallup, *The Gallup International Public Opinion Polls: Great Britain 1937-1975*, vols.1 and 2 (Random House, New York, 1976); in *The International Gallup Polls* (1978); and in *The Gallup Political Index* (1966-96).
15. British Broadcasting Corporation, *Religious Broadcasts and the Public* (Audience Research Department, BBC, 1955).
16. Ted Harrison, *Members Only?* (Triangle, SPCK, London, 1994).
17. *British Social Attitudes*, 1983-94.
18. Leslie J. Francis and William K. Kay, *Teenage Religion and Values* (Gracewing, Fowler Wright Books, Leominster, 1995).
19. Ronald Inglehart, *Culture Shift in Advanced Industrial Society* (Princeton University Press, New Jersey, 1990).
20. Cyril S. Rodd (ed.), *New Occasions Teach New Duties? Christian Ethics for Today*, (T & T Clark, Edinburgh, 1995).
21. Stephen Barton (ed.), *The Family in Theological Perspective* (T & T Clark, Edinburgh, 1996).
22. Adrian Thatcher and Elizabeth Stuart (eds.), *Christian Perspectives on Sexuality and Gender* (Gracewing, Fowler Wright Books, Leominster, 1996).
23. Susan Parsons, *Feminism and Christian Ethics* (Cambridge University Press, Cambridge, 1996).
24. Anne E. Patrick, *Liberating Conscience: Feminist Explorations in Catholic Moral Theology* (SCM Press, London, 1996).
25. ibid., p. 19.
26. ibid., p. 77.
27. ibid., pp. 78-9.
28. Vernon Robbins, *The Tapestry of Early Christian Discourse: Rhetoric. Society and Ideology* (Routledge, London, 1996).
29. ibid., p.39.
30. Robin Gill, *Moral Leadership in a Postmodern Age* (T & T Clark, Edinburgh, 1997).
31. *The Church and Human Sexuality* (Church of the Province of South Africa, 1995).
32. ibid., para B4.
33. ibid., para E6.